Media and Terrorism

Media and Terrorism
Global Perspectives

Edited by Des Freedman and Daya Kishan Thussu

Los Angeles | London | New Delhi
Singapore | Washington DC

SAGE Publications Ltd
1 Oliver's Yard
55 City Road
London EC1Y 1SP

SAGE Publications Inc.
2455 Teller Road
Thousand Oaks, California 91320

SAGE Publications India Pvt Ltd
B 1/I 1 Mohan Cooperative Industrial Area
Mathura Road
New Delhi 110 044

SAGE Publications Asia-Pacific Pte Ltd
3 Church Street
#10-04 Samsung Hub
Singapore 049483

Library of Congress Control Number: 2011930101

British Library Cataloguing in Publication data

A catalogue record for this book is available from the British Library

ISBN 978-1-4462-0157-2
ISBN 978-1-4462-0158-9 (pbk)

Typeset by C&M Digitals (P) Ltd, India, Chennai
Printed and bound by CPI Group (UK) Ltd, Croydon, CR0 4YY
Printed on paper from sustainable resources

CONTENTS

About the Editors vii
Notes on Contributors viii
Acknowledgements xiv

1   Introduction: Dynamics of Media and Terrorism 1
    Des Freedman and Daya Kishan Thussu

Part 1: Contexts **21**

2   Terror, War and Disjunctures in the Global Order 23
    Lena Jayyusi

3   Media, War and Information Technology 47
    Christian Fuchs

4   Public Diplomacy versus Terrorism 63
    Philip Seib

5   Propaganda and Terrorism 77
    David Miller and Rizwaan Sabir

Part 2: Global Representations of Terrorism **95**

6   Terrorism and Global Popular Culture 97
    Toby Miller

7   Hollywood, the CIA and the 'War on Terror' 116
    Oliver Boyd-Barrett, David Herrera and Jim Baumann

8   Terror, Culture and Anti-Muslim Racism 134
    Gholam Khiabany and Milly Williamson

9   Pictures and Public Relations in the Israeli–Palestinian Conflict 151
    Greg Philo

Part 3: Terrorism on the Home Front **165**

10 South Asia and the Frontline of the 'War on Terror' 167
    Daya Kishan Thussu

11   Covering Terrorism in Russian Media   184
      Elena Vartanova and Olga Smirnova

12   WikiLeaks and War Laws   206
      Stig A. Nohrstedt and Rune Ottosen

13   Television and Immigration in France   223
      Tristan Mattelart

14   The 'War on Terror' in Arab Media   241
      Helga Tawil-Souri

Part 4: Journalists and the 'War on Terror'   **255**

15   Terrorism and News Narratives   257
      Justin Lewis

16   Asylum-seeker Issues as Political Spectacle   271
      Jake Lynch, Annabel McGoldrick and Alex Russell

17   Media Myth and Ground Reality in Reporting from Iraq   289
      Dahr Jamail

18   Challenging the Media War   306
      Danny Schechter

Index   317

ABOUT THE EDITORS

Des Freedman is Reader in Communications and Cultural Studies in the Department of Media and Communications, Goldsmiths, University of London. He is the co-author (with James Curran and Natalie Fenton) of *Misunderstanding the Internet* (forthcoming 2012), author of *The Politics of Media Policy* (Polity, 2008) and *The Television Policies of the Labour Party, 1951–2001* (Frank Cass, 2003) and co-editor (with Daya Thussu) of *War and the Media: Reporting Conflict 24/7* (Sage, 2003). He is a co-editor of the SAGE journal *Global Media and Communication* and a member of the research team in the Goldsmiths Leverhulme Media Research Centre.

Daya Kishan Thussu is Professor of International Communication and Co-Director of India Media Centre at the University of Westminster in London. He is the Founder and Managing Editor of the SAGE journal *Global Media and Communication*. Among his main publications are: *Electronic Empires* (Arnold, 1998); *International Communication – Continuity and Change*, second edition (Arnold, 2006); *War and the Media: Reporting Conflict 24/7* (co-edited with Des Freedman; Sage, 2003); *Media on the Move – Global Flow and Contra-flow* (Routledge, 2007); *News as Entertainment* (Sage, 2007); and *Internationalizing Media Studies* (Routledge, 2009). He is series editor for two Routledge book series: Internationalizing Media Studies and Advances in Internationalizing Media Studies.

NOTES ON CONTRIBUTORS

Jim Baumann, PhD, is Assistant Professor in the Communication Department at St. Ambrose University, Iowa. His research interests include the adoption of emerging mediated communication technologies, communication theory and the political economy of communication. He received his doctorate from the School of Communication Studies at Bowling Green State University, Ohio, in 2009, where his dissertation investigated the social, economic, technological and application issues facing the public during the digital television transition in the United States. He is co-author with Oliver Boyd-Barrett and David Herrera of *Hollywood and the CIA* (Routledge, 2011).

Oliver Boyd-Barrett, PhD, is Professor of Journalism at Bowling Green State University, Ohio, and author/editor of 20 books and over 120 scholarly articles. Books include *The International News Agencies* (SAGE, 1980); *Contra-Flow in Global News* (with Daya Thussu; John Libbey, 1992); *Education Reform in Democratic Spain* (with Pamela O'Malley; Routledge, 1995); *The Globalization of News* (with Terhi Rantanen; SAGE, 1998); *Communications Media, Globalization and Empire* (John Libbey, 2006); *News Agencies in the Turbulent Era of the Internet* (Government of Catalonia, 2010); *Hollywood and the CIA* (with David Herrera and Jim Baumann; Routledge, 2011).

Christian Fuchs is Professor of Media and Communication Studies at Uppsala University, Sweden. He is editor of *tripleC – Cognition, Communication, Co-operation: Open Access Journal for a Global Sustainable Information Society* and board member of the Unified Theory of Information Research Group (UTI). His research interests are critical theory, critical theory of the media and the internet, critical political economy of the media and communication, media and society and critical information society studies. He is author of *Internet and Society: Social Theory in the Information Age* and *Foundations of Critical Media and Information Studies*. Website: http: //fuchs.uti.at.

David Herrera is a graduate student at the Missouri School of Journalism in Columbia, Missouri. His research interests include First Amendment law, mass communication theories and normative media theory. He worked as a web producer at the Detroit Free Press after graduating from Bowling Green State University, Ohio, where he studied journalism and popular culture. He is co-author, with Oliver Boyd-Barrett and Jim Baumann, of *Hollywood and the CIA* (Routledge, 2011).

Dahr Jamail is an independent journalist and author whose stories have been published with *Al-Jazeera English*, *The Independent*, the *Nation*, the *Sunday Herald* in Scotland, *The Guardian*, *Foreign Policy in Focus* and *Le Monde Diplomatique*. On radio as well as television, Jamail reports for *Democracy Now!*, has appeared on Al-Jazeera, the BBC and NPR, and numerous other stations around the globe. He was the recipient of the Lannan Foundation Writing Residency Fellowship in 2008. He is the author of, most recently, *The Will to Resist: Soldiers Who Refuse to Fight in Iraq and Afghanistan* (Haymarket, 2009) and *Beyond the Green Zone: Dispatches from an Unembedded Journalist in Occupied Iraq* (Haymarket, 2007).

Lena Jayyusi is Associate Professor at the College of Communication and Media Sciences at Zayed University, United Arab Emirates, and non-residential Senior Research Fellow at Muwatin: The Palestinian Institute for the Study of Democracy in Ramallah, Palestine. She has taught at Wellesley College, the University of Connecticut at Storrs and Cedar Crest College in Pennsylvania, where she was Chair of the Department of Communication Studies from 1990 to 1994. She worked between 1995 and 2002 in Palestine, doing research on Palestinian media discourse, and serving as a Senior TOKTEN consultant for the UNPD in Jerusalem and as Director of the Oral History Program at Shaml: The Palestinian Diaspora and Refugee Center. She is author of *Categorization and the Moral Order* (Routledge & Kegan Paul, 1984), which was translated into French (Economica, 2010). She has two edited volumes currently in press: *Jerusalem Interrupted: Modernity and Colonial Transformation 1917 – the Present* (Interlink Publishing) and *A Reader in Media and Democracy* (a Muwatin publication, in Arabic). She is currently preparing two original volumes: *Praxiologies* (a collection of studies in practical reasoning and communicative action) and a manuscript on Palestinian national discourse during the Oslo years.

Gholam Khiabany teaches in the School of Media, Film and Music at the University of Sussex. He is the author of *Iranian Media: The Paradox of Modernity* (Routledge, 2010), and co-author of *Blogistan* (with Annabelle Sreberny (I.B. Tauris, 2010).

Justin Lewis is Head of the School of Journalism, Media and Cultural Studies at Cardiff University. Before going to Cardiff in 2000 he worked for 12 years at the University of Massachusetts. He has written many books and articles about media, communication and politics. Recent books include *Climate Change and* *the Media* (co-edited with Tammy Boyce; Peter Lang, 2009) and *The Rise of 24 Hour News Television* (co-edited with Stephen Cushion; Peter Lang, 2010).

Jake Lynch is Director of the Centre for Peace and Conflict Studies at the University of Sydney and a pioneer in the emerging research field of Peace Journalism. He is also Secretary General of the International Peace Research Association. Before taking up an academic career, Lynch spent many years as a professional journalist, having worked as a presenter on BBC World television news; Political Correspondent for Sky News and Sydney Correspondent for *The Independent*.

Tristan Mattelart is Professor of International Communication at the Department of Culture and Communication of the University of Paris 8. His works include *La mondialisation des médias contre la censure: Tiers monde et audiovisuel sans frontières* (2002) and *Médias, migrations et cultures transnationales* (2007), as well as different articles and chapters published in English. In 2009, he coordinated a special issue of the electronic journal *tic&société* on 'ICTs and diasporas'. Currently, he is heading an international research project funded by the French National Research Agency (ANR) on 'Media and migration in the Euro-Mediterranean space'.

Annabel McGoldrick is studying for her PhD at the Centre for Peace and Conflict Studies at the University of Sydney, researching audience responses to Peace Journalism. She is also a qualified psychotherapist in private practice. She worked for many years in journalism, most recently as a reporter for SBS World News Australia, in Sydney. She chaired the Reporting the World meetings for professional journalists in London, and has facilitated training workshops for editors and reporters in many countries including Indonesia and the Philippines.

David Miller is Professor of Sociology at the University of Bath, the co-founder of Spinwatch (www.spinwatch.org) and the editor of Powerbase (www.powerbase.info), a wiki-based collaborative guide to power networks. His recent books include *Neoliberal Scotland: Class and Society in a Stateless Nation* (co-edited with Neil Davidson and Patricia McCafferty; Cambridge Scholars Publishing, 2010); *A Century of Spin – How Public Relations Became the Cutting Edge of Corporate Power* (with Willian Dinan; Pluto, 2008); *Thinker, Faker, Spinner, Spy: Corporate PR and the Assault on Democracy* (edited with William Dinan; Pluto, 2007); *Tell Me Lies: Propaganda and Media Distortion in the Attack on Iraq* (editor; Pluto, 2003).

Toby Miller works at the University of California, Riverside. He has written and edited more than 30 books and published articles in more than 100 journals and special collections. He runs a podcast, which can be found on iTunes under culturalstudies. Website: www.tobymiller.org.

Stig A. Nohrstedt is Professor at the School of Humanities, Education and Social Sciences at Örebro University, Sweden. His research interests include war and conflict journalism and journalistic ethics. He is the co-editor with Rune Ottosen of *Journalism and the New World Order: Gulf War, National News Discourse and Globalization* (Nordicom, 2001); *U.S. and the Others: Global Media Images on 'The War on Terror'* (Nordicom, 2004); and *Global War – Local Views: Media Images of the Iraq War* (Nordicom, 2005). He is editor of *Community Risks – Towards the Threat Society?* (Nordicom, 2011).

Rune Ottosen is Professor at Oslo and Akershus University College, Norway. He has written extensively on media coverage of conflicts. He is co-editor with Stig Arne Nohrstedt of *Journalism and the New World Order: Gulf War, National News Discourse and Globalization* (Nordicom, 2001); *Global Media Images on 'The War on Terror'* (Nordicom, 2004); and *Global War – Local Views: Media Images of the Iraq War* (Nordicom, 2005). Ottosen is leader in the Norwegian Association of Press and Media History and was President of the Norwegian Non-fiction Writers and Translator Association 2001–2005.

Greg Philo is Professor of Communications at Glasgow University and Research Director of the Glasgow University Media Group. His interests are in the area of the media and cultural reception and past research has centred on media presentations of industrial disputes and trade unionism, the economy, war, race and migration. Recent research includes ESRC, UKERC and other externally funded projects on political advertising, images of health and illness as well as risk, climate change, food scares and media presentations of international conflict, crime, sentencing policy and impacts on public belief. His books include *Message Received* (Longman, 1999), (with David Miller), *Market Killing* (Longman, 2001) and (with Mike Berry), *Israel and Palestine – Competing Histories* (Pluto, 2006) and *More Bad News from Israel* (Pluto, 2011).

Alex Russell has taught statistical and research methods in the University of Sydney's School of Psychology for five years. He is regularly in demand as a statistical advisor to research firms, marketing agencies and other educational institutions devising methodologies and reporting on quantitative and qualitative research. He is currently completing his PhD in Psychology at the University of Sydney, examining taste and smell perception, with an emphasis on wine expertise.

Rizwaan Sabir is a doctoral researcher in the School of Applied Social Sciences, University of Strathclyde, where he is researching British and Scottish government policy toward Muslims and Islam since 9/11, with a particular focus on counter-terrorism, propaganda and race-relations.

Danny Schechter is the editor of the New York-based media issues network Mediachannel.org. He is a blogger, author, filmmaker and troublemaker. He developed his techniques as a news dissector while a master's student at the London School of Economics during the Vietnam War. He is a graduate of Cornell University, has an honorary PhD from Fitchburg College and was a Nieman Fellow in journalism at Harvard University. His blog appears daily at NewsDissector.com and his latest film on the financial crisis as crime story, *Plunder: The Crime of Our Time*, is available though PlundertheCrimeofourtime. com. He contributes opinion commentaries to the Al Jazeera English website. Comments to dissector@mediachannel.org.

Philip Seib is Professor of Journalism and Public Diplomacy, Professor of International Relations and Director of the Center on Public Diplomacy at the University of Southern California. He studies linkages between media and war and terrorism, as well as public diplomacy issues. He is author or editor of numerous books, including *Headline Diplomacy: How News Coverage Affects Foreign Policy*; *Beyond the Front Lines: How the News Media Cover a World Shaped by War*, *Broadcasts from the Blitz: How Edward R. Murrow Helped Lead America into War*, *New Media and the New Middle East*; *The Al Jazeera Effect: How the New Global Media Are Reshaping World Politics*; *Toward a New Public Diplomacy: Redirecting U.S. Foreign Policy*; *Global Terrorism and New Media*; and the forthcoming *Real-Time Diplomacy: Politics and Power in the Social Media Era*. He is the series editor of the Palgrave Macmillan Series in International Political Communication, co-editor of the Palgrave Macmillan Series in Global Public Diplomacy and co-editor of the journal *Media, War, and Conflict*.

Olga Smirnova, PhD, is an Associate Professor at the Faculty of Journalism of Moscow State University. She is also the Deputy Dean and the Chair of Center for Gender and Media Studies. Her academic interests include journalism in Russia, digital divide and mass media and gender studies in mass media. She is editor of six research monographs and has authored more than 50 articles and book chapters.

Helga Tawil-Souri is Assistant Professor in the Department of Media, Culture, and Communication at New York University. Her research considers issues of globalization, media technologies, cultural expressions, and their relationship to economic and political change in the Middle East. She has published work on Arab and Palestinian broadcasting industries and cinema, internet development, video games, checkpoints and cultural/political spaces of resistance. She is also a photographer and documentary filmmaker.

Elena Vartanova is Professor, Dean and Chair in Media Theory and Media Economics at the Faculty of Journalism, Moscow State University. Her research interests include post-Soviet transformation of Russian media; media economics, information society and media systems in Nordic countries. Vartanova is author and editor of many books on Russian and Nordic media systems, information society and media economics. She has also published more than 100 research articles in Russian academic journals.

Milly Williamson is a Senior Lecturer in Film and Television Studies at Brunel University. She is the author of a number of articles on representations of Muslims in the media and of the film studies monograph *The Lure of the Vampire* (Wallflower, 2005).

ACKNOWLEDGEMENTS

Edited volumes are collaborative projects and we are fortunate to have been able to work with leading academics and journalists from different countries to provide a global spotlight on the complex relationship between terrorism and its mediation. We are deeply indebted to all our contributors as well as grateful to our colleagues in our respective departments for making this collection possible. Our gratitude too for Mila Steele at SAGE for her enthusiastic support for the project. Finally, we thank our families for their patience during our periods of absence.

Des Freedman and Daya Kishan Thussu

1

INTRODUCTION

Dynamics of Media and Terrorism
Des Freedman and Daya Kishan Thussu

Virtual or real, national or transnational, state-sponsored or executed by small groups, terrorism in all its forms remains a central concern for contemporary societies. It has not disappeared with the assassination of Osama bin Laden nor the emergence of a new narrative of democracy during the 'Arab spring' of 2011. Terrorism defines politics and international relations as well as social and cultural interactions in our globalizing world (Laqueur, 1977; Stepanova, 2008; Pape and Feldman, 2010; Foreign Policy, 2011; Schmid, 2011). According to the Global Terrorism Database compiled by the National Consortium for the Study of Terrorism and Responses to Terrorism (START), part of the Department of Homeland Security, more than 87,000 terrorist attacks took place worldwide between 1970 and 2008, attributed to over 2,100 terrorist groups. The US government data shows that, in 2009 alone, 11,000 terrorist attacks occurred in 83 countries, resulting in more than 15,700 deaths – the largest number taking place in South Asia.

As Table 1.1 shows, the countries afflicted most by terrorism are located in the global South, and yet terrorism remains a major geopolitical concern in the West, especially since 9/11. Media representations of terrorism are also skewed in favour of Western perceptions of and perspectives on the global and open-ended 'war on terror'. As we mark the tenth year after the events of 9/11, this book provides an opportunity to examine, in a global context, what the 'war on terror' has meant for media and its study. It is an appropriate time to evaluate the media's relationship to a changed geo-political environment and to pose questions about media performance and influence. In the years since 9/11, the world has witnessed two major conflicts – Afghanistan and Iraq – both continuing despite American 'combat operations' in Iraq being renamed as 'stability operations'. The NATO-led bombardment of Libya in 2011 is a continuation of the policy of 'regime change', which the US has enunciated and mainstream Western media largely endorsed.

Table 1.1   Top ten countries affected by terrorism, 1970–2008

Country	Number of fatalities
Colombia	6777
Peru	6038
El Salvador	5331
India	4323
Northern Ireland	3770
Spain	3176
Iraq	2968
Turkey	2695
Sri Lanka	2591
Pakistan	2529

Source: START, n.d.

As soon as President George W. Bush announced the official Global War on Terrorism (GWOT) on 20 September 2001, barely ten days after the attacks on New York and Washington, than the phrase 'war on terror' was snapped up by the US media. Given the latter's global reach and influence, the phrase gained worldwide currency, legitimizing the phenomenon, though how a state can wage a war against 'terror', which is neither an organization nor a state, remains, to put it mildly, deeply questionable.

The news media have played a crucial role in developing the narrative of the 'war on terror' as an ever-breaking global story, thus projecting the 'war on terror' as the most serious threat in our collective imagination. The conflict has given the media world a 'global vocabulary war' (Halliday, 2011: xi), with new words and phrases such as 'waterboarding', 'Shock and Awe' and 'extraordinary rendition'. The term 'war on terror' continues to be widely used in the media, though it is now officially given a less aggressive title under President Obama as 'overseas contingency operations'. Yet its open-ended, pre-emptive and global remit remains unchanged.

In the post-Cold War, post-Soviet world, the 'war on terror' has had an Islamic connotation. Unlike the Irish Republican Army (IRA) or Euskadi ta Askatasuna – Basque Fatherland and Liberty (ETA) (which are not labelled Catholic terrorists), or Sri Lankan Tamil separatists and Indian Maoists (not described as Hindu terrorist groups), the ubiquity and danger of 'Islamic' terrorism, exemplified by shadowy networks with their alleged links to 'rogue' states, are constantly invoked in the media. This view of Islamic militancy is undifferentiated: Islamist groups in different parts of the world – al-Qaeda (reputedly led by Osama bin Laden, himself partly a creation of the CIA which was also instrumental in his assassination in 2011) in Afghanistan/Pakistan, Hezbollah in Lebanon, Hamas in Palestine, al-Shabab in Somalia, Chechen groups, Lashkar-e-Toiba in Kashmir and Jemaah Islamiyah in

Indonesia – are all too often presented in the mainstream media as part of a seamless transnational terror network which links terrorist activities in such diverse locations as Madrid, Mumbai and Moscow.

Manuel Castells has suggested that the 'war on terror and its associated images and themes (al-Qaeda, Afghanistan, the Iraq War, radical Islamism, Muslims in general) constructed a network of associations in people's minds. They activated the deepest emotion in the human brain: the fear of death' (Castells, 2009: 169). It is undoubtedly the case that Islamic militant groups – in Palestine, Chechnya, Iraq, Pakistan, Afghanistan, India – have used terrorist activities (including suicide bombings) as an extreme manifestation of political protest. But what is the motivation which drives young men and women to sacrifice their lives? Is it extreme Islamist propaganda or, as Pape and Feldman have argued, that the rhetoric of Islamist extremist groups 'functions mainly as a recruiting tool in the context of national resistance' while the 'principal cause of suicide terrorism is resistance to foreign occupation, *not Islamic fundamentalism*' (Pape and Feldman, 2010: 20). Pape and Feldman's study of suicide bombings shows that 'over 95 per cent of the suicide attacks are in response to foreign occupation' (2010: 329). Hassan's extensive and comparative research on suicide bombers also points to the diversity of motives behind such acts and the specificity of a particular political situation in a given country (Hassan, 2010).

The vast majority of the world's one-billion Muslims have nothing to do with terrorism. Indeed, they are victims of this scourge and the 'war on terror' has brought misery and mayhem to large parts of the Islamic world. The death of Iraqis since the 2003 US invasion varies from an astonishing 1 million (as published in the *Lancet* in 2006) to the Iraq Body Count figure of more than 100,000 (Burnham et al., 2006). In other costs, the daily expenditure of the US military is estimated to be $1.75 billion, while the real cost of the Iraq invasion itself has been about $3 trillion, and arguably contributed to the economic downturn we are facing today (Stiglitz and Bilmes, 2008; Stiglitz, 2010). The US has increased its military spending by 81 per cent since 2001, and now accounts for 43 per cent of the global total, six times its nearest rival China, according to data from SIPRI (SIPRI, 2011).

Yet in a globalized world, the distinction between national and transnational terrorism has been disappearing. Traditionally, terrorists groups have depended on, and benefited from, the support – ideological, financial and political – from groups outside the national territory. There is a long history of such associations: from Russian socialist revolutionaries at the beginning of the 1900s (who planned attacks and procured material in France and Switzerland) to anti-colonial and other national liberation movements in the twentieth century which were internationalized. Cold War politics ensured that many socialist governments and European left-wing groups (such as Baader-Meinhof and the IRA) supported radical Palestinian organizations, while right-wing groups like the Nicaraguan Contras were funded by the CIA. Furthermore, just as the Soviet Union trained anti-Western movements in Africa and Arab world, the US supported *mujahideen* in Afghanistan and UNITA in Angola (Cronin, 2009).

However, in the post-Cold War, post 9/11 world a particular version of terrorism has come to dominate policy and media discourse internationally. The Kremlinologists have been replaced by the proliferation of 'jihadi studies', one leading exponent of which has baldly suggested that the 'war on terror' is going to be a generational event: *The Longest War* (Bergen, 2011). For the US, dealing with terrorism has become a major post-Cold War strategic priority. Given the primacy of the US as the world's largest economy and its formidable media, military and technological power, this strategic priority seems to have become a global political priority. By virtue of its unprecedented capacity for global surveillance, as well as its domination of global communication hardware and software (from satellites to telecommunication networks; from cyberspace to 'total spectrum dominance' of real space, and the messages which travel through these), the US is able to disseminate its image of terrorism to the world at large. 'What are the connections between technological innovations and Western imperialism?' asks Headrick in his latest book. His answer is 'the desire to conquer and control other peoples; a technological advantage is itself a motive for imperialism' (Headrick, 2010: 5). 'The Great American Mission', to borrow a phrase from the title of a book about America's global modernization effort – 9/11 and its aftermath – has given the US a pretext to shape the world to suit its own geo-strategic agenda (Ekbladh, 2009). It is difficult to disagree with the observations of the historian of US imperialism Richard Immerman:

> The empire that America constructed in the twentieth century is the most powerful empire in world history. Its rival Soviet empire, and its antecedent British Empire, pale in comparison. Its global leadership, when measured in terms of technological innovation, manufacturing, gross domestic product, or any other frame of reference, far eclipses all competitors. Its military superiority is breathtaking, and it continues to grow. It has assembled institutions – the North Atlantic Treaty Organization, the International Monetary Fund and World Bank, the Organization of American States, the World Trade Organization, and more – that provide potent mechanisms for global management. (Immerman, 2010: 12)

The majority of mainstream media enthusiastically take part in this global management process. Immerman notes that the phrase 'American empire' appeared more than 1,000 times in news stories during the six months prior to the 2003 Iraq invasion.

The global reach and influence of American media are well documented: from traditional newspapers and news magazines (*New York Times*, *Time*), to news networks (CNN International) to online news aggregators (Google, YouTube) (Thussu, 2007). The US vision and version of terrorism is therefore extended to reach a global audience. In Russia, the government has tried to link its Chechen problem with international terrorism, with the former Foreign Minister Igor Ivanov claiming that 'the war in Chechnya is against international terrorism – not Chechens, but international bandits and terrorists' (cited in Gilligan, 2009: 6). The suppression of Muslim minorities in China's north-western Xinjiang region was also framed as China's war on terrorism (Wayne, 2009). In India – one of the countries worst affected by terrorism-related violence – large sections of the media and intelligentsia have bought into the US 'war on terror' discourse. Across the Middle East, often unrepresentative governments have used the pretext of terrorism further to strengthen their grip on the levers of security states as well as to curtail civil and journalistic liberties. For example, during the 2011 NATO-led bombing of Libya, the government of Muammar al-Qaddafi claimed that the rebels in the Eastern part of the country were supporters of al-Qaeda.

Terrorism discourse has impacted on international aid policy. It has been suggested that 'development and aid policy, institutions and operations have been affected' by the 'shifting global politics driven and legitimated by the global war on terror regime' (Howell and Lind, 2009: 1293). Fighting terrorism has also been accompanied by the massive expansion of the so-called private military and security companies. This privatization of state-sponsored killings and outsourcing to private security networks has been presented as being more 'effective' in dealing with terrorism (Singer, 2003; Stanger, 2009). Among other key benefits of such a conflict is how it fills the coffers of the world's arms merchants: world military spending reached $1.6 trillion in 2010, according to SIPRI. The US remains the world's largest exporter of military equipment, accounting for 30 per cent of global arms exports in 2006–10 (SIPRI, 2011). Terrorism, and efforts to challenge it, thus remain central projects inside the global geo-political environment.

Defining 'Terrorism'

Yet despite its primacy in contemporary politics there is a distinct lack of agreement on how to define terrorism. There are, as a SIPRI study argues, 'objective reasons for the lack of agreement on a definition of terrorism – namely, the diversity and multiplicity of its forms, types and manifestations' (Stepanova, 2008: 5).

When Major Nidal Malik Hasan, the main suspect in the 2009 shooting of 13 army personnel at Ford Hood, Texas, was featured on the cover of *Time* magazine (23 November 2009), the word 'TERRORIST?' was emblazoned over his eyes. Jared Lee Loughner, accused of critically wounding Rep. Gabrielle Giffords and killing six others in Tucson, Arizona, also made it on to the cover (24 January 2011) but this time the headline focused on 'Guns. Speech. Madness'. The *Wall Street Journal* also treated the two incidents in very different ways: '[Sen. Joe] Lieberman Suggests Army Shooter Was "Home-Grown Terrorist"' was how it covered the Fort Hood story on 9 November 2009 while on 10 January 2011 the WSJ's headline was 'Suspect Fixated on Giffords'. The line between acts of terror and insanity was drawn very tightly. It seems so obvious, after all, that a Muslim targeting American soldiers must be a terrorist while a 22-year-old white native of Tucson must simply be disturbed.

Interestingly, the FBI stopped publishing official data on domestic terror attacks after 2005 so it is very difficult to find out how many other similar incidents have been classified as 'terrorist' or not. Annual reports on terrorism are now required by Federal law but only in relation to international terrorism. However, even the director of START, notes that:

> the gravity of excluding domestic attacks can be felt when we consider that two of the most noteworthy terrorist events of the 1990s – the March 1995 nerve agent attack on the Tokyo subway and the April 1995 bombing of the federal office building in Oklahoma City – would remain unrecorded in most event data bases because both lacked any known foreign involvement. (Quoted in NCTC, 2009: 73)

Data on US domestic terrorism is still compiled and the Global Terrorism Database (hosted by START) records that, between 2006 and 2008, 62 incidents of terrorism were recorded inside the US with eight fatalities. Of those perpetrators identified, not a single one was related to Islamist organizations while all were drawn either from the Ku Klux Klan, other neo-Nazi groups or the Animal Liberation Front (START, n.d.). In Europe, the other alleged theatre of 'Islamic terrorism' activity, out of 249 terrorist attacks carried out within the European Union in 2010, only three were attributed to Islamic extremists, according to the Europol's Terrorism Situation and Trend Report (Europol, 2011: 9).

This is where definitions matter and where the influence of the media in making things 'obvious' is particularly stark. By privileging certain associations – for example, of Islam as a 'violent' religion, of the West as a 'victim' of terrorist attacks, of terrorism itself as a form of violence carried out against 'democratic' states – the media assist in the naturalization of particular interpretations of terrorism and thus legitimize specific strategies used to confront terrorist actions. Such strategies might include passing domestic anti-terror legislation, curbing civil liberties in order to reduce the threat of terrorism and invading, occupying and bombing countries that are said to host terrorist elements – all in the name of a 'war on terror' conducted by a 'civilized' West against a less civilized 'other'.

The problem is that there is no single, commonly accepted definition of terrorism on which to base such associations and therefore no independent and reliable way of assessing what constitutes a terrorist act; hence the old adage that 'one person's terrorist is another person's freedom fighter'. There are instead interpretations: socially constructed understandings of events based on 'conscious efforts to manipulate perceptions to promote certain interests at the expense of others' (Turk, 2004: 490). Nevertheless, we have seen the emergence of an entire industry dedicated to defining terrorism that is populated by academics, government officials, judicial personnel, defence experts, security consultants and even the United Nations. After hundreds of thousands of pages and many dozens of competing definitions, there is still no consensus. For example, the US government's National Counterterrorism Centre still maintains that it is difficult to distinguish between terrorism and other forms of violence, such as sectarian attacks or hate crimes (NCTC, 2010: 4–5), while, in his 52-page report carried out for the UK government as the 'Independent Reviewer of Terrorism Legislation', Lord Carlile freely admits that '[h]ard as I have striven, and as many definitions as I have read, I have failed to conclude that there is one that I could regard as the paradigm' (Carlile, 2007: 4). This is only the latest defeat in the desperate search for the perfect definition, a failing that was initially identified by Walter Laqueur in his 1977 study of terrorism in which he insisted that 'a comprehensive definition of terrorism … does not exist nor will it found in the foreseeable future' (Laqueur, 1977: 5).

Of course, this lack of precision has not stopped interested parties from adopting their preferred perspectives on terrorism in order to justify their actions (in engaging in, responding to or simply trying to understand terrorism) nor has it prevented encyclopaedic efforts to map the multiple definitions that are used. Schmid and Jongman (2005) famously identified 109 separate definitions and also extracted data on the most common elements used in these definitions, of which 'violence', 'politics', 'fear' and 'threat' respectively dominated the top four (2005: 5). Michael Hoffman, from the US Military Academy at West Point, spends the first 40 pages of his influential book *Inside Terrorism* discussing definitions of terrorism and concludes with his own version: terrorism 'as the deliberate creation and exploitation of fear through violence or the threat of violence in the pursuit of political change' (Hoffman, 2006: 40).

This definition may be admirably concise in its linking of acts of terror and the generation of fear but it omits two rather important factors: the subjects and objects of terrorism. In relation to the latter, many definitions emphasize that the targets of terrorist violence are 'non-combatants'. Yet any historical guide to terrorism shows us that targets of terrorist attacks have included tsars, archdukes, presidents, generals and occupying soldiers, as well as civilians, so that the question of what constitutes a 'legitimate' target remains very much a subjective one. In part, this requires an appreciation of how what is described as 'terrorism' has been understood differently in different historical periods (Laqueur, 1977; Carr, 2006; Chaliand and Blin, 2007; Hoffman, 2006; Rubin and Rubin, 2008; Law, 2009). Laqueur, for example, discusses the operations of terrorist groups in the Roman and Persian Empires and argues that terrorism only 'became a term of abuse with criminal implications' (Laqueur, 1977: 6) following Jacobin rule in the French Revolution. This form of 'state terror' is quite different to the 'propaganda of the deed', targeted assassinations of powerful political figures that were pursued by anarchists in the nineteenth century, or the use of violence by nationalist groups against occupying forces in the following century. As Laqueur notes:

> No definition of terrorism can possibly cover all the varieties of terrorism that have appeared throughout history: peasant wars and labour disputes and brigandage have been accompanied by systematic terror, and the same is true of with regard to general wars, civil wars, revolutionary wars, wars of national liberation and resistance movements against foreign occupiers. (1977: 7)

But while the history of terrorism suggests that terrorist acts emanate from a range of both state and non-state actors, contemporary definitions increasingly limit the agents of terrorism to the latter, for example 'an organization with an identifiable chain of command or conspiratorial cell structure' or a 'small collection of individuals' (Hoffman, 2006: 40). This is precisely the definition used today by the US State Department that is based on Title 22 of the US Code, section 2656f(d)(2): 'The term "terrorism" means premeditated, politically motivated violence perpetrated against non-combatant targets by subnational groups or clandestine agents usually intended to intended to influence an audience.'

In the post 9/11 era, terrorism has all too often been reduced to acts of fanaticism and random brutality carried out by 'clandestine' groups against democratic states – this is the 'irregular warfare' that is distinct from the 'regular' military action (including the use of air strikes, psy-ops, rendition and waterboarding) conducted by elected governments. By definition, the former is illegitimate, the latter legitimate; the action is 'terrorist', the reaction is 'counterterrorist'. Conceived in this way, terrorism refers to acts of indiscriminate violence carried out against those with the power to define it in this way or, as Noam Chomsky put it, that 'the term applies only to terrorism against us, not the terrorism we carry out against them' (Chomsky, 2002: 131). Yet as Miller and Sabir argue in their chapter in this book, we should attempt as far as it is possible to adopt a 'literal' understanding of the concepts we use so that terrorism is defined not by the identity of the perpetrators but the nature of the deeds. When they argue that terrorism should be understood in relation to 'actions involving the creation of terror and usually the harming or perhaps deliberate targeting of civilians and non-combatants', this must necessarily involve both state and non-state actors, those of democratic and non-democratic regimes, small groups of people and official standing armies. The definition, they suggest, must be applied without discrimination.

However, without agreement on what terrorism refers to as well as the identity of its protagonists and victims, the use of such a slippery term is likely to have serious policy consequences. As Edward Said remarked following the events of 9/11, terrorism

> has become synonymous now with anti-Americanism, which, in turn, has become synonymous with being critical of the United States, which, in turn, has become synonymous with being unpatriotic. That's an unacceptable series of equations. The definition of terrorism has to be more precise, so that we are able to discriminate between, for example, what it is that the Palestinians are doing to fight the Israeli military occupation and terrorism of the sort that resulted in the World Trade Center bombing. (Quoted in Barsamian, 2001)

If 'terrorism' continues to be deployed in a 'propagandistic' way, as Miller and Tabir suggest it is all too often, then it follows that those who have definitional power in the West will continue to conflate many different political responses to perceived injustices – failing to distinguish, for example, between the attacks in London on 7/7 and the resistance to the occupation of Iraq – as 'terrorist' (and therefore illegitimate) and the West's attempts to pre-empt or challenge them as necessarily justified acts of 'counter-terrorism'. If this is the case, many countries in the West will be set to repeat the major foreign-policy mistakes of the last ten years.

Terrorism as Communication

We are concerned above all in this book to draw attention to the way in which existing definitions of and approaches to terrorism are naturalized through a range of institutions including, most centrally for us, the media. For the majority of people who are not directly subject to its violence or intimidation, terrorism has to be 'made to mean' and the media are crucial ideological vehicles in systematizing and organizing disparate 'acts of terror'. Indeed, media are not simply external actors passively bringing the news of terrorist incidents to global audiences but are increasingly seen as active agents in the actual conceptualization of terrorist events. They are credited, in other words, not simply with definitional but constitutive power: we now have 'mediatised terrorism' (Cottle, 2006), 'media-oriented terrorism' (Surette et al., 2009), 'media-ized warfare' (Louw, 2003) and 'mass-mediated terrorism' (Nacos, 2007).

In part this goes back to older debates about the symbolic character of the terrorist act: that it is aimed not simply to terrorize the immediate target but to create fear amongst wider groups through the re-circulation of the original event. 'Terrorism is a symbolic act designed to influence political behavior through extra-normal means' famously wrote former National Security Council member Thomas Thornton nearly 50 years ago (1964: 73). Yet the growing impact of electronic and, more recently, digital media has intensified the spectacular capacities of terrorism so that it has come to be described not simply in relation to media but, in itself, as a 'communicative act' (Hoskins and O'Loughlin, 2007: 9) and a 'symbolically organized event' (Blain, 2009: 24). When leading terrorism theorists Schmid and de Graaf first wrote in 1982 that 'an act of terrorism is in reality an act of communication. For the terrorist, the message matters, not the victim' (1982: 14), this was a clear demonstration that the symbolic character of the terrorist act had fused with the amplifying potential of new information and communication technologies to create a new and highly visible form of political struggle.

In an era of widespread media literacy, 24-hour news, satellite television, social media and decentralized online networks like WikiLeaks, entire sections on 'terrorism as communication' are now very familiar in contemporary studies of terrorism (cf Turk, 2004; Hoffman, 2006; McAllister and Schmid, 2011). As we have seen above, the State Department definition of terrorism actually highlights the notion that terrorists are communicating to specific audiences, a point reinforced by Louw's argument that 9/11 was purposefully aimed at three sets of audiences: Americans, al-Qaeda sympathizers and Muslims more generally (Louw, 2003: 214). For Kellner, 'September 11 could also only be a mega-event in a global media world, a society of the spectacle where the whole world is watching and participates in global media spectacle' (2002: 152).

Terrorism has thus come to be discussed inside media theory in a whole number of ways including the dynamics of its discursive construction (for example, Hodges and Nilep, 2007; Blain, 2009), the framing devices needed to 'furnish consistent, predictable, simple, and powerful narratives that are embedded in the social construction of reality' (Norris et al., 2003: 5) and that have contributed to a 'new model of the relationship between government and the media in the foreign policy process' (Entman, 2003: 416), and the mutual interest of both terrorists and media organizations to circulate dramatic images (Nacos, 2007). Hoskins and O'Loughlin (2007) write powerfully about how television in particular has become structurally fixated on terror and that broadcast news 'modulates' terror in the sense of simultaneously exaggerating its potential and containing representations of its threats. Television has become so dependent on terror in recent years that they ask the question: 'Is there a more effective means of spreading terror than through the news media's inability or unwillingness to prevent itself from being the principal publicity of those acts it abhors but which are key to its own economy?' (2007: 102).

These various approaches can all be valuable in opening up the relationship between media and terrorism but there is a significant danger in focusing too much on the mediated nature of terrorism and, in particular, on the idea of terrorism as the most spectacular form of modern political struggle: that we pay attention to only one, highly visible, form of modern terrorism, such as the attacks on the Twin Towers or the storming of the Taj hotel in Mumbai in 2008. According to James Der Derian, for example (2005: 24), 'Thanks to the immediacy of television, the internet and other networked information technology, we see terrorism everywhere in real time, all the time. In turn, terrorism has taken on an iconic, fetishised and, most significantly, a highly optical character'.

This emphasis on the 'optical' character of terrorism is certainly relevant to the major 'media events' of 9/11 and 7/7 but what about the less visible, far more mundane but no less terrifying bombing campaigns of civilians in Iraq and Afghanistan that were not accompanied by live pictures and Fox News commentaries? What of the individuals who 'disappeared' in Latin American and the Middle East without the aid of a media spotlight (let alone the refusal by President Obama to release pictures of the assassination of Bin Laden)? Of course 9/11 and other acts carried out by small groups who wish to use the amplifying powers of the media are evidence of a mediated form of terrorism but certainly not all forms of terrorism take place in and through the media.

Indeed, Schmid and Jongman – purveyors of the 109 definitions of terrorism – acknowledge this to be true: 'While insurgent terrorists and the media often seek each other out, state terrorists generally avoid publicity and attempt to conceal the regimes' repressive activities by media censorship and/ or disinformation' (Schmid and Jongman, 2005: 164). The traditional view was that terrorism would be more likely to take place in liberal democratic countries – 'in societies which have no censorship' (Laqueur, 1977: 110) – where, therefore, terrorists would be able to guarantee retransmission of their activities. But which country in the world today can claim – in the light, for example, of the hysterical reaction to WikiLeaks' release of diplomatic documents – to have no censorship or disinformation systems? Nacos solves this problem by simply excluding state terrorism from her analysis of 'mass-mediated terrorism' (Nacos, 2007), precisely because governments do not want to publicize violence against non-combatants and 'would rather limit media attention and even suppress public disclosure' (Nacos, 2007: 28). The bombing of Libya in 1986, as well as the invasion and occupation of both Afghanistan and Iraq in the subsequent decades, are thus seen collectively as 'counterterrorism' and not terrorism.

Media theorists need fully to contextualize terrorism: to recognize the ways in which media have been implicated in transformations of terrorist acts but also to acknowledge that terror is an essential part of unequal societies and an imbalanced world. We run the risk of mediatizing – and restricting – terrorism into an adjunct of symbolic systems rather than (geo)political conflicts. Of course terrorists understand the power of media which is why some of those who resort to terror do everything they can to stay beneath the media radar (to the extent that it exists and that all journalists are anxious to reveal terrorist activities especially when they may involve their own governments). It does not mean that terrorism requires a sophisticated understanding of framing and mediation for terrorist acts to take place. Perhaps we have been so stunned by the images of 9/11 that we focus on the spectacular and marginalize the banalities of the terror we do not, or are not allowed to, see.

Framing the 'War on Terror'

Media thus play a crucial role in perception and expectation management, particularly during a conflict such as the 'war on terror' that relates to a distant and ill-defined enemy (Hess and Kalb, 2003). As Baum and Groeling note: 'The credibility of media *messages*, their *sources*, and the *messengers* communicating those messages, as well as the *context* within which the messages are delivered, all mediate the influence of news on consumers' (Baum and Groeling, 2009: 3, italics in original).

How these sources and their messages cultivate an ideological framework, within which conflicts are defined and information about these disseminated, remains a crucial arena for media research. In his study of US media coverage of the Vietnam war, Hallin noted that anti-communism was an ideological trope, ensuring that 'journalists and government policymakers were united' behind the US policy of combating communism in Asia (Hallin, 1986: 24). Is the 'war on terror' (whatever its official title might be) a current ideological trope which unites policymakers and journalists?

Winning 'hearts and minds' of 'terrorists' is a key recommendation of the US military's Counterinsurgency Field Manual (COIN FM), released in 2006 (Kahl, 2007). This chimes with the message coming out of the official propaganda channels of the US government, including Al-Hurra, in operation since 2004 and funded by the Broadcasting Board of Governors (BBG), a federal agency that supervises all non-military international broadcasting. BBG's propaganda networks active on the 'war on terror' include Voice of America (VOA), Radio Free Europe/Radio Liberty (RFE/RL) and the Middle East Broadcasting Networks (MBN). Their content is also regularly carried by local transmitters in Iraq, Pakistan and Afghanistan on TV, FM and AM radio; in 2010, there were 360 affiliates for VOA and 62 for RFE/RL (BBG, 2011). The BBG is unambiguous in its goal: 'to create an increasingly effective and modern international broadcasting system that reaches significant audiences where most needed, in support of US strategic interests' (BBG, 2011: 7).

Apart from the official framing of news, the US entertainment industry too plays an important role in shaping global perceptions about terrorism. The Hollywood-dominated 'Military–Industrial–Media–Entertainment Network' has a major contribution in making the 'war on terror' an entertainment genre (Der Derian, 2009). As Shaheen has argued, the representations of Islam, and especially of Arabs, in most Hollywood films is deeply problematic in terms of racist stereotypes which contribute to a discourse where Muslims are projected as a threat to Western ways of life (Shaheen, 2008; see also Chapter 7 by Boyd-Barrett et al in this volume). Terrorism is also the prime subject of several popular American television series like *24*, *The Unit* and *Sleeper Cell*, which are all examples of intersections between popular entertainment and politics (Kellner, 2009).

The relationship between US entertainment industries and the military is also in evidence in the genre of video games. In 2004, the Institute for Creative Technology, affiliated with the University of Southern California, licensed *Full Spectrum Warrior*, which encourages gamers to coordinate military missions in an urban guerrilla situation in a fictional Arab country. Other popular games developed with a terrorist theme include *Conflict: Global Terror*, released in 2005 and the 2010 *Medal of Honour*, set in Afghanistan. The genre has also been popular as an app for smart phones; one example is *Arcade Super Sniper – War on Terror*, designed for iPhones and in operation since 2009. This 'militainment' has redefined terrorism as an object of consumer play, deployed by the Pentagon in association with the gaming industry (see Toby Miller's Chapter 6 in this book). As one commentator notes: 'Video game is increasingly both medium and metaphor by which war invades our hearts and minds' (Stahl, 2006: 127). It has been suggested that al-Qaeda too has taken a page from the Hollywood handbook. 'Its real expertise is not military damage, but media manipulation through sensational acts of special-effects terror that rivet attention …'(Gardels and Medavoy, 2009: 5).

Looking beyond the 'War on Terror'

Despite systematic and largely successful attempts to manage 'official' representations of terrorism, dissonances keep appearing. This is partly to do with the fact that, ten years after 9/11, the 'war on terror' narrative is simply harder to rationalize. The idea, for example, that the US and UK presence in Afghanistan is needed to make the world a 'safer' place is even tougher to justify after the killing of bin Laden in Pakistan. As the documentary filmmaker Adam Curtis put it in his response to bin Laden's death: 'One of the main functions of politicians – and journalists – is to simplify the world for us. But there comes a point when – however much they try – the bits of reality, the fragments of events, won't fit into the old frame' (Curtis, 2011: 29). The 'war on terror' frame is hardly convincing when significant parts of the Arab world are spilling onto the streets demanding democracy and not jihad.

Additionally, in the new digital media landscape where alternative messages travel globally and instantaneously (Nye, 2011; Shirky, 2011), the opportunities offered by Web 2.0-enabled mobile media will mean that the mediation of terrorism is likely to become more multi-layered and multi-lingual. Within international relations, pleas have been made to take blogs and social networking sites more seriously as new platforms for global communication (Carpenter and Drezner, 2010). For optimists:

> This global public square is the new space of power where images compete and ideas are contested; it is where hearts and minds are won or lost and legitimacy is established. It is a space both of friction and fusion where the cosmopolitan commons of the twenty-first century is being forged. (Gardels and Medavoy, 2009: 1)

However, a word of caution is in order. Apart from global media conglomerates such as Google and Facebook, with their formidable power over the aggregation and distribution of information, governments are determined to ensure that they control the global commons. The US Broadcasting Board of Governors, among others, is devising information technologies for 'maximized opportunities to spread content via viral marketing and use of social networking sites' (BBG, 2011), while the Obama administration's promotion of '21st Century Statecraft' depends on using social media to 'help individuals be empowered for their own development' (Clinton, n.d.). The 'virtual revolution in diplomatic and military affairs' which is 'enabled by networks not actors' demands new ways of looking at the framing of terrorism (Der Derian, 2009). As the phenomenon of the so-called CNN effect is supplemented by those of Al-Jazeera and YouTube effects, and mainstream media compete with subaltern media flows in a global theatre of images and ideologies (Thussu, 2007), the mediation of terrorism is likely to become increasingly contested. The advent of WikiLeaks – which has made international diplomatic and journalistic communication porous but also problematic – is a harbinger of what is to come (Davis et al., 2010; Keller, 2011). The civic and social media sector as witnessed during the anti-government demonstrations across the Middle East – the 'Arab spring' of 2011 – offers unparalleled opportunities for democratizing political communication. How is this feast of mobile videos and networked media to be harnessed? Who will distinguish facts from fiction, and half truths from rumours, and discriminate against both mediated hate and hagiography? The art of what Kovach and Rosenstiel term 'verification' (Kovach and Rosenstiel, 2010) is needed to ensure that, in the context of substantial pressure from propagandists on all sides, responsible media continue to sift through discourses of disinformation and work towards reconciliation and resolving the scourge of terrorism.

In geo-political terms, the diminished economic power of the US will make its version of terrorism discourse increasingly contested. As one leading US foreign-policy commentator notes: 'The rising power of China, India and other non-Western states presents a challenge to the old American-led order that will require new, expanded, and shared international governance arrangements' (Ikenberry, 2011: 31). In those altered governance arrangements how will terrorism, in all its versions, be framed? Both China and India represent civilizations whose roots are not in the Abrahamic religions and their perception of Islam therefore is less likely to be influenced by discourses that refer to the Crusades and the 'clash of civilizations'.

The other point worth keeping in mind is that if terrorism is essentially a political problem, as we have argued, it will eventually and inevitably have a political solution. The British experience of dealing with the IRA, the Peruvian government's dismantling of the Shining Path (Sendero Luminoso) guerrilla group and India's incorporation of the separatist Khalistan movement into democratic polity demonstrates that if underlying injustices are addressed terrorism-related problems can be resolved. It is also important not to discount the possibilities for political liberalization in the Islamic world, already exemplified by the cases of Turkey, Indonesia and Malaysia, among others (Hafez, 2010), let alone the emerging democracy movements in Tunisia, Egypt, Syria, Bahrain and elsewhere.

This book aims to provide a broader perspective on the relationship between media and terrorism: to recognize and discuss the ways in which media technologies and practices have helped to transform our understanding of terrorism (as well as the manner in which it operates) but also to highlight the full range of contextual factors that shape media's relationship to terrorism. The chapters that follow are divided into four parts, each with an introductory note.

Part 1 provides a historical and political context to the relationship between media and terrorism, from both Arab and Western perspectives. Part 3 links regional perspectives to global terrorism discourse with contributions covering South Asia, Russia, the Arab world and Scandinavia. The focus of the Part 2 is on representations of terrorism in the media. Two chapters in this section examine how popular culture – Hollywood and gaming industry – represent the 'war on terror'; two other chapters deal with how terrorism discourse has had a domestic impact on multiculturalism in Britain and France; while the final chapter in this section is based on a case study of the reception of the coverage of the 2008 Israeli attack on Lebanon. The final part of the book contains four essays that assess the relationship between journalism and the 'war on terror', two of which are written by working journalists with first-hand experience of reporting on terrorism. In addition, the section includes a chapter on news narratives on the war on terror and another on its impact on debates on migration and multiculturalism in Australia.

References

Barsamian, D. (2001) Interview with Edward Said, *The Progressive*, November. Available at: www.progressive.org/0901/intv1101.html (accessed 26 April 2011).

Baum, M. and Groeling, T. (2009) *War Stories: The Causes and Consequences of Public Views of War*. Princeton: Princeton University Press.

BBG (2011) *Fiscal Year 2010 Performance and Accountability Report*. Washington: Broadcasting Board of Governors.

Bergen, P. (2011) *The Longest War: The Enduring Conflict between America and Al-Qaeda*. New York: Simon & Schuster.

Blain, M. (2009) *The Sociology of Terrorism: Studies in Power, Subjection and Victimage Ritual*. Boca Raton: Universal Publishers.

Burnham, G., Lafta, R., Doocy, S. and Roberts, L. (2006) Mortality after the 2003 invasion of Iraq: a cross-sectional cluster sample survey. *Lancet* 368: 1421–1428.

Carlile, Lord (2007) *The Definition of Terrorism*, CM 7052. London: The Stationery Office.

Carpenter, C. and Drezner, D. (2010) International relations 2.0: the implications of new media for an old profession, *International Studies Perspectives* 11(3): 255–272.

Carr, M. (2006) *The Infernal Machine: A History of Terrorism from the Assassination of Tsar Alexander II to Al-Qaeda*. New York: The New Press.

Castells, M. (2009) *Communication Power*. Oxford: Oxford University Press.

Chaliand, G. and Blin, A. (eds) (2007) *The History of Terrorism: From Antiquity to Al-Qaeda*. Berkeley: University of California Press.

Chomsky, N. (2002) Who are the global terrorists? in K. Booth and T. Dunne (eds) *Worlds in Collision: Terror and the Future of Global Order*. Basingstoke: Palgrave Macmillan: 128–138.

Clinton, H. (n.d.) *21st Century Statecraft*, U.S. Department of State. Available at: www.state.gov/statecraft/index.htm (accessed 2 May 2011).

Cottle, S. (2006) *Mediatized Conflict: Developments in Media and Conflict Studies*. Maidenhead: Open University Press.

Cronin A. (2009) *How Terrorism Ends*. Princeton: Princeton University Press.

Curtis, A. (2011) Another goodies v baddies story has ended. Where will find the next? *Guardian*, May, p. 29.

Davis, N., Steele, J. and Leigh, D. (2010) Iraq war logs: secret files show how US ignored torture, *Guardian*, 22 October, p. 1.

Der Derian, J. (2005) Imaging terror: logos, pathos and ethos, *Third World Quarterly* 26(1): 23–37.

Der Derian, J. (2009) *Virtuous War: Mapping the Military–Industrial–Media–Entertainment Network*, second edition. New York: Routledge.

Ekbladh, D. (2009) *The Great American Mission, Modernization and the Construction of an American World Order*. Princeton: Princeton University Press.

Entman, R. (2003) Cascading activation, *Political Communication* 20: 415–432.

Europol (2011) *EU Terrorism Situation and Trend Report: TE-SAT 2011* Available at: www.europol.europa.eu/publications/EU_Terrorism_Situation_and_Trend_Report_TE-SAT/TE-SAT2011.pdf (accessed 2 May 2011)

Foreign Policy (2011) *The FP Survey: Terrorism, Foreign Policy*, January/February.

Gardels, N. and Medavoy, M. (2009) *American Idol after Iraq: Competing for Hearts and Minds in the Global Media Age*. Oxford: Wiley-Blackwell.

Gilligan, E. (2009) *Terror in Chechnya: Russia and the Tragedy of Civilians in War*. Princeton: Princeton University Press.

Hafez, K. (2010) *Radicalism and Political Reform in the Islamic and Western Worlds*. Cambridge: Cambridge University Press.

Halliday, F. (2011) *Shocked and Awed: How the War on Terror and Jihad Have Changed the English Language*. London: I. B.Tauris.

Hallin, D. (1986) *The Uncensored War: the Media and Vietnam*. Oxford: Oxford University Press.

Hassan, R. (2010) *Life as a Weapon: The Global Rise of Suicide Bombings*. London: Routledge.

Headrick, D. (2010) *Power over Peoples: Technology, Environments, and Western Imperialism, 1400 to the Present*. Princeton: Princeton University Press.

Hess, S. and Kalb, M. (eds) (2003) *The Media and the War on Terrorism*. Washington: Brookings Institution Press.

Hodges, A and Nilep, C. (eds) (2007) *Discourse, War and Terrorism*. Philadelphia: John Benjamins.

Hoffman, B. (2006) *Inside Terrorism*. New York: Columbia University Press.

Hoskins, A. and O'Loughlin, B. (2007) *Television and Terror: Conflicting Times and the Crisis of News Discourse*. Basingstoke: Palgrave Macmillan.

Howell, J. and Lind, J. (2009) Changing donor policy and practice in civil society in the post-9/11 aid context, *Third World Quarterly* 30(7): 1279–1296.

Ikenberry, J. (2011) *Liberal Leviathan: The Origins, Crisis, and Transformation of the American World Order*. Princeton: Princeton University Press.

Immerman, R. (2010) *Empire for Liberty: A History of American Imperialism from Benjamin Franklin to Paul Wolfowitz*. Princeton: Princeton University Press.

Kahl, C. (2007) COIN of the realm: is there a future for counterinsurgency? *Foreign Affairs* November/December, 169–176.

Keller, B. (2011) *Open Secrets: WikiLeaks, War and American Diplomacy: Complete and Expanded Coverage from The New York Times*. New York: nytimes.com/opensecrets.

Kellner, D. (2002) September 11, social theory and democratic politics, *Theory, Culture and Society* 19(4): 147–159.

Kellner, D. (2009) *Cinema Wars: Hollywood Film and Politics in the Bush–Cheney Era*. Oxford: Wiley Blackwell.

Kovach, B. and Rosenstiel, T. (2010) *Blur: How to Know What's True in the Age of Information Overload*. Washington: Bloomsbury.

Laqueur, W. (1977) *Terrorism*. London: Weidenfeld & Nicolson.

Law, R. (2009) *Terrorism: A History*. Cambridge: Polity.

Louw, P. E. (2003) The 'war against terrorism': a public relations challenge for the Pentagon, *Gazette* 65 (3): 211–230.

McAllister, B. and Schmid, A. (2011) Theories of terrorism in A. Schmid (ed.) *The Routledge Handbook of Terrorism Research*. New York: Routledge: 201–271.

Nacos, B. (2007) *Mass-Mediated Terrorism: The Central Role of the Media in Terrorism and Counterterrorism*. Lanham, MD: Rowman & Littlefield.

National Counterterrorism Center (NCTC) (2009) *2008 Report on Terrorism.* Washington, DC: NCTC. Available at: www.fas.org/irp/threat/nctc2008. pdf (accessed 26 April 2011).

National Counterterrorism Center (NCTC) (2010) *2009 Report on Terrorism.* Washington DC: NCTC. Available at: www.nctc.gov/witsbanner/docs/ 2009_report_on_terrorism.pdf (accessed 26 April 2011).

Norris, P., Kern, M. and Just, M. (2003) Framing terrorism in P. Norris, M. Kern and M. Just (eds) *Framing Terrorism: The News Media, The Government and the Public.* New York: Routledge: 3–23.

Nye, J. (2011) *The Future of Power.* New York: PublicAffairs.

Pape, R. and Feldman, J. (2010) *Cutting the Fuse: The Explosion of Global Suicide Terrorism and How to Stop It.* Chicago: University of Chicago Press.

Rubin, B. and Rubin, J. (2008) *Chronologies of Modern Terrorism.* Armonk, NY: M. E. Sharpe.

Schmid, A. (ed.) (2011) *The Routledge Handbook of Terrorism Research.* London: Routledge.

Schmid, A. and de Graaf, J. (1982) *Violence as Communication: Insurgent Terrorism and the Western News Media.* London: SAGE.

Schmid, A. and Jongman, A. (2005) *Political Terrorism: A New Guide to Actors, Authors, Concepts, Data Bases, Theories and Literature.* Piscataway, NJ: Transaction.

Shaheen, J. (2008) *Guilty: Hollywood's verdict on Arabs after 9/11.* Northampton, MA: Olive Branch Press.

Shirky, C. (2011) The political power of social media: technology, the public sphere, and political change, *Foreign Affairs* January/February, 28–41.

Singer, P. W. (2003) *Corporate Warriors: The Rise of the Privatized Military Industry.* New York: Cornell University Press.

SIPRI (2011) *SIPRI Yearbook 2011.* Stockholm: Stockholm International Peace Research Institute.

Stahl, R. (2006) Have you played the war on terror? *Critical Studies in Media Communication* 23(2): 112–130.

Stanger, A. (2009) *One Nation Under Contract: The Outsourcing of American Power and the Future of Foreign Policy.* London: Yale University Press.

START (n.d.) *Global Terrorism Database.* Available at: www.start.umd.edu/gtd/ (accessed 26 April 2011).

Stepanova, E. (2008) *Terrorism in Asymmetrical Conflict: Ideological and Structural Aspects*, SIPRI Research Report No. 23. Oxford: Oxford University Press.

Stiglitz, J. (2010) *America, Free Markets, and the Sinking of the World Economy.* New York: Norton.

Stiglitz, J. and Bilmes, L. (2008) *The Three Trillion Dollar War: The True Cost of the Iraq Conflict.* London: Allen Lane.

Surette, R., Hansen, K. and Noble, G. (2009) Measuring media oriented terrorism, *Journal of Criminal Justice* 37(4): 360–370.

Thornton, T. (1964) Terrorism as a weapon on political agitation, in H. Eckstein (ed.) *Internal War: Problems and Approaches*. New York: Free Press: 71–99.

Thussu, D. K. (2007) Mapping Global Media Flow and Contra-Flow, in D. K. Thussu (ed.) *Media on the Move: Global Flow and Contra-Flow*. London: Routledge: 11–32.

Turk, A. (2004) Sociology of terrorism, *Annual Review of Sociology* 30: 271–286.

Wayne, M. (2009) Inside China's war on terrorism. *Journal of Contemporary China* 18(59): 249–261.

PART 1
CONTEXTS

The opening section of the book attempts to map out some of the key contexts for an analysis of the relationship between media and terrorism. These include the geopolitical considerations that give rise to the use of violence to achieve political ends (such as resistance to foreign occupation or the struggle to control natural resources); religious and cultural objectives (that include campaigns over language rights and faith-based social orders); ideological debates concerning the interests of the various actors and the legitimacy of terrorism as a form of political struggle; access to the material resources of the media world; and, of course the potential of existing and emerging media forms to publicize and interpret terrorist actions for specific audiences.

In providing these contexts, we are keen to emphasize that terrorism is neither a wholly 'spectacular' affair, based on the production and circulation of images of explosions, beheadings and bombing raids, nor a matter simply of tactical decisions about how to pursue a particular political objective. To grasp the impact of the media on terrorist action requires an appreciation of both the geopolitical circumstances in which terrorism takes place as well as the possibilities afforded by communication technologies in the strategic calculation of the actors involved. To stress one at the expense of the other would be either to abstract 'mediated terrorism' from the wider political environment in which it has emerged or to exaggerate the symbolic character of contemporary terrorism where, as we have already noted, many assassinations, beatings, acts of torture and imprisonment take place off camera and are invisible to media audiences.

2

TERROR, WAR AND DISJUNCTURES IN THE GLOBAL ORDER

Lena Jayyusi

Lena Jayyusi situates her contribution in the context of a US-led 'war on terror' that has sought to link discursively Muslims and Islam itself to terrorism as part of a longer colonial project to terrorize and silence colonial subjects while presiding over their lands and resources. She argues that the 'war on terror' has served to re-designate Arab populations as a collective security 'threat' that has justified the near destruction of the social fabric over large swathes of the Middle East. 'Terror' in this context is a label used by the powerful to justify their own actions and to de-legitimize the response. This has required the mobilization of both physical and symbolic forms of pressure in which much of the mainstream media has been complicit, failing to identify the sources of violence and instability across the Arab world and reproducing negative stereotypes of Muslim populations. She describes the 'amnesia' of many journalistic reports of terror – that they are themselves de-contextualized – and argues that a dialectic of visibility/invisibility informs the new racism against Muslims and Arabs, and the logic of the terror wars directed at their region.

Ten years after the official launch of the 'war on terror', most people would agree that the symbolic environment within which we now live is a distinctly altered one from that in which we lived before. For some, the lived material environment has also been radically altered. This chapter will try to take stock of these changes and differences, to interrogate some crucial connections within them, and to explore what they mean and what they portend.

Today the terms 'Arab', 'Muslim' and 'Islam' have become discursively linked to the term 'terror'. To say that they are discursively linked does not simply mean that many people equate the two, but that even people who do not, who are mindful of the deeply problematic nature of such a position, find they have positively to assert the distinction. Even Arabs and Muslims find themselves called upon to demonstrate and accountably affirm that distinction repeatedly.[1] This is no mean achievement by the purveyors of the 'war on terror' and its administrative, political, cultural and military apparatus. This manifests and drives a distinct *discursive shift*. Though the figures of this shift are not radically new, their manifestations, usages and performative enactments do portend something new. Media discourse plays an agentive role in this: the mediating lens, representing, refracting and reflecting on events, on policies, and political and cultural figures, it constitutes the parameters of 'sense', normalcy and normativity for many.

The preoccupation of Western 'spokespersons' – politicians, academics, media personalities, religious leaders and reporters – with the Arab and Muslim world has now crystallized into an explicit configuration of thought and discourse, representable as the concern with 'Muslim/Islamic' difference. More than simply the threat of particular Muslim groups or organizations, it now appears as both a security threat for Western societies, as well as a civilizational one embedded in Islam itself, and irremediably marking the Arab world. For this to have developed has taken at least three decades, during which there have been moments that accelerated the process such as Samuel Huntington's 'clash of civilizations' thesis (1993, 1996). Even though, as Edward Said demonstrated (1978, 1994), Orientalist discourses, driven by and in turn driving colonial projects, have been a strategy of long standing, there is a difference: this time the 'civilizational threat' is deemed to be approaching, and itself encroaching upon, the territorial and lived domain of Western civilizational life. This development has been evident in the recent European discursive landscape, as well as the US landscape, and has even manifested itself in a telling way in the period during and after the Arab revolutions of 2011.

Preoccupying Signifiers, Corporeal Sites

Europe has recently occupied itself with heated discussions and pointed legislation to do with Muslim women's attire and bodily disposition: namely their veiling. This was most obviously the case in France, where in 2009 a French motion to ban the burqa and the niqab was introduced, provoking a heated public debate on the issue, that was explicitly tied into the question of what it is to be French. Yet, according to a French Internal Security Service Study (quoted in *The Independent*), out of a total population of adult Muslim women in France numbering 1,500,000 Muslims, only 2000 of them wear a burqa or niqab – a mere 0.13 per cent. Most of these happen to be younger women or French converts to Islam (see Lichfield, 2010). This, however, did nothing to dent the claims that the ban was based on the opposition to the oppression of women – here another somewhat paradoxical figure was embedded: the denial of agency, of choice, to Muslim women.

In Switzerland there was another heated public discussion, overshadowing other possible topics for public debate: this was on whether the construction of minarets, the towers from which the Muslim call to prayer is tradition-ally heard and which therefore can symbolize that call even when no physi-cal sounding takes place, should be allowed. The Swiss organized a plebiscite around this rather than other issues, emerging with a collective decision which ultimately violates the principles of the EU constitution and should have been seen as a violation of their own self-image as a pluralist and democratic society. The result of the vote was that 57.5 per cent supported a ban on minarets – this in a country which has only four minarets, none of which are used for the call to prayer. There are about 400,000 Muslims in Switzerland, mostly from Turkey and Kosovo, no more than four per cent of the population, and few of whom observe the most traditional mode of dress (Bremner 2009; Cumming-Bruce and Erlanger, 2009). Again, what is striking is the disproportionality of the action in relation to the context. Yet, in voting for a ban, the Swiss were clearly articulating a particular self-image, a European identity perceived to be essentially white and Christian, and not open to inflection by difference – not at least 'this' kind of difference. *An identity that is mooted as being at risk in the face of Muslim signs.* Again, curiously, Swiss feminists were mobilized in sup-port of the ban, on the grounds of their opposition to the oppression of women. They did not mind keeping company with the extreme right. In this context, one has to interrogate what is taken to constitute this European identity.

Perhaps the remarks of Pope Benedict XVI on Islam in his Regensburg lecture (12 September 2006) gives an insight. He quoted a fourteenth-century Byzantine emperor who made an unfavourable statement about Prophet Muhammad. Despite the assertion that these were not *his* words, but a quotation, the point of the quotation has to be analytically interrogated. In this case, the quotation (which he did not critique) was only used to serve his far more problematic larger claim. This was to do with the relationship between reason and faith, between God and reason, and between violence and religion. The distinction is made between Christian reason, embedded in the nature of

God, and Muslim obedience to an absolutely transcendent God, where reason is not paramount. This distinction is made in order to generate another one: the difference between conversion through reason (Christianity) and conversion through violence (Islam). The tropes of this discourse, if more sophisticated, are nevertheless isomorphic with the ones that shape the discourse of the European right on Islam and violence. For any member of the public, the quotation would be read in the context of the lecture's other points, and within the context of the issues being debated and given form in the public sphere at large. It is the *pragmatics* of this move that are significant. It can and will be read as effecting a particular kind of illocutionary act, and will expectably have an expectable perlocutionary uptake or effect (Austin, 1975).

A similar analysis needs to be made in relation to the Danish cartoon controversy. Casting the issues of the controversy in terms of 'freedom of speech' (versus censorship) is in some ways a self-validating argument: it is one which simply serves to reconstitute and reproduce the pragmatic implications of the act of publication itself: the advanced character of Western values over Muslim ones, their civilizational superiority, and the contrast between Western democracy and Muslim violence. This was a self-reproducing set of premises and conclusions, advanced from within a world-view deeply shaped by colonial histories, and imperial imaginaries. In the Arab and Muslim world, the view was that, if anything, the publication and re-publication of the cartoons was intended as a particular kind of performative act (Austin, 1975) – the assertion of superiority, the intent to be provocative and/or insulting – a move reflecting problematic values such as the lack of respect for other people's deeply held beliefs, belligerence, the lack of a sense of responsibility in relation to one's act of public discourse. Even deeply secular people in the Arab world were offended, given the circumstances.

Indeed, the insistence on the 'freedom of speech' issue as the prime one, notwithstanding the genuine belief in the principle, disingenuously neglects the pragmatics of utterance: that 'words are deeds' in the words of the philosopher of ordinary language, Ludwig Wittgenstein (1953/2001). Understood within that analytic frame, and thus read situatedly in the context of the public discourse at large, and the 'war on terror' with its violent trajectories, why would the publication not be read as a form of 'hate speech', even an incitement to hatred? Could the published cartoons not reasonably be expected to fuel anti-Muslim racism? Why would the kinds of violence in response to the publication by Muslims be factored into the judgments on the case, but not the imperial and colonial violence that was *already in place* at the time of the publication? A pragmatic analysis would help. Moreover, such an analysis suggests that, whilst publication of cartoons irreverent to Christianity may seem the same form of speech, it is not; unless, of course, it were published by an Arab newspaper circulating in the Arab world.

As in Europe, so in the USA: racial profiling is rampant, and Islamophobia is on the rise (Mujahid, 2010).[2] A small church in Florida, having publicly declared Islam to be 'of the devil', announced that it was going to ceremoniously burn copies of the Qur'an, one a day (Stacy, 2010). Plans to build a Muslim community center in New York City (the Park 51 Center) have run into a mounting wave of hostility and seemed to provoke rising tensions and more hate crimes against Muslims (ACLU, 2010).[3] The Congressional hearings of Rep. Peter King on 'The Extent of Radicalization in the American Muslim Community and that Community's Response' reminded many of McCarthy-era hearings (Fahrenthold and Boorstein, 2011). The projection of an American/Western identity that is Christian, and to which Islam is inimical, indeed which is put at risk by it, is thus elaborated in various practices, trajectories and discourses, converging into a particular configuration of thought, language and affect.

These are the markers of the current period, but they are the symptoms of a much deeper process: they represent the efflorescence of a body of affect and thought in which being Muslim (and of course being Arab or Iranian) is suspect in the Western popular imagination, and is seen as distinctively and fundamentally at odds with Western values. Clearly, there is in this also a definition of certain values as being fundamentally Western: freedom, and the respect for women are articulated in this way as is individuality, self-awareness, civility, and so on. There is a history of thought that underpins this, long before the 'war on terror' (Said, 1978, 1994; Shaheen, 2001). Interestingly, the term 'fundamentalism' is rarely applied to this configuration of thought and discourse, yet it essentializes both Western/Christian identity and Muslim identity, and, moreover, it essentializes these as a constituent of practical pursuits, politics and policy,[4] which is where the greater danger lies.

During this last decade, and as this discursive shift has been solidifying, there have been five major wars waged against Arab and/or Muslim populations: two against Iraq, one still ongoing in Afghanistan, one against Lebanon in July 2006 and another on Gaza in December 2008/January 2009. Each has competed with the ones before for scope of destruction and power of display: the corporeal and the symbolic enacted and enmeshed in the actual practice of violent (colonial) domination. Indeed all the major transnational wars of this century have been against populations that were predominantly Muslim, and mostly Arab. In the aftermath of these wars, talk of further ones persisted: Iran, Syria and Lebanon again, not to speak of the continuation of wars in Palestine and Iraq. Talk of completing combat troop withdrawal from Iraq by the end of 2011 underplays the large number of mercenaries deployed there – 'contractors' – that have been used to supplement troops and circumvent accountability and which, in June of 2009, according to a Pentagon report, numbered 132,610. Their numbers are expected to increase (Stoner, 2009).[5] Afghanistan has seen the expansion of operations, and the barely acknowledged yet constant death of civilians under the fire of US drones. Then there is the war that has effectively but silently been increasingly waged in Pakistan.

Through these wars, and the policies of blockade or sanctions that have been synergistic with them, there has been a 'catastrophization' of many populations: in Afghanistan, Iraq and Palestine. 'Catastrophization' is perhaps the wrong term, for it does not capture the crucial and central element in the process: *the undoing of a society's organic, self-reproducing fabric*. It is the disorganization and sundering of the social fabric and its self-organizing mechanism that is effected. The coherence and development of the whole is what is targeted. Saleh Abdel Jawwad, a Palestinian historian, used the term 'sociocide' to describe the policies of the Israeli occupation in the West Bank and Gaza (Abdel-Jawad 1998).[6] The term is an apt description for what has been taking place in all these countries and what has been set in motion by US (and allied) military campaigns and intervention: not only the constantly rising body count, nor just the destruction of infrastructure, but the dissolution of a coherent independent social fabric, the rupturing of communities from the inside. Instead, a fabric composed and woven by the occupying powers and their allies was to be inserted.

This is most clearly seen in the Iraq and Palestine cases, and involves the securitization of the spaces and places of social life in these locations, accompanied by the many other processes and policies of fragmentation, cantonization, bio-metric and informational surveillance. The securitization is co-extensive with the imperial grid of control that is its modus and instigator. It is particularly instructive when the increasing securitization of these places is seen within the frame of the accompanying corporatization and privatization of resources, and the installation of a new neo-liberal regime (Khalidi and Samour, 2011) for the benefit of an alliance of Western companies and contractors with local business elites. More generally, while there is talk of liberating women, bringing democracy to undemocratic regions, of the fight for freedom, and the fear of weapons of mass destruction in the hands of people not 'like us', civilians in Afghanistan, Pakistan and Iraq, after having endured the spectacular and molar dose of destruction heaped upon them in the original attacks, have daily been subject to aerial bombardment that rains unaccountable death and destruction,[7] and ever more impoverishment and de-development. It is a policy that leaves a ruined landscape, ruined lives and a deeply damaged social fabric.

It is not incidental that at the same time the discursive shift I reference here was being produced and manifested, these wars, and the militarized processes and politico-economic transformations embedded in them, were also taking place. The intensity, extensity and modus of the terms of this discursive shift were being massively generated from within and as part of the theatre of these wars. Derek Gregory traces the 'connections between the modalities of political, military, and economic power' (Gregory, 2004), demonstrating how the wars in the region are 'wired' together and involve the synergistic operation of the technical, the cultural and the politico-juridical registers to inscribe colonial cartographies of power and violence on the bodies of people and places. There is, in other words, an organic connection between the discursive shift, and the violent transformations imposed simultaneously with it, under the umbrella of the 'war on terror'. Graham (2006) shows how the production of a state of permanent insecurity and surveillance in the urban spaces of the 'homeland' is reflexively imbricated with the production of 'targeted' urban spaces in the Arab/Muslim world (the phenomenal 'hinterland') – most clearly in Iraq. One is a mechanism for producing the other. It is the same logic at work along the Israel/Palestine (Gaza) axis.

Over the last decade, then, the terms of the discursive shift have crystallized into a public discourse laminating the terms Arab/Muslim with 'terror', a discourse whose terms have functioned as the corollary of organized military violence against entire populations in geographic domains which are strategically located and/or resource rich, violence necessary to secure control of geostrategic assets, and remove what I have called ideo-strategic obstacles (Jayyusi, 2010). Hermann (1982, 2000) and Chomsky (1991) would describe this as 'wholesale terror' that ultimately further calls out and instigates the retail terror which alone, today, is dubbed terror in the domains of official and now popular discourse in the Western mainstream. There is a reflexive yet *disjunctive* relationship that is operative here, between the discourses of the war on terror (and the discursive shift driven by it) and the lived courses and settings of the subjects represented within them. The representational landscape, which is configured by the Muslim/Arab threat, is increasingly dislodged from the details and actualities of the war on terror as enacted and performed, and thus of the lived landscape of the places and peoples represented through it. This is a relationship of production: the assemblage of the 'regime of truth' effected through the various instrumentalities and fabulations of this war of imperial design.

The discourses on terror, the surveillance, the detentions and arrests, the pervasive security filters in various buildings and urban centres, and the terror alerts are all, as Graham (2006) shows, intended to remind you of the terror threat, whose locus is the cities of the Arab world, to make it visible and palpable. On the other side of this, its corollary, are the grim new realities produced and made in the lands and cities which are the objects (targets) of these imperial designs and fabulations in the first place. We are reminded here of 'the birth pangs of the new Middle East' with its imperially fabricated maps, announced by then Secretary of State Condoleeza Rice, as Israel launched its last war on Lebanon in 2006 (see Nazemroaya, 2006). The discursive environment that emerges is a product of practices and instrumentalities of power, and makes such power enactable, intelligible and assimilable, manifesting in official and popular stances and patterns of action that engender, on the other side of here and now, a social and political landscape that is starkly racialized, and increasingly repressive and deadly.

Disjuncture, Violence and Legitimacy

The contemporary condition under the sign of the 'war on terror' is, consequently, one of deep, systematic and systemic disjunctures. According to a report by Europol, Europe's Police Agency, there were in 2009 fewer than 300 terror attacks in mainland Europe, only one from an Islamist group.[8] Yet 'Islamist terrorism is still perceived as the biggest threat to most member states, despite the fact that only one Islamist terrorist attack – a bomb attack in Italy – took place in the EU in 2009' (Pop, 2010). The majority were actions committed by a variety of different groups or individuals, ranging from separatists, to radical leftists and environmentalists. The image most people in the West seem to have is that terror wears a Muslim face. Indeed, those who want to appear reasonable say that, while not all Muslims are terrorists, all terrorists are Muslim. For example, Leslie H. Gelb, Pulitzer Prize-winner, former correspondent for the *New York Times* and Board Senior Fellow of the Council on Foreign Relations, writes (2010):

> President Obama warns against "extremism." Former Vice President Dick Cheney declaims against "terrorists." But they hardly ever bark the essential word, the almost always absent critical adjective: Muslim. Almost all the terrorist and extremist violence in the world today is committed by Muslims—and in most instances, the victims are Muslims themselves. What's afoot here is Muslim extremism—despite the fact that the great majority of Muslims aren't radicals and condemn terrorism.

A particular representational landscape takes shape here. Admittedly, the terrorist attacks on 9/11 and the ones in London and Madrid were the most spectacular, sowing death and injury in large numbers, and leaving confusion and animosity in their wake. But that does not, by itself, account for this landscape. Despite 9/11, millions of people in the UK (a reported two million), in Europe and in the US took to the streets in early 2003 to protest against the projected war against Iraq at the time. Meanwhile, in the Arab world, many remained dubious about the origins of 9/11: putting aside the issue of 'conspiracy theory', the point is that this reflected the sense that these attacks were enabling of the new imperial onslaught on the region.

In the Arab and Muslim world, the perception is that were it not for US imperial interventionism there would not be serious transnational Islamist terrorism: the US, after all, through the CIA, funded, supported and trained the men who later formed al-Qaeda (Kellner, 2004; Mamdani, 2004), a group whose longest run of attacks since 9/11 (though perhaps, by some framings, not the most spectacular) have been in Arab and Muslim countries. The victims of the slaughter in the housing compounds of Saudi Arabia and the hotels in Amman were largely Arabs. In fact, as analysts at the Project on Defense Alternatives have argued, more terrorist activities and networks have developed after 'the war on terror' and in response to it than there were prior to it (Conetta, 2006). Moreover, the threat of 'terrorism' or of al-Qaeda, and the 'war on terror', have been every Arab dictator's gift, providing cover for the repression of any and all dissidents, and for the repression of all Islamic parties under the cover that they must all bring extremism and terror. Ben Ali, Mubarak and then Gaddafi all appealed for help against the popular revolutions shaking their regimes in the spring of 2011 with the pretext that Islamic fundamentalists or even al-Qaeda would be the victors if they lost. Beyond all that, it is actually in the Muslim/Arab world that massive devastation at the hands of US forces and their allies, and at the hands of the Israeli colonizing state, has become people's lived reality. It is a lived reality that, for people on the ground, is all too obvious, that resists all re-framings and rationales, all ideological makeovers, all the politics of justifications that draw on religious or other-histories. It is a reality that subverts excuses, inversions, or counter-simulations, a bodied reality that can be apprehended by anyone through the simple cross-cultural metric, the question: would you want this to be you?

In the Arab and Muslim world, then, there is a visceral perception, grounded in a contrapuntal reading of lived experience and the discursive production that is co-located with it, that the war on terror has not been primarily designed for locating and neutralizing real security threats; rather its actual design has been to target specific populations in strategically significant locales, by constituting them as all potential security threats – a design developed as a fundamental constituent of a project of colonial/imperial appropriation

One can point, then, to two major and overlapping disjunctures that exist as fault lines in the terms of contemporary discourse, and specifically the discourses of the 'war on terror'. The first is between who the agents of terror, the terrorists, are and the second is what counts as terrorism – how the actions of each side in this so-called war are to be constituted. These disjunctures appear clearly in the context of international law, and most prominently in the moment of its application: in the immunity from prosecution afforded to the agents of the imperial powers who wage the 'war on terror' (members of invading armies subduing whole cities; persons involved in rendition; parties to torture and those complicit in torture, and so on), agents who belong to a particular political community. These are all activities that would have been considered war crimes had they emanated from different political actors. It is a question of 'legitimacy': did the Germans have a right to occupy France? Were French resistors who ambushed German troops 'terrorists'? This is not a rhetorical question: it is the very 'order' of legitimacy here which is at stake, and it is a question which is central to the UN Charter, but which is always inflected differently under different situations. 'Legitimacy' is the creature simultaneously of power, law and morality, and manifests differently, therefore, in different articulations of these. Power will attempt to monopolize the constitution of 'legitimacy' but it can never completely succeed to contain or conceal its own excess which then provokes a different moment/equation of 'legitimacy' and of law.

There is, overall, an overwhelming consensus in the Arab (and Muslim) world, evident in public and private discourses alike, that the 'real terror network', to use Herman's phrase (1982), that is operative in the Middle East is that of the US/Israeli military–security complex. It is the policies and conduct of this team of actors in the region that manifest in, and as, terror inflicted on various populations. It is always the corporeal, the bodied outcome, the lived landscape, that is pointed to as the recalcitrant testimonial to this: the destroyed neighbourhoods and towns, from Fallujah to Khan Yunis, the broken threads of social life from Baghdad to Gaza. Thus the ability and the right to fight back, as well as the actual insistence on fighting back, are not construed as terrorism, but as resistance against occupation, invasion and dispossession.

This consensual conception emphasizes the distinction between terrorism and resistance – it does not efface that distinction. For the absolute majority, al-Qaeda is not resistance of any kind. Clearly some people do conceive of it that way, just as some Americans advocate 'nuking' Iran as a legitimate option (still a wholesale rather than retail imaginary of terror consonant with the kinds of power available to their political community). But the suggestion that because of that, a distinction between the two should not be made, as Kellner (2004) seems to suggest, is untenable as it simply delivers the dispossessed, the people whose lands and lives are plundered and violated on a systematic basis, up to the powerful who, after all, constitute any agency effected against them, any serious challenge to their power, armed or not, as terrorism or aid to terrorism. The higher the ability to fight back, to refuse, the greater the classification as 'terror threat'.

As Chomsky points out in his Eric Fromm lecture (2010: 5), the official definitions of 'terrorism' in US/UK law and army manuals (as violence for political ends) fail to exempt the violence of imperial wars or campaigns from being characterized as 'terror', and there have thus been countless conferences, studies and symposia attempting to define 'terrorism' in such a way as to exclude imperial state violence. In public discourse, however, 'Well-educated circles have internalized the special sense of 'terrorism' required for justification of state action and control of domestic populations' (ibid.: 6).

Certainly, under the rubric of the 'war on terror', the conventional usage of the term, generalized by mainstream media, covers all (and intendedly only) non-state violence, so as to condemn resistance against state forces, or invading armies (which in the region translates as any violence directed against the exercise of US imperial or Israeli colonial power). The distinction, however, embodies the insistence on a particular articulation of legitimacy, one that derives from a specific location in, and assessment of, the global order: it represents a systemic stance. However one defines 'terrorism', the distinction between that and resistance cannot be dismissed a priori: the real work is in where and how the two concepts are to be applied in practice. Most would apply the concept of terrorism to violence against civilians for political or ideological ends – this exempts imperial and colonial wars even less than the above definition that Chomsky referred to. The precise form of the distinction itself is an essentially contested one, in as much as the concepts of both terrorism and resistance are essentially contested concepts (Gallie, 1956).

Thus, by and large, there is in public Arab discourses, both popular and official (and certainly among most of the intellectuals of the Arab world), a different political and moral mapping of the contemporary moment, and the current conditions in the area, that is disjunctive with the mappings produced in and through the 'war on terror'. Time and again, however, the terms and referents of this war manifest themselves in the discourses and policies of political elites, when it comes to dealing with their own dissenters or opposition, as they did during the Arab revolutions of 2011. They also manifested in the discourses and stances of the Europeans, as well as the US administration, when these revolutions first broke out. The French foreign minister offered to send riot police and tear gas canisters to Ben Ali to help him quell the Tunisian revolution. The US administration was notably silent and at a loss for words when the Egyptians took to the streets, revolting against Mubarak's police state, the second largest recipient of US aid after Israel. In both cases, there was talk of the fear of Islamists taking over. The Western support for the terror inflicted by dictators in the Arab and Muslim countries on their own populations, further rationalized and amplified in and through the 'war on terror", did not figure in the conception of 'terrorism' that was being actively disseminated and generalized by politicians and mainstream media alike. When it became clear, however, that almost every Arab country was a candidate for popular change, it also became evident that the big powers intended to appropriate the revolutions: in Tony Blair's words (19th March 2010), the key was the development of "a strategic framework for *helping to shape* this revolutionary change sweeping the region" (italics added). Blair opined that "History, attitude and interests all dictate that we are players". The Libyan intervention (and the high toll of civilian casualties at the hands of NATO) is to be understood in this light.

The Terror of the Invisible

Perhaps it is in the discourse over Gaza that we can most sharply detect the lineaments of this discursive order, this new 'regime of truth', the order of legitimation embedded in it, and the parameters and contours of the representational landscape we are meant to inhabit in this brave new era. In Gaza, like many other locales in the Arab/Muslim world today, there is a ruined landscape, a deeply contaminated environment and wrecked lives: one and a half million people have been kept in an open-air prison for nearly five years, a siege made ever tighter, attempting to draw in ever more parties and complicities. People are visibly – and deliberately – kept just on the edge of disaster (see MSNBC, 2011), where materials from pencils to chocolate, medicine, cement and kerosene are on the banned list produced and organized by Israel (Hass, 2009). The most pressing question about this situation has been how to destroy the tunnels, described as Gaza's 'lungs', that the Palestinians have built and are building: the only arteries of life the population has. In the aftermath of the organized killing in the winter 2008–2009 war on Gaza, in which Israel used a range of deadly weapons on this open-air prison of its own creation, and where civilians were not even allowed to flee or find refuge away from the zone of death, the most prominent issue addressed by the representatives of the various Western powers who flew into the region was how to stop arms getting to the Palestinians in Gaza, not how to make Israel accountable for the killings, nor how to put an end to the brutal siege that was already two years old, nor how to work out a just resolution of the conflict in line with international law. In this context, of course, official political discourse in Europe and the US was clearly congruent with the frames of Israeli discourse, constituting the war as a response to terrorism, and Gaza's misery as essentially self-wrought. How many gave even a moment's attention to the kinds of discourse and open discussion of policies that took place unapologetically within Israeli circles?

In a 2004 interview, Arnon Soffer, advisor to Sharon, and the main architect and strategist of the Gaza 'disengagement plan', as well as of the demographic question (the numbers of Jews versus numbers of Arabs), had openly discussed how to deal with a closed-off Gaza after the Israeli 'withdrawal'. Soffer had said in that interview that what they (the Israelis) had to do 'was to kill, and kill, and kill, all day, everyday' (Blum, 2004). Soffer's single worry was how to make sure the Israeli soldiers who did the killing did not bring any of that back home to their own families. But it is obvious that this can work when you have managed to reconstruct the image of the other as a terrorist or always a would-be terrorist, whose actual discovery is ever in deferral, so that to pre-empt and destroy anyone who belongs to that species is an intelligible and reasonable solution. This after all was also the logic behind preventive war.

In the war on Gaza in the winter of 2008–9, the Israeli actions and discursive moves were strategically integrated to draw on the frames of the 'war on terror'. This was the logic of 'terror' or the 'terrorist' as inhabiting a space beyond the eye, beyond visibility, a phenomenon which justified the targeting of persons and communities despite their normal appearances. Charges of indiscriminately targeting civilians and civilian places and habitats were countered with the insistence that these places harboured 'terror': unseen, outside the places where one might expect to encounter it. It justified the bombing of hospitals, schools and homes. It excused the gunning down of civilians coming out of their places of hiding with their arms up. The virtual collapse of the category 'terror' into the category 'Palestinian' (and Arab) was complete.

In the initial IDF announcement of the war, the target for it was given as generic 'terror': 'The IDF will continue its operations against terror in accordance with constant state assessments held by the IDF Chief of General Staff' (Israel Defense Forces, 2008). The announcement went on:

> The Hamas government leaders and operatives, which activate terror from within civilian population centers, are the sole bearers of responsibility for Israel's military response. This response is crucial for preserving Israel's security interests.
>
> The IDF Spokesperson wishes to emphasize that anyone sponsoring terror, hosting terror in his house, housing terror in his basement and sending his wives and children to serve as human shields is considered a terrorist. (Ibid.)

Here, 'terror' is personified, a creature lurking in all kinds of normal spaces, inhabiting every place of ordinariness, invited and succored by the 'terrorist'. Note that the 'terrorist' in this construction is also thus deprived of even the horizon of subjective rationale for acting as s/he does, for he does it not on his own account but in the service of another monstrous creature: terror (the phrase 'terror operative' was very common in the Israeli discourse). In one sense, 'terror' here has the same standing and force as the notion of the 'devil' who possessed, where the possessed had to be 'burned' to get rid of the abomination. The 'terrorist' or 'terror operative' is presented as having a flattened agency: acting out of irrationality, subject to the will of another, subservient to a force that was deadly. At the same time, since 'terror' is everywhere, lurking behind the normal living spaces of this people, it reduces this population to one that is all contaminated.

This was a war in which the 'principle of distinction' central to international humanitarian law came openly under attack: the distinction between civilians and combatants; between lawful and legitimate targets, and unlawful and illegitimate ones; as well as between legitimate means and illegitimate means, between proportionate and disproportionate scales. This was co-terminous with the need to flatten the places of life of the other as spaces of monstrosity, redeemable only through fire. But this, the Israelis were insistent in affirming, was only something they shared with the rest of the world, with the 'international community'.

The Israelis were very clear in making an appeal to the commonality between their cause and the international 'war on terror' that the US and Europe was waging. In a briefing to the Diplomatic Corps on 8 January 2009 in Tel Aviv, while the war was still raging, Livni declared: 'But there is one thing that needs to be understood. This is a fight against terror – this is the same battle, the same war, the same ongoing, long war that the international community is waging in different parts of the world' (Livni, 2009).

The logic of Israeli discourse in the war on Gaza was the logic of an essential invisibility that constitutes entire populations as a potential security threat and as a source of danger, even in their most mundane manifestations. In the Israeli discourse, there is set up a systematic inability to tell the place or body of the threat, since it is everywhere, hidden by normal signs. To get at it, to protect oneself, one has not merely to ignore the signs of normalcy, but to suspect them systematically. This is a politics of organized suspicion, that in a transnational context becomes racism of a particular form. It is, ultimately, the constitution of a moral and epistemological order in which the attack on reason is systematic, predicating the operation of the transcendental invisible.

The above brings to mind Barthes's description of photographic meaning: the photograph, he suggested, is a polysemic text, producing 'a floating chain of signifieds' that is problematic, so that 'various techniques are developed intended to *fix* the floating chain of signifieds in such a way as to *counter the terror of uncertain signs*' (Barthes, 1977: 37, last phrase my emphasis). Of course, as I have elsewhere argued (Jayyusi, 1991), this is an argument of/in excess: no image that is recognizable is entirely uncertain; the 'floating chain of signifieds' is not indefinite but hovers between meanings and questions: who, where, when? It points to intelligible alternatives, prods specifiable questions, seeks specifiable empirical details, rather than entire structures of intelligibility. It rests within knowable and organized rationalities of knowledge: an African man being shot; a non-European child trying to pass through a crack in a high cement wall; a Muslim woman wailing for the loss of a child who has been shot. Though there may be an anxiety of a sort, we can recognize these: there is no real terror there, unless we abnegate what we know, what we share as knowledge of how things look, what they may mean, how courses of action can proceed, how people will act in routine family contexts, and so on. We deploy mundane knowledge, both of formal structures of activity and intelligibility, and of congeries of empirical facts.

The 'terror of uncertain signs' is a more fitting description for the constitution of the world from within the logic of essential invisibility. The latter suggests that you cannot know anything about the other (it does not apply to the self). It transforms the other into a creature of infinite darkness – beyond the human. It is particularly dangerous when it is projected at a popular level, as it is in the cultural imaginaries manufactured in Hollywood. Notably this same logic was already at work in relation to Arabs and Muslims prior to 11 September. The blatantly racist Hollywood film *Rules of Engagement* (2000), set in Yemen, turns on the self-same tropes of normal appearance versus a sinister threatening and hidden reality, to reconstitute the intentional killing of children, women and old people by US troops as self-defence. It is an argument for 'casting out' entire populations from the realm of the ordinary and of the human (see Gregory, 2004).

Though it might not seem so at first, this is a logic that is covalent to the logic of Islamophobia that is currently playing out in Europe and the US, and holds out the possibility of a future of potential horror. Despite the fact that for Muslim populations in the West the attack on Muslim signs and insignia seems to be based on 'visibility', the implications go deeper than that. For the visible sign to be banned and suppressed expresses and embodies the refusal to live with difference, and at the same time the constitution of a particular community of belief, and ethnic origin, as essentially different. In being essentially different, there is always the implication of an internal horizon of threat that those who carry this difference have. The appetite and desire for suppressing the signs of this difference will not be sated or satisfied: it will eventually be the *difference unseen* that will be targeted, that which is taken as the source and origin of the sign. It is the essence that is problematic – that carries a threat. If the visible sign is understood as a threatening one, and is suppressed, then the threat may be seen to have been only made invisible: the normal appearance begins to be suspect.

Here then is the terror of uncertain signs. But this terror of the uncertain is, in the next moment, turned into the certainty of threat, of evil. This rests on the *presumption of absolute difference*, of the incommensurability of ethical and political orientations and commitments. The visible and the invisible both become problematic: the one suspect, the other threatening, viewed as potentially murderous. Here indeed is also where the logic of preemptive prosecution emerges (see English, 2010; see also Korotzer, 2010), turning on the premise of a systematic opposition between appearance and reality. By contrast, the logic of visibility is what maintains ordinariness, the human compass of life.

The politics of fear (and attendant racial victimization) can turn on this dialectic of visibility/invisibility, on a supposition of a symbiotic and contradictory relationship at one and the same time between appearance and essence. This critique of the primacy of the logic of invisibility in these practices draws, of course, on Wittgenstein's insistence that mundane actions embody beliefs, that intentions are knowable from and in activities, that 'minds' are transparent to others (Wittgenstein, 1953/2001); that some items have the status of certainty in our forms of life; and that uncertainty has an end point grounded in shared understandings (Wittgenstein, 1979). All these modes of being and understanding within the human contexts of action and interaction, including those of conflict, belie the inter-subjective rationality of *systematic* doubt about any aspect of daily life. In our forms of life (rather than philosophy), systematic doubt is itself deemed irrational, even pathological.

Conclusion

One of the most distinctive aspects of this moment, and of the current global order, is the almost total integration of the politico-economic, the military–security and the cultural–media apparatuses in the practices of power. It promises the most intimate synchronization of sovereign politics and bio-politics, a synchronization that may be differentially accomplished, according to place and time. But this is also a moment in which there is heightened global struggle and contestation over both the 'lived' and the 'representational', about the shape and the perception of the world, and of its imaginaries, and its various conflicts, over rights and wrongs, desirable outcomes, just distributions, and conditions of possibility. Specifically, there has been a fierce struggle over the project of the new geo-strategic, and politico-cultural (re-)mapping of the region that was already envisaged by the neo-cons, with their Israel-centric agenda, at the end of the 1990s, laid out in the Project for a New American Century, but seriously launched after and as a result of 9/11 (see Dorrien, 2004). This project has, more than any previous imperial project, sought to integrate the various instrumentalities of power, as exemplified in the pursuit of the 'war on terror', very much an intrinsic mechanism of this attempted (re-)making of the region, and one of its more powerful instruments.

Under any hegemonic state, as in today's global imperium, the pressures produced for the production and dissemination of official history, as well as geographies of self and other, friend and foe, law and disorder, are powerful. Official histories and accounts require, not only the selection and emphasis of particular details, but the excision of other significant details that populate the actual world in which (and over which) struggle or contestation is waged. They require modes of 'forgetting'. To what extent do the Western mainstream media accounts incorporate the terms of official history and the discursive forms of producing the 'real' that emanate from them? What is the media's role in producing the conditions for, or indeed in inducing, 'amnesia'? What is the media's (and the contemporary intellectual's) role in the production and performance of empire, the production, not merely of imaginative geographies (Said, 1994) and/or counterfeit geographies, but of the enacted geographies envisioned by the neo-cons, the *performative* mappings that were the point of the spectacular wars waged on the region? What is their role in producing and maintaining an optic through which self and other are constituted in sharply asymmetric modes, engendering a sense of combined superiority/insecurity that may justify all outrage against that threatening other. How to avoid lending oneself to the apparatus of the 'war on terror', the apparatus of new imperial dominance and colonial difference?

Despite later recognition and admission of the falsity of the claims used to justify the war against Iraq (the weapons of mass destruction as 'clear and imminent danger', or that the Iraqi regime had links to al-Qaeda), this did not seriously impact on the way most mainstream US media framed and reported the war. Many scholars have described and critiqued the way the media conducted itself in the run-up to the Iraq war (for example, Kellner, 2002, 2004). What still largely remains to be analyzed in detail is how the media proceeded, nevertheless, to normalize the war and its consequences, and to be complicit in masking the agency which continued to enable or produce these consequences, from the sectarian market bombings of Iraq to the wastelands of the Gaza ghetto. The official US/UK discourse on the war, as it visibly encountered disjunctive perceptions and a disjunctive lived reality, branched and produced various new modalities that drew on the established symbolic repertoire of liberal democracies in the West: women's rights; electoral or representative democracy; freedom.

Despite the escalating violence and the sectarian geography inscribed by the invasion, and manifested in electoral politics as well as the regression of women's position, the lexicon, the news agenda and the frames of discourse were for the most part not seriously reconstructed accordingly in mainstream media. Rather, they continued instead to turn within the axes of official discourse, assimilating its claims and frames. For example, the Pentagon, and media discourse of 'foreign fighters' always referred to Arabs who enlisted in Iraq (not all in fact reducible to al-Qaeda fighters) and not to the Blackwater mercenaries who ranged free across Iraq, nor of course to the US soldiers who had invaded it. The disjuncture between discursive and material practice ('bringing democracy' on the one hand and killing people defending their city in 'the Sunni triangle' on the other) only exhibits these discourses as enabling, as productive: here the nexus between the military apparatus and the cultural apparatus is demonstrable. It demonstrates how 'truth' is, in Foucault's sense, produced through various regimens of power and constraint. This was a discourse disjoined both from the actual reality of the war, and from the reality of Iraqis on the ground, as well as from the standard norms of use of the concept of 'foreign'. It was a corrupted lexicon. But it was *effective* – especially over time.

These wars, and their embedded targets, aims and self-descriptions have by and large been naturalized in mainstream Western media, even as their details are obscured. Media discourses in the West, and wherever Western news agencies predominate, produce a world in which 'us' in the north are waging a war against insurrections and illegitimate fighters – insurgents and terrorists – in the south. Collateral damage is for the most part a result of *their* tactics. Civilian deaths are a part of *their* repertoire and their actions. They are engaged in religious, ethnic or denominational conflicts – it is a constituent of their backwardness. Thus the norms of reporting, and the frames of discourse which predominate, become ways and pressures to cultivate amnesia and complicity.

Greenwald (2010) details specific cases, showing how the media's reporting on the unlawful detentions of journalists was systematically one-sided, focusing on those held by opponent regimes (such as Iran) and largely ignoring or downplaying the much worse unlawful practices of detentions under the rubric of the war on terror. He gives as an example the detention of Sami al-Haj, the al-Jazeera reporter, who was held at Guantanamo for over six years. Al-Haj was never charged with anything specific, but was almost exclusively questioned about al-Jazeera. The case got comparatively little coverage. The pattern is repeated for other journalists, and one might say for numerous other issues. A few independent (and important) journalists manage to provide telling and contextualizing reports – but how many read or remember those? Given the flood of mainstreamed reporting across different media, the net effect is not changed. Journalism in the mode of amnesia dominates.

The issue here is not merely the 'double standard', neither is it simply the 'frames' used in media discourse; rather it is the *systemic production and naturalization of the frames* in the first place; the production of a discursive regime, itself embedded in imperial/colonial subjectivities, and synchronized with the imperial practices of the state, serving its self-image and reproducing it to effect. It is a productive order of affect, language and action. It operates across the range of cultural genres, from news reporting and talk shows to entertainment, including films and video games, to produce and naturalize the frames of a colonial/imperial optic, an entire industry working to produce the regime of official 'truth', and the popular conceptions, desires, fears and subjectivities which can enact and sustain it.

What is the grammar of such discourse? What is the lexicon used? What are the specific attributes of the affective, perceptual and discursive world that is produced through specific instances, and what horizon of action is embedded in it? Can the disassembling of the procedures and methods, of the deep grammar involved, tell us in detail about the nature of the politico-moral order being imaginatively established and implied? I would argue in the affirmative. It is still a task to be accomplished. It requires more media scholars to become public intellectuals. It needs more journalists to write from the stance of a 'species consciousness'. As Graham (2000) and Graham et al. (2004) suggest, the contemporary moment is the most discourse and media-reliant formation in history, but we stand at a fork between realizing our 'species being' and 'achieving self-annihilation' (2004: 29) – I would say descending into barbarism. They argue that 'the current malaise is primarily axiological (values-based)' and that discursive interventions 'at the axiological level are necessary in the policy field, in the multiple fields of mass media, and in every local field' (2004: 29). How precisely is that to be done in a media landscape locked under by a corporate economy of information and entertainment? In an environment which is shaped by the visions and practices of power inscribed by the 'military–industrial–media–entertainment network' (Der Derian, 2001)?

The above disjunctions which cleave the global landscape promote a meta-disjunctive condition: a preoccupation with, and a politics of negative difference that is recursive. They constitute a fault-line *within* Western modernity (between claims and stances/actions) and *between* its discourse/policy trajectories and the trajectories of peoples who refuse to be domesticated and refashioned unilaterally, cast out from the umbrella of humanity and from the spaces of modernity understood as the agency to shape one's own fate. This was evident in the 'Arab spring' of 2011, with the youth revolutions whose demands concerned simultaneously individual freedom, economic and social justice and national sovereignty. How is the agentive role of the media in shaping and maintaining the fractious and fractured realities of the global order to be reclaimed for a politics of truth against power? This is an urgent question. Given a world that is 'shared', but which is nevertheless riven by representational/symbolic constructions and stances, and the violent bodied policies enacted through them on behalf of imperial power, as discussed above, self-conscious intervention is needed. If no serious and consistent interventions are made, what can we hope for? We are all responsible for how the world will be on the other side of here, and on the other side of now.

Endnotes

1   In an interview on al-Jazeera Arabic channel, Tayyeb Urdogan, Prime Minister of Turkey, affirmed that 'there was no connection between Islam and terror as some claim'. This was on the programme *Without Frontiers* with Ahmad Mansour, broadcast on 12 January 2011.

2   See also Arab American Institute (2007) for details of a poll that finds more than three quarters of Arab Americans say they have encountered discrimination.

3   See ACLU (2010). The map shows reported anti-mosque attacks between 2006 and 2010. The reports listed start in 2006, and show a marked increase in 2009, with most incidents in 2010. Though this pattern may in part be a function of an increased rate of reporting in 2010, it still seems to suggest a rise in anti-Muslim sentiment, and in hostility to Islam as a religion.

4   Note that dictionary definitions of 'fundamentalism' all allude to the US Protestant movement that asserts the infallibility of the Bible and its literal interpretation, as well as to a broader notion that denotes strict adherence to some set of principles, usually religious. Most of these definitions give 'Islamic' fundamentalism as an example of the latter. See, for example, the Oxford Dictionaries online: www.oxford dictionaries.com/definition/fundamentalism?view=uk.

Yet a second look is needed at Protestant fundamentalism: not only is it alive and well, but it has expanded in scope and political impact: it is what feeds and finances the growth of settlement activity in Palestine (including east Jerusalem), and thus supports and promotes Jewish fundamentalism. The latter has arguably become the single most potent force that threatens peace in the Middle East, given its increasingly vigorous, aggressive and deeply exclusionary political agenda. Yet it receives little media coverage in comparison to Islamic fundamentalism. For more on Jewish fundamentalism see Israel Shahak and Norton Mezvinsky (1999). See also Ian Lustick (1988).

5   In fact, private military contractors, hired by the US government in the case of Iraq, are helping change the 'face' of military intervention and war. In the West Bank too, the US government has signed a five-year renewable contract with a company connected to Blackwater, one of the most notorious private security companies. The question is: why? See Kepler (2011).

6   The term 'sociocide' has been in use at least since John Galtung applied it in 1982. See Doubt (2007).

7   In October 2010 alone, in an escalating air war, a reported 1000 bombs were dropped on Afghanistan. See Associated Press reporter Deb Riechmann (2010). On the air war in Iraq see Turse and Engelhardt (2007).

8   According to the FBI, between 2002 and 2005 only about one out of 24 incidents of terrorism in the continental US was by Muslims, though terrorist prevention activities 'paint a more diverse threat picture', and global Jihadist actions were more significant, with most 'perpetrated by regional jihadist groups operating in primarily Muslim countries'. See FBI (2006).

References

Abdel-Jawad, S. (1998) 'War by other means', *Al-Ahram Weekly Online*. Available at: http://weekly.ahram.org.eg/1998/1948/359_salh.htm (accessed 1 March 2011).

ACLU (2010) Map – Nationwide Anti-Mosque Activity. Available at: www. aclu.org/map-nationwide-anti-mosque-activity (accessed 1 March 2011).

Arab American Institute (2007) 'AAI/Zogby poll on American Arab experiences and identity shows increase in discrimination among young Arab Americans', 16 July. Available at: www.aaiusa.org/page/-/Polls/r-2007%20 AA%20Identity%20poll%20-%20FINAL.pdf (accessed 3 March 2011).

Austin, J. L. (1975) *How to Do Things with Words, The William James Lectures on Philosophy and Psychology delivered at Harvard University in 1955*. Cambridge, MA: Harvard University Press.

Barthes, R. (1977) 'The rhetoric of the image', in *Image, Music, Text*. London: Fontana.

Blair, Tony (2010) 'We can't just be spectators in this revolution', Op-Ed, *The Times*, 19th March.

Blum, R. (2004) 'ONE on ONE: it's the demography, stupid', *Jerusalem Post*, 10 May.

Bremner, C. (2009) 'Swiss voters back right-wing minaret ban', *The Times*, 30 November.

Chomsky, N. (1991) 'International terrorism: image and reality', in Alexander George (ed.) *Western State Terrorism*. London: Routledge.

Chomsky, N. (2010) 'The evil scourge of terrorism: reality, construction, remedy'. Erich Fromm Lecture delivered at the International Erich Fromm Society, Stuttgart, Germany. 23 March. Available at: http://www.chomsky. info/talks/20100323.htm (accessed 21 October 2011).

Conetta, C. (2006) 'War & consequences: global terrorism has increased since 9/11 attacks', *Project on Defense Alternatives Briefing Memo #38*, updated 25 September. Cambridge, MA: Commonwealth Institute. Available at: www.comw.org/pda/fulltext/0609bm38.pdf (accessed 2 May 2011).

Cumming-Bruce, N. and Erlanger, S. (2009) 'Swiss ban building of minarets on mosques', *New York Times*, 29 November.

Der Derian, J. (2001) *Virtuous War: Mapping the Military–Industrial–Media– Entertainment Complex*. Boulder, CO: Westview.

Dorrien, G. (2004) *Imperial Designs: Neoconservatism and the New Pax Americana*, London: Routledge.

Doubt, K. (2007) 'Sociocide', in George Ritzer (ed.) *Blackwell Encyclopedia of Sociology*. Oxford: Blackwell.

English, S (2010) '"Preemptive prosecution" FBI entrapment of Muslims in the US', G*lobal Research*, 8 April. Available at: www.globalresearch.ca/index. php?context=va&aid=18549 (accessed 2 May 2011).

Fahrenthold, D. A. and Boorstein, M. (2011) 'Rep. Peter King's Muslim hearing: plenty of drama, less substance', *Washington Post*, 10 March.

FBI (2006) *Terrorism 2002–2005*. Washington: Federal Bureau of Investigation. Available at: www.fbi.gov/stats-services/publications/terrorism-2002-2005/ terror02_05#terror_0205 (accessed 2 May 2011).

Gallie, W. B. (1956) 'Essentially contested concepts', *Proceedings of the Aristotelian Society* 56: 167–198.

Gelb, L. H. (2010) 'Only Muslims can stop Muslim terror', *Daily Beast*, 7 January. Available at: www.thedailybeast.com/blogs-and-stories/2010-01-07/only-muslims-can-stop-muslim-terror/ (accessed 2 May 2011).

Graham, P. (2000) 'Hypercapitalism: a political economy of information idealism', *New Media & Society* 2(2): 131–156.

Graham, P. W., Keenan, T. and Dowd, Anne-Maree (2004) 'A call to arms at the End of History: a discourse-historical analysis of George W. Bush's declaration of war on terror', *Discourse & Society* 15(2–3): 199–221.

Graham, S. (2006) 'Cities and the "War on Terror"', *International Journal of Urban and Regional Research* 30(2): 255–276.

Greenwald, G. (2010) 'Limiting democracy: the American media's world view, and ours', *Social Research* 77(3): 827–838.

Gregory, D. (2004) *The Colonial Present: Afghanistan, Palestine, Iraq*. Oxford: Wiley-Blackwell.

Hass, A. (2009) 'Israel bans books, music and clothes from entering Gaza', *Haaretz*, 17 May.

Hermann, E. (1982) *The Real Terror Network*. Boston: South End Press.

Herman, E. (2000) 'The semantics of terrorism', *Global Dialogue* 2(4) – Terrorism: Image and Reality. Available at: www.worlddialogue.org/content.php?id=108 (accessed 15 April 2011).

Huntington, S. P. (1993) 'The clash of civilizations?', *Foreign Affairs* 72(3): 22–49.

Huntington, S. P. (1996) *The Clash of Civilizations and the Remaking of World Order*. New York: Simon & Schuster.

Israel Defense Forces (2008) 'IDF Launches Operation "Cast Lead".' 27 December. Available at http://idfspokesperson.com/2008/12/27/idf-launches-operation-cast-lead/ (accessed 15th April 2011).

Israeli Ministry of Foreign Affairs (2009) Briefing by FM Livni to the Diplomatic Corps. 8 January. Available at: www.mfa.gov.il/MFA/About+the+Ministry/Foreign+Minister+Livni/Speeches+interviews/Briefing_FM_Livni_Diplomatic_Corps_8-Jan-2009 (accessed 7 May 2011).

Jayyusi, L (1991) 'The reflexive nexus: photo-practice and natural history', *Continuum: Australian Journal of Media & Culture* 6(2): 25–52.

Jayyusi, L. (2010) 'The Arab world, the global moment and the struggle over representation', *Encounters: an International Journal for the Study of Culture and Society* 2: 153–182.

Kellner, D. (2002) 'September 11, the media and war fever', *Television & New Media* 3(2): 143–151.

Kellner, D. (2004) 'September 11, terror war, and blowback', in Joe. L. Kincheloe and Shirley R. Steinberg (eds) *The Miseducation of the West: How the Schools and Media Distort Our Understanding of Islam*. Westport: Praeger: 25–42.

Kepler, T. (2011) 'Blackwater related firm to provide "protective security" in West Bank', Alternative Information Center, 13 January. Available at: www.alternativenews.org/english/index.php/topics/news/3176-blackwater-related-firm-to-provide-protective-security-in-west-bank- (accessed 15 April 2011).

Khalidi, R. and Samour, S. (2011) 'Neolibralism as liberation: the statehood program and the remaking of the Palestinian national movement', *Journal of Palestine Studies* 40(2): 6–25.

Korotzer, F. (2010) 'Pre-emptive prosecution', *Next Left Notes*, 14 April. Available at: http: //nextleftnotes.org/NLN/?p=780 (accessed 15 April 2011).

Lichfield, J. (2010) 'France moves to outlaw the burka and niqab citing égalité', *Independent*, 8 January.

Lustick, I. S. (1988) 'For the land and the Lord: Jewish fundamentalism in Israel', Washington: Council on Foreign Relations. Available at: www.sas.upenn.edu/penncip/lustick/ (accessed 15 April 2011).

Mackey, R. (2009) 'Gaza's smugglers start digging new tunnels', *New York Times*, 22 January. Available at: http://thelede.blogs.nytimes.com/2009/01/22/gazas-smugglers-start-digging-new-tunnels/ (accessed 15 April 2011).

Mamdani, M. (2004) *Good Muslim, Bad Muslim: America, the Cold War and the Roots of Terror*. New York: Pantheon Books.

MSNBC.com (2011) 'Israel pushed Gaza to "brink of collapse": WikiLeaks', 5 January. Available at: www.msnbc.msn.com/id/40926651/ns/us_news-wikileaks_in_security/ (accessed 7 May 2011).

Mujahid, Abdul Malik (2008) 'Islamophobia statistics USA', Euro-Islam Info. Available at: www.euro-islam.info/2008/01/01/statistics-on-islamophobia-in-the-us/ (accessed 25 January 2010).

Nazemroaya, M. D. (2006) 'Plans for redrawing the Middle East: the project for a "New Middle East"', *Global Research*, 18 November. Available at: www.globalresearch.ca/index.php?context=va&aid=3882 (accessed 15 April 2011).

Pop, V. (2010) 'Terrorist attacks decrease in Europe', euobserver.com, 29 April. Available at: http://euobserver.com/9/29968 (accessed 7 May 2011).

Riechmann, D. (2010) 'Coalition ramps up air war in Afghanistan', MSNBC online, 30 November. Available at: www.msnbc.msn.com/id/40438569/ns/world_news-south_and_central_asia/ (accessed 15 April 2011).

Said, E. (1978) *Orientalism*. London: Vintage.

Said, E. (1994) *Culture and Imperialism*. London: Vintage.

Shahak, I. and Mezvinsky, N. (1999) *Jewish Fundamentalism in Israel*. London: Pluto.

Shaheen, J. G. (2001) *Reel Bad Arabs: How Hollywood Vilifies a People*. Northampton, MA: Interlink Publishing Group.

Stacy, M. (2010) 'Minister: "Burn a Quran day" to go as planned on September 11', *Huffington Post* 7 September.

Stoner, E. (2009) 'Mercenaries and murder in Iraq', *Guardian* 14 August.

The Israel Project (2009) 'US President Obama determined to stop Hamas weapons smuggling', 21 January. Available at: www.theisraelproject.org/

site/apps/nlnet/content2.aspx?c=hsJPK0PIJpH&b=689705&ct=6639147 (accessed 1 December 2010).

Turse, N. and Engelhardt, T. (2007) 'The Pentagon's secret air war in Iraq', AntiWar.Com, 8 February. Available at: http://antiwar.com/engelhardt/?articleid=10485 (accessed 15 April 2011).

Wittgenstein, L. (1953/2001) *Philosophical Investigations*. Oxford: Blackwell.

Wittgenstein, L. (1979) *On Certainty*, edited by G. E. M. Anscombe and G.H. von Wright. Oxford: Basil Blackwell.

3

MEDIA, WAR AND INFORMATION TECHNOLOGY

Christian Fuchs

Christian Fuchs interrogates the role of new information and communication technologies (ICTs) in recent transformations of capitalism – involving privatization, commodification and financialization – and, in particular, new forms of imperialism and empire. Adopting a Marxist view of technology as a profoundly contradictory phenomenon that simultaneously offers possibilities for both the powerful and the powerless, he assesses precisely how networked technologies have been incorporated into the structures of capitalism and contemporary warfare. He highlights an 'integrative' strategy in which ICTs are increasingly used to naturalize official perspectives of war (through, for example, the embedding of journalists) and also to mediatize war itself (through new military hardware which embeds communicative functions into surveillance and killing machines). Far from disappearing in an age of globalization, Fuchs argues that imperialism is re-asserting itself with the aid of networked technologies.

Lenin (1917) identified five characteristics of imperialism: economic concentration, the dominance of finance capital, the importance of capital export, the spatial stratification of the world as a result of corporate dominance and the political dimension of the spatial stratification of the world. This chapter argues that contemporary capitalism can be seen as a new form of imperialism marked by financialization, commodification, neoliberal privatization and the growth of transnational corporations. Financialization matches Lenin's emphasis on finance capital's role in imperialism, transnational corporations are an expression of capital export, and neoliberalism is the newest form of the political and economic stratification of the world (see Fuchs, 2010a, 2010b). It is also important, however, to tackle the communicative dimension of the rise of the new imperialism (Fuchs 2010c). This chapter contributes to this task by analysing the role of media technologies, especially networked digital information and communication technologies (ICTs), in the context of theories of new imperialism and global capitalism.

Lenin wrote his key text on imperialism, *Imperialism, the highest stage of capitalism* (Lenin, 1917), in the face of the First World War. In it, he stressed the role of war between nation states as one, but not the only, aspect of imperialism.

> Capitalism has grown into a world system of colonial oppression and of the financial strangulation of the overwhelming majority of the population of the world by a handful of 'advanced' countries. And this 'booty' is shared between two or three powerful world plunderers armed to the teeth (America, Great Britain, Japan), who are drawing the whole world into their war over the division of their booty. (Lenin, 1917: 28)

Lenin described the First World War as a 'war for the division of the world' (1917: 27) and argued that imperialism includes 'rivalry between a number of great powers in the striving for hegemony, i.e. for the conquest of territory, not so much directly for themselves, as to weaken the adversary and undermine his hegemony' (1917: 239). These great powers are not necessarily nation states but can also be military groups or corporations.

A notion of new imperialism that is grounded in Lenin's classic theory of imperialism shares with theories of empire, global capitalism and other concepts of new imperialism the insight that the global dimension of capital is a central characteristic of contemporary capitalism (see Callinicos, 2003a, 2003b, 2005, 2007; Hardt and Negri, 2000, 2004; Harvey, 2003, 2005; Panitch and Gindin, 2004, 2005; Robinson, 2004, 2007; Sklair, 2002; Wood, 2003a, 2003b; Zeller, 2004a, 2004b). My own approach is based on the assumption that theories of global capitalism, new imperialism and empire need to be grounded in critical social theory and in macroeconomic data that verify the theoretical assumptions (Fuchs, 2009, 2010a, 2010b).

New imperialism shows the characteristics of imperialism that Lenin described but takes on novel forms. Finance capital is now the dominant form of capital where insurance companies, pension funds, investment funds and new financial instruments play an important role in deregulated, volatile financial markets that resulted in the global world economic crisis of 2008. Capital export is today far more important than in the period 1945–1975. The world economy is highly stratified: developed countries dominate capital exports and world trade although North America's importance in capital and commodity exports has decreased. Europe is today the most important actor in the import and export of capital and goods while China has become a crucial exporting country and an important location for FDI inflows. In this changing situation, military conflicts – including the emergence of transnational 'terror' groups like Al-Qaeda – shape the new imperialism in which informatization is just one tendency besides financialization and hyperindustrialization. The discussion and analysis of media and information should, therefore, be situated within the context of the new imperialism.

ICTs in New Imperialism Theory

The task of this section is to analyse the role that various theories of new imperialism assign to the media and ICTs. The analysed theories focus on at least one of the notions of new imperialism, empire, or global capitalism. What they have in common is that they argue that there is a worldwide system of economic exploitation, that this system is globally networked, and a multi-level class system (with class division and exploitation being organized on the local, national, regional and global level). In order to grasp how new imperialism thinkers conceptualize the role of the media and ICTs, I searched systematically for passages containing at least one of the key words 'media', 'medium', 'communications', 'information', 'technology', 'internet', 'ICTs', 'IT' in significant publications.

First, there are approaches that see no relationship between capitalist development and ICTs/media. The latter are considered as rather unimportant factors in the analysis of capitalism. For example, there is not a single mention of either media or ICTs in the analysis by Leo Panitch and Sam Gindin (2004) of what they term 'American empire'. Second, there are approaches that stress that capitalist development has required and created the growth of the ICT sector because there was a need for new spheres of commodification and privatization and for increasing productivity and the speed of capital accumulation. ICTs are seen as the outcome of the development of global capitalism.

Sklair (2002), for example, focuses in his analysis of global capitalism on how capitalist globalization has transformed the media into more commercialized and commodified spheres: 'It is the capacity to commercialize and commodify all ideas and the products in which they adhere, television programmes, advertisements, newsprint, books, tapes, CDs, videos, films, the internet, and so on, that global capitalism strives to appropriate.' Habermas (1989) pointedly termed this 'the colonization of the lifeworld' (Sklair, 2002: 116).

Similarly, Robinson acknowledges the connection of globalization and ICTs. New communication technologies 'were "globalizing" in the sense that they allowed capital to "go global". New patterns of accumulation opened up by globalizing technologies both require and make possible economies of scale that are truly global and require a more generalized commodification of the world economy' (2004: 9).

In his opinion, the causal relation between ICTs and global capitalism takes on the form that the drive of capitalism to globalize and accumulate has brought about the need for the development of ICTs. So Robinson stresses that global capitalism was not caused by technological innovations and argues that the rise of ICTs 'has been caused by the drive, built into capitalism itself by competition and class struggle, to maximize profits by reducing labour and other "factor" costs' (2004: 21). The more general assumption behind this argument is that the 'technological effect is the effect of social forces' (2004: 102f.) and not their cause.

Third, there are approaches that stress that ICTs are a medium of the globalization and transformation of capitalism. So, for example, Wood (2003b: 135) says that 'the speed and extent of capital movements, especially those that depend on new information and communication technologies, have created something new' and the world has thereby become more interdependent. Wood does not give much focus to the media and ICTs and simply acknowledges in one sentence that ICTs have influenced the global extension and speed of capital accumulation.

Fourth, there are approaches that see ICTs and media as, on the one hand, as the result of the capitalist need for profit maximization and the development of commercialization, privatization and deregulation as central capitalist imperatives but, on the other hand, in the past decades also identify the transformative capacities of ICTs and media. The best examples are the approaches by Harvey and Hardt/Negri.

Harvey sees the rising importance of ICTs as a feature of the rise of a neoliberal capitalist regime: 'geographical expansion often entails investment in long-lived physical and social infrastructures (in transport and communications networks and education and research for example)' (2003: 88). Neo-liberalism and neoliberal globalization provide the contexts for the rise of ICTs that have resulted in the massive privatization and deregulation of communications so that they are no longer common goods, but private property. Indeed, this extends way beyond communications:

> Public utilities of all kinds (water, telecommunications, transpor-
> tation), social welfare provision (social housing, education, health
> care, pensions), public institutions (universities, research labora-
> tories, prisons) and even warfare (as illustrated by the "army" of
> private contractors operating alongside the armed forces in Iraq)
> have all been privatized to some degree throughout the capitalist
> world and beyond (for example in China). (Harvey, 2005: 160)

But Harvey sees not only a causal effect of capitalist restructuration on ICTs, but also identifies a reciprocal impact. ICTs are, according to Harvey, a medium of time–space compression of capitalism, in the sense that ICTs bring about a transformation of capitalism.

For Hardt and Negri (2000, 2004, 2009), capitalist development requires ever-newer forms of production, control and exploitation that have brought about the rise of information technologies and knowledge work as dominant forms of production. Reflecting on how capitalism exploits and commodifies communication and knowledge, they see a dialectic at work here in the sense that the advancement of the exploitation and commodification of knowledge and communication has resulted in a new mode of production that is based on immaterial labour. Immaterial labour, they argue, is labour 'that creates imma-terial products, such as knowledge, information, communication, a relationship, or an emotional response' (Hardt and Negri, 2004: 108).

Immaterial labour, however, could be highly co-operative and, with its immanent communist potentials, has the potential to question and threaten capitalist logic. It is the 'multitude' that produces knowledge in networks and is thus 'embedded in cooperative and communicative networks' (2004: xv). While they acknowledge the structural need for capitalism to bring about ever newer forms of production and technology (witness the rise of comput-ers and the internet as well as the culture industry), the core of their argu-ment is agency-oriented. The category of the multitude describes new forms of knowledge labour and struggle that produce communist potentials that go beyond capitalism and question its logic. For Hardt and Negri, immate-rial labour is dialectical: exploited by capital but also a communist activity of co-operation of the multitude. The liberating aspect of immaterial labour is best summarized in Hardt's and Negri's formulation that 'immaterial labour thus seems to provide the potential for a kind of spontaneous and elementary communism' (2004: 294).

Both the approaches of Harvey and Hardt/Negri stress that financializa-tion, neo-liberalism, privatization and commodification are aspects of capi-talism that have brought about the growth of the ICT and media sector and have shaped this sector according to capitalist imperatives. The main difference between them is that Harvey stresses the immanent development of the global development of capitalism whereas Hardt and Negri have a strong focus on elements that transcend capitalism. While the two approaches share the insight that ICTs in contemporary society are both media and outcome of capitalist development, Harvey focuses on the reproduction and development of capitalism while Hardt and Negri stress the explosive technological potentials that suggest the actuality of liberation.

Capitalist Development, ICT and Warfare

Perspectives that do not take into account an analysis of ICTs and the media in the development of capitalism ignore a fundamental dimension of human existence: humans not only have to eat and produce in order to exist, they also have to think, communicate and inform themselves in order to be able to manage their daily lives. Therefore each society has a communicative dimension and capitalist society needs to create means and relations of communication in order to be able to accumulate capital. Positions that only stress how capitalist processes of financializaton, privatization and commodification have formed the context for the emergence and diffusion of ICTs, fail to understand that technologies and communication are also part of the differentiation and development of social structures.

There is a risk here of taking a technologically deterministic position that reduces the development of society and the economy to technological factors alone and ignores the influence of other factors such as class structure, the distribution of wealth, ideology and world-views, education, and so on. Technology is an important dimension of human existence, but it is not the only dimension. Therefore its effects should neither be under- nor overestimated. Technology is conditioned, not determined, by society, and vice versa. This means that societal conditions, interests and conflicts influence which technologies will emerge, but technology's effects are not predetermined because modern technologies are complex wholes of interacting parts that are to certain extents unpredictable (Perrow, 1999).

A critical theory of technology and society proposes a mutual shaping approach that argues that technological development interacts with societal contradictions. A critical theory of media and technology is based on dialectical reasoning that allows us to see the relationship between media and technology as multi-dimensional and complex: a specific technology has, for example, multiple potential effects on society and social systems that can co-exist or stand in contradiction to each other. Which potentials are realized is based on how society, interests, power structures and struggles shape the design and usage of technology in multiple, and often contradictory, ways. As Marx put it (1867: 568f.):

> machinery in itself shortens the hours of labour, but when employed by capital it lengthens them; since it lightens labour, but when employed by capital it heightens its intensity; since in itself it is a victory of man over the forces of nature but in the hands of capital it makes man the slave of those forces; since in itself it increases the wealth of the producers, but in the hands of capital it makes them into paupers.

The economic diffusion of ICT in the current era is related to the crisis of global Fordism. As a reaction to the relative decline in the rates of profit in the 1970s, computerization and automation were introduced in order to save labour costs and increase profitability and flexibility, to speed up production and to create new spheres of accumulation. ICTs are both media and result of the economic globalization of capitalism. On the one hand, they support the overcoming of communication over spatial and temporal distances, hence local processes are influenced by global ones and vice versa, but they are also facilitate the territorial restructuring of capitalism.

The generation of networks of production that are typical for transnational corporations has been made much easier by ICTs that are heavily implicated in the movements of restructuring that are crucial for capital. These restructuring processes can be characterized as designing a flexible, neo-liberal regime of accumulation that is based on processes of globalization, privatization, commodification and financialization. These four processes are the core of the new imperialistic mode of capitalism (Fuchs, 2010a, 2010b). The aim of the economic globalization of production is to save labour costs and fixed capital costs by outsourcing parts of production to those regions of the globe where the most capital-friendly investment conditions are available. This can result in an undermining and competitive lowering and deterioration of working conditions and social conditions. If there are falling profits, then capital tries to find new spheres of accumulation.

One way of doing this is where publicly owned goods and services are transformed into privately owned resources and where new spheres of commodity production and sale are created. The rise of ICTs is related to the privatization of telecommunications and the formation of new software, hardware and internet industries. Financialization means that stocks, shares and various kinds of derivatives are created that are traded on the stock market. The main aim is to achieve high short-term financial profits. According to Harvey (2005: 33): 'A wave of innovations occurred in financial services to produce not only far more sophisticated global interconnections but also new kinds of financial markets based on securitization, derivatives, and all manner of futures trading. Neo-liberalization has meant, in short, the financialization of everything.'

The rise of the 'new media' industry in the 1990s was based on the heavy investment of finance capital. The problem with finance capital is that the financial market value of companies does not reflect the actual profits achieved in everyday production and commodity sales, but is partly based on the hope of future profits. The 'new economy' crisis in 2000 was caused by an explosion of the finance bubble that was created in this sector, i.e. a difference between financial market values and accumulated values.

Speculative ('fictive') capital that is detached from material production and constitutes fast, self-increasing, unstable ('bubble economy') global flows of capital is gaining importance. It is due to the fact that ICTs are able to dissolve temporal and spatial distances that corporations can flexibly manage production and make use of global interconnected flows of capital, technology, labour and information. Network organization is characteristic of a post-Fordist global capitalist economy composed of networks of firms, networks of suppliers and distributors, financial networks, strategic alliances, joint ventures and financial markets that are based on fast global flows of increasingly 'immaterial' speculative capital transmitted and manipulated digitally by making use of network technology.

ICTs make much easier the outsourcing, rationalization and decentralization of production, team work, the flexibilization of jobs and the flattening of organizational hierarchies. They have contributed to the shift of the employment sector from a focus on industrial jobs to service jobs. In most advanced countries the service sector today makes up two-thirds of total employment. The post-Fordist economy is a flexible regime of accumulation that is enabled by ICTs and based on a whole series of production trends that include: the outsourcing, decentralization and 'flexibilization' of production, lean management, just-in-time production, the flattening of internal hierarchies and growth of small organizational units, delegation of decision-making from upper hierarchical levels to lower ones, the rhetoric of participatory management, decentralization of organizational structures, team work, strategic alliances, innovation networks, semi-autonomous working groups, informatization, automation and rationalization.

Discussing ICTs as qualities of imperialist warfare should, therefore, be embedded into a discussion of the dialectic of technology and society. Many technological systems originated in a military context: the development of the computer was boosted by the decision of Allied Forces in the Second World War to develop powerful decryption and encryption technologies while the internet also originated in a military context, namely the attempt of the US in the 1960s to build a decentralized communication system that would withstand a Soviet nuclear attack. Warfare is the original context for the emergence of computers and the internet as technological innovations and their broader usage has emerged in the light of the crisis of Fordist capitalism as well as the rise of neo-liberalism and the new imperialism. Technological innovations that first had primarily military tasks were turned into an economic context, in which the dialectic of capitalist development and ICTs took effect.

There are several competing explanations for the US invasions of Afghanistan and Iraq (see Callinicos, 2003a, 2005, 2007; Harvey, 2005, 2006; Panitch and Gindin, 2004, 2005; Wood, 2003b): the desire to secure access to oil as a strategic economic resource, to establish worldwide geopolitical hegemony, to expand US economic power in the face of the challenges posed by Europe and China, to limit the influence of Islamic nations and groups that challenge Western dominance of the world, or to extend the existing model of neo-liberal capitalism all over the world. It is possible that the invasions were motivated by a combination of some or all of these elements. No matter which position one takes here, the discussion shows that capitalist development provides the broader context for wars in the early second millennium. It is also the context for the role of ICTs in new imperialist warfare. We can therefore say that new imperialism is, on the one hand, the context for information warfare but also that information warfare itself partly transforms the new imperialism. I want to point out some aspects of the role of ICTs in new imperialist warfare (for more details and a theoretical grounding, see Fuchs, 2008). In 1991, media coverage of the attacks on Iraq was dominated by pictures broadcast by CNN that mainly showed Baghdad by night illuminated by flashes and radar images, as well as military analyses. The situation was a bit different in the 2003 Iraq War. First, some large European countries, like France and Germany, opposed the war, which resulted in a certain number of mass media reports that were critical of the US role in the war. Al Jazeera had the role of an 'Arab CNN' and, to a certain extent, reached audiences in the West so that alternative views and kinds of reporting were available. Second, with the emergence of the internet as a new medium for alternative coverage, anti-war and pro-war blogs allowed citizens, independent journalists and alternative agencies to report directly from Iraq. Their importance and influence is unclear, but it is a fact that war-related user-generated content production has today become an immanent activity of wars, revolutions, protests and conflicts.

The coverage directly from the front further transformed media coverage of warfare into a spectacle that was designed to excite and thrill viewers but, all too often, the horrifying effects of horror were not shown. More than 600 reporters were 'embedded' with British and US troops and reported directly from the front. All of these journalists had to sign an agreement that defined 'ground rules' (see Katovsky and Carlson, 2003: 401–417) and set strict limits for coverage. One can question whether it makes sense to embed journalists and whether this results in a more balanced coverage. These journalists face all the dangers that the fighting soldiers are confronted with, and hence their reports might be distorted and might reflect their subjective fears and angers more than in traditional coverage. Can 'embedded' journalists report independently and impartially on warfare they are involved in personally? Can they adequately maintain distance from their objects of coverage? Which stories are shown on TV, which ones are missing? Does 24-hour live coverage and reports directly from the front democratize and pluralize media coverage or do they create yet a new dimension of hyper-reality, media spectacles and simulated, false, one-dimensional realities? The reality of death and destruction might get lost amid the high-tech imagery delivered by the mass media. Was the embedding experiment really 'a demonstration of democratic values and freedom of speech in action' (Katovsky and Carlson, 2003: xix), or rather an integrative strategy of manipulation?

Due to its experience in Vietnam, US governments in the following decades tried to keep the mass media out of war zones when it invaded countries. This was for example the case in Grenada and Panama. Since the 1990s and starting with the 1991 Gulf War, a different strategy has been employed: one that focuses on integration instead of repression. This shift is an expression of a larger ideological shift in society from the 'disciplinary society' to the 'society of controls' (Fuchs, 2008). Embedded journalism is an integrative strategy of media self-censorship, an expression of mechanisms of the Deleuzian society of control (Deleuze, 1995). The repressive political strategy tried to discipline the mass media while the integrative strategy in addition tries to provide a certain degree of flexibility (such as embedding journalists) and freedom of movement that is kept within clearly defined limits. It tries to produce identification between mass media and military strategists. The ground rules were able to invoke discipline, but in many cases there was no need to apply them due to the ideological identity established by the practice of embedding that was able to dissolve distance between reporter and military. This ideological shift can be observed not only in the mass media but also in the area of production where strategies of participative management aim at the ideological integration of the work force into corporations. Bonus systems, team work, share options, corporate identity, attractive design of the work place, construction of a community between management and workers (a 'we identity'), the advancement of a spirit of enterprise within the workforce, and so on, are all part of this strategy that constitutes significant features of this new disciplinary regime.

In 2003, there was no longer a CNN monopoly on war coverage. Rupert Murdoch's Fox News competed heavily with CNN, while there were alternative press institutions that mainly made use of the internet in order to provide alternative sources of war information. The competition for topical news and ratings between large channels such as Fox, CNN, ABC, CBS and MSNBC did not automatically result in a more democratic and pluralistic type of coverage. Indeed, the fierce battle for ratings helped to produce a competition as to who could present the war in the most sensationalistic and spectacular way. The result was not the proliferation of the representation of alternative views but mass one-dimensional coverage. The problem that alternative media are facing is that they are hardly recognized and little known, and that the war-waging parties try to control and influence information and war coverage.

Warfare, meanwhile, is increasingly informatized and digitized. While the US army pushes multi-player recruitment online games such as America's Army (cf. Bayer, 2006), military research in countries like the US, Israel and France focuses on the development of Unmanned Combat Air Vehicles (UCAVs) that work with precision-guided weapons. Unarmed UCAVs that monitor and collect data on enemy targets are in use in many armies. The Indoor Simulated Marksmanship Trainer is an example of a computer training system used in the US army in which soldiers fire with laser rifles at targets on a screen. In the 2003 Iraq War, the US used GPS (Global Positioning System) for navigating UCAVs and several thousand smart bombs (Webb, 2006). With the increasing importance of recognizing and monitoring enemy targets with the help of location technologies, C4I (Command, Control, Communications, Computers and Intelligence) has been renamed as C4ISR (Command, Control, Communications, Computer, Intelligence, Surveillance and Reconnaissance (see National Research Council, 2004).

Airborne Warning and Control System (AWACS) airplanes can now radar-detect targets and transmit the coordinates to bombers. The B-2 Stealth Bomber that can drop GPS-guided bombs was first used by the US army in the Kosovo war in 1999 and subsequently in Afghanistan in 2002 and in Iraq in 2003. Target coordinates collected by GPS satellites or UCAVs were transmitted to aircrafts and there was a real-time display of forces on computer screens (Larkin, 2006: 123). Joint Direct Attack Munitions (JDAMs) are smart bombs equipped with a guidance computer that permanently receives positioning data from GPS systems. The AGM-154 Joint Standoff Weapon (JSOW) is another GPS-guided smart bomb. Both types of weapons were dropped by B-2, B-1, B-52 and F-117A bombers on Iraq in 2003 (*Time*, 21 March 2003, 21 April 2003, *Newsweek*, 31 March 2003). Tomahawk cruise missiles that are guided by data that they receive from GPS were launched from ships and submarines (*Time*, 21 March 2003). The M1 Abrams battle tank, employed in the 2003 Iraq War, is equipped with a computerized fire-control system that, with the help of sensors, collects data, calculates target solutions for the gunners and can automatically fire at the target (*Time*, 21 March 2003). Joint Expeditionary Digital Information systems that link ground troops via satellite so that they can, for example, call in missile strikes are being developed by the US military (Rheingold, 2002: 162f.).

Hacking is also central to contemporary warfare. A dispute between China and the US involving the hacking of government websites and servers erupted in cyberspace after US forces accidentally bombed the Chinese embassy in Belgrade during the Kosovo war on 7 May 1999. The attack was carried out by a misguided bomb which shows that such weapons are still prone to technological errors (for example if the GPS signal connection to the satellite fails and the bombs hits a wrong target because the position could not be dynamically actualized) and human error (for example if there is a wrong input of initial target coordinates) and that a bloodless cyber-war is hence unlikely. After a US spy plane collided with a Chinese fighter jet and had to make a forced landing on Chinese territory in April 2001, a war between Chinese and American hackers, who disabled and defaced websites, erupted.

Networked warfare frequently makes use of technological networks for communication. So, for example, the US military uses the SIPRNET (Secret Internet Protocol Router Network) for transmitting classified information and the NIPRNET (Non-classified Internet Protocol Router Network) for transmitting unclassified information. The reality of information war today involves network warfare, media manipulation, smart weapons, virtual reality training, encrypted communication and hacking. The targets of war are still material and human – war has not become a pure simulation as sometimes claimed in postmodern theories. War is mediated by information technology so that there is less direct human contact and more possibility of long-distance air attacks. Humans control and operate war technologies, but they gain more distance from their enemies whom they attempt to wipe out with the help of information technologies. There are no purely virtual battlefields with virtual soldiers.

Conclusion

Privatization, commodification, globalization and financialization form the core processes of the new imperialism. They are drivers of ICT development but, at the same time, also partly driven by these technologies. ICTs are therefore both medium and outcome of capitalist development processes. ICTs as aspects of warfare play a key role in the new imperialism in relation to, for example, the coverage of war, recruitment games, military communication networks, and especially the development and deployment of weapon systems. ICTs, like computers and the internet, had their origin in a military context and were then diffused into capitalist economies where they both intensified and were shaped by processes of capitalist development. They are now used as a specific means of waging the struggle against new forms of terrorism but also, of course, by the terrorists themselves.

The US-led wars in Iraq and Afghanistan are the practical validation of the presence of the fifth characteristic of Lenin's concept of imperialism: struggles for the control of the world today. Military conflicts that aim at territorial control and global hegemony and counter-hegemony are immanent features of the new imperialism. Lenin (1917: 264) argued that imperialism is leading to annexation and increased oppression and consequently also to increased resistance. 9/11 and the rise of global terrorism can be interpreted as a reaction to global US economic, political and cultural influence. It resulted in a vicious cycle of global war that creates and secures spheres of Western influence and global terrorism that tries to destroy Western lifestyles and Western dominance.

The history of capitalism after the First World War did not bring an end to warfare. Since then we have seen major conflicts including, for example, the Second World War (1939–1945), the Vietnamese War of Independence (1946–1954), the Cold War (1945–1990), the Korean War (1950–1953), the Vietnam War (1959–1975), the invasion of Grenada (1983), the invasion of Panama (1989–1990), the Persian Gulf War (1990–1991), the War in Afghanistan (2001–), and the War in Iraq (2003–). In many of the bloodiest wars of the twentieth and twenty-first centuries, North American and European nations have been involved. This is not an abstract example but empirical evidence that war is an inherent means of the expansion of capitalism that creates spheres of economic and political influence. It is one element of imperialism. The end of the Soviet Union has not brought an end to the threat of global war, but new geopolitical conflicts all over the world that have shaped capitalism since the 1990s.

The First World War was the expression of the political-economic conflict between what Lenin termed imperialism's 'great powers' (1917: 239). Imperialism is necessarily a system of political-economic competition between great powers. In contemporary conditions, the military conflicts do not always coincide with economic conflicts. Arab nations and groups question Western hegemony through military means, while Asian nations such as China challenge the West through economic means. Lenin spoke of imperialism as the conflict between great powers, which does not imply that these great powers need only be nation states but also corporations and various ideologically driven groups. Military wars have economic dimensions and economic wars can, and in many cases do, result in military wars, but if and when exactly this happens is not predetermined but a matter of the contingent complexity of societal power struggles. We simply do not know, for example, if in the future there will be a military war between China and Western nations for political-economic hegemony. The future cannot be predicted, but we can say, looking back to the past, that it is highly likely that if the twenty-first century does not establish alternatives to the global rule of capitalism, that it will be another century of violence with new territorial wars waged for political and economic reasons.

References

Bayer, M. (2006) Virtual violence and real war, in E. Halpin et al. (eds) *Cyberwar, Netwar and the Revolution in Military Affairs*. Basingstoke: Palgrave Macmillan: 12–31.

Callinicos, A. (2003a) *An Anti-Capitalist Manifesto*. Cambridge: Polity.

Callinicos, A. (2003b) Toni Negri in perspective, in G. Balakrishnan (ed.) *Debating Empire*. London: Verso: 121–143.

Callinicos, A. (2005) Imperialism and global political economy, *International Socialism* 108, online version: http://www.isj.org.uk/index.php4?id=140& issue=108

Callinicos, A. (2007) *Social Theory*. Cambridge: Polity.

Deleuze, G. (1995) Postscript on the societies of control, in *Negotiations*. New York: Columbia University Press: 177–182.

Fuchs, C. (2008) *Internet and Society: Social theory in the information age*. New York: Routledge.

Fuchs, C. (2009) *A Contribution to Critical Globalization Studies*. Centre for the Critical Study of Global Power and Politics Working Paper CSGP 09/8. Peterborough, Canada: Trent University.

Fuchs, C. (2010a) Critical globalization studies: An empirical and theoretical analysis of the new imperialism, *Science & Society* 74(2): 215–247.

Fuchs, C. (2010b) Critical globalization studies and the new imperialism, *Critical Sociology* 36(6): 839–867.

Fuchs, C. (2010c) New imperialism: Information and media imperialism? *Global Media and Communication* 6(1): 33–60.

Fuchs, C. and Zimmermann, R. (2009) *Practical Civil Virtues in Cyberspace: Towards the utopian identity of civitas and multitudo. Munich Series in Design Science Volume 5*. Aachen: Shaker.

Giddens, A. (1990) *The Consequences of Modernity*. Stanford: Stanford University Press.

Habermas, J. (1989) *The Structural Transformation of the Public Sphere*. Cambridge, MA: MIT Press.

Hardt, M. and Negri, A. (2000) *Empire*. Cambridge, MA: Harvard University Press.

Hardt, M. and Negri, A (2004) *Multitude*. New York: Penguin.

Hardt, M. and Negri, A (2009) *Commonwealth*. Cambridge, MA: Harvard University Press.

Harvey, D. (1990) *The Condition of Postmodernity*. Cambridge, MA: Blackwell.

Harvey, D. (2003) *The New Imperialism*. Oxford: Oxford University Press.

Harvey, D. (2005) *A Brief History of Neo-Liberalism*. Oxford: Oxford University Press.

Harvey, D. (2006) *Spaces of Global Capitalism. Towards a theory of uneven geographical development*. London: Verso.

Harvey, D. (2007) In what ways is the 'new imperialism' really new? *Historical Materialism* 15(3): 57–70.

Hofkirchner, W. (2007) A critical social systems view of the Internet, *Philosophy of the Social Sciences* 37(4): 471–500.

Katovsky, B. and Carlson, T. (eds) (2003) *Embedded: The media at war in Iraq*. Guilford, CT: Lyons Press.

Larkin, B. (2006) Nuclear weapons and the vision of command and control, in E. Halpin et al. (eds) *Cyberwar, Netwar and the Revolution in Military Affairs*. Basingstoke: Palgrave Macmillan: 113–138.

Lenin, V. I. (1917) *Imperialism, the Highest Stage of Capitalism*. Sydney: Resistance Books.

Marx, K. (1867) *Capital: Volume 1*. London: Penguin.

National Research Council (2004) *Army Science and Technology for Homeland Security. Report 2: C4ISR*. Washington, DC: National Academies Press.

Negri, A. (2008) *Reflections on Empire*. Cambridge: Polity.

Panitch, L. and Gindin, S. (2004) *Global Capitalism and American Empire*. London: Merlin Press.

Panitch, L. and Gindin, S. (2005) Finance and American empire, *Socialist Register* 41, 46–81.

Perrow, C. (1999) *Normal Accidents: Living with high-risk technologies*. Princeton: Princeton University Press.

Rheingold, H. (2002) *Smart Mobs*. New York: Basic Books.

Robinson, W. (2004) *A Theory of Global Capitalism*. Baltimore: Johns Hopkins University Press.

Robinson, W. (2007) The pitfalls of realist analysis of global capitalism. A critique of Ellen Meiksins Wood's Empire of Capital, *Historical Materialism* 15(3): 71–93.

Sklair, L. (2002) *Globalization: Capitalism & its alternatives.* Oxford: Oxford University Press.

Webb, M. (2006) *Illusions of Security: Global surveillance and democracy in the post-9/11 world.* San Francisco: City Lights.

Wood, E. M. (2003a) A manifesto for global capitalism? in G. Balakrishnan (ed.) *Debating Empire.* London: Verso: 61–82.

Wood, E. M. (2003b) *Empire of Capital.* London: Verso.

Zeller, C. (2004a) Die globale Enteignungsökonomie, in C. Zeller (ed.) *Die Globale Enteignungsökonomie.* Münster: Westfälisches Dampfboot: 9–20.

Zeller, C. (2004b) Ein neuer Kapitalismus und ein neuer Imperialismus? in C. Zeller (ed.) *Die Globale Enteignungsökonomie.* Münster: Westfälisches Dampfboot: 61–125.

4

PUBLIC DIPLOMACY VERSUS TERRORISM

Philip Seib

The final two chapters of the section should be read together as a debate over the kinds of strategies used to manage terrorism and counter-terrorism, most notably in relation to public diplomacy and 'soft power'. Philip Seib argues that the widespread take-up of social media has ensured that public diplomacy – the use of non-military means to secure political objectives – is no longer a 'sideshow' to official diplomacy but a struggle undertaken by a range of actors including governments, terrorists, NGOs and multinational corporations. Insisting that conventional approaches to diplomacy must take on board the persuasive powers of the media and providing examples from Al-Qaeda's use of media to international versions of *Sesame Street*, Seib adopts a perspective that public diplomacy can be an essential part of winning back the ground on which terrorism is nurtured.

Public diplomacy tends to be underrated as a counter-terrorism tool. As a preventive measure, it offers an alternative to military or police force because it seeks to reduce the level of enmity between those who might commit such acts and their potential victims. Dealing with terrorism tends to be left primarily to exponents of hard power. That approach makes sense in some instances, but defeating terrorism will require more complex and carefully crafted measures that address the mass publics from which terrorists draw their recruits and support. These publics may be exposed to increasingly sophisticated media messages from terrorist groups, and such messages must be countered.

Public diplomacy should be at the heart of such efforts. This chapter addresses how governments – particularly the government of the United States – have approached this task since the attacks on New York and Washington in 2001, and why some methods have been more successful than others. Among the issues and strategies worth examining are the role of international broadcasting, use of new media technologies, the roles of virtual states and diasporic populations, and the importance of linking public diplomacy efforts to specific policy initiatives. Terrorists' use of soft power is also analyzed.

Considering Public Diplomacy

To begin, let us settle on a simple – perhaps too simple – dictionary definition of public diplomacy: 'that element of diplomacy that involves a government reaching out to a public, rather than to another government'. A more complete definition recognizes that it need not be a 'government' that reaches out, multinational organizations, NGOs, corporations and the like may do so as well.

The significance of public diplomacy has grown exponentially during the past decade, partly because of the pervasiveness of new media. To an unprecedented extent, publics that previously were difficult or impossible to reach can now be contacted in cyber cafés and on their mobile phones. Governments that do not want their publics to be in touch with outsiders can impede this – for a while – but they might as well be trying to hold back the tide. In the contest between obstruction and technology, technology will sooner or later prevail.

Not only do governments have this tool of public diplomacy, but publics expect them to use it. To varying degrees, people feel intellectually and politically liberated by the technologies that enable them to be part of the larger world. A nation that does not reach out through public diplomacy today will not be considered a global leader, and it will not be adequately serving its own international interests.

The need for greater attention to public diplomacy is partly a function of globalized communication, which has sharpened the points at which policy and public meet. Proliferation of satellite television and the internet means that people know more and know it faster than at any previous time. This can produce quick explosions, such as during the Danish cartoon controversy of 2006, and it has increased volatility among the denizens of 'the Arab streets', 'the Chinese streets' and other publics. This restiveness affects domestic politics in these countries and complicates the tasks of diplomacy.

Less dependent on government-tied media for information, publics search for information on their own and must be courted directly rather than exclusively through their governments. This courtship is also important because a government concerned that a large part of its population is antagonistic toward the United States, for example, may be reluctant to cooperate with US policy. Public diplomacy could help reduce this problem.

The 'public' to which public diplomacy is directed is vast, curious and less inhibited about challenging the information they are given. As one public relations guru has noted, we have moved from an 'authority-driven' to an 'experience-driven' world. This is a world far beyond the niceties of old-fashioned diplomacy that could be conducted exclusively among comfortable elites, occasionally letting their decisions trickle down to the public. New media have opened a reconfigured diplomatic process to much of the world, and these new participants will never allow themselves to be shut out. Using platforms provided by social networking media, members of the global public are, more than ever before, persistent players in the previously closed world of foreign affairs.

For public diplomacy practitioners, new media realities change the nature of their work. The days of stately diplomatic process are long gone, and a public diplomacy initiative that lags too far behind the media flow may be ineffective. Transparency, long considered annoying and even dangerous by many diplomats, is increasingly expected and can be driven by YouTube, Twitter and other social media. As technological divides narrow, more of the world knows more of what is going on. The diplomatic pouch gave way first to the BBC, CNN and Al Jazeera, then to web-based forums, and now social media such as Facebook and YouTube. This means that when policy determinations are made, the world may learn about them within minutes. A parallel public diplomacy plan must be ready for implementation, which means public diplomats must participate fully in the policy-making process.

In addition to quickness, public diplomacy requires imagination in devising ways to capture the attention of global publics. Advancing women's rights, facilitating microcredit programmes, championing environmental protection, upgrading public health and public education, and more such ventures are essential in meeting the needs of the publics that a country wishes to influence.

A more creative approach to public diplomacy might encourage the rest of the foreign-policy establishment to become more creative itself. Pulling such efforts together will require remapping bureaucratic turf, which is never an easy job but is an essential one if any nation's public diplomacy is to have the coherence and breadth that it requires. This will require political leadership from the highest levels.

Public Diplomacy as Counter-terrorism Tool

Those who dismiss public diplomacy as a sideshow are correct if public diplomacy efforts have little purpose beyond image construction or 'branding'. But an argument can be made that public diplomacy has larger roles, including as a valuable counter-terrorism tool.

Let us look at terrorism as a pyramid. At the tip are Osama bin Laden (until his death), Ayman al-Zawahiri and a relatively small number of others who will never turn aside from the path of violence and must be dealt with accordingly. But as we move towards the base of the pyramid, the numbers grow larger and the commitment to violence lessens. Here are the people – many of them young – who can still be reached.

They are certainly being reached by Al Qaeda and other terrorist groups. Drop into a cyber café in Tangier or Amman and you are sure to find some 15-year-old boys watching videos showing American soldiers being killed while a stirring martial soundtrack plays and alluring promises are made to those who would join the fight.

One of the essential tasks of public diplomacy is to provide counter-programming to offset the messages of proponents of hatred and violence. Establishing dialogue that involves peers, respected leaders, moderate clerics and others is part of this. But an argument is convincing only if it is backed up by policy that can ensure that the promises made in such dialogue become reality. This underscores the importance of bringing public diplomacy into the heart of foreign policy, not leaving it as a satellite in distant orbit, glimpsed only occasionally.

As new media have fostered exponentially expanded information flows and pervasive interactive communication, public diplomacy's importance has increased. Superpowers do it, small states do it, NGOs do it, corporations do it, and so do quasi-states such as Al Qaeda. An example of Al Qaeda's public diplomacy was Aymen al-Zawahiri's online 'open meeting' in 2008, during which he responded to questions selected from nearly 2,000 submitted through the al-Ikhlas and al-Hesbah websites. The responses were presented in a one-hour-43-minute audio statement, with Arabic and English transcripts, released by Al Qaeda's As-Sahab media production company.

The exercise was apparently a response by the Al Qaeda leaders to their deteriorating standing within the base of the 'pyramid' described above. Zawahiri ignored the most frequently asked questions, which were about the dynamics of Al Qaeda's leadership, and instead focused on political competitors, principally Hamas and the Muslim Brotherhood (although the latter was mentioned in only one per cent of the questions) (Brachman et al., 2008). Nevertheless, this outreach was notable for its creating at least the appearance of accessibility and accountability. The mystique of remoteness wears thin after a while, particularly when the competition – such as Hamas – is so much a part of public life.

The Al Qaeda leaders also may have recognized that they had fallen behind the pace of technology development. Daniel Kimmage, an analyst at Radio Free Europe/Radio Liberty wrote that originally, 'the genius of Al Qaeda was to combine real-world mayhem with virtual marketing'. But now, added Kimmage: a more interactive, empowered online community, particularly in the Arab-Islamic world, may prove to be Al Qaeda's Achilles heel. Anonymity and accessibility, the hallmarks of Web 1.0, provided an ideal platform for Al Qaeda's radical demagoguery. Social networking, the emerging hallmark of Web 2.0, can unite a fragmented silent majority and help it find its voice in the face of thuggish opponents, whether they are repressive rulers or extremist Islamic movements (Kimmage, 2008).

While Al Qaeda tries to adapt to the changes in the online world, counter-terrorism agencies are also working to keep pace with technology. In Britain, the Research, Information and Communication Unit (RICU), which is based in the Home Office, produced a report, 'Challenging Violent Extremist Ideology through Communications', calling for a two-part strategy: 'channelling [anti-Al Qaeda] messages through volunteers in Internet forums' and providing the BBC and other media organizations around the world with propaganda designed to 'taint the Al Qaeda brand' (Travis, 2008b).

The RICU report called for targeting the 'Al Qaeda narrative', which it said 'combines fact, fiction, emotion, and religion and manipulates discontent about local and international issues. The narrative is simple, flexible, and infinitely accommodating. It can be adapted to suit local conditions and may have a disproportionate influence on understanding and interpretation of local or global events.' Challenging this narrative, noted the report, would reduce the ability of terrorists to exploit the social grievances of the various publics Al Qaeda and other such groups count on for support. The report said, 'The objective is not to dismiss 'grievances' but undermine Al Qaeda's position as their champion and violent extremism as their solution' (Travis, 2008a).

This British strategy reflects recognition by counter-terrorism planners that new and traditional media platforms must be used in loose combination to ensure comprehensive reach of their efforts. By being assertive, it also forces the hand of Al Qaeda and other terrorist organizations that want to maintain their popular bases. Drawing the likes of Zawahiri into the (relative) open provides, at the very least, a chance for counter-terrorism analysts to acquire information and insights about what the enemy is doing.

More general public diplomacy programs are needed in addition to counter-terrorism efforts. The United States has been notably unsuccessful in developing a comprehensive, first-rate public diplomacy strategy suitable for the environment of Web 2.0 (and beyond). US Secretary of Defense Robert Gates said in 2007:

> Public relations was invented in the United States, yet we are miserable at communicating to the rest of the world what we are about as a society and a culture, about freedom and democracy, about our policies and our goals. It is just plain embarrassing that al-Qaeda is better at communicating its message on the internet than America. As one foreign diplomat asked a couple of years ago, 'How has one man in a cave managed to out-communicate

the world's greatest communication society?' Speed, agility, and cultural relevance are not terms that come readily to mind when discussing US strategic communications. (Gates, 2007)

Although the Obama administration promptly made high-tech diplomacy more of a priority than it had been in previous years, these efforts have still suffered from bureaucratic resistance to technological change and problems of scale. This has limited the US government's ability to reach numerous audiences. Creative ventures, such as providing unfiltered 'C-SPAN-type' news to the Muslim world and elsewhere, exist but have failed to gain traction. Instead, Cold War theories hold sway, as can be seen in the largely archaic US international broadcasting strategy, and so do remarkably unsophisticated views of most online efforts. Partly because of the public's memories of terrorist attacks, the hard power approach is politically far easier to embrace than is a broader, more subtle strategy grounded in soft power.

Outside of governments, however, progress is happening. The Mideast Youth Foundation is one example and defines its work this way:

> In a region where the freedom to explore freely and formulate informed opinions are greatly constrained and dissent is neither welcomed nor tolerated, the Internet has provided youth with an avenue to break through the barriers. Through utilizing the inherent powers of the Internet, MideastYouth.com built the region's most diverse forum, where we challenge each other on a daily basis....Governments no longer hold a monopoly over information; together we built an independent news outlet for the people and by the people.

Among the projects with which the foundation is involved is the March 18 Movement, which commemorates the day in 2009 when Omid Reza Mir Sayafi, Iranian blogger and journalist, died in Evin Prison in Tehran. The December before his death, he was sentenced to two and half years in prison for allegedly insulting religious leaders and engaging in 'propaganda' against the Islamic Republic of Iran:

> The March 18 Movement aims not only to make sure that Omid Reza is remembered, but also that other persecuted bloggers around the world do not disappear into interrogation rooms and prison cells. The March 18 Movement would like to become a voice for bloggers everywhere who are in risk of being crushed under the heavy machinery of repression. (www.mideastyouth. com/projects; www.march18.org)

Other online voices discuss Facebook as a way to bring about digital democracy within non-democratic countries (international.daralhayat.com/

internationalarticle/44327) and yet others anticipate greater internet use once URLs in the Latin alphabet are joined by those in Arabic, Chinese, and other alphabets. Facebook, Twitter, YouTube and other online venues offer opportunities to demystify 'the other', and if this can be done, some people who occupy the midsection and base of the terrorism pyramid might begin drifting away and into more constructive pursuits.

The importance of persistent efforts along these lines was underscored in November 2009 when 57 per cent of voters in a Swiss referendum endorsed a ban on construction of new minarets (although not mosques themselves) anywhere in the country. About 400,000 Muslims live in Switzerland in what had been presumed to be a relatively well-integrated society. *The Economist* observed that the Swiss voters supporting the minarets ban believe 'that the world really does divide into Huntingtonian blocks, where one religion or another prevails, and the rest exist on sufferance' (*The Economist*, 2009a).

Responses to the vote were peaceful: public protests, political lobbying and no violence. Nevertheless, the election pointed out that religious tensions exist, even if below the surface. The Swiss vote was a sign that better connections between Muslims and non-Muslims would be useful in reducing mutual distrust, and not just in Switzerland.

In terms of creating intercultural connections, one of the best-known bridge-building efforts comes from some of the best-known citizens of the world, the Muppets. *Sesame Street* was born in the United States during the 1960s after studies showed that early childhood education was crucial to a child's later learning. Sesame Workshop, the programme's creative home, has continued to grow, and by 2010 versions of the program were seen in more than 130 nations, with local co-production taking place in 30 countries. These localized versions feature characters addressing local issues. In South Africa, for example, where 11 per cent of children are AIDS orphans, Takalani Street includes a Muppet who is an HIV-infected AIDS orphan and who demonstrates a vibrant and positive approach to dealing with HIV/AIDS issues.

One of Sesame Workshop's most ambitious ventures has been the Palestinian-produced version of *Sesame Street*, which evolved after *Sesame Stories* – showing segments created by Palestinian, Israeli and Jordanian production teams – ran afoul of intifada-related politics. The wholly Palestinian *Shara'a Simsim* began production in 2006, and although all the show's content must be approved by Sesame Workshop, it addresses realities of Palestinian children's lives. UNICEF found that as of June 2007 children in nearly a third of Palestinian families were experiencing anxiety, phobia, or depression, coupled in many cases with poor nutrition and poor general health.

The executive director of the Palestinian programme, Daoud Kuttab, observed that young Palestinian boys are particularly in need of positive messages, given the cultural pressures they face, and the programme's content advisor, Dr Cairo

Arafat, said, 'We want to show boys that they can enjoy life, share and participate without having to prove that they are tough and without reverting to violence.' Kuttab added, 'I would say 3-, 4-, 5-year olds – if we don't catch them at that early age, we do risk losing them to all kinds of propaganda, whether it's conservative, religious, or fundamentalist' (Shapiro, 2009).

Sesame Workshop is careful to avoid direct references to the politics and conflict of the region, but the show teaches lessons grounded in real events. One storyline portrayed the community working together to recover from a serious storm that had caused much destruction and loss. Although there were no military symbols to be seen, the story could easily be interpreted as representing the aftermath of the 2008–9 Israeli attacks on Gaza. Compare this to the episode of a programme on Hamas's Al Aqsa channel in which a leading character of the show is portrayed as dying as a result of this conflict and calling for revenge against Israel.

The example of *Shara'a Simsim* is not just a 'feel-good' story. It is an example of constructive pushback against the pressures young people feel that can nudge them toward violence. Hate-filled children's programming from Al Aqsa television and other sources cannot be allowed to stand unchallenged without increasing the risk of their viciousness taking hold in a generation that either can be the next recruiting ground for terrorists or can provide people who will work against violence.

This kind of message is also important in countries that have known recent violence that has subsided. In Northern Ireland, the increasing diversity of the population is emphasized. In Kosovo, the programme appears in Albanian (*Rruga Sesam*) and Serbian (*Ulica Sezam*), and tries to make the 'other' more humanized and less threatening. In addition to Albanian and Serbian children the programme includes Roma, Bosnian and Turkish youngsters. Because Albanians, who use the Latin alphabet, do not want to even see the Cyrillic letters used by Serbians, Sesame Workshop had to find a way to conduct its instruction about vocabulary in a way different from the usual *Sesame Street* method. Producers came up with a 'visual dictionary' that shows children saying words without the words appearing on the screen.

As they dealt with such matters, the Sesame Workshop producers kept the primary focus on relieving children from the burdens of hatred that if allowed to exist without a response would increase the likelihood of another cycle of violence in Kosovo. One of the producers, Basia Nikonorow, said: 'Hate is a learned trait. Children don't naturally hate someone of another ethnicity; this is taught to them or they pick it up from snippets of conversation and stereotyping' (Sesame Workshop).

Programming such as this can serve as a model for what might be a softer companion to 'antiterrorism' and classified as 'terrorism prevention', reaching the base of the terrorism pyramid described above. Using Sesame Workshop's creations as a paradigm, similar work could be commissioned to meet particular needs in particular places. This will not be a cure-all; the child who is well adjusted at age five could certainly embrace violence by age 16. But to do nothing to shape children's attitudes about cooperation and problem-solving would be to leave the door to violence open just a bit wider.

For young people and others, at no time should a vacuum be allowed to exist, because experience has shown that extremists will be quick to fill it with their messages. Further, merely reacting to extremist initiatives is insufficient; a proactive strategy that embraces innovative tactics is essential in dealing with foes whose own creativity has consistently been underestimated. Sesame Workshop's efforts, which draw financial support from USAID, are a paradigm for what governments and NGOs might accomplish. Selecting the media to use in such efforts should be determined by the audience's information consumption habits.

In much of the Middle East, satellite television is the most popular medium. (Scan the urban landscape of a city such as Cairo and you will see evidence of this in the thousands of satellite dishes.) For large parts of the world, internet use is increasing, but still trails far behind television. Another medium, in public use for a hundred years, is still dominant in areas of the world that are less wired and less connected. Radio still holds sway in countries such as Afghanistan, and, given the realities of global terrorism, radio's importance should not be ignored.

In Afghanistan, Mullah Fazlullah, also known as 'Mullah Radio', has used an FM transmitter to threaten with beheading those who do not support the Taliban (*The Economist*, 2009a). This is reminiscent of Rwanda's Radio Mille Collines, which contributed to the 1994 genocide by broadcasting a stream of hate-filled messages urging Hutus to kill Tutsis. The worst thing to do in such a case is to leave such radio broadcasts unanswered. In Afghanistan, Americans have worked with Afghans to prepare their own local-oriented programming and given residents crank-powered radios so they can listen to the voices that are trying to drown out the Taliban's exhortations.

The Taliban leaders do not limit themselves to radio. Apparently with coaching by Al Qaeda's media experts, the Taliban have produced websites, electronic magazines, DVDs with combat scenes, and even downloadable Taliban ringtones (Coghlan, 2009). (The Taliban ringtones are non-musical, featuring instead passages from the Qur'an.) Even as they condemn modernism on religious grounds, the Taliban recognize the military and political necessity of using the media they claim to despise. In late 2009, Al Qaeda itself began its 'Al-Ansar Mobile Team', which uploads text, audio and photographs for reception on mobile telephones (al Saleh, 2010).

As was seen in the November 2008 terror attacks in Mumbai, perpetrators and victims alike rely on new media. The terrorists used the internet in planning the strikes and in communicating with each other, and those caught up in the attacks used Twitter, mobile-phone cameras and other tools to report what was going on as it happened. The examples are many. Mumbai, Bali, Madrid, London, Nairobi, New York – wherever terrorists have attacked or gained a foothold, the many facets of extremism have become inextricably linked to media technologies and networks.

Toward an End of Terrorism

Thomas Friedman has suggested that at contemporary terrorism's heart is an anti-American narrative that is 'the cocktail of half-truths, propaganda, and outright lies about America that have taken hold in the Arab-Muslim world since 9/11. Propagated by jihadist websites, mosque preachers, Arab intellectuals, satellite news stations, and books – and tacitly endorsed by some Arab regimes – this narrative posits that America has declared war on Islam, as part of a grand 'American–Crusader–Zionist conspiracy' to keep Muslims down (Friedman, 2009). The results of this narrative range from the youngster in an internet café responding to an extremist video that is based on this world-view, to a mentally unbalanced American army officer, Major Nidal Malik Hasan, who killed 13 people at Fort Hood, Texas in 2009 partly because he had heard an interpretation of that narrative from an extremist Muslim cleric.

That narrative, in one form or another, has taken hold far beyond the Islamic world, and if anti-Americanism is not a sufficient motivating force, anti-globalization can serve as a supplement or substitute. Joseph Nye has pointed out that the democratization of technology allows terrorists to do much more than sulk and plot in isolation. To counter extremists' influence, wrote Nye, 'democratic leaders must use soft or attractive power to disseminate a positive narrative about globalization and the prospects for a better future that attracts moderates and counters the poisonous jihadist narratives on the Web' (Nye, 2005).

Such a strategy must recognize the generational aspects of extremism, which are reflected in the use of new media. Although Osama bin Laden remains the world's best-known terrorist, it was Abu Musab al-Zarqawi, almost ten years bin Laden's junior, who most thoroughly exploited online venues. Zarqawi understood the value of maintaining a consistent media presence by systematically disseminating 'news' about his activities. He may have alienated people with his infamous Berg execution video, but he established himself as America's chief nemesis within Iraq and a focus of journalistic attention.

When he was killed in 2006 (at age 39), much of the Western news media treated his death as a far more significant event than it really was, partly because he had been so skilful at self-promotion. He had done tremendous damage – killing many more Iraqis than Americans – and used his sophisticated appreciation of new media to leverage his position within Al Qaeda's loose-limbed international network. Although many American news organizations responded to this story with exultant headlines about Zarqawi's elimination signifying 'turning the corner' in Iraq, his death in a US bombing raid was merely useful, not determinative, in efforts to combat the Al Qaeda in Iraq organization. Zarqawi was successfully targeted by a combination of intelligence work and military skill, and the American missile-carrying drones in South Asia have killed additional terrorists.

But this approach will not eradicate terrorism. Every time an influential terrorist is killed, someone is certain to take his place. The ranks in the lower parts of the 'pyramid' discussed earlier include many committed to the causes terrorists claim that they champion. Until extremist groups' ranks are thinned, terrorism will continue.

Debate continues about how best to reduce those ranks. A RAND Corporation study published in 2008 examined 648 terrorist groups operating between 1968 and 2006 and found that most groups ended because their members joined the political process or their numbers were substantially reduced because members were arrested or killed by local police or intelligence agencies. Military force was largely ineffective, according to the study: 'It usually has the opposite effect from what is intended: it is often overused, alienates the local population by its heavy-handed nature, and provides a window of opportunity for terrorist-group recruitment' (Jones and Libicki, 2008: xiii, xvii).

Ratcheting down counter-terrorism from a military to a police/intelligence level makes sense, as does changing the rhetoric of counter-terrorism. The RAND study recommended abandoning use of the phrase 'war on terror' because:

> The phrase raises public expectations … that there is a battlefield solution to the problem of terrorism. It also encourages others abroad to respond by conducting a jihad (or holy war) … and elevates them to the status of holy warriors. Terrorists should be perceived and described as criminals, not holy warriors. (ibid.: xvii)

If counter-terrorism strategy were to shift away from a 'hard power' effort toward a more political approach, the significance of media-based tactics would increase. A first task along these lines would be to make non-violent political change seem more appealing, but that could only happen if governments alter their own institutions sufficiently to attract an expanded constituency. This is something the United States, in particular, must finally grapple with because so many of its allies have political systems that can most charitably be called 'rigged'. Until that situation changes, extremism, including violent acts, will seem justifiable even to many who would prefer another route toward change. When alternatives are not available, desperation can take hold.

These matters are crucial because terrorism around the world shows no signs of withering away on its own. Although spectacular attacks – such as those in the United States, Indonesia, Spain, the United Kingdom, India and elsewhere – have apparently subsided (as of late 2009), it would be dangerously foolish to relax. Al Qaeda has shown that it is not inclined to rush its planning for major attacks. Somalia and Yemen are well on its way to becoming the next Afghanistans, with strong Al Qaeda-related activity in both countries as 2010 began.

In Somalia, the Shabab embrace many of the same repressive measures that the Taliban have employed in trying to dictate how Afghans should live their lives. The Shabab's relationship with Al Qaeda is hard to precisely determine, but they share malignant intent, at the very least. The enormous cost, in lives and money, of the war in Afghanistan could continue indefinitely, with the next battlegrounds being Somalia and Yemen, and then – who knows where?

New media will be part of this. In December 2009, five American men were detained in Pakistan as they apparently tried to join Al Qaeda to fight against US forces in Afghanistan. They had been recruited online, with initial contact coming after one of the men had repeatedly commented positively about YouTube videos showing attacks on American troops. A US Department of Homeland Security official said, 'Online recruiting has exponentially increased, with Facebook, YouTube, and the increasing sophistication of people online.' Another apparent factor in the increase in online contacts is the success of intelligence agencies in scrutinizing activities at mosques, community centers, and other real – as opposed to cyber – world places where recruiting might occur (Witte et al., 2009). Somalia's Shabab have also engaged in recruitment within the United States (United States Senate, 2009).

As disturbing to counter-terrorism officials as this story may be, the greater fear is that this recruitment will lead not to such young men going overseas to fight, but rather finding targets close to home. As was seen in the 2005 London bombings, 'homegrown terrorism' is a threat that is difficult to deter, at least through conventional security methods.

Late 2009 also saw the emergence on the global stage of Anwar al Awlaki, the American-born Yemeni sheikh who had been implicated in the shootings at Fort Hood, Texas in November of that year. After a failed attempt to firebomb a Northwest Airlines flight from Amsterdam to Detroit, it was found that the would-be bomber, a young Nigerian named Umar Farouk Abdulmutallab, had frequently visited Al-Awlaki's website. As more attention focused on Al-Awlaki, ties were also found to the men who planned to attack the US Army base at Fort Dix, New Jersey in 2008 and to the Britons who carried out the 7/7 London bombings in 2005. More than 2,000 Al-Awlaki clips could be found on YouTube, which as of the end of 2009 had been viewed about three million times (Stalinsky, 2009).

Journalist Abdul Rahman Al-Rashed wrote that Al-Awlaki 'is the bin Laden of the Internet'. Noting Al-Awlaki's influence, Al-Rashed argued that 'Al Qaeda is an ideological problem rather than an organizational one. Whilst there is a lot to do on the ground in order to eradicate this malignant disease, the first priority should be to confront extremist ideology, its theorists and scholars before its students and soldiers' (Al-Rashed, 2009).

Al-Awlaki became the terrorist media star of the moment, but lost in most of the news coverage of his role in terrorist enterprises was the thread of his persistent and successful use of the internet to connect with existing and prospective followers and inspire them to action. Without the internet, Al-Awlaki would be far less of a menace. Discouraging news about the growth of terrorist operations in Somalia, Yemen and elsewhere continues to accumulate but, on the other hand, polling data showing the decline in popular support for violent actions, whatever their rationale, provides encouragement to those who believe that the destructive nihilism at the heart of terrorism may be receding. Perhaps the new communication technologies can help bring an end to, or at least significantly reduce, the fierce threat of terrorism.

No magic formula exists to reach this result. To get under way, the best plan may be to create a comprehensive strategy that will use in a coordinated way the many component elements of new media to counter the work of terrorists. So far, extremists who embrace violence have done a better job of mastering these media, but there is no reason they should be allowed to continue to hold the upper hand.

This takes us back to the fundamentals of public diplomacy. If terrorist organizations draw their support from a large public, they should not be allowed to access that public without competition from those who want to bring terrorism to an end. Conventional diplomacy operates on too narrow a wavelength to compete in this way, but well-designed public diplomacy can reach large numbers of the political public and can challenge terrorism at its base.

References

Al-Rashed, Abdul Rahman (2009) In Search of the Instructor in Yemen, *Asharq Alawsat*, 29 December.

al Saleh, Huda (2010) Al Qaeda Continues Using Modern Technology to Recruit Youth, *Asharq Alawsat*, 5 January.

Brachman, Jarret, Brian Fishman and Joseph Felter (2008) *The Power of Truth: Questions for Ayman al-Zawahiri*, Combating Terrorism Center, United States Military Academy, 21 April.

Christensen, Jen (2009) Reaching the Next Generation with 'Muppet Diplomacy', 13 August,www.cnn.com/2009/world/meast/08/13/generation. islam.gaza.muppets/index

Coghlan, Tom (2009) Taliban Spin Doctors Winning Fresh Ground in Propaganda War with NATO, *The Times*, 12 November.

Economist, The (2009a) The Return of the Nativists, 5 December, p. 71.

Economist, The (2009b) Crackles of Hatred, 25 July, p. 60.

Friedman, Thomas (2009) America vs. the Narrative, *New York Times*, 28 November.

Gates, Robert (2007) Robert M. Landon Lecture, Kansas State University, November 26, www.defense.gov/speeches/speech.aspx?speechid=1199

Jones, Seth and Libicki, Martin (2008) *How Terrorist Groups End*, Santa Monica, CA: RAND.

Kimmage, Daniel (2008) Fight Terror with YouTube, *New York Times*, 26 June.

Mideast Youth, www.mideastyouth.com/projects; www.march18.org

Nye, Joseph S. (2005) How to Counter Terrorism's Online Generation, *Financial Times*, 13 October.

Sesame Workshop to Palestinian Children 'Shara'a Simsim Spreads Hope and Empowerment www.sesameworkshop.org/aroundtheworld/palestine

Sesame Workshop Rruga Sesam/Ulica Sezam Humanizes the 'Other' in a Recovering Region, www.sesameworkshop.org/aroundtheworld/kosovo

Shapiro, Samantha (2009) Can the Muppets Make Friends in Ramallah? *New York Times Magazine*, 4 October.

Stalinsky, Steven (2009) Deleting Online Jihad and the Case of Anwar Al-Awlaki, *MEMRI Inquiry and Analysis Series*, No. 576, 30 December.

Theyabi, Jameel (2009) Does Facebook Threaten Arab Governments? *Al Hayat*, August 3, www.international.daralhayat.com/internationalarticle/44327

Travis, Alan (2008a) Battle against Al Qaeda Brand Highlighted in Secret Paper, *Guardian*, 26 August.

Travis, Alan (2008b) Revealed: Britain's Secret Propaganda War Against Al Qaeda, *Guardian*, 26 August.

United States Senate Hearing (2009) Violent Islamist Extremism Al-Shabab Recruitment in America, 11 March, http://hsgac.senate.gov/public/index. cfm?FuseAction=Hearings.Hearing&Hearing_ID=35e68562-1606-409a-9118-3edfbb8e87c8.

Witte, Griff; Jerry Markon and Shaiq Hussain (2009) Terrorist Recruiters Leverage the Web, *Washington Post*, 13 December.

5

PROPAGANDA AND TERRORISM

David Miller and Rizwaan Sabir

David Miller and Rizwaan Sabir take a very different approach to Seib in the previous chapter and equate public diplomacy, strategic communications and psychological operations as forms of propaganda designed to promote the military capacities of those who advocate them. Propaganda, for Miller and Sabir, is far from simply a question of ideas but a matter of 'political action' that ties together practices of persuasion and coercion. Identifying four key areas of propaganda – its institutions, doctrine, practice and its outcomes – in relation to contemporary examples concerning counter-terrorism raids in the UK, terrorism statistics across Europe and the government organizations dedicated to producing propaganda, they conclude that techniques like public diplomacy and propaganda are far from benevolent forms of political action but part of the 'weaponization of information'.

Key Message 1

Positive: Terrorism is a real and serious threat to us all.

Negative: Terrorism is not a real and serious threat to us all. The terrorist threat is exaggerated by the UK government

Research Information and Communications Unit, Home Office, UK Government 2010

Introduction

The 'key messages' of the UK (and US) government on terrorism can be ana-lysed in terms of their relationship with truth and/or selectivity. However, any analysis of government communications on terrorism must do more than ana-lyse the role of dishonesty by commission (or omission). To illustrate this we need to start with some comments on definitions. Both the terms 'terrorism' and 'propaganda' are heavily contested. Both have, in general usage, a consider-able negative charge. Both are subject to argumentation on definition, on who or what is the real 'terrorist' or 'propagandist'.

Although there is much to be said on the problems of definition, both terms can be used in a neutral way – so long as a 'literal' and not a 'propagandist approach' is adopted (Chomsky, 1992: 119). In this sense, we need to immedi-ately introduce the distinction between interest-linked communications where particular definitions are used as 'a weapon to be exploited in the service of some system of power' (Chomsky, 1992: 119) and those which aspire to stick to the facts.

Terrorism, conceived of as actions involving the creation of terror and usually the harming or perhaps deliberate targeting of civilians and non-combatants, is of course something that can be undertaken by both state and non-state actors. Although the term has unavoidably negative connotations, it is not in principle impossible to distinguish between terrorism and non-terrorism by empirical means and using social scientific methods (or even ordi-nary logic). That is, we must take a literal as opposed to a propagandist approach to terrorism that applies definitions in the same way to groups whether the analyst is opposed, neutral or sympathetic. This sounds elementary, but the history of the discipline of 'terrorism studies' in the academy (never mind in policy or popular discourse) and both open and disguised commitments to great power shows matters are not so simple (Miller and Mills, 2009).

Similarly, the term propaganda carries a heavy negative ballast especially, but not exclusively, from its use in the 1914–18 and 1939–45 wars. It should be noted that as a result, even early in the twentieth century, there were those who aspired to create a profession out of propaganda but who recognized the neces-sity of renaming it, in order to avoid the negative associations. Thus the term 'public relations' was born (Miller and Dinan, 2008) followed by a whole host of other terms such as psychological operations, public diplomacy and strate-gic communication. For some, the negative associations accumulated since the early twentieth century have rendered propaganda a term that we must 'think beyond' (Corner, 2007: 676).

Maybe so, but in the era after 11 September 2001 in which propaganda has returned to spectacular effect and in which determined efforts are made by 'propagandists' to reshape our understanding of the term, the case seems less than persuasive. Corner's case is marred by its narrow focus on the content and meaning of propaganda output – he lists six aspects, all of which fall under this rubric. He does allow that there might be an argument concerning 'motives', but quickly dismisses this. Propaganda needs to be seen in its institutional context – that is as a specific communicative practice. It has outputs, but these are only a product of specific institutions which themselves stand in need of study and explanation.

Focusing only on the content of what is produced misdirects attention from the institutional basis of propaganda. Any definition of propaganda that laboured to categorize it in terms of the range of aspects outlined by Corner would miss much, perhaps most, propaganda activity. Mainstream analysts such as Philip Taylor understand this well enough, noting the distinction between 'white', 'grey' and 'black' propaganda (i.e. depending on the degree to which the source is open, disguised or falsified as opposed to whether the content itself is true or false or a mixture) (Taylor, P., 2006).

In practice, descriptions in play are themselves tainted by their involvement in or relationship with legitimation strategies ('propaganda'). It is precisely these strategies that ought to be at the centre of studying propaganda today. These will involve examining communication and no doubt 'discourse', but they should not be limited to that. 'Public diplomacy' is inadequate as a replacement term since it deals only with state appeals to mass (mainly foreign) publics as opposed to the full range of audiences and activities that a proper definition of propaganda entails (see, for example Seib's Chapter 4 in this volume).

Propaganda is more than a question of communication or ideas or discourses. It is a communicative practice, in that it requires and can only be enacted by humans in specific social relations. Torture and killing – or the avoidance of such practices – can be examples of propaganda. Indeed as we will see in this chapter, they are viewed as central parts of propaganda activities by official practitioners. This is encapsulated in the phrase of a leading counter-insurgency theorist, David Kilcullen, as 'armed propaganda' (quoted in Miller and Mills, 2010: 206).

Whatever term is used for 'propaganda', it must be capable of seeing the phenomenon as an 'organic' process, as something which can enable certain interests to be advanced and others limited. This is more than Corner's (2007: 670) reference to 'the metaphorical sense of propagation, of sowing'. It is to suggest the organic process of organizing and developing conduct and outcomes. Propaganda is, in other words, not simply a matter of discourse but a matter of concrete material action by particular institutional interests. It is these properties that make propaganda – still – a superior term to its available alternatives because it captures its catalytic role in social relations that can result in the propagation of both ideas and outcomes.

Thus, a proper analysis must involve research evidence in relation to these key areas:

1   Institutions: the people and organizations that create or pursue propaganda and the material resources on which they draw.
2   Doctrine: the philosophy and doctrine which theorizes, codifies and organises propaganda efforts.
3   Practice: the activities and outputs of the institutions.
4   Outcomes: in other words the question of impacts.

In what remains we review these four areas.

Propaganda Institutions

There is very little public debate on the propaganda apparatus and few people are fully aware of the extensive machinery that has been built up following 11 September 2001. This machinery has a number of parallel elements between the US and UK, partly through the co-ordination globally between the US and UK. In the US, George W. Bush created the Office of Global Communications in July 2002 which is based on the experience of the Coalition Information Centers (CIC) that operated during the Kosovo and Afghanistan adventures. These drew on the propaganda expertise of the British government and are reported to have been the idea of Alastair Campbell, Director of Communications to Tony Blair (Foreign Affairs Select Committee, 2003). The CIC, for the Afghanistan campaign, was launched in October 2001 with offices in Washington, London and Islamabad and was designed to co-ordinate propaganda activity across time-zones and to ensure that the US and UK (and other governments) 'sang from the same hymn sheet' (Day, 2002). The CIC was made permanent under the auspices of the White House with the creation of the Office of Global Communications (OGC). It was the OGC which fed out the lies about the threat posed by the Saddam Hussein regime in Iraq. This included the faked and spun intelligence information supplied by the UK and by the secret Pentagon intelligence operation, the Office of Special Plans, set up by Defense Secretary Donald Rumsfeld to bypass the CIA, which was reluctant to go along with some of the lies (Prados, 2004).

From the White House the message was cascaded down to the rest of the propaganda apparatus. The Office of Public Diplomacy in the State Department is responsible for overseas propaganda while in the UK the Ministry of Defence

(MoD) and the Foreign and Commonwealth Office (FCO) have the biggest propaganda operations of any government departments. Co-ordination with Downing Street is accomplished by means of a cross-departmental committee known as the Communication and Information Centre, later changed back to the Coalition Information Centre as it had been in the Afghan campaign. It is administratively based in the Foreign Office Information Directorate, yet was directed by Alastair Campbell and run from Downing Street (Rammell, 2003: 816). Campbell also chaired a further cross-departmental committee in Downing Street: the Iraq Communication Group. It was from here that the campaign to mislead the media about the existence of weapons of mass destruction was directed. In particular it oversaw the production of the 'September dossier' on WMD and the second 'dodgy' dossier of February 2003 that was quickly exposed as plagiarized.

The propaganda apparatus below this has four main elements. The first is the external system of propaganda run by the FCO; internal propaganda focused on the alleged 'terrorist threat' is co-ordinated in the Cabinet Office by the Civil Contingencies Secretariat; next is the operation 'in theatre' in Iraq; finally, US and UK military psychological operation teams undertake overt and covert operations inside Iraq and Afghanistan. All of these operations have their own contribution to make in the 'war on terror' although most public debate (in the US and UK) in 2003–4 focused on the system of embedding journalists and latterly (in the UK) on the Downing Street operation overseen by Campbell (see Miller, 2004).

In the years since the invasion of Afghanistan and Iraq, and in particular since the London bombings of July 2005, the UK has further developed its internal propaganda apparatus. This has been done with the assistance of a range of military personnel with career experience and practical and theoretical knowledge of 'information operations', 'information superiority' and 'strategic communications', all of which are terms that have specific doctrinal meanings. The most important element of this internal propaganda battle was the creation in 2007 of the Research Information and Communications Unit (RICU) inside the Home Office, albeit with funding and influence from the Department for Communities, the FCO and latterly the MoD. RICU is part of the Office for Security and Counter Terrorism (OSCT) and describes itself as a 'strategic communications unit' (Home Office, 2009). According to the *Guardian*, the OSCT is 'widely regarded in Whitehall as being an intelligence agency' (Dodd, 2009: 1). This suggests similarities between RICU and the covert FCO-based propaganda outfit the Information Research Department (Lashmar and Oliver, 1998). On the launch of RICU, the *Sunday Times* reported that 'officials deny this is in any way a propaganda department, although one conceded: "It does sound horribly cold war"' (Correra, 2007).

RICU's back story links it to two key military figures in Whitehall: Steve Tatham and Jamie Macintosh. Tatham is the MoD lead on matters of strategic communication. In 2009, he was seconded to the Strategic Horizons Unit (SHU), a unit created in September 2008 and housed in the Cabinet Office (Maude, 2009). SHU is part of the Joint Intelligence Organisation and is charged with scoping future threats. Tatham developed his thinking on strategic communications while at the Defence Academy think tank ARAG, where his 'boss' was Dr Jamie Macintosh who, while at the Defence Science and Technology Laboratory, made 'strategic and operational contributions in the emerging fields of Information Superiority and Information Operations (IS-IO)' (Defence Academy, 2008)

Macintosh co-authored the White Paper and undertook conceptual research design that led to the creation of the Civil Contingencies Secretariat in 2001. This was the body involved in issuing information about the alleged threat to Heathrow Airport and about the 'Ricin plot', which turned out not to involve any Ricin (Miller, 2006). Indeed, according to Archer and Bawdon (2010), nor was there any 'plot'.

Before being appointed the Head of ARAG, Macintosh spent over a year as the personal advisor on Transformation and National Security to Home Secretary John Reid. An MoD biographical note claims that he was 'instrumental' in the creation of the Office for Security and Counter Terrorism (OSCT) and its strategic communications division, the Research, Information and Communications Unit (RICU) (Defence Academy, 2008).

We can conclude from this that there is a significant and co-ordinated propaganda network and that key elements of internal propaganda machinery have been developed by those with experience of propaganda activities in the military. We turn next to the philosophy of propaganda.

Propaganda Doctrine

Information dominance is the name given to the doctrine that integrates propaganda into overall US and UK global strategy. It is a central component of the US aim of 'full spectrum dominance' (Joint Chiefs of Staff, 2000: 61–63) that plays a key role in US military strategy and foreign policy. It is best expressed in the Pentagon's Joint Vision 2020 which 'implies that US forces are able to conduct prompt, sustained and synchronized operations with combinations of forces tailored to specific situations and with access to and freedom to operate in all domains – space, sea, land, air and information' (2000: 61).

The presence of information on the list indicates that the US Army views it as 'an element of combat power' (Department of the Army, 2003: iii). To the outsider, the official debate about how 'information dominance' differs from 'information superiority' might seem arcane, but it is nevertheless revealing. For example, according to Jim Winters and John Giffin of the US Space and Information Operations Directorate, information superiority alone is insufficient: 'at some base point "superiority" means an advantage of 51–49, on some arbitrary metric scale. That is not enough of an advantage to give us the freedom of action required to establish "Full Spectrum dominance"' (Winters and Giffin, 1997). Dominance, instead, implies 'a mastery of the situation' while superiority provides 'only an edge': 'We think of dominance in terms of 'having our way' – 'Overmatch' over all operational possibilities. This connotation is 'qualitative' rather than 'quantitative'. When dominance occurs, nothing done makes any difference. We have sufficient knowledge to stop anything we don't want to occur, or do anything we want to do' (Winters and Giffin, 1997).

This could hardly be any clearer about the agenda of the US military. Traditional conceptions of propaganda as persuasive communication fail to do justice to current conceptions of information war. They incorporate the gathering, processing and deployment of information including via computers, intelligence and military information (command and control) systems. Now propaganda and psychological operations are simply part of a larger information armoury. As Colonel Kenneth Allard has written, the 2003 attack on Iraq 'will be remembered as a conflict in which information fully took its place as a weapon of war' (Allard, 2003). Allard tells a familiar story in military writings on such matters:

> in the 1990s, the Joint Chiefs of Staff began to promote a vision of future warfare in which C4ISR (command, control, communications, computers, intelligence, surveillance and reconnaissance) systems would be forged into a new style of American warfare in which interoperability was the key to information dominance – and information dominance the key to victory' (Allard, 2003).

This is a conception shared by the UK military: 'maintaining moral as well as information dominance will rank as important as physical protection' (Ministry of Defence, 2000).

Propaganda on the home front also takes place under this conceptual umbrella. Although it has gone by a variety of names since 11 September 2001 – including public affairs, information support, information operations and public diplomacy – the emerging term which commands significant policy traction is 'strategic communication', a term used in official circles both in the US and UK (Corman et al., 2008; Tatham 2008). This might sound a relatively benign phrase and it certainly has less negative connotations than possible alternatives like 'Psyops', 'propaganda' or 'political warfare', but it does have a specific meaning in official thinking. Indeed, the Ministry of Defence has an official 'lead' for strategic communication, Commander Steve Tatham, who has written extensively on what it involves (see Miller and Sabir, 2011; Tatham, 2008). In his view, strategic communication is more positive than the alternatives, by which he means approaches based mainly or solely on force or 'kinetic' power – a term used widely in military circles as a synonym for physical destruction and killing.

Tatham argues that the term strategic communication is widely misconstrued because it is understood as a replacement term for 'spin', Media and Information Operations or propaganda. Tatham describes these as 'emotive and often inaccurate terms'. Use of such terms is, he writes, 'unhelpful and mires understanding' (Tatham, 2008: 5). Strategic communication, on the other hand, is 'an extremely powerful tool that may hold the key to the dilemma of 21st century conflict, the power of information and opinion and its ability to enable behavioural change' (2008: 20).

This emphasis on behavioural change is central to the 2009 Ministry of Defence counter-insurgency doctrine, which opens its section on 'Information Operations' with a quote from the doyen of contemporary counter-insurgency theorist, David Kilcullen (Ministry of Defence, 2009: 6–2: 'Traditionally, in the course of conventional operations we use information operations to explain what we are doing, but in Counterinsurgency we should design operations to enact our influence campaign.' This distinction between explaining and enacting is absolutely critical to understanding strategic communication. It suggests that propaganda is viewed as part of 'kinetic' operations, an impression reinforced by the MoD discussion of I-Ops (2009: 6–5): 'Information operations will on occasions require an aggressive and manipulative approach to delivering messages (usually through the PSYOPS tool). This is essential in order to attack, undermine and defeat the will, understanding and capability of insurgents.'

Likewise, Tatham suggests that any definition of the concept must 'recognise that the success of non-kinetic effect is amplified by threats of kinetic activity' (Tatham, 2008: 15). In other words, strategic communication is integrated with an overall kinetic strategy and is itself part of a coercive strategy. As Tatham himself puts it: 'Influence does not mean the exclusion of hard power', nor is it only directed at 'external' audiences or at an 'enemy' (2008: 15), but is also directed at 'internal' audiences, meaning sections or all of the general public (2008: 4). This is a programme not just of persuasive communication – propaganda as traditionally understood – but a highly coercive strategy intended to manage the behaviour of the British public.

Propaganda in Practice

Propaganda in practice does involve the production of 'information', but also crucially involves its dissemination. We see propaganda as a matter, in part at least, of coercion – the 'science of coercion' as Christopher Simpson (1996) termed it in his classic book of the same name. Let us take two examples of the use of pysops in Iraq to illustrate the point. Psyops is presented as an attempt to save lives, thus Major Taylor, the head of 42 Commando Royal Marines psyops unit, described it as follows: 'The main thing is that we are trying to save these peoples lives' (cited in Edwards, 2003). This account is in itself part of the propaganda war as the rest of what Major Taylor had to say reveals:

> We use tactical and strategic methods. Tactically, on the first stage, we target the military by dropping leaflets stating the inevitability of their defeat, telling them they will not be destroyed if they play our game and exactly how they can surrender. On the second wave we show them pictures of Iraqi officers who complied. On the third wave we show them pictures of those people who did not. (Quoted in Edwards, 2003)

The meaning of the messages depends in part, therefore, on the coercive firepower of the coalition. We are in the presence here of coercive threats as opposed to 'persuasion' or 'dialogue'. Any theory of propaganda as a matter of 'persuasive communication' cannot fully accommodate the 'weaponization' of information.

A similar tale can be told about the scandal of the photos from Abu Graibh. These were not really trophy pictures and nor were they pictures of torture in the normal sense of the word. Certainly, they capture images of the degradation of Iraqi prisoners, but what were the photos produced for? Celebrated investigative journalist Seymour Hersh revealed that this operation ran by the name of 'Copper Green' (Hersh, 2004). According to one of his sources 'the purpose of the photographs was to create an army of informants, people you could insert back in the population' (Hersh, 2004). The source also claimed: 'It was thought that some prisoners would do anything – including spying on their associates – to avoid dissemination of the shameful photos to family and friends' (Hersh, 2004). Private Lyndie England, who was in the photos, added further detail saying: 'I was instructed by persons in higher rank to "stand there, hold this leash and look at the camera." The pictures were for PsyOps reasons … They'd come back and they'd look at the pictures and they'd state, "Oh, that's a good tactic… This is working. Keep doing it, it's getting what we need"' (cited in Ronson, 2005: 166–7). The Abu Ghraib photos are not, therefore, just a record of torture, but an active part in the process of torture – again an illustration of the coercive nature of this kind of propaganda.

Turning now to domestic propaganda efforts in the UK we can note that the pre-eminent body used to 'taint the Al Qaeda brand' (Travis, 2008: 8) is RICU. It does this by co-ordinating and issuing regular guidance on lines to take across central and local government and beyond, by providing advice on language to use and by conducting research on Islam, British Muslims and communication issues. Its four key messages in 2007/8 (with the positive message first and the opposite negative second) were:

> Terrorism is a real and serious threat to us all. Terrorism is not a real and serious threat to us all. The terrorist threat is exaggerated by the UK government

> Terrorists are criminals and murderers. Terrorist attacks against the UK are legitimate

> Terrorists attack the values that we all share. Terrorist attacks are justified by 'Muslim values'

> We all need to work together to tackle the terrorist challenge. The terrorist challenge is primarily a problem for Muslims or Muslim communities to address. (TNS Media Intelligence, 2008)

These messages are core to RICU's activities and frame much official communications. Indeed, in one study conducted for RICU it was concluded that only one government press release in the period January 2007–March 2008 was not 'on-message' (2008: 4). RICU has issued guidance on how to communicate its messages which includes specific advice on ensuring that the government is not thought to be exaggerating the terror threat.

Amongst their other activities, RICU has also funded research on Muslim communities. Between 2007 and 2010, for example, RICU commissioned work on Muslim 'identity and sense of belonging', 'how young British Muslims use the internet', 'how Government messages are perceived by Muslim communities,' 'Islamic Blogs' and 'The Language of Terrorism' (Fanshaw, 2009). One project was funded by an Economic and Social Research Council award to Dr David Stevens of Nottingham University to study 'radical blogs' in a secondment to RICU (see Powerbase, 2011). The report published a list of the top 20 'Islamic' blogs with the inference that these were in some senses 'radical'. However, a number of those listed were not 'radical' or 'Islamic' at all. The *Guardian* noted a number of examples:

> … the man identified in the report as Britain's third most influential 'pro-Islamic' blogger is actually an atheist based in the United States. As'ad Abukhalil, a Lebanese-American professor of

political science at California State University who blogs as 'The Angry Arab' is furious about it. 'How ignorant are the researchers of the Home Office?' he writes. 'How many times does one have to espouse atheist, anarchist, and secular principles before they realise that their categorisation is screwed up?'...Top spot in the league table of Britain's most influential 'pro-Islamic' bloggers goes to Ali Eteraz, a Cif [Comment is Free] contributor. Back in 2007, he wrote a series of articles for Cif, from a liberal perspective, about reforming Islam. (Whitaker, 2010)

It seems that this project – whatever the intentions behind it – ended up by exaggerating the threat from 'radical' blogs. It is to the key issue of the wider media politics of the terror threat that we now turn.

Outcomes

In this section we draw attention to the impacts of propaganda. In line with our argument that sees information and propaganda as integrated into the military and coercive apparatus of the state, we see this as a question not simply of influence on media agendas and content or on public ideas or beliefs, but on the relative balance of forces and concrete policy, military, policing and other outcomes. We focus here on the mid-level case of impacts on media reporting in order to demonstrate how the approach outlined above can be seen as operating via mass media reporting.

It is clear that there is a threat of political violence in the UK from 'Islamist' or 'Jihadi' political violence as evidenced in the London bombings of 7 July 2005, the failed London bombings two weeks later and the attack on Glasgow airport in 2007. The 'official' threat assessment, which was first made public in 2006, claimed that there is a 'severe national security threat' from this source (MI5, 2011). However, data published by Europol (the EU's serious and organized crime prevention agency) and obtained under the Freedom of Information Act shows that the most serious and sustained threat of violence in the UK stems from armed groups in Northern Ireland (both Republican and Loyalist) and not from 'Jihadis'. This data shows that across the EU in the years 2006, 2007, 2008 and 2009 there were a total of 472, 583, 515 and 294 'failed, foiled or successful' attacks, respectively. Of these specifically 'Islamist'-related incidents amounted to one, four, zero and one in each year. Thus according to Europol, based on figures supplied by member states, 'Islamist' incidents accounted for 0.002 per cent, 0.006 per cent, 0 per cent and 0 per cent of 'terrorist' incidents in the whole of the European Union. In the UK, the pattern is slightly excluded due to the UK government's refusal to give a breakdown for its figures in the year 2008 and 2009 (see Europol, 2011: 9–10). FoI requests to the

Table 5.1   British national press items on 'Islamist' and
'Northern Irish' related political violence and 'terrorism'
2006–2008

Year	Islamist	Northern Irish
2006	3594	1859
2007	3239	1391
2008	2615	1309

Police Service of Northern Ireland produced a very full statistical breakdown
of 'terrorist' related activities (Reid, 2010a, 2010b). The Home Office refused
to give any breakdown, though we got official confirmation that there were no
Jihadist attacks in 2009 (Fisher, 2010; Lister, 2010). We thus calculated that in
the four years from 2006 to 2009, there were 371 attacks (defined as shootings,
bombings and incendiaries) in the UK related to Northern Ireland (Europol,
2011; Reid 2010) and two attacks by 'Jihadists' (Fisher, 2010). In other words,
in a total of four years, 99.5 per cent of UK political violence came from armed
Northern Irish groups and 0.5 per cent from Jihadists (Fisher, 2010).

Nevertheless, it is Islamist terrorism that is at the forefront of government
pronouncements. We can also show that this is the case in media reporting. Table 5.1 shows the number of items in the British national press on
'Islamist' and 'Northern Ireland' related political violence and 'terrorism' for
each of the years.

The figures show that the government's emphasis on 'Islamist' terrorism has
been translated into a similar over-emphasis in the press, though the degree of
over-emphasis is not as stark. Given the apparent lack of data on even 'failed' or
'foiled' plots and the reluctance of the government to state openly the basis of
its threat assessment, we analysed the number of plots said by official sources to
have existed from 2006 until 2008 (using full text searches on Nexis UK) and
found that the numbers were irregular and inconsistent.

- June 2006, 'at least 20 major plots' (Rayment, 2006: 4)
- July 2006 '70 plots'(Taylor, B. 2006: 20)
- August 2006, 74 plots (Steele et al, 2006: 1)
- September 2006 70 plots (Johnston, 2006: 1)
- November 2006, 30 'major [Jihadist] terrorist plots'(Norton-Taylor, 2006: 1)
- July 2007, 30 plots (Rayment, 2007: 1)
- July 2008, '80 separate terror plots' (McDonald, 2008: 6)
- December 2008, 30 plots (Hartley, 2008: 13)

In the press reports that we used to obtain these figures, there was never any explanation for the fluctuations, nor was any explanation or definition of a terrorist 'plot' given.

Taken together, this suggests strong circumstantial evidence that official pronouncements on the alleged threat from 'Islamist' political violence mis-states the relative risk. However, it also suggests that, on the one hand, security forces are able to regularly disrupt significant numbers of plots while at the same time significant numbers of new plots emerge. On the other hand, it suggests that the definition of 'plot' may be elastic enough to respond to the needs of strategic communication work. We can gain some clues to this by examining the factual basis of one of the most high profile plots reported in this period.

The 'anti-terrorism' raid on a home in Forest Gate in London (codenamed 'Operation Volga') occurred in the early hours of 2 June 2006 after 'security sources' were reported to be acting on intelligence which indicated a 'viable' chemical bomb was being built by two Muslim brothers (BBC News, 2006a). 'Intelligence had suggested', reported the BBC, that it was 'a fatal device that could produce casualty figures in double or even triple figures' (BBC News, 2006a). *The Sun* reported that 'senior officers are convinced' of 'an "imminent" attack in the UK' either 'by a suicide bomber or in a remote-controlled explosion' (Sullivan, 2006). Throughout the raid, and the subsequent investigation, an air-exclusion zone was imposed which banned aircraft from flying 2,500 feet above the house (BBC News, 2006a).

After eight days of enquiries, no chemical weapon was found and no evidence emerged to suggest that the men had ever been involved in terrorism. Both men were released without charge. 'Intelligence sources' told the *Guardian* that the police did not have 'time to bug the house' – 'Intelligence is patchy. Even if it suggests a 5% likelihood of something nasty, we can't take that risk' (Dodd et al., 2006: 1). During the raid, Abdul Kahar Kalam was shot and injured by an armed officer. The story from official briefings was that a struggle between the officer (known only as B6) and the two brothers broke out, in which one of the men tried snatching the gun; resulting in a shot being fired (Panton and Sabey, 2006). Kalam maintained that he was shot without warning or signal (IPCC, 2006: 3; BBC News, 2006b).

The *News of the World* reported a 'highly-placed Whitehall source' as saying: 'the officers are adamant that they did not pull the trigger and have told bosses at Scotland Yard the DNA evidence will prove this' (Panton and Sabey, 2006). Eventually the Independent Police Complaints Commission (IPCC) reported that the shot had been fired by the officer as a 'mistake'; perpetuated by the 'bulky clothing and gloves' (IPCC, 2006: 6). They also stated that 'no identifiable fingerprints [were] found on the weapon except those attributed to the officer who would have handled the weapon' (2006: 4). In other words, contrary to the claims made by the *News of the World*, neither of the brothers had touched the weapon.

We can conclude from this that official briefings on alleged 'plots' are not always reliable, whether by mistake or design. Certainly they suggest that official sources' account of the threat from 'Islamist' terrorism is likely to exaggerate the threat. The extent to which this is a deliberate and inevitable or the result of errors or mistakes is difficult to tell. The pattern of misinformation and deception involved is hardly incompatible with a strategic communication approach to terrorism.

Conclusions

What this tells us is something more than an answer to the question of the role of the state in practising an economy of actualité. We think that it suggests that understanding propaganda in an holistic way allows us to move beyond the narrow conceptualisation of propaganda as a matter of distorted communications to see it in its whole institutional context and to see it as – in fact as it is seen by professional propagandists – a matter of political action. In doing so we have moved beyond seeing it as simply a matter of communication to seeing it as a material and indeed coercive practice: no longer just a matter of 'signification' but a complex mixture of coercion and consent. The issue is not whether this or that piece of propaganda output (or this or that propagandist) is misleading or whether a whole class of communication is 'systematically distorted' (Habermas, 1970) but a matter of a systematic propaganda management of society (Miller, 2005). It is not only a question, in other words, of whether, Tony Blair, Alastair Campbell, George Bush or Colin Powell lied, but of whether they are guilty of war crimes. In that question is a more complex conceptual point which is that there is no fixed barrier between communication and action, between coercion and consent, and between – in the end – propaganda and terrorism.

References

Allard, Kenneth (2003) Battlefield Information Advantage, *CIO Magazine*, Fall/Winter. Available at: www.cio.com/archive/092203/allard.html (accessed 14 March 2011).

Archer, Lawrence and Bawdon, Fiona (2010) *Ricin! The Inside Story of the Terror Plot That Never Was*. London: Pluto.

BBC News (2006a) Raid police hunt chemical device, 3 June. Available at: http://news.bbc.co.uk/1/hi/uk/5042724.stm (accessed 6 March 2011).

BBC News (2006b) In quotes: terror raid brothers, 13 June. Available at: http://news.bbc.co.uk/1/hi/uk/5075618.stm (accessed 14 March 2011).

Chomsky, Noam (1992) International terrorism: image and reality, in Alexander George (ed.) *Western State Terrorism*. Cambridge: Polity.

Corman, S., Tretheway, A. and Goodhall Jr., H. L (eds) (2008) *Weapons of Mass Persuasion: Strategic Communication to Combat Violent Extremism*. New York: Peter Lang.

Corner, John (2007) Mediated politics, promotional culture and the idea of 'propaganda', *Media Culture and Society* 29(4): 669–677.

Correra, Gordon (2007) Don't look now, Britain's real spooks are right behind you, *Sunday Times*, 2 December.

Day, Julia (2002) US steps up global PR drive, *Guardian*, 30 July.

Defence Academy (2007) Dr. J. P Macintosh, Available at: www.da.mod.uk/our-work/governance/board-biogs/dr-j-p-macintosh (accessed 6 May 2009).

Defence Academy (2008) Dr. J. P Macintosh, Retrieved from the Internet Archive of 15 April 2008, accessed 12 August 2011 http://web.archive.org/web/20080415124622/; www.da.mod.uk/our-work/governance/board biogs/dr-j-p-macintosh

Department of the Army (2003) Information operations: doctrine, tactics, techniques, and procedures, November, FM 3–13 (FM 100–6). Available at: www.adtdl.army.mil/cgi-bin/atdl.dll/fm/3-13/fm3_13.pdf (accessed 14 November 2011).

Dodd, Vikram (2009) Government anti-terrorism strategy spies on innocent, *Guardian*, 17 October.

Dodd, Vikram, Laville, Sandra and Norton-Taylor, Richard (2006) Intelligence behind raid was wrong, officials say, *Guardian*, 6 June.

Edwards, Richard (2003) The propaganda war in Iraq, *Guardian*, 26 March

Europol (2011) Terrorism Situation and Trend Report (TE-SAT) 2010. Available at: www.europol.europa.eu/publications/EU_Terrorism_Situation_and_Trend_Report_TE-SAT/Tesat2010.pdf (accessed 23 February 2011).

Fanshaw, J. (2009) Direct Communications Unit, Home Office, Freedom of Information response – Ref 11707, Annex A Details of RICU Research, 10.08.

Fisher, L (2010) Number of terrorist attacks that occurred in the United Kingdom and Northern Ireland – Freedom of Information Act 2000 Request, Ref. 15683, email to Rizwaan Sabir from Home Office, 26 August.

Foreign Affairs Select Committee (2003) *The Decision to go to War in Iraq*, Ninth Report of Session 2002–03, Volume I, HC 813-I. London: The Stationery Office.

Habermas, Jurgen (1970) On systematically distorted communication, *Inquiry* 13(1): 205–218.

Hartley, Lodagh (2008) Unite now to cut off terrorism, *The Sun*, 15 December.

Hersh, Seymour (2004) The Gray Zone: how a secret Pentagon program came to Abu Ghraib, *New Yorker*, 24 May.

Home Office (2009) *Security and Counter Terrorism Science Business Plan 2009–2012*. Available at: www.homeoffice.gov.uk/documents/science-innovation-strategy09-12/security-business-plan2835.pdf?view=Binary (accessed 24 March 2010).

Independent Police Complaints Commission (IPCC) (2006) IPCC Independent Investigation into the Shooting of Muhammad Abdulkahar in 46 Lansdown Road, Forest Gate on Friday 2 June 2006, 3 August. Available at: http://webarchive.nationalarchives.gov.uk/20100908152737/ipcc.gov.uk/report.pdf (accessed 07 March 2011).

Joint Chiefs of Staff (2000) *Joint Vision 2020: America's Military – Preparing for Tomorrow*, Strategy Division, Directorate for Strategic Plans and Policy (J-5), Joint Staff, Washington DC: U.S. Government Printing Office. Available at: www.dtic.mil/doctrine/jel/jfq_pubs/1225.pdf (accessed 14 March 2011).

Johnston, Phillip (2006) Yard is watching thousands of terror suspects, *Daily Telegraph*, 2 September.

Lashmar, Paul and Oliver, James (1998) *Britain's Secret Propaganda War: Foreign Office and the Cold War 1948–1977*. Gloucestershire: Sutton Publishing.

Lister, Ian (2010) Request for information about the number of terrorist attacks that occurred in the United Kingdom and Northern Ireland under the Freedom of Information Act 2000, Ref. CR14289, email to Rizwaan Sabir from Home Office, 30 September.

McDonald, Henry (2008) Bombs and death threats: dissidents step up efforts to derail power-sharing, *Guardian*, 28 July.

Maude, Francis (2009) Strategic Horizons Unit: Manpower Cabinet Office, written answers, 26 June. Available at: www.theyworkforyou.com/wrans/?id=2009-06-26c.249902.h (accessed 17 January 2011).

MI5 (2011) International Terrorism. Available at: www.mi5.gov.uk/output/international-terrorism.html (accessed 22 February 2011).

Miller, David (2004) The propaganda machine, in David Miller (ed.) *Tell Me Lies: Propaganda and Media Distortion in the Attack on Iraq*. London: Pluto.

Miller, David (2005) Propaganda managed democracy: the UK and the lessons of Iraq, in L. Panitch and C. Leys (eds) *Telling the Truth: Socialist Register*, 2006. London: Merlin Press.

Miller, David (2006) Propaganda and the 'terror threat' in the UK, in Elizabeth Poole and John Richardson (eds) *Muslims and the News Media*. London: I. B. Tauris.

Miller, David and Dinan, Will (2008) *A Century of Spin*. London: Pluto.

Miller, David and Mills, Tom (2009) The terror experts and the mainstream media: the expert nexus and its dominance in the news media, *Critical Studies on Terrorism* 2(3): 414–437.

Miller, David and Mills, Tom (2010) Counterinsurgency and terror expertise: the integration of social scientists into the war effort, *Cambridge Review of International Affairs* 23(2): 203–221.

Miller, David and Sabir, Rizwaan (2011) Counterterrorism as counterinsurgency in the UK 'war on terror', in David Whyte and Scott Poynting (eds) *Counter-Terrorism and State Political Violence: The 'War on Terror' as Terror*. London: Routledge.

Ministry of Defence (2000) Soldiering: The Military Covenant, Chapter 2, Operational Trends. Available at: http://replay.waybackmachine. org/20060824091437/; www.army.mod.uk/servingsoldier/usefulinfo/values general/adp5milcov/ss_hrpers_values_adp5_2_w.html (accessed 14 March 2011).

Ministry of Defence (2009) *British Army Field Manual Volume 1 Part 10 Countering Insurgency*, Army Code 71876, October. Available at: www.scribd. com/doc/28411813/British-Army-Field-Manual-Counterinsurgency-2009?in_collection=2383030 (accessed 12 January 2011).

Norton-Taylor, Richard (2006) MI5: 30 terror plots being planned in UK, *Guardian*, 10 November.

Panton, Lucy and Sabey, Ryan (2006) Bomb suspect shot by brother, *News of the World*, 4 June. Available at: http://notwats.blogspot.com/2006/06/bomb-suspect-shot-by-brother.html (accessed 6 March 2011).

Powerbase (2011) Estimating network size and tracking information dissemination amongst Islamic blogs. Available at: www.powerbase.info/index. php/Estimating_network_size_and_tracking_information_dissemination_amongst_Islamic_blogs (accessed 6 January 2011).

Prados, John (2004) *Hoodwinked: The Documents that Reveal how Bush Sold Us a War*. New York: The New Press.

Rammell, Bill (2003) Iraq, *Hansard*, 9 July. Availale at: www.publications. parliament.uk/pa/cm200203/cmhansrd/vo030709/text/30709w08.htm (accessed 14 March 2011).

Rayment, Sean (2006) MI5 fears silent army of 1,200 biding its time in the suburbs in the wake of terror raid; Injured man's solicitor claims police gave no warning before opening fire, *Sunday Telegraph*, 4 June.

Rayment, Sean (2007) Britain on highest alert ever after attack at airport; Two arrests as car explodes at Glasgow terminal, *Sunday Telegraph*, 1 July.

Reid, Gordon (2010a) Statistics of the Security Situation Report – Freedom of Information Act 2000 Request F-2010-00710, email to Rizwaan Sabir from Police Service Northern Ireland, 24 March.

Reid, Gordon (2010b) Number of Shootings carried out by Terrorists/ Paramilitaries – Freedom of Information Act 2000 Request F-2010-02146, Email to Rizwaan Sabir from Police Service Northern Ireland, 24 August.

Ronson, Jon (2005) *The Men Who Stare at Goats*. London: Picador.

Simpson, Christopher (1996) *Science of Coercion: Communication Research and Psychological Warfare, 1945–1960*. Oxford: Oxford University Press.

Steele, John, Helm, Toby and Derbyshire, David (2006) Reid warns as he cuts threat level to 'severe'; Tempers fray as the airport misery goes on, *Daily Telegraph*, 14 August.

Sullivan, Mike (2006) Police in toxic bomb hunt, *The Sun*, 3 June.

Tatham, Steve, A. (2008) Strategic Communication: A Primer, Advanced Research and Assessment Group, *Defence Academy of the United Kingdom*, Special Series, 8(2), December. Available at: www.carlisle.army.mil/ dime/documents/DAUKARAG08(28)Strategic%20Communication.pdf (accessed 08 February 2010).

Taylor, Ben (2006) Security bosses keep terror watch on 1,200 home grown fanatics, *Daily Mail*, 4 July.

Taylor, Philip (2006) Strategic communications and the relationship between governmental 'information activities', in the Post 9/11 World, *Journal of Information Warfare* 5(3): 1–25.

TNS Media Intelligence (2008) The Language of Terrorism: Analysing the Public Discourse and Evaluating RICU's Impact, January 2007 – March 2008. Research, Information and Communications Unit (RICU), April 2010

Travis, Alan (2008) Battle against al-Qaida brand highlighted in secret paper, *Guardian*, 26 August.

Whitaker, Brian (2010) Not much blog for your buck: Home Office research has thrown up some blindingly obvious insights into the Muslim blogosphere. Why did they bother? *Guardian*, 25 March. Available at: www. guardian.co.uk/commentisfree/belief/2010/mar/25/blogs-islamic-home-office-report (accessed 15 January 2011).

Winters, Jim and Giffin, John (1997) Information Dominance Vs. Information Superiority, 1 April. Available at: www.iwar.org.uk/iwar/resources/info-dominance/issue-paper.htm (accessed 14 March 2011).

PART 2
Global Representations of Terrorism

Apart from dominating international news for a decade, the 'war on terror' has also been variously represented in the world of entertainment. The formidable corporate and technological power of US cultural industries can ensure that American versions of terrorism and how to deal with it have been circulating across global digital superhighways, being avidly consumed in multiplexes as well as via multimedia and mobile platforms. Arguably, an entertainment-driven media have a much greater global currency than news and current affairs, given that the audiences for the latter are minuscule in comparison to the $50 billion electronic gaming industry and the omnipresent Hollywood whose hegemony continues to shape popular culture across the world – in its original, cannibalized or hybridized forms.

Chapters in this part of the book examine how a range of media – including entertainment and news forms – have responded to the 'war on terror' and how the terrorism frame has been embedded into the narratives and texts of everyday media cultures. Among the themes covered are the war-gaming industry and popular filmic representations of the CIA, as well as racism in terms of domestic demonization of Muslims and distortions in foreign reporting, based on a case study of the coverage of the 2008 Israeli invasion of Gaza.

6

TERRORISM AND GLOBAL POPULAR CULTURE

Toby Miller

In this chapter, Toby Miller analyses the backdrop to US imperialism and militarism by examining the often neglected genre of electronic gaming, which makes the 'war on terror' an entertaining and pleasurable commodity that also helps recruit American soldiers. In a spirited argument, Miller points to the well-established relationship between sections of US academia and the US military, going back to the First World War, through the Cold War years and the 'war on terror', and how complicit campuses have formed a symbiotic ideological and material relationship with the Pentagon, promoting US interests worldwide as a 'de-territorialized overlord'.

Imperialism: US-style

Take the world's most powerful sea, air and land force with you wherever you go with the new America's Navy iPhone app. Read the latest articles. See the newest pics and videos. And learn more about the Navy – from its vessels and weapons to its global activities. You can do it all right on your iPhone – and then share what you like with friends via your favorite social media venues. (US Navy homepage, www.navy.com)

Blackwell is what his creators call an interactive virtual character – a life-sized, 3-D simulation of a person whose mission is to help train real soldiers. He inhabits FlatWorld, a kind of theme-park version of a war zone run by the University of Southern

California's Institute for Creative Technologies (ICT). At a time when Hollywood is often tagged by those on the political right as a liberal bastion, ICT teams the military and the entertainment biz for defence projects, funded by a five-year, $100 million grant from the Pentagon – the largest the university has ever received (Hebert, 2005).

This chapter analyses the backdrop to US imperialism and militarism – crucial aspects of the contemporary debate about terrorism and how to represent it. Then I consider a topic that is usually excluded from discussions of media coverage – electronic gaming – because it promotes warfare and implicates media studies in the latter-day project of imperialism.

US imperialism poses many complexities – for opponents, analysts and fellow-travellers alike. It has involved invasion and seizure (as per the Philippines and Cuba); temporary occupation and permanent militarization (think of Japan); ideological imperialism (consider the Monroe doctrine and Theodore Roosevelt); febrile anti-Marxism ('All the Way with LBJ' and 'Win One for the Gipper'); and ideological anti-imperialism (for example, Franklin Delano Roosevelt and Barack Obama).

Yanqui imperialism differs from the classic nineteenth-century model exemplified by the UK. It is much harder to gain independence from the US than it was from Britain, because US imperialism is indirect and mediated as well as direct and intense. This produces fewer dramatic moments of resistive nation-building than the painful but well-defined struggles towards sovereignty which threw off conventional colonial yokes across the twentieth century.

The difference arose because Yanqui imperialism began at a more fully developed stage of industrial capitalism and led into the post-industrial age as Washington sought to break colonialism down and gain access to labour and consumption on a global scale. This coincided with a Cold War that favoured imperial proxies over possessions, due to both prevailing ideology and the desire to avoid direct nuclear conflict with an apparent equal. Once the Soviet Union collapsed, the free markets that had been undermined by classic imperialism in 1914 were re-established as rhetorical tropes, confirming the drive towards a looser model of domination.

This does not mean the US variety of imperialism lacks the drive and horror of old-world imperialism. The country that advertises itself as the world's greatest promise of modernity has been dedicated to translating its own national legacy, a nineteenth-century regime of clearance, genocide and enslavement as much as democracy – a modernity built, as each successful one has been, on brutality – into a foreign and economic policy with similar effects and, at times, methods. But it has principally done so through overhanging ideological, military and commercial power rather than comprehensive colonization. Spain's *conquista de América*, Portugal's *missão civilizadora* and France's *mission civili-satrice* saw these nations occupy conquered peoples then exemplify approved conduct up close; *gringos* invade if necessary, then instruct from afar.

Today's United States is both a territorial state and a de-territorialized overlord – worried about immigration and terrorism, yet obsessed with its right to indirect rule of the globe's material resources and supply of labour and loans. These identities merge in Washington's blend of discourse and warfare. The embarrassingly penile metaphors of mainstream US international relations describe culture as 'soft power', a partner to the 'hard power' of force and economics (Nye, 2002).

The unfortunate, newly modish, term 'public diplomacy' appealed to the Federal government in its search for an answer to the plaintive cry uttered by a refugee from las Torres Gemelas after 11 September: 'Why do they hate us?' Public diplomacy is supposed to transcend the material impact of US foreign policy and corporate expropriation by fostering communication at a civil-society level. Linking citizens directly across borders purportedly galvanizes foreign publics in the interest of the US government, but without the connotation of propaganda.

Then along came WikiLeaks. Materials that generally become available to historians of democracies some 50 years after the fact have fallen into our collective lap spontaneously, products of the folly of an intranet available to millions of US government workers, the majority of whom are not schooled in the ways and means of diplomacy. For the moment, at least, it has destabilized the semi-private world of international relations, of oleaginous schmoozing at cocktail parties, notes taken on napkins, conspirators briefed behind cupped hands, and gossip exchanged about health and sex – in short, an insiders' club. It has made private diplomacy public and, in the process, compromised the propaganda of official public diplomacy (Barber, 2010).

The WikiLeaks scandal foregrounds gender, as a consequence of the accusations of sexual violence made about its narcissist-in-chief. It also places a focus on nationalism, so evident in the vapidly vicious reactions from US officials, conservatives and liberals. Most of all, though, it emphasizes the pettiness, triviality and shallowness of what passes in the US for the strategic analysis of international politics – a quaint mixture of self-interest and high moralism that is central to the way the country speaks of itself on the global stage, the parochial television screen and the university campus.

Diplomats will still need to do something with the notes they have made on napkins at cocktail parties; will still see themselves as a sacerdotal elite of the elect and will still regard what they do as above the ken of ordinary people. But if WikiLeaks has achieved anything by its revelations, it is to disclose the triviality of this elect group via their soap-operatic, amateurish pronouncements on affairs of state. That has given an unlikely global audience insights into international relations – a form of studying up, where ethnography turns its gaze onto the powerful rather than the powerless (Nader, 1972).

Just as 'soft power' is revealed to be a very old concept in new form, Washington has reached back across history to mobilize Cold War tactics through a renewed doctrine of deterrence. This is not the rational-actor model of mutually assured destruction, which warned the Soviets of what a nuclear attack would mean. Rather, the new line stresses the material retribution that will follow non-state violence directed against the US, and the fact that anti-US assaults are condemned by most of Islam.

As the bumper sticker of the 1960s read: 'Visit the United States before it visits you.' This form of deterrence basks in asymmetry – minus the grudging respect accorded to rivalrous state actors, and plus a gruesome Christian–Muslim history that predates modern sovereignty, albeit leavened by the credo of religious tolerance that is central to Yanqui mythology.

The other factor we must address is the US public. Why did it take so long for the population to turn against obviously ill-advised wars in Afghanistan and Iraq? Why did anyone favour these misadventures, which were as predictable in their outcome as their vengeful animation? I am excluding lapdog apparatchiks and coin-operated think-tanks from such a query. We know what they will say before they speak. Instead, I shall focus on the public's taste for state violence aimed at Muslim countries that are not client states.

This kind of foreign-policy jingoism is frequently misunderstood as the benign product of 'American exceptionalism'. This concept began as an attempt to explain why socialism had not taken greater hold in the US. It has since turned into an excessive rhapsody to Yanqui world leadership, difference and sanctimony (Brown, 2005) that can take almost comic forms. For instance, the convicted Watergate conspirator G Gordon Liddy decries association football on his radio talk show because it 'originated with the South American Indians'. He asks: 'Whatever happened to American exceptionalism?' and his guests from the Media Research Center argue that football is 'a poor man or poor woman's sport' that 'the left is pushing … in schools across the country' (quoted in Media Matters for America, 2010). Such a dialogue is laughable until one recognizes it as a widespread form of hyper-nationalism and messianic self-righteousness. Surveys that address popular knowledge of US foreign policy again and again disclose the public's deluded assumption that the state's primary overseas role has been helping others or securing the nation from attack (Miller, 2007).

How could such naïveté prevail in a country that has a million warriors across four continents, 702 military facilities in 132 sovereign-states, battleships in every ocean, a much-vaunted desire to mount wars on two international fronts at the same time as ensuring domestic security, and a 'defence' budget greater than the next twelve biggest countries put together? How many destabilized governments and rigged elections will it take, from Lebanon, Indonesia, Iran and Vietnam in the 1950s, through Japan, Laos, Brazil, the Dominican Republic, Guatemala, Bolivia and Chile in the 1960s, Portugal, Australia and Jamaica in the 1970s, and Central America in the 1980s, before *gringos* realize that US imperialism is bellicose, bloodthirsty, anti-democratic – and their responsibility (Miller, 2007)?

Clearly, the poor quality of US journalism, specifically its coverage of military conflicts, is significant here. These failings are produced by four forces, which I have analysed elsewhere in depth: transformations in the wider political economy of journalism; financialization – over-reportage of news from the perspective of capital; emotionalization – the emphasis on news from a feelings point of view; and a chronic dependency on official sources – the Pentagon as truth-teller (Miller, 2007). But we must equally understand public ignorance in the light of nationalism. A long history of popular thought in the US dates from the simultaneously anti-British, anti-imperial rhetoric and locally-imperialistic conduct of early White invaders (Pope, 2007). The violence of the country's origin is added to endlessly iterated justifications for adventurism that invoke the Second World War, which supposedly saw the US save the globe from Fascism. That story excludes the approximately 20 million Soviet citizens who died in the conflict, for example, but why bother with such details? I well recall my 2009 exam to become a US citizen. I was required to list the countries that won WWII. The correct answer was 'England,' (whatever that is), the US, and France.

Today, the mythology of exceptionalism finds expression through hyper-Christianity and the latest Great Awakening, which has been articulated, like other Great Awakenings before it, to a stalling economy and accelerating immigration (Miller, 2008). This both results from and helps reproduce a radical disarticulation between public anti-statism, which finds so many people loathing US governmental institutions, and their sanguine view of – let's say, their orgasmic cathexis onto – the military.

The opening epigraph to this chapter comes from the US Navy's promotional strategy, a multi-media campaign orchestrated since 2009 around the notion of being 'A Global Force for Good™' (as opposed to the previous recruiting technique, which promised young people it would 'Accelerate Your Life').[1] Examples of this newly beneficent, if still speedy, work are offered in television commercials that show Navy personnel capturing Somali pirates, treating Haitian earthquake survivors and handing toys to impoverished children. But there is always another side to this notion. An unbridled nationalism rides side-saddle with civil-society mythology. The Navy twins these duties via its trite but revealing slogan 'First to Fight, First to Help', and insists that '[t]he strength and status of any nation can be measured in part by the will and might of its navy' (US Navy, n.d.).

The formation of public opinion is not only achieved through such broad-brush ideology. It also relies on a poverty draft and the militarization of everyday life. The military is the nation's premier employer of 17–24-year-old workers (Verklin and Kanner, 2007). Throughout the country, there is an extraordinary reliance of working-class people on military welfare as a source of work, whether through making weaponry – the nation's principal manufacturing export – or via direct employment as servants of the Pentagon, be it in the field, the hospital, or the bureau.

Consider the student body I teach. Located just east of Los Angeles, it is working class economically and diverse culturally. There is no ethnic majority on campus, with White students comprising less than a fifth of the population. Unsurprisingly, many folks serve in the military or have relatives doing so. California has a million-person majority voting for Democrats in Presidential elections – and every person, at every moment, is never further than 70 kilometres from a military establishment. That is quite a multiplier effect, both economically and ideologically. Everyday life in this putatively progressive part of the United States is not a site of resistance, as per the romantic wishes of many on the left, but a site of militarization. Similar things could be said across the country, especially in poverty zones (see Goldberg, 2010).

To join the US military, it is not necessary to be a citizen – obtaining citizenship is a potential benefit that attracts recruits. Killing and dying are culturally trans-territorial, with 38,000 US soldiers being aliens. Neo-conservatives even call for the Pentagon to recruit undocumented residents and people who have never been in the US, under the rubric of a 'Freedom Legion'. The reward for service would be citizenship, following similar gifts to anti-communist East Europeans in the 1950s. Plus US military recruiters highlight free or cheap elective plastic surgery for uniformed personnel and their families (with the policy alibi that this permits doctors to practise their art) (Amaya, 2007; Fifield, 2009; Miller, 2007, 2008). I do not suggest that those serving are beyond ideology – far from it – but that they are 'beneficiaries' of our only real welfare system (outside massive aid to prop up Israel).

The result? The role of warfare in the economy and society cannot be overestimated. A weak president like Obama is no counter to this tendency, even if he wanted to be. When that is linked to the horrors of 11 September 2001 and a supine and incompetent news media, the outcome is hardly surprising – it is exactly what Osama bin Mohammed bin Awad bin Laden counted on.

Clearly, the United States is not a monolith, despite its imperial history and successful incorporation of the working class into military life. It is too large, too diverse and too educated for ideology to have complete hold. Counters to the dominant tendency include anti-imperialist talk-show hosts, like Thom Hartmann and Bob McChesney; progressive magazines, such as *Mother Jones*, *In These Times* and *Counter Punch*; agile meta-reports on media coverage, for example the organization Fairness and Accuracy in Reporting and Al Jazeera-in-English's TV show *The Listening Post*, fronted by Richard Gizbert, fired by ABC for refusing to report from Iraq during the war; many internet sites and blogs – think of juancole.com or dahrjamailiraq.com; a few politicians – consider Senator Bernie Sanders; feminist groups, including Code Pink; and peace organizations, notably Iraq Veterans Against the War. And as the US media and political establishment dithered over the centrality of the alleged weapons of mass destruction as alibis for the invasion of Iraq, and in the wake of revelation after revelation of White House duplicity through exaggeration and perhaps worse, the most effective 2003 search team for this mythic material proved to be Google – Figure 6.1 shows what was offered to those who typed in the search term 'weapons of mass destruction'. Designed to resemble an error message, this ran for months, sometimes logging a million visits a week. Clicking on the 'Bomb button' took viewers to an advertisement for the DVD of *Doctor Strangelove: Or, How I Learned to Stop Worrying and Love the Bomb* (Stanley Kubrick, 1964) (Reuters, 2003). Military veteran Micah Ian Wright adopted a similarly deconstructive counter-strategy, taking right-wing posters and redisposing them at www.antiwarposters.com. Wright's inspiration was his discovery that the National Security Agency was borrowing from Schutzstaffel (i.e. SS) recruiting tactics (Reuters, 2003: 22).

Despite these worthy forms of opposition, the militarization of everyday US existence is pervasive. I will, therefore, focus in the remainder of this chapter on links between broad-brush ideology and the poverty draft and the role of militarized electronic games in recruiting and training the proletariat, courtesy of partnerships between the Pentagon, capital and universities.

Electronic Games

I am including games within 'media' because I see the latter term as a portmanteau word that covers a multitude of cultural and communications machines and processes. There is increasing overlap between the sectors, as black-box techniques and technologies, once set away from audiences, increasingly become part of public debate and utilization. Consumer electronics connect to information and communications technologies and vice versa: televisions resemble computers; books are read on telephones; newspapers are written through clouds; and so on. Genres and gadgets that were once separate are now linked (Malmodin et al., 2010).

ℹ These Weapons of Mass Destruction cannot be displayed

The weapons you are looking for are currently unavailable. The country might be experiencing technical difficulties, or you may need to adjust your weapons inspectors mandate.

Please try the following:

- Click the 🔃 Regime change button, or try again later.
- If you are George Bush and typed the country's name in the address bar, make sure that it is spelled correctly. (IRAQ).
- To check your weapons inspector settings, click the **UN** menu, and then click **Weapons Inspector Options**. On the **Security Council** tab, click **Consensus**. The settings should match those provided by your government or NATO.
- If the Security Council has enabled it, The United States of America can examine your country and automatically discover Weapons of Mass Destruction.
  If you would like to use the CIA to try and discover them, click 🔍 Detect weapons
- Some countries require 128 thousand troops to liberate them. Click the **Panic** menu and then click **About US foreign policy** to determine what regime they will install.
- If you are an Old European Country trying to protect your interests, make sure your options are left wide open as long as possible. Click the **Tools** menu, and then click on **League of Nations**. On the Advanced tab, scroll to the Head in the Sand section and check settings for your exports to Iraq.
- Click the 💣 Bomb button if you are Donald Rumsfeld.

Cannot find weapons or CIA Error
Iraqi Explorer

Bush went to Iraq to look for Weapons of Mass Destruction and all he found was this lousy T-shirt.

This page supports The Euston Manifesto.

Figure 6.1

Outsiders probably think of electronic games in one of two ways. Either they are the newest means of rotting the brains of the young or they are exciting new educational forms that will improve learning. In terms of the role that research universities should play in them, we perhaps imagine that scholars evaluate the potential for harm in real life caused by players of violent first-person shooter games or the potential for benefit through conflict-resolution gaming and peaceful virtual worlds. We might even think about those wacky folks over in creative industries making their own games as part of the suddenly benign ghost of Schumpeter that haunts their work.

Here is the real scoop: the political economy of the global gaming industry sees a working mythology of consumer power; massive underwriting by the state through militarism and universities; and domination by large firms that buy up or destroy small businesses and centralize power in the metropole (Kerr and Flynn, 2003). The role of academia in militaristic electronic games is particularly meaningful, as it represents significant complicity with the delivery and support systems of US imperialism by lackey faculty. This is in keeping with a long and sorry history.

Technocratic from the First, the two World Wars provided US higher education with additional pump-priming and premia on practicality from the Federal government. Large research schools even expanded their capacity during the Depression (Aronowitz, 2000). The shop was really set up to cater to corporate and military research and development in the late 1950s via the Cold War, a trend that has largely continued unabated, albeit with associated ethico-political controversies. In anthropology, there have been struggles over espionage and briefings for empire. Psychology has colluded in torture by the US military. Or we might consider political scientists plotting the downfall of socialism (Project Camelot in the 1960s); biomedical researchers (relations with pharmaceutical companies); sociobiologists (defences of male sexual violence); nuclear physicists (Red-baiting of scientists); CIA-funded anti-Marxist leftism; and the Iraq invasion's 'Human Terrain Teams'. The same complicity has supported some supposedly radical work: Noam Chomsky's linguistics, the basis for his scientific reputation, was underwritten by the Pentagon through the US military's Joint Services Electronics Programs, while the Defense Department also supported Harold Garfinkel's research on transgender identity, which has been foundational in queer studies (González, 2008; Miller, 1998).

Many critics have expressed shock that US journalists embedded with the US military for the Iraq invasion compared the experience to a video game (Power, 2007: 271). They should not be so taken aback, because gaming has been crucial to war and vice versa since the late nineteenth century, when the US Naval War College Game simulated Prussian and French field tactics.

Such methods gained popularity when they predicted Japanese strategy in the Pacific from 1942 (Der Derian 2003: 38–39).

In the 1950s, computers were utilized to theorize and play these games and political science and warcraft scientized the study and practice of crisis decision-making via game theory. It was founded on a rational-actor model of maximizing utility reapplied to states, soldiers and diplomats to construct nuclear-war prospects (Der Derian, 2003). With the decline of Keynesianism in the 1970s, game theory's ideal-typical monadic subject came to dominate economics and political science more generally. Utility maximization even overtook parts of Marxism, which had tended to favour collective rather than selfish models of choice. Games were in, everywhere you looked.

That notion of individuals out for themselves remains in vogue, re-stimulated through electronic games (which were invented for the US military by defence contractors). The Pentagon worked with Atari in the 1980s to develop Battlezone, an arcade game, as a flight simulator for fighter pilots, at the same time as it established a gaming centre within the National Defense University (Power, 2007: 276). In the early 1990s, the end of Cold War II wrought economic havoc on many corporations involved in the US defence industry. They turned to the games industry as a natural supplement to their principal customer, the military. Today's new geopolitical crisis sees these firms, such as Quantum 3-D, conducting half their games business with the private market and half with the Pentagon (Hall, 2006). Players of the commercial title Doom II can download Marine Doom, a Marine-Corps modification of the original that was developed after the Corps commandant issued a directive that games would improve tactics. Sony's U.S. Navy Seals website links directly to the Corps' own page. TV commercials, now deleted from www. usarmy.com, have depicted soldiers directly addressing gamers, urging them to show their manliness by volunteering for the real thing and serving abroad to secure US power.

It should come as no surprise, then, that visitors to the Fox News site on 31 May 2004 encountered a 'grey zone'. On one side of the page, a US soldier in battle gear prowled the streets of Baghdad. On the other, a Terror Handbook promised to facilitate 'Understanding and facing the threat to America' under the banner: 'WAR ON TERROR sponsored by KUMA WAR' (a major gaming company). The Kuma War game includes online missions entitled 'Fallujah: Operation al Fajr', 'Battle in Sadr City' and 'Uday and Qusay's Last Stand'. Its legitimacy and realism are underwritten by the fact that the firm is run by retired military officers and used as a recruiting tool by their former colleagues. Both sides benefit from the company's website, which invites soldiers to pen their battlefield experiences – a neat way of getting intellectual property gratis in the name of the nation (Deck, 2004; Power 2007: 272; Turse 2008: 137).

The site features 'Quotes from Players in the Trenches' and a re-creation of the mission that assassinated Abu Musab al-Zarqawi. It boasts that:

> Kuma War is a series of playable recreations of real events in the War on Terror. Nearly 100 playable missions bring our soldiers' heroic stories to life, and you can get them all right now, for free. Stop watching the news and get in the game! (www.kumawar.com)

Such ideological work became vital because the military–diplomatic–fiscal disasters of the 2001–07 period jeopardized a steady supply of new troops. So at the same time as neophytes were hard to attract to the military due to the perils of war, recruits to militaristic game design stepped forward – nationalistic designers volunteering for service. Their mission, which they appeared to accept with alacrity, was to interpellate the country's youth by situating their bodies and minds to fire the same weapons and face the same issues as on the battlefield (Power 2007: 282; Thompson, 2004).

Universities have applied their idée fixe of rational-actor theory to these developments. In 1996, the National Academy of Sciences held a workshop for academia, Hollywood and the Pentagon on simulation and games. The next year, the National Research Council announced a collaborative research agenda on popular culture and militarism. It convened meetings to streamline such cooperation, from special effects to training simulations, from immersive technologies to simulated networks (Lenoir 2003: 190; Macedonia, 2002).

Today, untold numbers of academic journals and institutes on games are closely tied to the Pentagon. They test and augment the recruiting and training potential of games to ideologize, hire and instruct the population. For example, the Center for Computational Analysis of Social and Organizational Systems at Carnegie-Mellon University in Pittsburgh promulgates studies underwritten by the Office of Naval Research and the Defense Advanced Research Projects Agency (DARPA), whose wonderful slogan is 'Creating & Preventing Strategic Surprise'. Similar work around the country and the globe is proudly paraded by the Association for the Advancement of Artificial Intelligence (a 'scientific society'), while military sites such as www.goarmy.com/downloads/games.html and www.airforce.com/games-and-extras offer games that simulate life as both killer and enabler.

The Naval Postgraduate School's Modelling, Virtual Environments and Simulation Academic Program developed a game called *Operation Starfighter*, based on the 1984 film *The Last Starfighter*. The next step was farmed out for participation by George Lucas' companies, inter alia. America's Army was then launched, with due symbolism, on 4 July 2002 – doubly symbolic, in that Independence Day is a key date in Hollywood's summer release of feature films. The military had to bring additional servers into play to handle 400,000 downloads of the game that first day. Gamespot PC Reviews awarded it a high textual rating, and was equally impressed by the 'business model'. America's Army takes full advantage of the usual array of cybertarian fantasies about the new media as civil society, across the gamut of community fora, internet chat, fan sites and virtual competition. And the game is formally commodified through privatization – bought by Ubisoft to be repurposed for games consoles, arcades and cell phones, and turned into figurines by the allegedly edgy independent company Radioactive Clown. Tournaments are convened, replete with hundreds of thousands of dollars' prize money, along with smaller events at military recruiting sites (America's Army 2008; Lenoir, 2003: 175; Power 2007: 279–80; Turse 2008: 117–18, 123–24, 157).

A decade later, AA remains one of the ten most-played games on line, and has millions of registered users. Civilian developers regularly refresh it by consulting with veterans and participating in physical war games, while paratexts provide promotional renewal. With over 40 million downloads, and websites by the thousand, the message of the game has travelled far and wide – an excellent return on the initial public investment of $19 million and $5 million for annual updates. Studies of young people who have positive attitudes to the US military indicate that 30 per cent formed that view through playing the game – a game that sports a Teen rating, forbids role reversal via modifications (preventing players from experiencing the pain of the other) and is officially ranked number one among the Army's recruiting tools (Craig, 2006; Mirrlees, 2009; Nieborg, 2004; Ottosen, 2008, 2009a, 2009b; Shachtman, 2002; Thompson, 2004).

DARPA likes to spread the fiscal-developmental joy around universities (see, for instance, www.darpa.mil/Opportunities/Universities), deploying its $2 billion annual budget to examine, as one example, how social networking of the game can uncover:

> top America's Army players' distinct behaviors, the optimum size of an America's Army team, the importance of fire volume toward opponent, the recommendable communication structure and content, and the contribution of the unity among team members. (Carley et al., 2005)

And the Agency refers to Orlando as 'Team Orlando' because the city houses Disney's research-and-development 'imagineers', the University of Central Florida's Institute for Simulation and Training, and Lockheed Martin (the nation's biggest military contractor) (Team Orlando, n.d.).

In Los Angeles, the University of Southern California's Institute for Creative Technologies (ICT) articulates faculty, film and television producers, game designers and the Pentagon to one another. Formally opened by the Secretary of the Army and the head of the Motion Picture Association of America in 1998, it began with $45 million of the military's budget, a figure that was doubled in its 2004 renewal. ICT uses military money and Hollywood muscle to test out homicidal technologies and narrative scenarios – under the aegis of film, engineering and communications professors, beavering away in a workspace thoughtfully set up by the set designer for the *Star Trek* franchise. By the end of 2010, its products were available on 65 military bases (Deck, 2004; Hennigan, 2010; Silver and Marwick 2006: 50; Turse, 2008: 120). I guess that is convergence.

ICT collaborates on major motion pictures, for instance the 2004 *Spider-Man 2*. But more importantly, the Institute produces Pentagon recruitment tools such as *Full Spectrum Warrior* that double as 'training devices for military operations in urban terrain': what's good for the Xbox is good for the combat simulator. The utility of these innovations continues in the field. Many off-duty soldiers play games. The idea is to invade their supposed leisure time and wean them from skater games in favour of what are essentially training manuals. The Pentagon even boasts that *Full Spectrum Warrior* was the 'game that captured Saddam', because the men who dug Hussein out had been trained with it. At a more macro-level, electronic games have become crucial tools because fewer and fewer nations now allow the US to play live war games on their terrain (Andersen, 2007; Burston, 2003; Harmon, 2003; Kundnani, 2004; Stockwell and Muir, 2003; Turse 2008: 122, 119).

To keep up with the Institute's work, podcasts are available from Armed with Science: Research Applications for the Modern Military at the Defense Department's website (http://science.dodlive.mil/). Listeners learn that the Pentagon and ICT are developing UrbanSim to improve 'the art of battle command' which is aptly described as a small shift from commercial gaming: 'instead of having Godzilla and tornados attacking your city, the players are faced with things like uncooperative local officials and ethnic divisions in the communities, different tribal rivalries', to quote an Institute scholar in the pod (DoD, 2010). How annoying that pesky locals in places one has invaded can be uncooperative. Curse them.

In short, gaming, universities and militarism are connected through 'techno-logical nationalism' (Charland, 1986). Complicit campuses have thereby formed a symbiotic ideological and material relationship with the globe's leading polluter – the US Department of Defense. Military expenditure on electronics, information technologies, games and special effects links the 'war against terror' to orgiastic use of fossil fuels, destruction of terrain and infrastructure, radiation, conventional pollution, buried ordinance, defoliants, land use, anti-personnel mines, carcinogenic chemical deposits and toxic effluents. The Pentagon claims to be 'going green', yet remains the world's largest user of petroleum (Corbett and Turco, 2006; Jorgenson et al., 2010; Leaning, 2000; Shachtman, 2010).

For the scholarly advocates of corporate culture who proliferate in game studies, none of this appears to be a problem: 'games serve the national interest by entertaining consumer-citizens and creating a consumer-based demand for military technology' that is unrelated to actual violence (Hall, 2006; Power 2007: 277). But academics who are involved with these delightful paymasters would do well to read some scientific history. In his testimony to the US Atomic Energy Commission, J. Robert Oppenheimer, who led the group that developed the atomic bomb, talked about the instrumental rationality that animated the people who created this awesome technology. Once these scientists saw that it was feasible, the device's impact lost intellectual and emotional significance for them – overtaken by what he labelled its 'technically sweet' quality (United States Atomic Energy Commission, 1954: 81).

'Technically sweet' qualities animate innovation, adoption and the mix of the sublime – the awesome, the ineffable, the uncontrollable, the powerful – with the beautiful – the approachable, the attractive, the pliant, the soothing. In philosophical aesthetics, the sublime and the beautiful are generally regarded as opposites. But gaming technologies have brought them together for denizens of the ICT and their friends across campus.

Virtual blowback is under way, with Al Qaeda reportedly learning tactics by playing these games and developing counters of their own; the Global Islamic Media Front releasing Quest for Bush (Power, 2007: 283; Vargas, 2006); and the artist Joseph DeLappe creating counter-texts online by typing the details of deceased soldiers into the game under the moniker 'dead-in-Iraq' (see Delappe, n.d.).

What does this mean for media researchers? Many of us feel comfortable criticizing media effects studies – from a comfortable distance – as crude, unproven, anti-child and anti-pleasure. But we need to address, for example, the fact that the American Academy of Pediatrics (2009) denounces the mimetic force of violent electronic games on young people, yet fails to describe how this is preyed upon by the Pentagon. Are we prepared to criticize games that promote death, at the same time as we criticize scientists' neglect of this tendency when it abets empire?

That should lead us to a next step: transcending laptop critique. Whilst I am all in favour of using political economy, textual analysis and audience research to comprehend and teach how the media cover militarism, our efforts should turn not only to publishing and pedagogy but the very fabric of research, notably in the US. As per the brave actions taken by professional bodies in anthropology and – belatedly – psychology against their co-optation by the US war machine (see AAA, 2006; APA, 2009), we should shame universities for their role in electronic-game militarism. For example, USC and Carnegie-Mellon academics should protest the bloody work of Empire undertaken on their campuses, collectively and publicly. We must all work to counter DARPA's ideological incorporation of untenured faculty, whom it seeks to engage via the 'Young Faculty Award'. The goal is 'to develop the next generation of academic scientists, engineers and mathematicians in key disciplines who will focus a significant portion of their career on D[epartment]o[f]D[efense] and national security issues' (DARPA, n.d). Faculty in other countries should boycott military-endowed US universities and researchers if we fail to contest these murderous paymasters. The task is massive, and it will require people with progressive politics to collaborate as never before. They must do so with an appreciation of the history of imperialism, the experience of militarization, the play of games and the complicity of higher education.

Pretty clearly, the US is in monumental decline as a global suzerain. Its death throes may be violent. We need to restrain and retrain it. If that fails, let us help ease this tortured and torturing nation into a well-deserved rest home where it can conclude its last great game.

Endnote

1   Yes, the Navy has sought to trademark 'Global Force for Good' www.navytimes.com/news/2009/10/navy_slogan_update_100209w.

References

AAA (American Anthropological Association) (2006) Anthropologists Weigh In on Iraq Torture at Annual Meeting, news release, 11 December. Available at: http://aaanet.org/pdf/iraqtorture.pdf (accessed 17 March 2011).

Amaya, Hector (2007) Dying American or the Violence of Citizenship: Latinos in Iraq, *Latino Studies* 5: 3–24.

American Academy of Pediatrics, Council on Communications and Media (2009) Policy Statement-Media Violence, *Pediatrics*, 124(5): 1495–1503.

America's Army (2008) AA: Sf Tops 9 Million User Mark, 10 February. Available at: http://beta.americasarmy.com/press/news.php?t=70 (accessed 17 March 2011).

Andersen, Robin (2007) Bush's Fantasy Budget and the Military/Entertainment Complex, *PRWatch*, 12 February. Available at: http://prwatch.org/node/5742 (accessed 17 March 2011).

APA (American Psychological Association) (2009) APA Board Reiterates Its Stance on Interrogations, *Monitor on Psychology*, September, 40(8). Available at: www.apa.org/monitor/2009/09/interrogations.aspx (accessed 17 March 2011).

Aronowitz, Stanley (2000) *The Knowledge Factory: Dismantling the Corporate University and Creating True Higher Learning*. Boston: Beacon Press.

Barber, Ben (2010) WikiLeaks and the Sham of 'Public Diplomacy', *Salon*, 4 December. Available at: www.salon.com/news/politics/war_room/2010/12/04/wikileaks_public_diplomacy (accessed 17 March, 2011).

Brown, S. F. (2005) Exceptionalist America: American Sports Fans' Reaction to Internationalization, *International Journal of the History of Sport*, 22(6): 1106–35.

Burston, Jonathan (2003) War and the Entertainment Industries: New Research Priorities in an Era of Cyber-Patriotism, in Daya Thussu and Des Freedman (eds) *War and the Media: Reporting Conflict 24/7*. London: SAGE. 163–75.

Carley, Kathleen, Moon, Il-Chul, Schneider, Mike and Shigiltchoff, Oleg (2005) *Detailed Analysis of Factors Affecting Team Success and Failure in the America's Army Game*. CASOS Technical Report.

Charland, Maurice (1986) Technological Nationalism, *Canadian Journal of Political and Social Theory* 10(1): 196–220.

Corbett, Charles J. and Turco, Richard (2006) *Sustainability in the Motion Picture Industry*. Report prepared for the Integrated Waste Management Board of the State of California, November. Available at: http://personal.anderson.ucla.edu/charles.corbett/papers/mpis_report.pdf (accessed 17 March 2011).

Craig, Kathleen (2006) Dead in Iraq: It's No Game, *Wired*, 6 June. Available at: www.wired.com/gaming/gamingreviews/news/2006/06/71052 (accessed 17 March 2011).

DARPA (n.d.) Opportunities at DARPA: Young Faculty Award. Available at: www.darpa.mil/Opportunities/Universities/Young_Faculty.aspx (accessed 17 March 2011).

Deck, Andy (2004) Demilitarizing the Playground, *Art Context*. Available at: http://artcontext.org/crit/essays/noQuarter/ (accessed 17 March 2011).

DeLappe, J. (n.d.) 'Dead-in-Iraq' project. Available at: http://unr.edu/art/DELAPPE/DeLappe%20Main%20Page/DeLappe%20Online%20MAIN.html (accessed 17 March 2011).

Der Derian, James (2003) War as Game, *Brown Journal of World Affairs* 10(1): 37–48.

DoD (Department of Defense) (2010) Armed with Science: Research Applications for the Modern Military, Podcast, 3 March. Available at: www.defense.gov/Blog_files/Blog_assets/20100303_AWS_Episode57_tran-script.pdf (accessed 17 March 2011).

Fifield, Jessica (2009) Just War and Citizenship: Responses to Youth Violence, *International Journal of Communication* 3: 668–82.

Goldberg, David Theo (2010) A Conversation with David Theo Goldberg, Cultural Studies podcast, 18 August. Available at: http://culturalstudies.podbean.com/2010/08/18/a-conversation-with-david-theo-goldberg (accessed 10 March 2011).

González, Roberto J. (2008) 'Human Terrain': Past, Present and Future Applications, *Anthropology Today* 24(1): 21–6.

Hall, Karen J. (2006) Shooters to the Left of Us, Shooters to the Right: First Person Arcade Shooter Games, the Violence Debate, and the Legacy of Militarism, *Reconstruction: Studies in Contemporary Culture* 6(1). Available at: http://reconstruction.eserver.org/061/hall.shtml (accessed 17 March 2011).

Harmon, Amy (2003) More Than Just a Game, but How Close to Reality?, *New York Times*, 3 April. Available at: www.nytimes.com/2003/04/03/technology/more-than-just-a-game-but-how-close-to-reality.html (accessed 17 March 2011).

Hebert, James (2005) Band of Brothers, *San Diego Union-Tribune*, 6 November. Available at: www.signonsandiego.com/uniontrib/20051106/news_lz1a06ictech.html (accessed 17 March 2011).

Hennigan, W. J. (2010) Computer Simulation is a Growing Reality for Instruction, *Los Angeles Times*, 2 November.

Jorgenson, Andrew K., Clark, B. and Kentor, J. (2010) Militarization and the Environment: A Panel Study of Carbon Dioxide Emissions and the Ecological Footprints of Nations, 1970–2000, *Global Environmental Politics* 10(1): 7–29.

Kerr, Aphra and Flynn, R. (2003) Revisiting Globalisation Through the Movie and Digital Games Industries, *Convergence: The International Journal of Research into New Media Technologies* 9(1): 91–113.

Kundnani, Arun (2004) Wired for War: Military Technology and the Politics of Fear, *Race & Class* 46(1): 116–25.

Leaning, Jennifer (2000) Environment and Health: 5. Impact of War, *Canadian Medical Association Journal* 163(9): 1157–61.

Lenoir, Timothy (2003) Programming Theaters of War: Gamemakers as Soldiers, in Robert Latham (ed.) *Bombs and Bandwidth: The Emerging Relationship Between Information Technology and Security*. New York: New Press. 175–98.

Macedonia, Mike (2002) Games, Simulation, and the Military Education Dilemma, in *The Internet and the University: 2001 Forum*. Boulder: Educause. 157–67.

Malmodin, Jens, Moberg, Åsa, Lundén, Dag, Finnveden, Göran and Lövehagen, Nina (2010) Greenhouse Gas Emissions and Operational Electricity Use in the ICT and Entertainment & Media Sectors, *Journal of Industrial Ecology* 14(5): 770–90.

Media Matters for America (2010) As the World Cup Starts, Conservative Media Declare War on Soccer, 11 June. Available at: mediamatters.org/research/201006110040 (accessed 14 March 2011).

Miller, Toby (1998) *Technologies of Truth: Cultural Citizenship and the Popular Media*. Minneapolis: University of Minnesota Press.

Miller, Toby (2007) *Cultural Citizenship: Cosmopolitanism, Consumerism, and Television in a Neoliberal Age*. Philadelphia: Temple University Press.

Miller, Toby (2008) *Makeover Nation: The United States of Reinvention*. Cleveland: Ohio State University Press.

Mirrlees, Tanner (2009) Digital Militainment by Design: Producing and Playing *SOCOM: U.S. Navy SEALs*, *International Journal of Media and Cultural Politics* 5(3): 161–81.

Nader, Laura (1972) Up the Anthropologist – Perspectives Gained from Studying Up, in Dell H. Hymes (ed.) *Reinventing Anthropology*. New York: Pantheon Books. 284–311.

Nieborg, David B (2004) America's Army: More Than a Game, in Thomas Eberle and Willy Christian Kriz (eds) *Transforming Knowledge into Action Through Gaming and Simulation*. Munich: SAGSAGA. CD-ROM.

Nye, Joseph S. (2002) Limits of American Power, *Political Science Quarterly* 117(4): 545–59.

Ottosen, Rune (2008) Targeting the Audience: Video Games as War Propaganda in Entertainment and News, *Bodhi: An Interdisciplinary Journal* 2(1): 14–41.

Ottosen, Rune (2009a) The Military–Industrial Complex Revisited, *Television & New Media* 10(1): 122–5.

Ottosen, Rune (2009b) Targeting the Player: Computer Games as Propaganda for the Military–Industrial Complex, *Nordicom Review* 30(2): 35–51.

Pope, S. W. (2007) Rethinking Sport, Empire, and American Exceptionalism, *Sport History Review* 38(2): 92–120.

Power, Marcus (2007) Digitized Virtuosity: Video War Games and Post-9/11 Cyber-Deterrence, *Security Dialogue* 38(2): 271–88.

Reuters (2003) Search for WMD Finds 'Bomb' on Internet, 4 July. Available at: www.commondreams.org/headlines03/0704-06.htm (accessed 17 March 2011).

Shachtman, Noah (2002) Shoot 'Em Up and Join the Army, *Wired*, 4 July.

Shachtman, Noah (2010) Green Monster, *Foreign Policy*, May/June.

Silver, David and Marwick, Alice (2006) Internet Studies in Times of Terror, in David Silver and Adrienne Massanari (eds) *Critical Cyberculture Studies*. New York: New York University Press. 47–54.

Stockwell, Stephen and Muir, Adam (2003) The Military–Entertainment Complex: A New Facet of Information Warfare, *Fibreculture*, 1. Available at: http://one.fibreculturejournal.org/fcj-004-the-military-entertainment-complex-a-new-facet-of-information-warfare (accessed 17 March 2011).

Team Orlando (n.d.) Team Orlando: Improving Human Performance Through Simulation. Available at: http://teamorlando.org/about/index.shtml# (accessed 17 March 2011).

Thompson, Clive (2004) The Making of an X Box Warrior, *New York Times Magazine*, 22 August.

Turse, Nick (2008) *The Complex: How the Military Invades Our Everyday Lives.* New York: Metropolitan Books.

United States Atomic Energy Commission (1954) *In the Matter of J. Robert Oppenheimer. Transcript of Hearing Before Personnel Security Board.* Cambridge, Mass.: MIT Press.

US Navy (n.d.) A Global Force for Good. Available at: www.navy.com/about/gffg.html (accessed 14 March 2011).

Vargas, Jose Antonio (2006) Way Radical, Dude, *Washington Post*, 9 October.

Verklin, David and Kanner, Bernice (2007) Why a Killer Videogame is the U. S. Army's Best Recruitment Tool, *MarketingProfs*, 29 May. Available at: www.marketingprofs.com/articles/2007/2377/why-a-killer-videogame-is-the-us-armys-best-recruitment-tool (accessed 17 March 2011).

Wright, Micah Ian (2003) *You Back the Attack! We'll Bomb Who We Want! Remixed War Propaganda.* New York: Seven Stories Press.

7

HOLLYWOOD, THE CIA AND THE 'WAR ON TERROR'

Oliver Boyd-Barrett, David Herrera and Jim Baumann

Hollywood's depiction of the CIA and the 'war on terror' is the theme of this chapter by Oliver Boyd-Barrett, David Herrera and Jim Baumann. The piece, based on their recent study of the representations of the CIA in Hollywood movies, underlines the important contribution of the world's most famous entertainment industry to normalization of the 'war on terror' on screen and the justification of espionage and covert operations in foreign nations. Their survey of CIA-themed movies produced in the last decade demonstrates that such movies generally manifest an ideological sub-text, even when this is disguised by dramatic representations of 'realism', 'truthiness' or 'limited hang-outs': in the garb of action-packed celluloid entertainment, their narratives represent an imperial vision of contemporary conflicts and in the process the films legitimize US geo-political and economic interests.

This chapter examines representations of the CIA in Hollywood theatrical movies from 2000 to 2010 and considers the importance of the CIA as a narrative driver, the ideological work the movies perform, their relationship to the historical moments of production, and whether representations of the institution and of CIA protagonists are favourable or unfavourable. Numbers of 'CIA movies' increased significantly in the 2000s. Initial searches established 25 each for the 1960s and 1970s, 26 for the 1980s, 23 for the 1990s and over 40 for the 2000s. Here, we select 13 movies that we have judged to have strong pretensions to 'realism' (via allusions to demonstrable historical events including the 'war on terror' and other theatres of war), even though more fantastical narratives typically played on presumptions of audience knowledge as framed through American or western interests. In particular, we ask how did the movies relate to their historical moment of production and whether (and how) they served identifiable ideological or propaganda functions.

These movies frequently rewrite history to support US interests or soften potential critique. Some are supportive of the institutional CIA, CIA protagonists and US foreign policy. Some favour only one or two of these three. Occasionally a movie is critical of all three. Movies commonly acknowledge popular disquiet with CIA methods while quietly endorsing the authority of its 'parent', the global hegemon. Spying and covert activity are unquestionably 'normal'. If 'normalization' was Hollywood's only ideological work, this alone would contribute to US empire. Hollywood provides more variety of representations and moral positions than we expected. Variety co-exists with the deeper ideological work of normalization. Yet covert operations, thriving on secrecy, are deeply problematic for democracy, regularly counterproductive to public interest and frequently amoral and/or criminal.

Chronologically, the first movie is *Spy Game* (2001), directed by Tony Scott. This engages with three 'moments' of CIA history. First is 1960s Vietnam, before protagonist Bishop (Brad Pitt), has been recruited by Muir (Robert Redford) into the CIA. Muir, working within the Phoenix programme, judges Bishop to be a competent replacement for the sniper he had been promised. The target is a friend of the enemy, a Chinese general. No reference is made to the violent, indiscriminate nature of the Phoenix programme of torture and assassination. Muir's superiors, interrogating him about this episode, ask whether he had had Presidential clearance, but their interest as CIA bureaucrats is in finding reasons for not saving Bishop from Chinese incarceration. They fear that if Bishop is 'outed' as an ex-agent this may undermine an upcoming US–China trade deal.

In Cold War Berlin, Muir assigns Bishop to escort an asset from East to West Berlin. Bishop is unaware that this is a set-up to entrap a female mole in the US embassy. Although he is frustrated and angry when ordered to abandon his asset in the East, Muir had trained him to obey, and to be alert to the possibility that an asset who has been 'chosen' may actually be choosing his 'recruiter' as asset.

In 1980s Beirut, Muir and Bishop enlist the doctor of a Hezbollah-supported refugee camp where Bishop's girlfriend, Elizabeth Hadley (Catherine McCormack) tends to orphans. Hadley has a previous 'terrorist' association, protesting against Chinese human rights abuses. Muir and Bishop convince the doctor that a sheikh whom they want to assassinate had killed the doctor's parents. The sheikh is believed responsible for bombings of US embassies. The doctor is to administer poison, so that US involvement will not be detected. Should this 'quiet way' fail, a Lebanese militia group is prepped to car-bomb the sheikh's apartment block. Something goes awry: a terrorist bombing (possibly Israeli?) at the camp requires the doctor's presence. Worried that the sheikh will exit his safe house before the doctor arrives, Muir orders the militia to proceed. The car bomb brings down half a block, inflicting much 'collateral damage'. Appalled, Bishop resigns.

Muir later sells out Bishop's girlfriend in a 'trade' with the Chinese for a captured CIA agent. He fears that Hadley, left in Beirut, might expose CIA identities. Bishop discovers the trade, tracks Hadley to her Chinese prison and is apprehended. Muir spends his final days before retirement covertly orchestrating a rescue that costs him his life savings. Muir earlier recommended Bishop to a British agent in Hong Kong as someone MI6 might hire. Through this channel Bishop learned that Hadley was incarcerated and Muir was alerted to Bishop's imprisonment.

The film uncritically adopts a US-framed list of 'good' and 'bad' nations, reinforcing a world view that synchronizes with US policies. North Vietnamese sympathizers are 'bad' in the Vietnam War: no call for ethical qualms over torture and death visited upon neutrals and nationalists alike by Phoenix. East German communists are 'bad', so no need to worry about abandoning an Eastern bloc asset and killing an agency mole. CIA incompetence in mishandling agents in the Soviet bloc is irrelevant. Islamic fundamentalists in Beirut are 'bad'. Israel and Palestine are invisible. The visiting of US terrorism upon its enemy, in collaboration with Lebanese Christian militia, often Israeli allies, is vindicated. China is self-evidently a thorn in US flesh, from Vietnam to the 'present'. Because Bishop's girlfriend engaged in illegal action for a 'good' cause against China's human rights record, she earns sympathy, deserving of heroic efforts to free her. Her association with Hezbollah is overlooked within the movie's political and emotional logic because she relies on Hezbollah help to care for orphans.

Mike Salomon's *The Company* (2002), adapted from a television mini-series, connects to many historical personalities, including James Angleton, Allen Dulles, Dwight Eisenhower, Sam Giancana, Mikhail Gorbachev, E. Howard Hunt, Lyndon B. Johnson, John F. Kennedy, Joseph P. Kennedy, Snr, Robert F. Kennedy, Nikita Khrushchev, H.A.R. 'Kim' Philby, Frank Sinatra, Harry Truman and Boris Yeltsin. The narrative runs World War II to the end of the Cold War, dwelling on post-war Berlin, the Soviet invasion of Hungary 1956 and the Bay of Pigs in 1961. The principal themes are trust and betrayal, and penetration of western intelligence, especially the CIA, by the KGB. Many characters, American and Russian, CIA and KGB, are represented sympathetically, but the protagonist, recruited by the CIA at a Yale Skull and Bones initiation, is Jack McAuliffe (Chris O'Donnell). It is McAuliffe and his colleagues – CIA head of counter-espionage James Angleton (Michael Keaton),

Berlin CIA bureau chief Harvey Torriti (Alfred Molina), and rising agency star Leo Kritsky (Alessandro Novili) – who occupy most screen time. The world is seen through McAuliffe's idealistic eyes. The Oedipal theme common to this genre pits a young, competent recruit (McAuliffe eventually identifies Kritsky as Sasha, the mole, punishes and ultimately absolves him) against veterans who are more ruthless (Torriti), deceitful (Kritsky) or paranoid (Angleton).

A Soviet parallel emerges between McAuliffe's Yale contemporary, Soviet-born Yevgeny Tsipin (Roy Cochrane) and his KGB controller, Starik Zhilov (Ulrich Thomsen). The film uses McAuliffe to whitewash, on the grounds that the US, fictionally at least, had previously warned it would not intervene, US/CIA 'failure' to support Hungarian resistance to Soviet occupiers in 1956 or expatriate Cuban rebels in the Bay of Pigs in 1961. McAuliffe warns Hungarian resistance leader Arpad Zelk (Misel Matirevic) not to expect US help; he warns Bay of Pigs' leader Roberto Escalona (Raoul Bova) that the US will not aid his men if they run into trouble. He does not explain the 'real' reason is that CIA counter-espionage chief James Angleton calculates that while the CIA has a mole, 'Sasha', there is no point to CIA intervention, since 'Sasha' will leak the plans. The movie rewrites history to vindicate Angleton's paranoia: his suspicion that Kritsky is 'Sasha' is confirmed, although only after colleagues have forced Angleton's retirement.

That Angleton was mistaken not to suspect his friend, MI6 spy Kim Philby, as a KGB double agent, and that he questioned the loyalties of politicians such as Averell Harriman and Henry Kissinger, should invite the conclusion that his judgements were unsound. There is other whitewashing of the CIA and US foreign policy. The catastrophic mismanagement of the CIA's post-war Soviet assets (Weiner, 2007) is overlooked. Recounting of the Bay of Pigs shows no appreciation for its grave consequences (acquiescence of Cuba to Russian nuclear missiles, and planetary near-annihilation) nor for the entitlement of the Cuban people to have overthrown the Batista regime and defend themselves against northern aggression.

Least favoured main characters include double agent (and historical figure) Kim Philby, whose retirement in Moscow is represented as pathetically short of paradise; Leo Kritsky (who ends up in Moscow where his life is spared by McAuliffe, an act of compassion which is mixed with contempt and pity); and McAuliffe's 'asset' and Berlin mistress, Lili (Alexandra Maria Lara), who shoots herself. All worked for the KGB. Starik Zhilov's scheme to bring down US capitalism is a damp squib (hardly comparing with the self-destructive capacity of finance capitalism, unravelling in 2008). Cinematic claims to realism notwithstanding, the movie celebrates US power and intelligence services. As virtuous protagonist, McAuliffe may entertain doubts, but the commanding words are those of the 'realist', Berlin boss Harvey Torriti: the CIA were 'good guys' simply because they won. The struggle for power, whether benign or otherwise, will come with compromises and failures. Men of goodwill, like McAuliffe, suffer pangs of conscience; realists like Torriti get on with the game.

Strongly negative in its assessment of the CIA as imperial agent, Phillip Noyce's *The Quiet American* (2002) captures the 1950s moment when novelist Graham Greene, then a war correspondent in Saigon, weaved a novel around his intuition that US flexing of post-war imperial muscle was dirtier than suggested by its pose as defender of democracy. The movie resonates with the moment of its exhibition: a story about US facilitation of terrorist bombing of innocents in support of neo-imperial foreign policy in Vietnam strikes an uneasy chord against popular doubts surrounding the official record of 9/11 and its relationship to a previously formulated neo-conservative policy of aggressive overseas interventionism (Griffin et al., 2004).

The Quiet American presciently critiques US foreign policy. Alden Pyle (Brendan Fraser), undercover CIA station chief, nurtures the political ambitions of an authoritarian Vietnamese army commander seen by the US as suitable leader of the 'Third Way' between French imperialism (still underwritten by the US), and communism. Young Pyle seems polite, moral and sensitive yet audaciously undermines the happiness of his new friend, middle-aged British journalist Thomas Fowler (Michael Caine), wedging himself between Fowler and Fowler's young mistress, Phuong (Do Thi Hai Yen). This is a metaphor for the US wedge inserted between a dying European imperialism and a lush 'Orient' now vulnerable to the anti-capitalist ideologies of the Soviet Union, China and possibly India against which old western imperialism, whose mouthpiece is Fowler's establishment newspaper, is pathetically ill-equipped. Unbowed by the self-knowledge of established imperialists, Pyle seems barely shaken by the pain his actions have helped to inflict, content in the certainty that he has acted for the long-term good of the Vietnamese and the world.

A contemporary critique, *Syriana* (2005), directed by Stephen Gaghan, constructs an imbroglio that links the US government, the CIA, Middle Eastern oil-producing countries, US energy multinationals, and 'Jihadist' terror, in a global setting in which US supremacy is threatened by China. The main target of critique is US dependency on Middle Eastern oil and the bonds between US oil and political establishments (powerful enough to strangle antitrust investigations), represented as inimical to long-term US interests.

The protagonist, CIA agent Bob Barnes (George Clooney) is assigned to assassinate Nasir (Alexander Siddig), progressive prince of an oil state. Upon discovering the likely consequences, Barnes later tries, vainly and at the cost of his own life, to save Nasir, the movie's true hero. Enlightened son of an emirate sheik, his vision is diversified production, distributed dependence (favouring China over the US) and democracy. His predilections are not free of western influence, since he is advised by American representative Bryan Woodman (Matt Damon) – of a Swiss-based energy consultancy. Nasir's father, however, wants continued US dominance, and anoints as successor his younger, dissolute son who is clearly unfit to rule. In response, Nasir plans a coup, but he and his family are assassinated by US predator drone, despite Barnes' attempts to forewarn him.

US political and corporate interests are represented unfavourably. The oil company Killen has secured rights to drill for oil in Kazakhstan by means of bribery. As it merges with the larger, gas-drilling company Connex, the conglomerate diverts anti-trust scrutiny from the Department of Justice by sacrificing two internal scapegoats (on the advice of a Justice insider). Through its attorney Dean Whiting (Christopher Plummer) the conglomerate attempts unsuccessfully to thwart the CIA's relentless assassination-by-drone policy, since it deems this counter-productive, possibly favouring the forces both of moderation and of radicalism. The scheming of US corporate and political interests is rendered pathetic by the initial ability of the Chinese to win gas-drilling rights in Nasir's emirate, ahead of the US, and by the human consequences, notably for Pakistani expatriate oil workers Saleem Ahmed Kahn (Shahid Ahmed) and his son Wasim (Mazhar Munir). Upon being laid-off from Connex-Killen, Wasim trains for a suicide attack against a Connex-Killen LNG tanker, using the US anti-tank missile that Barnes had reported missing after his attack on Iranian arms dealers at the movie's start.

On the circuitous route to death at the hands of his own agency that deems him 'rogue', Barnes is a victim of the simplicity of his cultural presumptions in discounting the possibility that his accomplice for the assassination, Mussawi (Mark Strong), now working for the Iranians, will make no connection between the politics of Hezbollah (whom Barnes is trying to pacify) and the assassination of a progressive Arab leader. It is an agent of Hezbollah that rescues Barnes from beheading by Mussawi. Yet the movie is otherwise negative towards Iran, associating it with terrorism, and in this respect supports the US administration's insistent drumming for war against Iran.

The Good Shepherd (2006), directed by Robert de Niro, appears to be a serious movie seeking historical and emotional truths about OSS and CIA involvement in important events, seen mainly through the perspective of a fictionalized character, Edward Wilson (Matt Damon, again), whose career raises critical doubts about the efficacy of intelligence and its impact on the integrity of the political system it serves. Founding father of the CIA Bill Sullivan (Robert de Niro) expresses concern to his protégé about this tension between the CIA's covert nature and democracy (Wilson is aghast at the very idea of congressional oversight). Significant historical events with which the film deals include the interrogation of captured Nazis at the end of World War II, relations with allied and enemy intelligence services, elite recruitment to the agency through Yale University's Skull and Bones initiation rites, the agency's destabilization of Central American and Caribbean republics including Cuba, Soviet penetration of the CIA and illegal methods of interrogation.

Posing as a frank examination of the agency's origins, the movie consistently softens its critical edge. While some Nazi prisoners may have been tricked into giving up valuable information before consignment to execution or imprisonment, as occurs here, there is no reference to Nazis protectively recruited to assist the US in such fields as atomic power and bioterrorism (Blum, 2005). The movie misleadingly suggests it was only Soviets who sought Nazi scientists, while Americans mainly sought Jewish ones. The film fictionalizes the 'betrayal' of the 'Bay of Pigs' – the botched 1961 US invasion of Cuba – supposedly by means of an advance leak to the Cubans by an agency mole. Rather than seriously represent the historical reasons for the failure, it has Wilson's son accidentally overhear the plan and, through accident or naiveté, reveal it to his girlfriend, whom his father is later led to believe is a Soviet spy. There is no reference to President Kennedy's refusal to supply air cover or call in the marines (a possible provocation to Kennedy's assassins), nor even to Castro's wiliness (Raffy, 2004). Rather, the movie assumes an indulgent, insider, conservative point of view. Nobody questions the wisdom of the operation or recognizes its ramifications, namely that it drove Cuba to acquiesce to the stationing of Soviet nuclear missiles which, in turn, nearly triggered a nuclear armageddon.

Representation of CIA water-boarding, while it critically suggests routine illegality by US secret services, has curious resonance (given the film's release soon after Abu Ghraib torture, and rendition exposures of the 'war on terror') with scandals of the Bush Jnr presidency involving encouragement and condoning of torture. The argument that 'we've always done it, it's not that unusual' is propaganda whose purpose, under the smokescreen of 'tradition', is to inoculate against the shock of violations of national and international law.

Depicting one of the CIA's first 'successes', namely the destabilization in 1954 of the democratically elected regime of President Jacobo Arbenz in Guatemala, the movie focuses on use of biological weapons (in this instance, locusts) to destroy the country's principal crop – presented in this movie as coffee, averting attention from the role in the conspiracy of the United Fruit Company (UFC) and its banana interests. By emphasizing the presence of Wilson's Soviet nemesis, 'Ulysses' in the Arbenz entourage, the movie conveniently endorses dubious US accusations of undue Soviet influence over that regime. Blum (2005) argues that the communist presence in the Arbenz cabinet was token and the Soviets, far from seeking to intervene, were anxious not to give the US excuse for retaliation. A more compelling reason for US intervention was UFC's plea for assistance to President Eisenhower and his new CIA Director Allen Dulles (whose Guatemala campaign took advice from Edward Bernays, founding father of public relations; cf. Curtis 2007). The UFC's banana interests had been undermined by Arbenz's policies of land redistribution and crop substitution. Eisenhower's view was that US business interests equalled US national interests. The suggestion in the movie that Wilson's boss was taking a cut from private corporate interests is not translated into direct recognition of the political determination of US foreign policy by corporations such as UFC.

If releasing locusts over coffee exemplifies CIA nefariousness, it is a gentle example. Why did the movie not deal with the more important CIA 'success' one year previously, namely the toppling of the democratically elected regime of Mohammad Mossadegh, prime minister of Iran – an act that occasioned massive 'blowback' for the following half century (Johnson 2004)? The movie succumbs to its myth of the CIA as a gentlemanly club of sincere, intelligent Americans, recruited from the country's elite amidst the ritualistic rites de passage of Yale's Skull and Bones, defending civilization at great personal sacrifice. The movie has Wilson's son conduct his affair in Leopoldville in the Congo, without reference to the possible CIA role in the 1961 assassination of democratically elected and first Prime Minister of the Congo, Patrice Lumumba, and CIA support for his replacement, the corrupt dictator Joseph Mobutu. The narrative is propelled by the game of wits between Wilson and his Soviet nemesis, Ulysses. This frames CIA operations as Herculean battles in the decades-long Cold War against the evil Soviet empire, rather than as gambits in which communism was a pretext for destabilizing regimes that resisted US pressure for privileged access to internal markets. Wilson's personal tragedy, that in the process he condones and perhaps even instigates the murder of his CIA son's pregnant fiancée, pays witness to a moral price sometimes paid by those caught in the paranoiac vortex of uncertain trust and betrayal that is the fate of serious practitioners of espionage.

Within the rare (for Hollywood) context of Pakistan, Michael Winterbottom's *A Mighty Heart* (2007) docudrama's focus is *Wall Street Journal* reporter Daniel Pearl, and the desperate attempts of his wife, his newspaper, the US diplomatic security service and Pakistani CID to track down Pearl's kidnappers before his execution. Given that the tragedy of Jewish Daniel Pearl (like that of Israeli Olympic victims in Speilberg's *Munich*, 2005) is its principal focus, the entire movie is framed through compassion for Pearl as victim, the stoic anguish of his pregnant wife and of his US family.

The film adopts an intensely personalized perspective on complex historical events. We are invited to its narrative on the presumption that Pearl and his wife are worthy of compassion, to identify with their agony as threatened strangers in a hostile land. The film is unflattering of deeply ineffective US efforts to help. Given their familiarity with the context, Pakistani security forces emerge more favourably if, in the end, as ineffectively. There is no sustained attempt to see events other than through the eyes of the victims and their helpers. Excluded are the mainly Muslim casualties of US aggression in Afghanistan in its war against the Taliban on the pretext (since there were many other motives and agendas in play) of some kind of (disputed) responsibility of the Taliban for harbouring Osama bin Laden, and the implications of this war for Pakistani intelligence and security in a country that just a few years later was disintegrating under US military incursions. Ordinary citizens of the dystopian society of Pakistan, deeply divided and unequal, are largely absent.

While the CIA is a marginal force here, the movie has interesting things to say about intelligence work, including the US Diplomatic Security Service, represented by Randall Bennett (Will Patton) and Pakistan's CID, represented by Javed Habib (Irfan Khan), and about the 2001 9/11 attacks. After Pearl's abduction in Karachi, the efforts of Mariane Pearl (Angelina Jolie) and her husband's assistant Asra Nomani (playing herself) are augmented with the arrival of *Wall Street Journal*'s Central Asian correspondent, Steve Levine. Levine is emailed a story from the *Journal*'s London bureau, picked up from the (British) *Independent* (24 January 2000, headed 'Briton linked to al-Qa'ida behind Calcutta killing'), about Ahmed Omar Saeed Sheikh. It told how Sheikh was rumoured to be the person instructed by Lt General Mahmoud Ahmad, head of Pakistan's military intelligence agency Inter Services Intelligence (ISI) – to which, curiously, no reference is made in the film, even though ISI works closely with the CIA – to wire $10,000 to Mohamed Atta, the supposed lead 9/11 hijacker, shortly before the 9/11 attacks. This is a rare instance of a mainstream medium referencing a central mystery of 9/11, mentioned without much by way of later comment. Those in Karachi to whom the story is sent appear totally uninterested in the 9/11 dimension, focusing only on Saeed Sheikh's reputation of being a kidnapper of westerners. Saeed Sheikh (Alyy Khan) is shown being interrogated about the circumstances of Pearl's abduction, and is eventually sentenced to death (three co-defenders were sentenced to life imprisonment), from which he later appealed. There is only one further, oblique reference to his (or to ISI's) possible ties to 9/11 when Steve Levine speculates whether US attempts to get Pakistan to hand over Saeed Sheikh and the dismissal by President Musharraf of Lt General Ahmad of ISI on 7 October 2002 may have been connected to the timing of Pearl's abduction. By 2007, perhaps, the makers of the movie were likely aware that Khalid Sheik Mohammed had also confessed to the murder, following extensive water-boarding (although many well-placed sources doubted KSM's confession; see Mayer 2007), as apparently had at least one other Guantanamo detainee, while members of Lashkar-e-Jhangri were being arrested in connection with the crime as late as 2009.

Mariane Pearl criticizes *Wall Street Journal* foreign editor John Bussey (Denis O'Hare) for the newspaper's earlier decision to hand the CIA a computer containing details of 'shoe bomber' Richard Reid's alleged attempts to blow up an airliner, and then, by broadcasting this cooperation, indicating possible collusion between the newspaper and the CIA. Bussey says the *Journal* had no choice. He earlier informed Mariane that the CIA had publicly confirmed the *Journal*'s assurances that Pearl worked neither for government nor the CIA. Within the movie there is a showing of Colin Powell's press statement intimating that the US government would not accede to the kidnappers' requests, and that detainees in Guantanamo were being treated humanely. This suggests that the kidnappers were bargaining for the release of at least some Guantanamo detainees in return for their release of Pearl, that the US government did not want to negotiate and had anyway protested that its methods of detention were humane, despite evidence of severe abuse and murder of detainees, including torture by CIA interrogators – including of Khalid Sheik Mohammed, who was water-boarded 183 times, according to details from a 2005 Justice Department legal memorandum, published by the *New York Times* in 2009 (Shane, 2009).

Charlie Wilson's War (2007), directed by Mike Nichols, is fairly faithful to the triumphal George Crile narrative on which it is based. Both lionize the efforts of congressional Democrat Charlie Wilson (Tom Hanks), his career already in jeopardy, to secure the resources that Afghanistan *mujahideen* need to oust the occupying Soviet army of the 1980s. Wilson manoeuvres a significant increase of congressional funding, and secures Stinger missile launchers. The accomplishment requires unlikely alliances. These include President (by virtue of military coup) Mummad Zia-ul-Haq of Pakistan – who a decade later might have earned the epithet 'fundamentalist' – and both Israeli and Egyptian intelligence (which provide weaponry donated to Egypt by the Soviets, so that the US is not seen to be directly implicated). Wilson depends on critical help from two people who loathe one another: Gust Avrakotos (Phillip Seymour Hoffman), a dirty-mouthed street-fighting renegade in charge of the CIA's Afghanistan desk who scorns the status presumptions of his patrician CIA bosses, and a sensuous, wealthy Texan widow with evangelical Christian tendencies – Joanne Herring (Julia Roberts). At the end of the movie (as in real life) Wilson's accomplishment is acknowledged in a highly unusual CIA award ceremony.

The narrative endorses the view that Soviet defeat by the *mujahedin*, and withdrawal in 1988, triggered the implosion of the Soviet Union in 1991. There is anxious soul-searching at the conclusion, when Wilson worries that US neglect of national reconstruction of Afghanistan is a wasted opportunity that may create future problems (with a subtle nod towards 9/11). This is disingenuous, to say the least. The movie does not speak to CIA involvement in the destabilization of Afghanistan designed, in part, to provoke Soviet intervention (Parenti, 2004); nor to the murderous, reactionary character of *mujahedin* warlords and their dependency on the opium trade; nor to the role of Islamic fundamentalism, nor to the CIA's attempts to 'weaponize' or bastardize Islam to imbue it with a militancy foreign to the Koran and inspire more intense hatred of the Soviets (Prados, 2002). It does not speak to the role of Pakistan's intelligence agency, ISI, in channelling arms to the *mujahedin* (nor its later support for the Taliban), nor to the role of Osama bin Laden and his ties to the CIA during this period (Gasper, 2001). It does not identify US strategic interests in Central Asian and Caspian sea oil, gas and minerals, nor the usefulness of Afghanistan for transit of both oil and gas from the Caspian to western-friendly (i.e. not Iranian, not Soviet) sea ports (Rozoff, 2009). In short, *Charlie Wilson's War* applies a simplistic narrative to complex historical events that continue to exercise disastrous blowback for the US. Arguably, the early 1980s CIA policy of caution – which this movie rubbishes – had merits, but the movie has no inclination to explore them. It is incurious, finally, about the scope for manoeuvre allowed the agency's head of the Afghanistan desk, or about the power of a wealthy Texan widow to sway the foreign policy of the most powerful nation of the world, a supposed democracy, from behind the scenes.

The narrative of Ridley Scott's *Body of Lies* (2008) unfolds within a wealth of iconic references to 'war on terror' discourse, including: 'Middle East' props (desert, dusty open-air markets, Muslim and Arab headwear), Arab terrorists, and covert US intelligence operations, without reference to a broader context and history of US–Arab relations. The threat of Jihadist terrorism is part of the natural order of things. The film commiserates with its Western heroes and justifies its one-sided focus with on-screen representations of fictional acts of terrorism in Sheffield, Manchester and Amsterdam. The CIA field agent Roger Ferris (Leonardo DiCaprio) and his handler Ed Hoffman (Russell Crowe) are quick-thinking, creative and heroic, aided by sophisticated technologies, including unmanned surveillance drones. With the principal exception of US ally and head of Jordanian General Intelligence Hani Salaam (Mark Strong), Arab characters and especially the main villain Al-Saleem (Alon Abutbul) – his base is conveniently located in favourite western bogeyman country, Syria – are a sleazy crowd. Ferris' local girlfriend, Aisha (Golshifteh Farahani), a non-Arab, Iranian, has nephews who prefer hamburgers to their mother's cooking. Hoffman sums it up: 'nobody likes the Middle East'.

The package of Middle Eastern terrorism comes complete with Al-Saleem's torture and planned video beheading of Ferris. The apparent disparity of resources between American intelligence and their enemy is casually discounted by Hoffman for whom terrorist 'cunning' (shades of Said's 'Orientalism') in evading western technology with Stone Age methods explains their strength (a meme that draws sustenance from the official but disputed narrative of 9/11, though undermined by an abundance of four-wheel drive vehicles at the terrorists' disposal). An (unintended?) negative representation of US policy and

CIA tactics is the 'false flag' operation conceived by Ferris, which nets the terrorist but takes the life of an innocent decoy. Ferris' plan is to set up a bogus terrorist group that will attract the attention of the CIA's real target (it does, but not as anticipated). A Jordanian architect, Omar Sadiki (Ali Suliman), is chosen, without his knowledge, to be leader of the bogus group: his profile might suggest he has terrorist connections. A covert CIA operative stages a 'terrorist' act on US property, Incirlik Air Base, in Turkey, supplying unclaimed local bodies as props. News of the 'attack' is fed to mainstream media who, playing to a script they have been fed by CIA sources, attribute it to a previously unknown terrorist group led by Omar Sadiki. As planned, the terrorist, Al-Saleem, contacts Sadiki.

Sitting uneasily between promoting the US 'war on terror' and being against it is Gavin Hood's *Rendition* (2007), which begins and ends with the (same) suicide bomb attack in North Africa. The perpetrator, Khalid (Moa Khouas), seeks to avenge the killing of his younger brother, killed in a prison run by Abasi Fawal (Yigol Naor). Fawal, a high-ranking army officer, US collaborator and aggressive interrogator, is the target. The movie invites sympathy not so much with Khalid, but with his girl friend Fatima (Zineb Oukach), Abasi's innocent daughter who dies in the explosion while trying to dissuade Khalid and save her father. CIA analyst Douglas Freeman (Jake Gyllenhaal), posted in the same country, participates in the interrogation of innocent 'rendered' suspect, Anwar El-Ibrahimi (Omar Metwally). Douglas determines that a confession extracted from Anwar is false, delivered under duress, and that Anwar is innocent. Against orders, Douglas arranges for Anwar's escape and leaks details to the press so as to pre-empt retaliatory action by CIA boss Corrine Whitman (Meryl Streep).

The movie essentially argues that bad things happen but that good people in the US, supported by First Amendment rights and a fearless press, put them right. The movie is critical of the 'war on terror', not by contesting its basic premises, but because it finds rendition and torture cruel, repugnant and counterproductive as torture extracts false information from an innocent victim. The CIA is incompetent because it has incorrectly and unjustly assumed that records of calls from a known terrorist to Anwar's cell phone are sufficient grounds for suspecting Anwar of terrorist collaboration, and is unreasonably uncompromising in error, since Whitman is unmoved by the pleas of Anwar's pregnant wife, Isabella (Reese Witherspoon). The film invites compassion for an innocent man unjustly accused, rather than anger at rendition and torture that are illegal and cruel in and of themselves, regardless of the guilt or innocence of victims. In further concession to US sensibilities, Anwar is a handsome middle-class professional, married to an American wife who is also pregnant. The presumption that a leak to the press will ensure Anwar's safety is a fairy-tale whose origin is complacent mythologizing about Watergate. This bears no relationship to contemporary reality in which corporate US media have responded with timidity to the degradation of US respect for national and international law and human rights. More apt would be the response of CIA agent J. Higgins (Cliff Robertson) to Joseph Turner (Robert Redford) at the end of *Three Days of the Condor* (1975), 'How do you know they will print it?'

Nothing But the Truth (2008), written and directed by Rod Lurie, exemplifies a Hollywood thriller constructed to resonate with recent events, which it fictionalizes in a manner that is significantly if not diametrically at variance with the original events. A reporter, Rachel Armstrong (Kate Beckinsale), has learned (from the neighbour's own child) that neighbour Erica Van Doren (Vera Farmiga) is the CIA agent who provided evidence that the White House launched an illegal war against Venezuela on the bogus pretext that Venezuela had planned to assassinate the President (a highly unlikely fantasy that would have resonated well with White House anti-Chavez propaganda). Armstrong persuades a disaffected ex-staffer from the White House to confirm that Van Doren is indeed a CIA agent. Armstrong, who works for a high-prestige publication such as the *Washington Post* or *New York Times* (and whose African-American female editor might seem a sop to 'liberal media' fantasies) writes her story. This prompts the establishment of a leak investigation and the appointment of a special prosecutor whose name is 'Pat' Dubois (Matt Dillon), to be confused, of course, with Pat Fitzgerald of the Judith Miller case.

Dubois is unreasonably overbearing in making life acutely uncomfortable for Armstrong, having no qualms about sending her to jail if she fails to reveal her sources. She remains silent. Her marriage disintegrates. She decides against having her young son visit her in prison as she believes that it is not good for him (dubious this, but a narrative tear-wrencher). She has a friend in her legal representative (Alan Alda) but he gets nowhere. In the meantime, Van Doren is abandoned by the CIA and later assassinated by a crazed, right-wing gunman. The Armstrong case goes to the Supreme Court. Armstrong's lawyer weaves a fine but fruitless argument: if reporters are forced to disclose their sources, no-one will risk talking to the press, and it will be impossible to hold powerful wrong-doers to account. He offers as an example a soldier who has condoned torture (an allusion that might have been extended, in angrier hands, to a vice-president, Director of the CIA, or a national security adviser). The Supreme Court finds in favour of the prosecution. The original judge says he will now release Armstrong. The point of holding her was to force her to reveal her sources, he says, and since she is manifestly not going to do that, nothing is served by continuing to hold her. But Dubois hauls Armstrong back to court. Even though she is presented with waivers from all White House staffers – 'just in case' – she refuses to reveal the source, arguing that such waivers were doubtless, in effect, 'coerced', not even relenting when the actual ex-administration source goes on record in court as having been the source. The prosecutor then charges that because it was Armstrong who had asked the source to confirm the identity of the CIA agent, then the reporter clearly knew from some other source, beforehand, and therefore someone else had illegally leaked the information. But Armstrong is not going to endanger Van Doren's young daughter. So she is sentenced to two years in jail, and has already spent a year in custody.

How totally different is all this from the Judith Miller saga that had supposedly 'inspired' the movie (see Boyd-Barrett, 2004 and 2010 for fuller accounts)? Why did the director and writer Rod Lurie not make a movie about the actual Judith Miller story or one that ran exactly parallel to it (see *Fair Game* below)? Miller the reporter and her paper were arguably the villains: instead of doing their job to expose as bogus the administration's pretexts for an illegal invasion and occupation of a sovereign country, they created the case for war using anonymous and bad sources (Boyd-Barrett, 2004, 2010). Miller was hauled to court not because she herself had published information about a CIA agent (Valerie Plame) but because she was believed to have information related to the leak inquiry. Miller refused to testify most likely because she was protecting a source (Lewis Libbey), one who had already given her a waiver. Libbey was found guilty of a crime, possibly instigated by a more senior authority in the White House whose purpose was to humiliate an opponent, the husband of Valerie Plame and ex-ambassador Joseph Wilson. Wilson had exposed as false the administration's 'evidence' of Iraq's purchase of 'Yellow Cake' as a pretext for war. Miller spent 83 days in jail. She did not have a young child nor, as far as we are aware, did she have any children, and was married to a man well into his seventies. The special prosecutor, Pat Fitzgerald, far from being a vengeful establishment figure was arguably a popular hero (although see Peter Lance, 2009, for a different view, in relation to previous cases in which Fitzgerald was involved), one of the few people in a position of power who could and did try, in some limited way, to hold the administration accountable for war crimes as well as for crimes of a lesser magnitude. Valerie Plame's cover was blown, but she was not assassinated, and to all accounts her (not inconsiderable) suffering was mainly limited to the ending of an otherwise promising and purposeful career.

We should note in passing that the defects of this account are in part compensated for by the 2010 Doug Liman drama-documentary, *Fair Game*, based on separate books written by Valerie Plame (Wilson, 2007) and by her husband, Ambassador Joseph Wilson (2004), who are played, in the movie, by Naomi Watts and Sean Penn. The CIA is depicted through a conventional, patriotic, heroic lens that lends unquestioning and naive support to the administration's dubious 'war on terror' discourse. The film barely touches the trial of Scooter Libby, nor the role in this trial and in the original build-up towards the 2003 invasion and occupation of Iraq, of (then) *New York Times* correspondent

Judith Miller. Miller herself has been critical of the movie (Miller, 2010), and Doug Liman has made a fulsome response to her criticisms (Liman, 2010).

Both Roman Polanski's *The Ghost Writer* (2009) and Paul Greengrass' *Green Zone* (2010) represent fictional attempts to represent profoundly important contemporary political crises (rendition in the first film; the false pretexts given for the US invasion and occupation of Iraq, in the second), with many references, direct and indirect, to historical persons and events, and the CIA is central to both. In the first, a ghost writer (unnamed, played by Ewan McGregor) is hired to complete the memoirs of British Prime Minister Adam Lang (Pierce Brosnan). Lang is accused by a cabinet minister of supporting rendition and may be charged by the International Criminal Court. The ghost writer stumbles upon evidence that Lang's wife, Ruth (Olivia Williams), was originally 'planted' into his life by the CIA with a view to directing his political career and influencing his decisions to ensure a good fit with US foreign policy (comparable methods have been used by intelligence services; see Raffy 2004). The ghost writer's predecessor had been assassinated by the CIA to stall the investigation, and although he has better success in eluding his CIA pursuers for a time, he meets with a fatal car 'accident' before he has time to broadcast his discovery.

The film has the merit of calling attention to what for many Britons is the mysterious tie that seems to require UK complicity with all major US foreign-policy objectives no matter how repugnant, and throws out a potential clue, not so unreasonably, in the general direction of the intelligence services and how these may serve to coalesce the policies of both countries' respective 'secret governments'. On the downside, the film targets the lesser crime of rendition (bad enough) rather than the greater crime of complicity in an illegal war. Lang's personal attempt to explain his actions in terms of being tough on terrorism is as illogical and superficial as it was perhaps intended to sound.

Green Zone (2010) represents a classic 'limited hangout' rewrite of history, perhaps intended to soften the blow from an increasingly indefensible and murderous US policy of invasion and occupation to US prestige and credibility, for both domestic and foreign consumption. Chief Warrant Officer Ray Miller (Matt Damon) is searching unsuccessfully for WMD in post-invasion Iraq and realizes that official intelligence is highly suspect. His superiors do not want to know. Only local CIA representative Martin Brown (Brendon Gleeson) seems interested in the truth. Miller finds himself up against Pentagon Special Intelligence in the form of Clark Poundstone (Greg Kinnear), whom it is easy to mistake, both in the film and in real life, for Paul Bremer, who was head of the Coalition Provisional Authority at the time of the disbandment of the Iraqi army. Both Miller and Poundstone are on the hunt for ex Baathist General Al-Rawi. Miller's motivation is at first to track down someone he calculates will head up the Baathist underground resistance, but later realizes that Poundstone wants to kill Al-Rawi because it was Al-Rawi, as Poundstone's inside source of

Baathist intelligence, who informed him there were no WMD left in Saddam Hussein's arsenal. Poundstone, wanting an invasion, had lied to his superiors, telling them that there were indeed WMD and attributing this information to a fictitious source, 'Magellan', and passing on the 'Magellan' revelations to gullible *Wall Street Journal* correspondent Lawrie Dayne (Amy Ryan). Miller confronts Poundstone with the truth. While Poundstone is untouchable, he comes to realize the futility of the policy of invasion and occupation.

The movie is complicit with power in several ways; we will mention four. It places the blame for the exploitation of lies about WMD as a pretext for an illegal invasion and occupation on the shoulders of a mid-ranking intelligence operative, at a time when it had been already been beyond reasonable dispute for several years before production of this film, that the architects for this policy and for the fabrication or manipulation of intelligence resided in the White House, Department of Defense, State Department and CIA. Second, the movie presents the CIA as passionately interested in the truth, whereas it was George Tenet, as CIA Director, who lent his support and physical presence to the half-truths, deceptions and showmanship of Secretary of State Colin Powell's 'WMD' address to the UN Security Council in February 2003. Yes, there were voices within the CIA and in other agencies that were sceptical of these narratives. But such voices were drowned out – and this is the third level of deception – by a US media cacophony favouring White House war policy, stirred up in particular by *New York Times* correspondent, Judith Miller and by her newspaper. *Green Zone* not only attributes the Miller-role to the *Wall Street Journal*, but presents her as naive and timid, which Judith Miller certainly was not (see Boyd-Barrett, 2004). While the movie is therefore critical of the media, its criticism is at the level of naivety or stupidity, not complicity, and leaves the audience to presume that once Chief Warrant Officer Ray Miller (a strange confusion of names to provoke a misleading audience sensation of recognition?) gets the truth to the news agencies, the world will be put to rights, a highly unlikely presumption. Fourth, although US media eventually became more critical of US policy in Iraq, this happened too late to prevent the worst damage and did not hold the powerful to account for war crimes. Late conversion to a 'terrible mistake' script obscures the ways in which the policy has actually been 'good' for corporate America, notably in re-opening Iraqi oil fields to western oil companies (mainly) who had been shut out of the country by Saddam Hussein's policies of nationalization.

Conclusion

Our survey of 'CIA movies' has indicated various ways in which the genre appears to work ideologically in favour of US foreign policy and empire. The single most consistent way in which this work occurs is through the 'normalization' of espionage and covert operations, sometimes through portrayals that appear quite faithful to known techniques of 'spycraft' despite the clear conflicts of interest these also pose to the maintenance of democratic governance. The agency's 'enemies' are generally those of the US, past or present. Frequently, movies re-write established histories so as to whitewash or reconstruct the work of the agency or its operatives. On the other hand, we also find evidence of significant elements of critique, sometimes robust, in the midst of complex narrative: critique of the CIA as an institution, of particular CIA characters, or of the foreign policies, elite or corporate interests that they serve. Movies often target one or even two of these three possible foci, which are then redeemed by positive portrayal of the second or third: the virtues of a young CIA protagonist frequently compensate for the corruption of his bosses or institution. We can also argue that Hollywood provides 'dialogue' within a cluster of movies that deal with similar issues or themes (e.g. both *Nothing But the Truth* and *Fair Game*). But even the most critical movies see the world through the lenses of western, and usually US, eyes, and indulge an exaggerated confidence in the willingness of the US press to expose wrongdoing and hold the powerful to account.

References

Blum, W. (2005) *Rogue state: A guide to the world's only superpower*, 3rd edition. Monroe, ME: Common Courage Press.

Boyd-Barrett, O., Herrera, D. and Baumann, J. (2011) *Hollywood and the CIA: Cinema, Defense and Subversion*. London: Routledge.

Boyd-Barrett, O. (2004) Judith Miller, the *New York Times*, and the propaganda model, *Journalism Studies* 5(4): 435–449.

Boyd-Barrett, O. (2006*) Communications media, globalization and empire*. London: John Libbey.

Boyd-Barrett, O. (2010) Recovering agency for the propaganda model: The implications for reporting war and peace' in R. Keeble (ed.) *Peace Journalism, War and Conflict Resolution*. London: Peter Lang, 31–48.

Curtis, A (2007) *The century of the self*. Transmitted 29 April–2 May. London: BBC.

Gasper, P. (2001) Afghanistan, the CIA, bin Laden, and the Taliban. *International Socialist Review*, Nov.–Dec.: 2–9.

Griffin, D., Ray, D. and Falk, R. (2004) *The new Pearl Harbor: Disturbing questions about the Bush Administration and 9/11*. New York: Olive Branch Press

Johnson, C. (2004) *Blowback: The costs and consequences of American Empire*, 2nd edition. New York: Holt Paperbacks.

Lance, P. (2009) *Triple cross: How Bin Laden's master spy penetrated the CIA, the Green Berets and the FBI.* London: Harpers.

Liman, D. (2010) *Fair Game* director Doug Liman responds to Judith Miller, *Columbia Journalism Review*, 14 December

Mayer, J. (2007) The black sites: A rare look inside the CIA's secret internment program, *New Yorker*, 13 August.

Miller, J. (2010) The Plame affair, Hollywood style, *Wall Street Journal*, 9 December.

Parenti, M. (2004) *The terrorism trap, September 11 and beyond.* San Francisco: City Lights.

Prados, J. (2002) Notes on the CIA's secret war in Afghanistan. *Journal of American History* 89(2): 466–471.

Raffy, S. (2004) *Castro el desleal.* Madrid: Aguilar.

Rozoff, R. (2009) Afghanistan: Training ground for war on Russia, Global Research, www.globalresearch.ca/index.php?context=va&aid=14538 (accessed 18 March 2011).

Shane, S. (2009) Waterboarding used 266 times on 2, *New York Times*, 19 April.

Wilson, J. (2004) *The politics of truth: Inside the lies that put the White House on trial and betrayed my wife's identity.* New York: Carroll & Graf.

Wilson, V. P. (2007) *Fair game: My life as a spy, my betrayal by the White House.* New York: Simon & Schuster.

8

TERROR, CULTURE AND ANTI-MUSLIM RACISM

Gholam Khiabany and Milly Williamson

The 'war on terror' has had a profound impact on social relations, government policy towards minorities, and discourses of race and religion. Writing about how the 'war on terror' has shaped debates about multiculturalism, Gholam Khiabany and Milly Williamson examine how in Britain, Islam has been redefined in cultural terms – a binary of 'us' vs. 'them' – within the mainstream media as well as in the realm of state policy. The chapter explores how the perceived threat from global jihad has been used to circumscribe the civil rights of British Muslims, who face a high degree of discrimination and, in many instances, demonization in the media, and not just within its right-wing, as Islamophobia cuts across the political spectrum.

This chapter examines the use of 'culture' to frame and legitimize state terror and violence, both in the West and elsewhere – most obviously Iraq and Afghanistan. In particular it examines how the religion of Islam has been redefined in cultural terms in the media and in government circles and highlights how imperialist interventions are justified in the name of culture (the idea of 'our' culture versus 'theirs'). It also explores how the perceived threat from abroad is used to terrorize people of that 'culture' (Islam) at home (in Britain), examines the prominent role that security has been given in the context of the neoliberal restructuring of public life and reflects on how this process of culturalization naturalizes anti-Muslim racism in Britain. In short this chapter sets out to look at the culturalization of acts of violence and the subsequent de-contexualization of the 'war on terror'.

The Culturalization of Terror

In Britain, the 'debate' about Islam is rarely out of the headlines. Elizabeth Poole has identified the huge increase in articles about Muslims in the British press since 9/11. The tone of the reportage is one which emphasizes Muslim difference from the 'host' culture and, as Poole suggests, this is linked to the concerns of powerful groups in society (Poole, 2002: 81). Such is the inflammatory character of the press coverage of Islam in the UK that the Press Complaints Commission has received record numbers of complaints in the last ten years about articles that equated Islam with barbaric practices (Petley, 2006). The British tabloid press have been at the forefront of anti-Muslim journalism. Trevor Kavanagh, the former political editor of the best-selling British tabloid paper *The Sun*, regularly used his column to link Islam to violence and backwardness. For example, in an article entitled 'Beware the rise of Muslim hardliners', Kavanagh opined:

> THOUSANDS of vicious thugs are on the streets when they should be in jail. Gun crime is out of control. Ministers want to cut prison numbers because, embarrassingly, they are Europe's biggest. But that's because we have the highest crime rate in Europe, too. That is not embarrassing – it's humiliating. CAN you imagine women walking the streets of Britain wearing Taliban-style burkas? The stoning of adulterous wives? The amputation of limbs for theft? Of course not. It would be barbarous and unthinkable. Yet a new poll shows four out of ten British Muslims now favour strict Sharia law for their communities. The religious law can be interpreted liberally or harshly, but the mood of the Muslim community across Europe is already veering towards the harsh. (*Sun*, 20 February 2006)

This conflation of the rise in gun crimes and the increase in number of prisoners with Muslims, stoning and the burka is not accidental. The simplistic equation of Islam with barbaric practices is a key aspect of the culturalization of terror and violence. However, this is not confined to the journalism of the tabloid press, but spans the British media to include journalism from the liberal media and 'respectable' broadsheet press. The line of argument found in the broadsheets is based around 'blame discourse', according to which 'Muslims are to blame for their discrimination and deprivation through their own antiquated practices' (Poole, 2002: 81). One prominent voice has been that of Polly Toynbee, columnist for the liberal *Guardian* newspaper. Toynbee regularly uses the language of feminism to construct Islam in binary opposition to Western secular values and human rights. For instance, in an article following 9/11, Toynbee exclaimed:

> Islamophobia! No such thing. Primitive Middle Eastern religions
> (and most others) are much the same – Islam, Christianity and
> Judaism all define themselves through disgust for women's bod-
> ies...Religions that thrive are pliable, morphing to suit chang-
> ing needs: most Christianity has had to moderate to modernise.
> Islamic fundamentalism flourishes because it too suits modern
> needs very well in a developing world seeking an identity to defy
> the all-engulfing West. And the burka and chador are its battle
> flags. (*Guardian*, 28 September 2001)

Arun Kundnani (2008) has pointed out that it is not just the conservative
and neoconservative wing of politics that sets Islam in opposition to the West.
Kundnani identifies the above style of reportage as belonging to a new 'aggressive liberalism' which has clear differences from the neoconservative view of
Islam as inherently backwards and violent. This new liberalism targets not Islam
per se as the problem, but 'Islamism' which is identified as a modern political
movement akin to totalitarianism. Kundnani suggests that, '[w]hereas the neo-
conservatives see Muslims *en masses* as inherently anti-modern, the new liberals
see individuals choosing the wrong kind of modern politics' (Kundnani, 2008:
42). This is less a 'clash of civilizations as a clash within civilizations between
extremist and moderates' (ibid: 42). This distinction enables new liberals to
refute charges of racism on the basis that they are attacking Islamism and not
Islam and 'extremists' rather than 'moderates' with the result that there is now
a broad Islamophobic consensus in the UK which spans the political spectrum.
In this new consensus, neoconservative and liberal approaches reinforce each
other and are often conflated.

In this climate many liberal intellectuals, with very little or no knowledge
of Islam, have been given space to express their views and offer their solutions
to this perceived crisis and threat. The views of the celebrated author Martin
Amis offer one particularly revealing example:

> What can we do to raise the price of them doing this? There's
> a definite urge – don't you have it? – to say, 'The Muslim com-
> munity will have to suffer until it gets its house in order.' What
> sort of suffering? Not letting them travel. Deportation – further
> down the road. Curtailing of freedoms. Strip searching people
> who look like they're from the Middle East or from Pakistan...
> Discriminatory stuff, until it hurts the whole community and
> they start getting tough with their children. They hate us for
> letting our children have sex and take drugs – well, they've got
> to stop their children killing people. It's a huge dereliction on
> their part. I suppose they justify it on the grounds that they have

suffered from state terrorism in the past, but I don't think that's wholly irrational. It's their own past they're pissed off about; their great decline. It's also masculinity, isn't it?' (*Times* Magazine, 9 September 2006)

Similar views have had wide airing in the British media. For instance, when the *Evening Standard* asked a number of prominent figures in London whether or not Islam is good for London, Rod Liddle (former editor of the BBC's *Today* programme) replied following the well-worn path in the British press which aligns Islam with barbarism:

> Islam is masochistic, homophobic and a totalitarian regime. It is a fascistic, bigoted and medieval religion. I have plenty of friends who are Muslims and I know other Muslims I don't get along with. I may be Islamophobic but I am not against the religion. As long as we're able to say what we think about Islam and Muslims without fear of censorship, being accused of racism or having our heads cut off then we're heading in the right direction. (*Evening Standard*, November 14, 2007)

These wildly self-contradictory, yet inflammatory comments overtly connect religion to derogatory stable cultural/racial attributes (masochistic, homophobic, fascistic, bigoted and medieval) while managing, with the mentioning of having heads cut off, to imply that 'we' are at threat from 'their' barbarity. In the same newspaper piece, even those commentators who responded positively to the question still played into the rhetoric of equating Islam with backwardness. For instance, while Professor Michael Burleigh thought Islam was good for London, he finished his statement having to 'agree with Mr. Liddle that Islam is masochistic and homophobic'.

The prevalence of an anti-Muslim consensus in the UK is such that the first female Muslim cabinet member, Conservative Baroness Sayeeda Warsi, delivered a high-profile speech at Leicester University on 19 January 2011 condemning the growing acceptability of anti-Muslim racism. Although there was some support for the views expressed in Warsi's lecture, including the *Telegraph*'s chief political commentator, Peter Oborne (2011), the most prominent responses were comments from Prime Minister David Cameron who reaffirmed Britain's commitment to fighting terrorism and who distanced the coalition government from Warsi's views. Also prominent were the comments from Conservative ex-cabinet minister Lord Tebbit in which he claims that the British did not discuss Islam before 'large numbers of Muslims came here to our country' and advised Warsi to take a 'period of silence' (Tebbit, 2011).

However, anti-Muslim racism predates immigration from Muslim-majority countries to the UK or the 'war on terror'. The image of Arabs and of

Muslim-majority countries as being backward, atavistic, barbaric and fanatical emerged several centuries ago in the context of imperialism and the coloniza- tion of the Middle East and North Africa by Western imperialist powers in order to justify their so-called 'civilizing mission'. But these ideas have been re-animated after 9/11 and Islam has been redefined in entirely cultural terms. There have been three important elements in this process. The first is the reduc- tion of diverse Muslim populations across the globe into a single homogenized Islam. What is generally presented under the banner of the 'Islamic world' actually ranges from Indonesia to Nigeria and Sudan, as well as to countries with large Muslim populations such as India and China. As Aziz Al-Azmeh has suggested, there are 'as many Islams as situations that sustain it' (1993: 1). So the perceived homogeneity of 'Muslimness' is created not by the real diver- sity of geography, history, politics, language and the broader contexts of mate- rial life found in this range, but by discursive practices which define a singular Islam. Rather than Muslims being an homogenized block that are hostile to democracy, tolerance, liberalism, individualism, and so on, Muslims in Britain, Europe and elsewhere are differentiated on a variety of criteria including ethnic and national origins, class and generation. While levels of religiosity and the range of political affiliations are as diverse as the population itself (Zubaida, 2003), this process of reducing diverse Muslim populations to a single set of characteristics has occurred in relation to British and European Muslims too.

The second element has been to redefine this homogenized version of Islam as a 'culture' and an ethnicity. It has been noted that terms such as 'Muslim culture' and 'Islamic' are now used in official welfare documentation as well as academic and journalistic articles as markers of identity and ethnicity (Alexander, 1998; Wilson, 2007). Amrit Wilson observes that populations that were once identified by language or region are now identified above all else by their religion (Wilson, 2007: 31). Anne-Marie Fortier suggests that there is a 'taxonomic shift in Britain, from "ethnic minorities" in the 1970s to "minority faith communities" today', which highlights 'beliefs, morals and values [as] the primary site for the marking of absolute difference' (2008: 5).

The third element is that a homogenized Islamic culture is set in opposition to another invention – Western culture and, in the UK, 'British culture' (despite the claim by Fryer (1984) that the idea of a unified British culture is a myth). The best-known formulation of this idea was offered by Samuel Huntington who, in his version of the realities of the post-Cold War era, located the main source of global conflicts in culture. In his *Clash of Civilizations* (Huntington, 1996) he asserted that the iron curtain of ideology had been replaced by the velvet curtain of culture. While the US policy of 'Shock and Awe' and the carpet bombing of Afghanistan and Iraq hardly can be called a 'velvet curtain of culture', Huntington and his enthusiastic followers are not alone in this exaggerated assumption of cultural essentialism as this notion has, as we have already seen, been taken up by politicians and journalists across the political spectrum. The result has been the definition of societies and communities in terms of some deeply embedded cultural ethos and the counter-posing of a supposed rational Occidental culture against a rigid, stagnant Oriental culture and religion. That Huntington's next big project (Huntington, 2004) turned to the impact of immigrants in the United States, and specifically Hispanic communities, was an indication of his actual concerns.

Concerns about demographic changes in Europe and the US have often been expressed in scaremongering language in the media. A recent article in *The Economist* (2011) warns that Europe is in danger of becoming 'Eurabia' due to a projected 'surge' in the Muslim population. The article draws on recent research from the Pew Research Centre to claim that the world Muslim population will 'soar' by three per cent in the next 20 years. The article is ostensibly about the growth of the Muslim population across the globe; however, it pays particular attention to the Muslim population and its perceived cultural characteristics in Europe: 'Europe's Muslims should, by 2030, have become articulate and effective political bargainers. But with nativism on the march, it is also highly possible that Muslims will come to feel they have less in common with their fellow citizens than with their growing band of co-religionists elsewhere (*The Economist*, 2011).

The article strips European Muslims of their 'Europeaness' by stressing deep and unchangeable cultural traits (i.e. co-religionists) and by insisting that their cultural identification lies abroad. *The Economist* inverts European racism by claiming that Muslim 'nativism' is a block on integration.

It is important to note that in pointing at Muslims and Islam as the principal threat to what Huntington calls 'Western Civilization' he was, in fact, not pointing at Islam or Muslims in the Middle East and North Africa, but rather at large Muslim communities (of all nationalities and ethnicities) who are living in the 'West'. Muslims make up about two per cent of the European population dispersed in predominantly 17 European countries (Al-shahi and Lawless, 2003: 103). But not all Muslims in Europe are immigrants or 'foreigners'. A large number have become citizens through naturalization, marriage or other means. Many, second- or even third-generation, are European born and are European citizens. Hence what is presented in the press as an alien culture and a foreign threat is actually a European issue.

It is also significant that the national/ethnic composition of Muslims in different European countries is determined by the legacy of colonialism. It is no accident that the majority of Muslims in France are of Maghrebian (Algeria, Tunisia and Morocco) origin; in Germany they are predominantly of Turkish origin and in Britain of Indian, Pakistani and Bangladeshi origin. In the case of

Britain and France, the Muslim populations originate from countries which were part of the French and British Empires and recruited either as soldiers or labourers. Turkish workers began to arrive in Germany after the two countries signed labour accords in 1961 followed by similar treaties between Turkey and France, Belgium, Holland, and so on (Al-shahi and Lawless, 2003; Zubaida, 2003).

Diasporic Muslim communities, therefore, rather than being detached, free-floating (and essentialized) subjects outside of history, are marked by colonialism and imperialism. The economic downturn in the latter half of twentieth-century Europe has had an impact on levels of unemployment which has resulted in a rethinking of labour-exchange agreements with various countries of the global South. However, the Muslim residents of Europe were joined by new arrivals from the 1980s that began to migrate due to political violence and instability, and among those were Iranians, Lebanese, Iraqis, Turks, Somalis and Bangladeshis. In addition, family reunification, political prosecutions and the increased demand for workers employed in the domestic and cleaning sectors have meant a rapid increase in the numbers of women of MENA (Middle East and North Africa) origins in Europe. The politics of 'regime change' in Iraq and elsewhere has only added to number of refugees. None of these developments can be understood outside of the history of imperialism and colonial interventions, nor can the responses of European Muslims to these international events.

Another point to consider is that the Muslim population of Europe is very young and predominantly European born (Al-shahi and Lawless, 2003: 116). If, as is claimed by Amis and others, the problems of 'extremism' lie with 'Muslim youth' then this is a European population, not a foreign one. Rather than pointing to a 'foreign threat' or to the elders of 'foreign' Muslim communities in Europe, the question of the politicization of Muslim youth must be discussed in relation to the experiences of European Muslims in their countries of birth. Many come from poor and marginalized backgrounds (although living conditions and levels of citizenship vary), and many suffer racism as a direct result of politics of 'us' versus 'them'. As Alex Callinicos argues: 'In a familiar move in which the oppressors' categorization is taken up and turned against him by his targets, many British Asians have now adopted the label of Muslim as a basis of collective identity and political mobilization' (2008: 145–6). The attacks on so-called Islamic 'culture' serve to camouflage the desire by the government to drive Muslims, who have been 'goaded into self-assertion' (2008: 144), back into political silence and marginality. This does not seem to have worked given the large numbers of Muslim youth (along with others) who have become politicized in response to foreign and domestic policies in recent years.

Like Samuel Huntington, Francis Fukuyama was also disturbed by demographic changes within North America and Europe. Even when he began to distance himself from the disastrous invasion of Iraq, he argued that: 'Meeting the jihadist challenge is more of a "long, twilight struggle" whose core is not a military campaign but a political contest for the hearts and minds of ordinary Muslims around the world. As recent events in France and Denmark suggest, Europe will be a central battleground' (Fukuyama, 2006).

Needless to say, this 'contest for the hearts and minds' of Muslims in Europe is less a battle for 'soft power' than it is a codename for a wholehearted attack on civil liberties of ordinary citizens in Europe, Muslims or otherwise. The intention of neo-conservative writers and policymakers was always to silence these poor and marginalized communities who, naively assuming they were living in the land of economic plenty and liberal tolerance, demanded louder than before more 'civilized' treatment. The 'clash of civilizations' thesis was about them.

The culturalization of terror brushes aside, or seeks to naturalize, the terrorizing policies and acts of the so-called coalition in Afghanistan and Iraq and tries to obscure imperialist interests and interventions. Framing terror in terms of culture and cultural differences deflects attention from the broader socio-economic context of its production. In this formulation of terror, it is culture and not colonialism, imperialism, exploitation, inequality and injustice that takes centre stage. It becomes the all-encompassing, determining and sole signifier in the realm of public life.

Terrorizing Culture

Not only does this process of culturalization serve to justify imperialist wars abroad, it also terrorizes a section of the population in Britain by defining them as belonging to a culture of violence in opposition to 'British culture'. Defining 'them' as terrorists, either in the neo-conservative 'clash of civilizations' guise or the new liberal mode of opposing Islamism and then collapsing Islamism and Islam, serves to justify a more authoritarian state which potentially terrorizes the overwhelming majority of the population. Fear of cultural diversity and difference has long shaped policies and politics in the UK, as have celebrations of 'Britishness' (Barker: 1981). Since 9/11 both Labour and Conservative politicians have connected talk of 'terror' to that of 'culture'. For example, just as Tony Blair argued that the 'best defence of our security lies in the spread of our values' (Blair, 2004), Gordon Brown, his successor as Prime Minister, also insisted that 'the days of Britain having to apologise for our history are over. I think we should move forward. I think we should celebrate much of our past rather than apologise for it and we should talk, rightly so, about British values' (Brown, 2005).

In a similar vein, David Cameron, when he was Shadow Education Secretary, argued that 'we need to re-assert faith in our shared British values which might help guarantee stability, tolerance and civility' (Cameron, 2005). As part of his general programme which included tighter border controls, citizenship tests and monitoring of what is taught at Islamic schools, he suggested that the school curriculum should avoid 'politically correct' criticisms of empire:

> We need to be much more rigorous in ensuring that all children are taught to be proud of Britain, our history and our values. This doesn't mean just cherry picking proud achievements – such as Britain's role in ending slavery – any more than it should mean glossing over shameful episodes. But you don't have to be Colonel Blimp to worry about political correctness in the teaching of history. (Cameron, 2005)

Today the centre and right of the political spectrum have been joined by the liberal left in their nationalist condemnation of multiculturalism. Christopher Hitchens, well-known one-time radical of the 1968 generation, wrote an essay for *Vanity Fair* in 2007 entitled 'Londonistan calling' which contrasts British 'tolerance' with those extremists who would 'exploit' it. Fondly painting Britain as a 'country of warm beer and cricket', a country 'proud of their tradition of hospitality and asylum', Hitchens wondered how London had become 'a place of arms for exotic and morbid cults'. The culprit, according to Hitchens, is multiculturalism:

> For the British mainstream, multiculturalism has been the official civic religion for so long that any criticism of any minority group has become the equivalent of profanity. And Islamic extremists have long understood that they only need to suggest a racial bias – or a hint of the newly invented and meaningless term 'Islamophobia' – in order to make the British shuffle with embarrassment. (Hitchens, 2007)

It is hard to square this rather quaint description of the British state with Britain's imperial history; of the British invasion, colonization and partition of Ireland and India, or of the present-day incarceration in detention centres of asylum seekers and their often British-born children.

The consequence of this neo-conservative/liberal consensus on the alleged role of multiculturalism in enabling terrorism can be found in a configuration of the British state which curtails individual freedoms and potentially criminalizes those who refuse to 'assimilate'. While such views emanating from the right are no surprise, what is new is that those on the right have now found new allies on the centre and left of British politics. As Kundnani points out, it is now 'Muslims who are routinely singled out: it is their cultural difference which needs limits placed on it; it is they who must subsume their cultural heritage within "Britishness"; it is they who must declare their allegiance to (ill-defined) British values' (2007: 26). This is a significant shift away from the liberal view of multiculturalism which underpinned public policy for many years and which was expressed in the late 1960s by Roy Jenkins, then Home Secretary, as: 'equal opportunity accompanied by cultural diversity, in an atmosphere of mutual tolerance' (quoted in Lloyd, 2002).

Today liberal authors such as Martin Amis express views that, as we have already seen, are in harmony with the virulently anti-Muslim English Defence League (EDL). According to Amis:

> '[T]he only thing the Islamists like about modernity is modern weapons. And they're going to get better and better at that. They're also gaining on us demographically at a huge rate. A quarter of humanity now and by 2025 they'll be a third. Italy's down to 1.1 child per woman. We're just going to be outnumbered.' (Quoted in Dougary, 2006)

Contrast this statement with the thoughts of the EDL in its regular 'Jihad Watch' blog:

> The massive, catastrophic problem that is the presence of tens of millions of Muslims in Europe is finally dawning on the other citizens of that continent. Fitfully and unevenly, they are stirring themselves to find that they have invited a dangerous enemy into their home, who has no intention of leaving, or ceasing to act aggressively. (EDL, 2011)

Terry Eagleton (2007) and Ronan Bennett were lonely voices in condemning Amis. Bennett described Amis's views as 'symptomatic of a much wider and deeper hostility to Islam and intolerance of otherness' and claimed that Amis, 'got away with as odious an outburst of racist sentiment as any public figure has made in this country for a very long time. Shame on him for saying it, and shame on us for tolerating it' (Bennett, 2007). Liz Fekete (2004: 4) argues that the government's response to the notion that 'we' are in 'mortal danger' 'marks the first stage in Europe's assumption of a fundamentally different authoritarian paradigm of the state [that] …is based on a concept of national security that is shot through with 'xeno-racism''.

Muslims are the main target here; they are treated as the 'enemy within' and their very presence in Europe is now supposedly threatening European values, legitimizing the introduction of a raft of new legislation that curtails civil liberties and shifts attention on to the significance of security.

In the case of Britain it is crucial to remember that emergency measures to deal with terrorism are nothing new. Indeed such measures have been the norm for decades and 'temporary' or 'emergency' legislation has been eroding civil liberties for many years (Hillyard, 1993). As Mark McGovern and Angela Tobin (2010) have pointed out, we can trace British emergency legislation back to the nineteenth century which saw successive British governments introduce no less than 105 Coercion Acts in response to Irish political and agrarian agitation (2010: 16). When Ireland was partitioned in 1920, the government introduced the Restoration of Order Act (1920), followed by Civil Authorities act in 1922 (also known as Special Powers Act) which allowed for internment (arrest without charge and detention without trial) and gave the British state the power to ban associations and publications. This initially temporary act became permanent in 1933. The provisions of the Act were widely used after 1969, including the introduction of interment in 1971 which resulted in the detainment of 2000 people, predominantly Catholic/Nationalists, almost all of whom were later released without charge.

The first act containing the term 'terrorism' was the Prevention of Terrorism (Temporary Previsions) Act, introduced in 1974, which replaced the Special Powers Act. The Prevention of Terrorism Act was ostensibly a 'temporary' measure but was extended in 1984 with the excuse of meeting the challenge of the increasing prevalence of international terrorism in Britain. In fact both Acts became the basis for a whole range of current legislation and emergency measures to combat terrorism. They include the following:

- The Terrorism Act (2000) which allows for the disbanding of any organisation perceived of as 'terrorist'. Protestors at an arms trading fair in London were arrested under its provisions in 2003 (BBC 2003). This Act also extended stop and search powers and this was the first time that an act relating to the prevention of terrorism did not contain a 'sunset clause' requiring periodic review – that it is permanent from the outset.
- The Regulation of Investigatory Powers (2000) which allows for the surveillance of all kinds of communications devices.
- The Anti-terrorism and Security Act (2001) which allows for the indefinite detention of non-British nationals.
- The Criminal Justice Act (2003) which removed the statute ensuring that a person cannot be tried for the same crime twice.
- The Civil Contingencies Act (2004) which allows the government in an 'emergency' to deploy armed forces anywhere in the country.
- The Serious Organised Crime and Police Act (2005) which demands the advanced notification of protests up to 1 km away from parliament.
- The Prevention of Terrorism Act (2005) which permitted control orders to be imposed on suspects of terrorism. Breach of such order without valid justification is considered a criminal offence and meets a sentence of up to five years.
- The Terrorism Act (2006) created a number of new offences such as Acts Preparatory to Terrorism, Encouragement to Terrorism, Dissemination of Terrorist Publications and Terrorist Training Offences. It introduced warrants

to enable the police to search any property owned or controlled by a terrorist suspect, extended terrorism stop-and-search powers to cover bays and estuaries, extended police powers to detain suspects after arrest for up to 28 days, extended search powers at ports, increased flexibility of the proscription regime, including the power to proscribe groups that glorify terrorism. This is a major violation of human rights to liberty and personal security.

This brief look at the history of emergency legislation demonstrates that anti-terror policies in Britain predate 9/11, although without a doubt September 2001 was a watershed in this long history of demonizing communities and curtailing civil liberties. In this respect there are a number of interrelated issues about the role of the state in Britain that merit attention. First, as Fekete (2006) rightly suggests, it is precisely within this context that the shift away from multiculturalism and towards assimilation across Europe needs to be understood. In the drive towards assimilation and integration, racism is justified in terms of cultural 'values', and this in turn justifies an increasingly violent and authoritarian state. Cameron has recently made these links explicit in a speech attacking 'the doctrine of state multiculturalism'. It was no accident that Cameron chose the Munich International Security Conference as the venue to announce a significant shift in British state racial policy. Cameron was addressing the right-wing press at home and signalling his support for the European right when he adopted the language of Angela Merkel and the German Christian Democratic party which equates 'security' with mono-culturalism and assimilation. Liz Fekete (2011) points out that Cameron is indicating a shift in counter-terrorism policy which locates all Muslims and Muslim organizations on a 'spectrum of radicalisation' which includes any non-violent Muslim organizations that oppose government policy.

The second concern relates to the way in which the state has tried to find a focal point by invoking a 'proud' and glorious past in order to stir up nationalist sentiments and to provide a new basis for the social legitimacy of the state. As the economic crisis, drastic cuts on public spending and the increasing gap between rich and poor eat away at the existing legitimacy of the state, the image of a 'great nation under threat' has been nurtured in the media in order to attach the public to a new authoritarian state, in part by providing an anti-Islamic 'common purpose'. Throughout British history various communities have served this function; Muslims are the latest embodiment of such 'suspect' communities.

The treatment of terror suspects and their coverage in British media illustrates a high degree of discrimination and demonization as well as a selective interpretation of the law (Banakar, 2010; Kundnani, 2009). For instance, in 2007 the British government created the Office for Security and Counter-Terrorism Strategy (OSCT) as a new department in the Home Office as part of its counter-terror strategy. In making counter-terrorism one of the main priorities of the Home Office, OSCT established the Preventing Violent Extremism Pathfinder Fund in 2007 which, with a budget of £6 million, aimed at preventing extremism by winning the hearts and minds of Muslims. Within a year the budget of this programme had increased to £140 million. A significant part of the Prevent programme is to cultivate 'moderate Muslims' in order to isolate extremists, to promote a moderate version of Islam and to encourage 'shared values'. The use of public money to promote particular readings and interpretations of Islam is based on a false dichotomy which separates Muslims according to their degree of commitment to the British state. This battle for the 'hearts and minds' of Muslims as the political/cultural dimension of both 'shock and awe' and anti-terror legislation, not only 'conceives of Muslims as living in a moral universe that is separate from the rest of the population', as Kundnani argues (2009: 40), but also has the potential of not seeing Muslims as citizens to which the state is accountable and responsible.

Such an approach overstates the ideological struggle between different and competing versions of Islam and casts Muslims as an enemy of the state. According to Kundnani, '[t]his intentional dimension means that the attention focused on this "extremism" is of a completely different kind to that focused on, say, right-wing extremism, which is taken to be no more than a public order threat' (2009: 40). Two particular cases of right-wing extremists, Martyn Gilleard and Terrence Gavan, demonstrate this. The home of Gilleard, a member of the National Front and the White Nationalist Party, was initially searched for child pornography in 2008 but, in addition to 39,000 indecent images of children found, the police also found four homemade nail bombs, other weapons and racist literature. Gilleard was not under surveillance for terrorist activities, and he was not regarded as a threat to national security, and his case did not attract the attention of British media. The printed version of *The Times* did not even carry a report on this case on 25 June 2008 (Banakar, 2010). In the case of Terrence Gavan, the police found 12 firearms, 54 explosive devises plus a large number of bomb making manuals and literature in his home in Yorkshire. Gavan was a member of the neo-fascist British National Party but his case was not regarded by the police or the judge as an ideological threat. This case also failed to attract much media attention. Banakar argues that a comparison of the cases of Gilleard and Gavan with the way that Muslim suspects are treated and widely reported upon 'gives further support to the thesis regarding the symbolic effects of the UK's anti-terrorism policy and legislation … [and] suggest[s] that anti-terrorism laws operate in a racially selective fashion' (Banakar, 2010: 210).

There are obvious contradictions in the functions of the neo-liberal state. For despite the theoretical commitment to the downsizing of the state and proposals in favour of a 'small state' and 'big society', it is clear that European states in general, and the British state in particular, are increasingly using their coercive powers not to monitor the power of capital but to punish those who have suffered most from it. Strong support for individual property rights in neo-liberal states has gone hand in hand with suppressing the individual freedom of citizens. The privatization of public assets has happened at the expense of collective rights and of collective forms of association and protest; the withdrawal of the state from public concerns such as health, education, jobs, pensions and welfare has been replaced with more aggressive policing and elevating security (nationally and internationally) as the most significant role of the state. In short, the emphasis on a more 'liberal' economy has led to very 'illiberal' politics.

Although it is Muslims who are at the forefront of these attacks, they are attacks to which we all must respond because these are attacks on our liberties way beyond 'Muslimness'. The government has used the culturalization of Islam and its perceived opposition to Western liberty to attack those liberties. The atmosphere is one of a permanent state of emergency; for this is a war with no clear enemy in a conventional sense or a clear boundary. This ambiguity allows for powerful states to become garrison states, to declare anyone the enemy, any space the battlefield and any attack justified. This is a war with no end. A 'war on terror' that is defined in terms of culture is not about preserving our 'way of life' but instead becomes a 'way of life'. This is what we mean by terrorizing culture and both this 'way of life' and the racism upon which it rests must be opposed.

References

Abbas, T. (ed.) (2005) *Muslim Britain: Communities under Pressure*. London: Zed Books.

Ahmad, A. (2008) Islam, Islamisms and the West, in L. Panitch and C. Leys (eds) *Global Flashpoints: Reactions to Imperialism and Neoliberalism*. New York: Monthly Review Press.

Al-Azmeh, A. (1993) *Islams and Modernities*. London: Verso.

Al-Azmeh, A. (2007) Afterward in A. Al-Azmeh and E. Fokas (eds) *Islam in Europe: Diversities, Identities and Influence*. Cambridge: Cambridge University Press.

Alexander, C. (1998) Re-imagining the Muslim community, *Innovation* 11(4): 439–450.

Allievi, S. (2003) Islam in the public space: social networks, media and neo-communities, in S. Allieve and J. S. Nielsen (eds) *Muslim Networks and Transnational Communities in and across Europe*. Boston, MA: Brill.

Al-shahi, A. and Lawless, R. (2003) Introduction, *Immigrants & Minorities* 22(2/3): 99–126.

Anwar, M. (2005) Muslims in Britain: issues, policy, practice, in T. Abbas (ed.) *Muslim Britain: Communities under Pressure*. London: Zed Books.

Banakar, R. (2010) Pre-empting terrorism? Two case studies of the UK's anti-terrorism legislation, in R. Banakar (ed.) *Rights in Context: Law and Justice in Late Modern Society*. London: Ashgate.

Barker, M (1981) *The New Racism: Conservatives and the Ideology of the Tribe*. London: Junction Books.

Baxter, K. (2006) From migrants to citizens: Muslims in Britain 1950s–1990s. *Immigrants & Minorities* 24(2): 164–192.

BBC (2003) Legal challenge to arms fair policing, BBC News, 10 September. Available at: http://news.bbc.co.uk/1/hi/england/london/3093412.stm (accessed 1 March 2011).

Bennett, R. (2007) Shame on us, *Guardian*, 19 November. Available at: www.guardian.co.uk/uk/2007/nov/19/race.bookscomment (accessed 1 March 2011).

Blair, T. (2004) Full text: Tony Blair's speech, 5 March. Available at: www.guardian.co.uk/politics/2004/mar/05/iraq.iraq (accessed 2 February 2011).

Brown, G. (2005) Brown seeks out 'British values', 14 March, BBC News. Available at: http://news.bbc.co.uk/1/hi/programmes/newsnight/4347369.stm (accessed 1 March 2011).

Callinicos, A. (2008) Marxists, Muslims and religion: Anglo-French attitudes, *Historical Materialism* 16: 143–166.

Cameron, D. (2005) Full text: Cameron's speech, *Guardian*, 24 August. Available at: www.guardian.co.uk/politics/2005/aug/24/conservatives.faith schools (accessed 1 March 2011).

Cesari, J. (2007) Muslim identities in Europe: the snare of exceptionalism, in A. Al-Azmeh and E. Fokas (eds) *Islam in Europe: Diversities, Identities and Influence*. Cambridge: Cambridge University Press.

Dirlik, A. (2004) Intimate others: [private] nations and diaspora in an age of globalization, *Inter-Asia Cultural Studies* 5(3): 491–502.

Dougary, G. (2006) The voice of experience, *The Times*, 9 September.

Eagleton, T. (2007) *Ideology: An Introduction*, 2nd edition, London: Verso.

Economist, The (2011) A waxing crescent, 27 January. Available at: www.economist.com/node/18008022 (accessed 14 March 2011).

English Defence League (EDL) (2011) The new Muslim conquistadors, 25 January. Available at: http://theenglishdefenceleagueextra.blogspot.com/2011/01/new-muslim-conquistadors.html (accessed 1 March 2011).

Fekete, L. (2004) Anti-Muslim racism and the European security state, *Race & Class* 46(1): 3–29.

Fekete, L. (2006) Enlightened fundamentalism? Immigration, feminism and the right, *Race & Class* 48(2): 1–22.

Fekete, L. (2011) Cameron's Munich speech marks securitisation of race policy, Available at: www.irr.org.uk/2011/february/ha000009.html (accessed 14 March 2011).

Fortier, A. M. (2008) *Multicultural Horizons: Diversity and the Limits of the Civil Nation*. London: Routledge.

Fryer, P. (1984) *Staying Power: The History of Black People in Britain Since 1504*. London: Pluto.

Fukuyama, F. (2006) After Neoconservatism, *New York Times*, 19 February. Available at: www.nytimes.com/2006/02/19/magazine/neo.html?_r=1&pagewanted=all (accessed 18 February 2011).

Hillyard, P. (1993) *Suspect Community: People's Experience of the Prevention of Terrorism Acts in Britain*. London: Pluto.

Hitchens, C. (2007) Londonistan calling, *Vanity Fair*, June. Available at: www.vanityfair.com/politics/features/2007/06/hitchens200706?current (accessed 18 February 2011).

Huntington, S. (1996) *The Clash of Civilizations and the Remaking of World Order*. New York: Simon & Schuster.

Huntington, S. (2004) *Who are We? The Challenges to America's National Identity*. New York: Simon & Schuster.

Kundnani, A. (2007) *The End of Tolerance: Racism and the 21st Century*. London: Pluto.

Kundnani, K. (2008) Islamism and the roots of liberal rage, *Race and Class* 50(2): 40–68.

Kundnani, K. (2009) *Spooked! How not to Prevent Violent Extremism*. London: Institute of Race Relations.

Lloyd, J. (2002) The end of multiculturalism, *New Statesman*, 27 May. Available at: www.newstatesman.com/200205270012 (accessed 1 March 2011).

Martiniello, M. (2003) The state, the market and cultural diversity, *Immigrants & Minorities* 22(2/3): 127–140.

McGovern, M. and A. Tobin (2010) *Countering Terror or Counter Productive? Comparing Irish and British Muslim Experiences of Counter-insurgency Law and Policy*. Lancashire: Edge Hill University.

Oborne, P. (2011) Baroness Warsi was right to speak out: hatred of Muslims is one of the last bastions of British bigotry, *Daily Telegraph*, 20 January.

Peach, C. (2005) Muslims in the UK, in T. Abbas (ed.) *Muslim Britain: Communities under Pressure*. London: Zed Books.

Petley, J. (2006) Still no redress from the PCC, in E. Poole and J. E. Richardson (eds) *Muslims and the News Media*. London: I. B. Tauris.

Poole, E. (2002) *Reporting Islam: Media Representations of British Muslims.* London: I. B. Tauris.

Tebbit, N. (2011) Baroness Warsi should think twice before accusing Christians of bigotry. *Daily Telegraph* online, 20 January. Available at: http://blogs. telegraph.co.uk/news/normantebbit/100072696/baroness-warsi-should-think-twice-before-accusing-christians-of-bigotry/ (accessed 18 February 2011).

Wilson, A. (2007) The forced marriage debate and the British state, *Race & Class* 49(1): 25–38.

Zubaida, S. (2003) Islam in Europe, *Critical Quarterly* 45(1/2): 88–98

9

PICTURES AND PUBLIC RELATIONS IN THE ISRAELI–PALESTINIAN CONFLICT

Greg Philo

Mainstream representations of Muslims may arguably contribute to the way majority populations in countries such as Britain perceive 'distant' conflicts involving Muslim populations, as Greg Philo shows in this chapter. Based on research into British TV news coverage of the Israeli attack on Gaza in December 2008 and January 2009, Philo and his team demonstrate that preconceived notions about Palestinians and their perceived proclivity for violence is blamed for the crisis, while the Israeli position that it was reacting to Islamist terrorists, is normalized in Western media discourses – with a little help from a well-oiled public relations war machine from the Israeli side.

Can every picture tell a story? Yes, but what story it tells can often depend on who is telling us how to understand the picture. This chapter is based on new research that analysed TV news accounts of the Israeli attack on Gaza in December 2008 and January 2009 and examined audience understanding of these events using focus groups and questionnaire responses.[1]

In analysing news coverage, we identified key explanatory themes which underpinned the reporting of events. These themes were in effect the central explanations which underpinned how the conflict would be understood in terms of its origins, causes and the legitimacy of different parties within it. Such themes are of course contested and the main purpose of propaganda in such a conflict is to achieve dominance for particular ways of understanding.

The Israelis invested very heavily in public relations in the period before and during the attack on Gaza (see, for example, Shabi, 2009). The essence of the Israeli account was that they were forced to respond to unwarranted rocket attacks from Gaza by the Palestinian group Hamas. The motivations for the attacks were found in Islamic extremism and terrorism. Israel was part of the free world, while Hamas was not. In this perspective, the reasons for the conflict were not located in the military occupation of Palestinian territories by Israel from 1967 or the war in 1948 and the creation of the state of Israel. The Israeli account begins rather in 2005 with their pull-out from Gaza. Its argument is that the Palestinians, instead of building a new state, voted instead for Hamas and the conflict, because their primary interest is in killing Jews. From the perspective of Hamas and the Palestinians, the causes of the conflict were very different. Their narrative focused on the loss of homes and land to Israel, its military occupation of Palestinian land and the economic blockade on Gaza imposed by Israel.

Writing in the *Guardian*, Toni O'Loughlin (2008: 7) describes the development of the blockade: 'Having built a wall around Gaza before disengagement, Israel then imposed a progressively tighter blockade, by barring Gazan labourers from entering Israel in late 2005, then by banning Gazan commercial trade in 2006, and finally, in mid-2007, by squeezing humanitarian aid.'

The consequences on the living conditions of the people were dramatic. The Liberal Democratic MP Sarah Teather visited Gaza nine months before the Israeli attack. She spoke of her experiences on the BBC Radio 4 programme *Any Questions*:

> I was absolutely appalled by the conditions there, really terrible. The level of poverty is unimaginable. You see as you first go into Gaza, the area in the north of Gaza has been bombed to nothingness. It is wasteland and then as you drive into the city the first thing that hits you is the smell of sewage because it lies in raw lakes on the north side of the city and we went to visit peoples homes that are as good as slums. They are huts that people are crammed into and you cannot rebuild these homes (even though) the UN has the money to rebuild. Because of the siege on Gaza, Israel won't allow construction materials to go across the border (9 January 2009)

Israel regards Hamas as a terrorist group which has killed civilians through suicide bombing and rocket fire. These are clearly designated as war crimes. But many Palestinians regard Israel as state terrorists and a report by Amnesty International in the aftermath of the Gaza attack accused both sides of war crimes (Amnesty International, 2009)[2].

Israel, however, was able to use its dominance of international news media to legitimize its own actions by establishing a specific version of the history and sequences of events which led to the conflict. Chris McGreal, writing in the *Observer*, summarised the key elements of the Israeli position: 'In briefings in Jerusalem and London, Brussels and New York, the same core messages were repeated: that Israel had no choice but to attack in response to the barrage of Hamas rockets; that the coming attack would be on "the infrastructure of terror" in Gaza and the targets principally Hamas fighters; that civilians would die, but it was because Hamas hides its fighters and weapons factories among ordinary people' (McGreal, 2009: 2).

The message was promoted via the National Information Directorate of Israel, which was set up early in 2008. A key element in such a narrative is that Israel is consistently seen as 'responding' to attacks upon it which are initiated by the Palestinians. One side starts the trouble, the other 'responds'. In promoting this view, the Israelis had powerful allies in political figures who could command media coverage and reinforce the central message. For example on 3 January 2009, George Bush in the last days of his presidency intervened to press the Israeli case:

BBC Correspondent:	Israel says it's targeting the Islamist movement here. President Bush in his weekly radio address has blamed the Islamic movement for what has been happening in Gaza.
President Bush:	This recent outburst of violence was instigated by Hamas. A Palestinian group supported by Iran and Syria which calls for Israel's destruction. Eighteen months ago Hamas took over the Gaza strip in a coup and since then has imported thousands of guns and rockets and ordinance. (BBC1 early evening news, 3 January 2009)

And again on 5 January;

President Bush:	Hamas decided to use Gaza to launch rockets to kill innocent Israelis. Israel has obviously decided to protect herself and her people. (BBC1 main news, 5 January 2009)

It has been strongly argued that Hamas would have halted the rocket fire in exchange for the lifting of the blockade. Ephraim Halevy, the former head of the Mossad Intelligence Service stated in the Israeli press that the 'government in Jerusalem could have stopped the rocket attacks long ago by lifting its siege of

Gaza' (quoted in McGreal, 2009). But Israel's key interest was in undermining Hamas in favour of its rival Fatah, seen as a more amenable partner in negotiations. Hamas and the Palestinians of Gaza would also reject the view that it was they who broke the cease-fire. They point to an Israeli incursion in November 2008 in which six Palestinians were killed. Writing in the *Observer*, Chris McGreal notes that 'even during the cease-fire, Israel killed 22 people in Gaza, including 2 children and a woman' (2009: 4).

In practice, however, Israel was able to dominate the news agenda in the crucial area of how the origins and causes of the conflict were explained. This can be illustrated through quantitative analysis. The news bulletins which we examined were transcribed and the numbers which we give here relate to the lines of text on specific explanations. We can see on the BBC, for example, that the themes of 'ending the rockets', the 'need for security' and to 'stop the smuggling of weapons' received a total of 316.5 lines of text. Others, such as the need to 'hit Hamas' and that 'Hamas and terrorists are to blame', received 62 lines. The total for Israeli explanatory statements on the BBC is 421.25. This compares with a much lower total for Hamas/Palestinian explanations of just 126.25. There is another important point to make here which is that the bulk of the Palestinian accounts do not explain their case beyond saying that they will resist. They are mostly declamatory statements saying for example that 'Gaza is a graveyard for Israel' or that 'Israel will face a dark destiny' (68.5 lines). These may have a function in terms of rallying supporters but as we will see they do little to inform wider audiences about the nature of the conflict. Crucially, many of the core elements of the Palestinian rationale for their actions are very sparsely represented. There are just 14.5 lines referring to the occupation and only 10.5 on the ending of the siege/blockade. The same pattern occurs in ITV's coverage with over 302 lines relating to Israeli explanatory statements and just 78 for Hamas/Palestinians.

The importance of the Israeli dominance of such accounts is that key moments in the reporting of events are accompanied by a coherent statement which contextualizes and has the potential to legitimize Israeli action. We can see this by examining specific examples of news text. The opening lines of the BBC early evening news on the first day of the bombing contain a clear statement from Israel that the air strikes are 'in response' to missile attacks, while from Hamas we hear that they 'have vowed revenge':

Newscaster: Israeli war planes have carried out a wave of attacks on the Gaza strip in one of the bloodiest days of the conflict. Palestinian officials say more than 200 people have been killed in the raids. Israel says the air strikes were in response to missile attacks on its country and now is the time to fight. The targets were security compounds belonging to Hamas, the militant group that controls Gaza. They vowed revenge. (BBC1 early evening news, 27 December 2008)

The Israeli narrative is followed in other ways. In the example above, the targets are referred to as 'security compounds'. They are said to belong to Hamas, described as 'the militant group that controls Gaza'. This is the perspective of Israel and others who are critical of Hamas. It takes no account of the fact that Hamas won the Palestinian elections and in that sense had a degree of democratically given authority. The 'security compounds' described here were police stations, which in international law may be regarded as civilian. This is a point on which the *Guardian* commented at the time:

> The targets were not the training camps of Hamas's military wing, which were empty when the jets struck, but rather police stations. The raids were intended to destroy the infrastructure on which Hamas builds its administrative as much as its military hold over Gaza. But that means killing policemen not just the militants who assemble and fire the rockets. Presumably it also means targeting judges, officials, and doctors too. (*Guardian*, 2008)

The BBC news, however, classes the targets as military. After referring to a police station, it states 'there were civilian casualties too' and says there were homes and families near to 'every military target':

> More than 100 tonnes of bombs were dropped, Israel said, on dozens of targets. This was one, a Gaza city police station. A badly injured man recites the Muslim prayer for those about to die. The Gaza police chief himself was also killed. There were many civilian casualties too including children. Gaza is one of the most crowded places on earth, every military target has homes and families close by. (BBC1 early evening news, 27 December 2008)

We found in our audience studies that some people drew a clear distinction between Hamas and the Palestinians and were unaware that Hamas had won the elections of 2006. This perspective was assumed in headlines and commentaries which presented the Israeli attack as being directed only at Hamas, and this is certainly how Israel wished it to be seen. Consider the following examples:

- 'The bombardment continues on Hamas targets' (BBC1 early evening news, headline 31 December 2008).
- 'The offensive against Hamas enters its second week' (BBC1 early evening news, 3 January 2009).
- 'Israeli ground forces enter Gaza in the second phase of their offensive against Hamas' (BBC1 late news, 03 January 2009).

- 'Israel said it will continue its assault on Gaza until Hamas puts down its rockets' (ITV early evening news, headline 28 December 2008).
- 'Israel shows no sign of letting up in its onslaught against Hamas' (ITV early evening news, 05 January 2009).

From the Palestinian side, it was argued that a key purpose of the Israeli action was to weaken support for Hamas. There were many who believed that to do so involved killing and terrorizing people in the civilian population.[3] But such a view was rarely expressed on the news. The dominant explanation for the attack was that it was to stop the firing of rockets by Hamas. The offer that Hamas was said to have made, to halt this is in exchange for lifting the blockade (which Israel had rejected), was almost completely absent from the coverage. So the news perpetuated a one-sided view of the causes of the conflict, by highlighting the issue of the rockets without reporting the Hamas offer and by missing the alternative Palestinian view on the purpose of the attack.

Explanations

What accounts for the lack of balance in this area of news? The key factors are: the power of Israeli public relations, the political and commercial links between Britain, the US and Israel, and how these are used to produce extremely effective lobbying. Mearsheimer and Walt (2008) have produced a major study of the Israeli lobby and its impact on US foreign policy. In 2009, the Channel 4 programme *Dispatches* also produced an extended account of the impact of pro-Israel lobbying on British political life and the media. It noted the close relationship between lobby groups and political parties in the Westminster Parliament:

> So how does the lobby work? Money plays a big part. Millions of pounds in donations from businessmen and others into the bank accounts of politicians and political parties. The Conservative Friends of Israel is one of Westminster's most active lobbying groups. It claims that its members include 80 per cent of all Conservative members of Parliament…Aside from raising cash some of the pro-Israeli lobbies in Parliament pay for and arrange trips to Israel. They have sent almost as many MPs and candidates on trips to Israel as have been made by all MPs to the United States and Europe combined over the last eight years ('Inside Britain's Israel Lobby', *Dispatches*, Channel 4, 16 November 2009).

Tony Blair, after being Prime Minister of the UK was appointed in 2007 as Middle East envoy in the search for peace. Yet his lack of neutrality is sometimes manifest. Consider this interview which was filmed during the Israeli attack on Gaza in January 2009. The ITN correspondent begins by stating:

Correspondent: Mr. Blair believes that the key to a ceasefire lies in stopping Hamas smuggling weapons through these tunnels into Gaza.

Blair then gives his very critical view of Hamas, noting how Gaza can be used as a base for directing rockets at civilians in Israel:

Tony Blair: Either Hamas agree to be part of the solution, or alternatively Hamas stay in Gaza, using Gaza as a base for operations, directing rockets at civilians in Israel, in which case they are not part of the solution, they are part of the problem.

He is then repeatedly asked if he will also condemn Israel's use of force on Gaza as 'disproportionate' to which he first replies:

Tony Blair: The most important thing for me to do as international community representative is to try and get this thing stopped.

And then:

Tony Blair: Look there is nothing that can take away the fact that when military action of this sort happens there are innocent civilians that suffer and the people of Gaza are suffering badly. The most important thing for me to do, rather than condemning one side or the other, is actually get the thing sorted and that's what I am trying to do. (ITV early evening news, 6 January 2009)

So when Hamas fires rockets and 13 Israelis are killed, they are part of the problem, but when Israel attacks Gaza and more than 1,000 Palestinians are killed, then this is the sort of 'thing' that happens when military action takes place. It can be seen that journalists who do try to feature both sides of the conflict are facing something of an uphill task. There is less to fear in criticizing the Palestinians, but to criticize Israel can create major problems and journalists have spoken to us of the extraordinary number of complaints which they receive. We have presented our findings to many groups of media practitioners. After one such meeting a senior editor from a major BBC news programme told us that 'we wait in fear for the phone call from the Israelis'. He then said that the main issues they would face were from how high up had the call come (e.g. a monitoring group or the Israeli embassy) and then how high up the BBC had the complaint gone (e.g. to the duty editor or the director general). He described how journalists had checked with him minutes before a programme was broadcast on which words to describe the conflict should now be used. On another occasion, the journalist and filmmaker John Pilger told us of the storm of criticism which followed the broadcast of his film *Palestine is Still the Issue* in 2002. The film was attacked by supporters of Israel and by Michael Green, the chairman of Carlton Television. At the time, Pilger wrote in the *Guardian*: 'What is disquieting is that Green had actually seen the film before it went to air and had not alerted the programme makers to his concerns, waiting until the Jewish Board of Deputies, the Conservative Friends of Israel and the Israeli embassy expressed their outrage' (Pilger, 2002).

He told us how he had received 20,000 emails and letters and that many of the most critical were sent to the governing body of Independent Television. Pilger had then to stop other projects and spend six weeks writing a defence of the programme. In this he was able to show that many of the critical emails had come from the US where the programme had not actually been shown. His work was cleared but the point here is that many journalists, when faced with such a climate, are likely to be cautious. The simplest approach is to avoid areas which will attract criticism. This does not mean that they will all be pro-Israeli, but there is a tendency, as we show here, to focus critical commentary in the areas where they are on the strongest ground such as the discussion of civilian casualties.

Civilian Casualties and Audience Response

The coverage of casualties was very extensive. On the BBC, there were just over 300 lines devoted to those of the Palestinians, and on ITV the figure was over 450. For the BBC this represents about five times the amount given to Israeli casualties and for ITV over seven times. But since the number killed on the Palestinian side was around 100 times that of the Israelis, the amount of coverage given is not proportional to the harm inflicted. In these terms it can be seen that there is a disproportionate representation of Israeli casualties. The news on both BBC and ITV explores extensively the effect of the rockets on Israeli civilians. But there is also a very intense and critical focus on the effects of Israel's attack on the population of Gaza. The issue of civilian casualties and their inevitability in such an operation is raised very early in the news. In this example a report on the killing of five sisters from a Palestinian family is followed by an Israeli claim about the avoidance of civilian casualties. This, however, is then effectively dismissed by the journalist, citing the UN:

> BBC Correspondent: Mourners braved Gaza's deadly streets to bury five sisters from [this] family. They were killed by an Israeli attack while they were sleeping last night. Israel talks about pinpoint strikes avoiding civilians, but the UN said this is what happens when massive force is used in Gaza's overcrowded densely packed refugee camps. (BBC1 early evening news, 29 December 2008).

The words 'terror' and 'horror' are used in headlines about Israeli actions:

Newscaster: Inside Gaza, an eyewitness account of the terror of the bomb-
               ings from the heart of the conflict. (ITV main news headline, 16
               January 2009)
Newscaster: Horror on the streets of Gaza. At least 40 people die as schools
               come under attack. The UN controlled buildings were shelter-
               ing civilians taking refuge from the Israeli assault. Tonight no
               sanctuaries in Gaza, dozens were killed in the very place they
               were supposed to find safety. (ITV early evening news headline,
               6 January 2009)

Journalists should of course highlight the dreadful effects of war against
civilians. But in this coverage as a whole, the images are presented without the
Palestinians' explanation of why this is happening. This is in large part because
of the pressure journalists experience in this area. There was almost nothing
in this news to explain the key issues to which the Palestinians object such as
the taking of land and water by Israel, extra-judicial killing, the curfews, economic control or mass arrests and imprisonment. In essence what is missing is
a perspective of people who have lost their homes and land and who are trying
to throw off the economic and military rule to which they are subject. It does
not take long to include such information but to do so in the climate which
journalists currently work is to risk controversy. So in practice what happened is
that journalists stayed on the most secure ground by focusing on civilian casualties. This meant that they were 'balancing' the Israeli account of the causes
of the conflict against the effects of Israeli actions upon civilians. The result in
term of public understanding is clear. Some people can 'fill in' the gaps in the
news accounts by recourse to other sources of information. But for many in
our samples, the impact of the Israeli account was to explain and legitimize the
attack. It was seen as a retaliation and a response, albeit sometimes a 'disproportionate' one. The consequences for the Palestinians were understood and the
visual images of suffering and death were seen as shocking, but nonetheless the
Palestinians were believed to have 'started' the trouble and therefore in some
way brought the trouble upon themselves.

In 2009, we asked young people in higher education this question about
their attitudes to the images from the conflict: 'In the Gaza conflict, many pictures were shown of civilians, women and children killed in Gaza. When you
see these, whose fault do you think it is?'

In answering this, 29 per cent blamed Israel and 11 per cent Hamas and
the Palestinians. The majority, 52 per cent blamed both equally. These figures
are based on the views of students studying social science, just after the attack
on Gaza, at a time when university campuses featured a great deal of protest

against the Israeli actions. This might have been expected to have increased support for Palestinians, yet the figures show that when looking at the images, 63 per cent either blame the Palestinians or blame both sides equally.

Our next task was to unpack these beliefs and to understand how they were constituted. A key issue is the apparent success of the Israelis in establishing a link between the breaking down or ending of the ceasefire and the firing of rockets by Palestinians. We therefore asked: 'Before the conflict of Dec. 08–Jan. 09, there was a ceasefire. Who broke it?'

In answering this 44 per cent stated that it was Hamas and the Palestinians, while 36 per cent replied that it was Israel. The following year, in 2010, we asked more specific questions to another group of over 100 students. They were asked how many believed the ceasefire had been broken because of rockets fired at Israel and how many had heard of the Israeli attack and the killing of six Palestinians in November 2008. Of 104 replies, 45 per cent answered yes to the first while the figure for the second was just 20 per cent. We explored this in the focus groups and, again, found a strong current of belief relating the onset of violence in December 2008 to rocket fire:

> I was pretty sure that it was the Palestinians who started the conflict with the rocket attacks because I've seen it on TV. Every report on TV I seem to remember it being that the Israelis were responding to the Palestinian rocket attacks and not so much the other way around. (Student, 2009)

> I thought the rockets were catalytic for their thing most recently. (Student, 2009)

The following responses were given by students in another group, who were asked who broke the ceasefire:

Participant 4: Hamas as they fired missiles.
Participant 3: Yeah, I thought that too as Hamas fired missiles into an Israeli village.
Participant 2: I did that too.
Participant 6: Hamas rocket attacks.
Participant 1: I wrote that too. (Students, Group 4, 2009)

And in the group of those in full-time work, when asked about the ceasefire:

Participant 2: Wasn't it Hamas that broke the ceasefire?
Participant 3: I think so, I think it was Hamas.
Participant 4: Me too, I think it was a suicide bomb.
Participant 5: I think it was Hamas as I seen[sic] on the news that Hamas were firing rocket launchers. (In-work, Group 6, 2009)

Since the Palestinians are seen as initiating the violence, it follows that Israel is 'retaliating' or 'responding'. This is very much the pattern which we identified in news coverage and on which we have previously written (Philo and Berry, 2004). We can see in the following comment from a respondent how the belief that the Palestinians have a grievance is tempered by the assumption that they are somehow starting the violence, to which the Israelis 'retaliate':

> I definitely think that the Palestinians have a grievance against Israel. They do have a right because of what Israel has done to try to break free from that oppression so I can understand why they're doing that but then again if you're asking who is to blame for the casualties exclusively, then people firing rockets maybe to have to take part of the blame for that because if they hadn't fired the rockets then maybe Israel maybe wouldn't have retaliated and went[sic] in so heavy handed. (Student 2009)

The logic of this leads to the argument on whether the Israeli 'response' was 'disproportionate'. The discussion in the following group show very clearly the success of the Israelis in establishing key elements of their perspective and the effect of these being relayed uncritically in media accounts. There is a sequence of assumptions which can become part of commonly held beliefs about responsibility. These are that the Palestinians have started the violence through rocket fire, that it is Hamas that is inflexible and wants to destroy Israel, and therefore that 'Hamas cannot blame Israel for Palestinian casualties':

Moderator: Who was to blame for the current conflict?

Participant 1: Hamas weren't willing to renew the cease fire as they were firing rockets and didn't want to compromise as they wanted to destroy the state of Israel but they would effectively need to compromise. But I also think it's hard to get over the scale of destruction of the retaliation.

Moderator: You think Israel retaliated to Hamas?

Participant 1: Yeah but I think it's difficult to separate. Israel clearly are separated this occasion, as they were retaliating.

Participant 2: The images shown just made me feel sad, but I didn't feel anything in particular about cause or blame.

Moderator: Had you heard about rockets being fired in to Israel?

Participant 3: Yeah, but I just thought they can't have expected Israel to have retaliated any other way. The scale of Israel's retaliation was too much though; it seems like Israel is trying to destroy the people, it seems to have went beyond political.

Participant 4: Yeah, if Hamas had fired rockets at a school then they must expect Israel to respond. So Hamas cannot blame Israel for

Participant 5:

Participant 6:

Palestinian casualties as they are only retaliating to what they started.

I find it hard to remove this context from the historical context in which I would blame Israel, but in this conflict they are both to blame. Hamas still wants to destroy the Israeli state, so it is more complex now and more compromise is needed to achieve a goal of securing a Palestinian state.

Israel's responses are massively disproportionate. (Student Group 4 2009)

There is a sense amongst some that the disparity between the powers of each side is 'unfair'. But what is missing from most of this audience is the Palestinian perspective, that, for example, Palestinians have been subject to continuous killings even during the ceasefire. The Israeli historian Avi Shlaim has noted that in the three years after the withdrawal from Gaza, 11 Israelis were killed by rocket fire. But he goes on to comment that 'in 2005–07 alone, the IDF killed 1,290 Palestinians including 222 children' (Shlaim, 2009: 4). We asked all the members of the focus groups if they had heard these figures and were aware of the scale and disparity of the killing. Less than a quarter said that they were. In these groups, no one recalled or mentioned the view that Israel could have had a ceasefire if they lifted the blockade. Knowledge of the siege was mostly very limited. We read to the groups the description of the conditions under which Palestinians lived, which had been given by Sarah Teather, including the reference to 'lakes of sewage' (quoted on p. 152). Again, less than one quarter of those in the groups knew of this.

Conclusion

The key point is that the gaps in audience knowledge very closely parallel the absences in news reporting. On the other hand, many elements of what is assumed to be true are exactly the points which were highlighted in Israeli public relations and reported uncritically on the news. Crucially, this can affect how audiences apportion blame and responsibility and also influence how the images of civilian casualties were interpreted. One participant who was in full-time work expressed this as follows:

> When I saw the pictures of the dead children, it was dreadful, I was in tears but it didn't make me feel that the Palestinians and Hamas were right … I think the Palestinians haven't taken the chance to work towards a peaceful solution. Hamas were offered the chance to sit down and talk and they haven't taken it and they called an end to the last cease fire. (In work, 2009)

This participant cited BBC Radio 4 as their main source of information on these issues and was very surprised to hear the view that the rockets could have been stopped by lifting the siege. We wish to emphasize the point that the ability to control understanding of relations of cause and effect as well the history of events gives the power to influence how new actions will be understood. This can ameliorate audience perceptions of even the grimmest outcomes and reduce the allocation of blame to those who perpetrate them. Pictures do not automatically tell any story and for journalists to show images of victims is not the same as explaining the case of both sides. Ultimately, we are offered a one-sided account of the causes and origins of the conflict, which can then have profound impacts on audience beliefs to the detriment of any rational public debate on how this crisis may be resolved.

Endnotes

1   The news content sample for the study was BBC1 and ITV early evening and main news programmes from the first day of the conflict 27 December 2008 until the announcement by Israel of a ceasefire on 17 January 2009. For the audience sample we interviewed 40 people in focus groups and gave questionnaires to 236 young people in higher education aged 17–23. This work was part of an extensive study of news content and public understanding of the Israeli–Palestinian conflict conducted 2000–2010 for which we have analysed nearly 300 news items and questioned over 1,000 people using questionnaires, focus groups and in-depth interviews (see Philo and Berry, 2011). This chapter focuses on reporting the results of our studies rather than explaining their links to theoretical issues in mass communications. For a discussion of these in relation to content analysis and discourse theory see Philo (2007) and for their relationship to reception theory see Philo (2008).

2   The BBC News online account of the report refers to it as saying 'Israel committed war crimes and carried out reckless attacks and acts of wanton destruction in its Gaza offensive' and that the report 'also calls rocket attacks by Palestinian militant's war crimes' (BBC News online, 2 July 2009). Amnesty was also reported in February 2009 to have new evidence that Hamas forces perpetrated a 'campaign of abductions, deliberate and unlawful killings, torture and death threats against those they accuse of "collaborating" with Israel, as well as opponents and critics'. The evidence was said to corroborate witness accounts given to the *Guardian* and an investigation by the Palestinian Centre for Human Rights (McCarthy, 2009a: 31).

3   This was also seen by many to be the purpose of the blockade, as a form of collective punishment imposed with increasing stringency after Hamas became the governing body of Gaza. For this reason journalists at Al-Jazeera, the Arab television news service, were told in their guidelines that when referring to the embargo or sanctions, they should say 'the embargo against the Palestinians and not the embargo against the Palestinian government of Hamas'. The guidelines go on to say that 'the embargo is not confined to the government, everybody is affected in Palestine' (Al-Jazeera internal guidelines cited in Barkho, 2010).

References

Amnesty International (2009) Israel/Gaza, Operation 'Cast Lead': 22 Days of Death and Destruction. *AI Index: MDE 15/015/2009.*

Barkho, L. (2010) *News from the BBC, CNN and Al-Jazeera – How the Broadcasters Cover the Middle East.* Cresskill, NJ: Hampton Press.

Guardian (2008) Killing a two-state solution for Israel and Palestine, editorial, 29 December.

McCarthy, R (2009a) Hamas murder campaign in Gaza exposed, *Guardian* 14 February.

McCarthy, R (2009b) Shifting sands: Hamas police patrol the beaches in move to enforce conservative dress code, *Guardian* 19 October.

McGreal, C. (2009) Why Israel went to war in Gaza, *Observer* 4 January.

Mearsheimer, J. J. and Walt, S. M. (2008) *The Israel Lobby and US Foreign Policy.* London: Penguin.

O'Loughlin, T. (2008) Israel mounts PR campaign to blame Hamas for Gaza destruction, *Guardian* 28 December.

Philo, G. (2007) Can discourse analysis successfully explain the content of media and journalistic practice? *Journalism Studies* 8(2): 175–196.

Philo, G. (2008) Active audiences and the construction of public knowledge, *Journalism Studies* 9(4): 535–544.

Philo, G. and Berry, M. (2004) *Bad News from Israel.* London: Pluto.

Philo, G. and Berry, M. (2011) *More Bad News from Israel.* London: Pluto.

Pilger, J. (2002) Why my film is under fire, *Guardian* 23 September.

Shabi, R. (2009) Special spin body gets media on message, says Israel, *Guardian* 2 January.

Shlaim, A. (2009) Israel and Gaza: rhetoric and reality, *Open Democracy*, 7 January. Available at: www.opendemocracy.net/article/israel-and-gaza-rhetoric-and-reality (accessed 15 September 2010).

PART 3
Terrorism on the Home Front

More often than not, the study of terrorism – its politics, sociology or mediation – has been conducted within a rather narrow Anglo-American ambit. The US-defined and disseminated discourse on terrorism has had a global impact: this dominant narrative has tended to neglect terrorism-related activities in other parts of the globe. In fact, terrorism has had its most violent manifestations in the world outside the radar of the US–UK 'news duopoly'. Contributors to this part of the book aim to broaden the remit of such discussion and to consider the various ways in which the relationship between media and terrorism is played out in specific non-Anglo-American contexts: in South Asia, the Arab world, France, Russia and Scandinavia.

Chapters examine the impact of the global 'war on terror' on domestic political agenda, for example in terms of representation of Muslim minorities in France and coverage of terrorism in Russian newspapers. Regional perspectives on terrorism are presented with examples from South Asia – the epicentre of the 'war on terror' – as well as the Arab and Nordic regions. The chapters aim to avoid a media-centric approach, preferring to provide an often neglected geo-political, legal and policy framework for the analysis of terrorism.

10

SOUTH ASIA AND THE FRONTLINE OF THE 'WAR ON TERROR'

Daya Kishan Thussu

In this chapter, Daya Thussu suggests that one of the worst affected regions for terrorism-related violence is South Asia. He places the terrorism narrative within the broader geo-political framework of the region – home to centrifugal and centripetal tendencies, emanating from religious, ethnic and geo-linguistic factors, rooted in a history shaped by colonialism and often accentuated by contemporary political-economy of development. Although what he calls the 'Talibanization of terrorism' in Afghanistan and parts of Pakistan gave it global currency, the major terrorist-related violence in the region has more political rather than religious significance: Tamil terrorism in Sri Lanka and Maoist insurgency in Nepal and parts of India are prime examples. Nevertheless, Thussu argues that terrorism coverage in the region has been profoundly influenced by the US-defined 'war on terror'. Given the exponential growth in the media in the region – India alone has 80 dedicated news channels – the coverage of terrorism has been hostage to an infotainment-driven news media. This has resulted in terrorism being presented as a spectacle influenced by the imagery of Bollywood.

The dramatic assassination of Osama bin Laden by US 'Navy Seals' in 2011 has brought the global media spotlight on Pakistan as the main theatre of terrorism. International as well as the regional media have been focusing on

Table 10.1   Top ten locations for suicide attacks, 1991–2008

Country/location	Number of suicide attacks
Iraq	626
Afghanistan	190
Pakistan	116
Israel	113
Sri Lanka	80
West Bank and Gaza Strip	54
Russia	32
India	28
Turkey	28
Algeria	17

Source: START, 2009–10

the success of the US-led operation to decapitate Al-Qaeda and get rid of the world's most wanted terrorist. As Americans celebrate, the fall-out is likely to affect the country which hosted bin Laden. Ten times more people have died in terrorist-related violence in Pakistan than in the US – 30,000 since 9/11.

Such disparities rarely get noticed in the mainstream international media. Away from the world's television cameras, South Asia has been on the receiving end of the global war on terror. In 2009, of the nearly 11,000 terrorism-related reported attacks worldwide, about 4,850, or 44 per cent, occurred in South Asia, accounting for approximately 6,270 fatalities, or 42 per cent of the worldwide total for that year. The country with highest number of suicide bombings was Afghanistan with 99, followed by Pakistan with 84. Of the top ten countries afflicted by suicide attacks between 1991 and 2008, four were in South Asia – see Table 10.1 (START, 2009–10).

As the assassination of bin Laden has demonstrated, the war on terror has its epicentre in the South Asian region, with Al-Qaeda having safe havens in the Pakistan–Afghanistan border. One fall-out of the US invasion of Afghanistan in 2001 – Operation Enduring Freedom – and the resultant overthrow of the Taliban regime in Kabul has been that Al-Qaeda-affiliated terrorists as well as Afghan insurgents have been forced to move to Pakistan's Federally Administered Tribal Areas (FATA), Baluchistan and the North West Frontier Province.

While 'Islamic' terrorism that such groups represent has received the widest possible media coverage both internationally and within the region, South Asia has experienced many different forms of terrorism-related violence, particularly in the last two decades. In this chapter, I aim to provide the geo-political context to the scourge of terrorism in South Asia and argue that in most instances there are political rather than religious reasons for its existence. After providing a historical context to the terrorism discourse in the region, the chapter will explore how the media revolution in the countries of the region – especially in India – has contributed to an infotainment-driven coverage of terrorism.

Terrorism in South Asia

Terrorism in South Asia has a complex and contested history, manifested in the types of terrorism organizations, their motives and mechanisms. Their social organizations and strategies have been documented by various studies (Chellaney, 2001; Bajpai, 2002; Gupta, 2008; Jaffrelot and Gayer, 2009). As the dominant country in the region, India has a long history of terrorism-related violence: according to the Global Terrorism Database, 4,108 terrorist incidents and 12,539 terrorist-related fatalities occurred in India between 1970 and 2004, by 56 terrorism-related groups – an average of almost 360 fatalities per year. In 2009 alone, the country experienced 1,000 deaths attributed to terrorist attacks, primarily in Kashmir, the northeast and the Maoist-affected 'Red Corridor' in the country's central and eastern regions (START, 2009–10).

The terrorist campaign of the Maoist-inspired Naxalite Movement represents one of the longest histories of extreme political violence in India, with its origins in momentous peasant uprising in 1967 in the village of Naxalbari in the state of West Bengal. The main leaders of this anti-state and anti-bourgeoisie revolt – notably Charu Mazumdar and Kanu Sanyal – had a sizeable following within India's diverse left-wing groups with roots in anti-colonial movements, many of which were inspired by the extremist vision, especially in Bengal (Heehs, 1993). As Nivedita Majumdar's recent anthology shows, the interest in the leftist cause was deep and not just confined to political parties and groups – its manifestations could be found in other cultural expressions, in theatre, literature and cinema (Majumdar, 2009).

The Indian government, which blamed China for supporting the Maoists, both materially and ideologically, was able to crush the movement, which splintered into factional politics and to irrelevance. In the 1990s, and partly as a reaction to globalization and the resultant exploitation of forest lands and minerals by both Indian and transnational corporations, a new version of Maoist insurgency – ostensibly engaged in a violent struggle on behalf of landless labourers and tribals – has resurfaced in interiors of east and central India. It is claimed that groups affiliated with the Maoist insurgency have been operating in 165 districts in India (Chakravarti, 2008). Notable Maoist groups include the People's War Group (PWG), mainly active in the southern Andhra Pradesh state, and the Maoist Communist Centre of West Bengal and Bihar. In 2004, the two merged to form the Communist Party of India – Maoist.

As journalist Sudeep Chakravarti shows in his recent book, the Maoists have taken up a cause which has resonance among many educated Indians, although the mass media tend to ignore the plight of the dispossessed (Chakravarti, 2008). Unlike stories of 'Islamic' terrorism, such socio-politically significant coverage does not interest the media, as most Maoist activities are confined to rural areas in some of India's poorest districts, away from the media spotlight and of little interest to global media: one notable exception being the 2010 massacre of 76 police personnel in Dantewada in eastern India, which was widely reported in Indian media, especially by news networks such as NDTV 24x7. The threat from Maoists is considered a serious one for India and indeed for the region (Gupta, 2004). The issues that the Maoists raised in India – gross inequality, massive exploitation of both natural and human resources of rural poor – also received favourable echoes across the border in Nepal, one of the world's poorest countries. Maoist-inspired terrorism was one of the chosen tactics of the Communist Party of Nepal (Maoist) during its insurrection in the 1990s (Hutt, 2004). Eventually, the Maoists joined the electoral process and came to power in 2008.

Another type of terrorism to afflict India was the one perpetrated by the pro-Khalistan (a homeland for India's Sikh minority) groups in the border state of Punjab in the early 1980s, aggravated by domestic politics as well as aided and abetted by forces across the border in Pakistan. The demand for Khalistan was led by such terrorist organizations as the Khalistan Commando Force, Babbar Khalsa and Bhindranwale Tiger Force of Khalistan. The suppression of the movement culminated in the storming of the Golden Temple in Amritsar and the assassination of India's Prime Minister Indira Gandhi, in 1984 by her Sikh bodyguard. On its northeastern border too, India has had to contend with separatist movements based on ethnicities, representing centrifugal tendencies. Some of these have deployed terrorist tactics, claiming more than 6,000 lives since 1992 in the states of Nagaland, Assam, Manipur and Tripura. Among the dozens of insurgent groups active in the northeast include the United Liberation Front of Assam; the Nationalist Social Council of Nagaland; the National Liberation Front of Tripura; the National Democratic Front of Bodoland. Although some of these continue to be active they receive very limited coverage in the media in India and indeed globally (Sonwalkar, 2004).

On India's southern border, another version of terrorism has been prevalent. In Sri Lanka, the Liberation Tigers of Tamil Eelam (LTTE) launched a campaign in 1972 to create a separate Tamil homeland in the Sinhalese-majority island (DeVotta, 2004). The 26-year-long civil war which claimed as many as 100,000 lives, ended in 2009 with the military defeat of the LTTE (Lewis, 2010). India, which has its own sizeable Tamil population, was supportive of the Tamil cause until an LTTE female suicide bomber assassinated

Indian Prime Minister Rajiv Gandhi in 1991, one of the first cases of the then unknown 'human terrorist bombs'.

Although these regional varieties of terrorism have been covered by national and regional media, they rarely make it into the global news. More often than not, such attacks are seen as isolated incidents of regional discontent, precipitated by socio-political inequalities, as well as ethnic and linguistic chauvinism rather than religion, which scarcely enters the political or media discourse. However, the most dominant media discourse of terrorism, and one that fits in with the global 'war on terror' narrative, is the Islamic version.

In the Indian context, Islamist terrorism is manifested by groups such as the Pakistan-based Lashkar-e-Taiba (or 'Army of the Pure') demanding freedom from India of Kashmir – the only Muslim-majority province in secular India. The dispute over Kashmir – divided since 1948 by a Line of Control separating India's Jammu and Kashmir state and Pakistan-controlled Azad (Free) Kashmir – has remained unresolved and has contributed to four wars between India and Pakistan – in 1948, 1965, 1971 and 1999. New Delhi has consistently argued that anti-India insurgency in Kashmir could not survive without Pakistani support for 'cross-border terrorism', in terms of providing arms and training to militants, a claim, however, refuted by Islamabad. Pakistan insists its support for 'freedom fighters' in Kashmir is a moral resistance to Indian rule (Haqqani, 2005).

The anti-India insurgency in Kashmir, which erupted in 1989, was led in its initial phase by the indigenous Jammu and Kashmir Liberation Front. However, it grew in intensity, being affected also by the geo-political situation in the region, triggered by the withdrawal of Soviet troops from Afghanistan and the rise of US-funded, Pakistan-supported Taliban in neighbouring Afghanistan (Swami, 2007). In such an environment, extremist groups such as Lashkar-e-Taiba and Jaish-e-Mohammad (or 'The Army of Mohammad') became increasingly involved in Kashmiri terrorism (Jamal, 2009; Tankel, 2011). As Islamic fundamentalism became state policy in Pakistan under the then military dictatorship of General Zia-ul Haq, such political parties as Jamaat-i-Islami acquired prominence and got involved in Kashmiri politics. One manifestation of this involvement was infiltration of schools and media outlets in Kashmir by what one commentator called the 'industrial scale production of propagandistic literature' (Swami, 2007: 123).

In December 2001, the US included the Lashkar-e-Taiba as a Foreign Terrorist Organization, shortly after it was implicated by Indian government for an audacious terrorist attack on the Indian Parliament. The Indian government has also blamed Pakistan for terrorist activities beyond Kashmir: in 1993 more than 250 people died in bomb attacks across Mumbai, believed to be in retaliation for the demolition by Hindu radicals of a historic mosque at Ayodhya; while in 2006, nearly 200 people were killed in terrorist blasts on local trains in Mumbai. The most spectacular terrorist activity was the 26 November 2008 attack in Mumbai – 26/11 or the so-called India's 9/11 (see p. 177). Sections of the Indian media and security establishment have blamed the 'Indian Mujahideen' group, a pseudonym of the Students Islamic Movement of India, for complicity with international terror networks in providing local logistical support for terrorism-related atrocities.

Such suspicions have undermined the Muslim communities in India which have been tarred with the brush of terrorism. Muslims have lived in India since the eighth century and form part of what is known as India's 'composite culture' (Hasan and Roy, 2005). During the colonial period, the politicization of religion and its exploitation by the 'divide and rule' policy of British colonialism created deep divisions, contributing to a separatist Muslim nationalism which led to the Partition in 1947 and the creation of Pakistan, the first modern state founded on the basis of religion. Since then Muslims in India have not fully benefited from India's economic growth, as the Sachar Committee, established by the Indian Prime Minister, has noted: 'Muslims, the largest minority community in the country, constituting 13.4 per cent of the population, are seriously lagging behind in terms of most of the human development indicators' (Government of India, 2006: 2). In terms of terrorism discourse, a disproportionate number of Muslim youth have been arrested under the Prevention of Terrorism Act (POTA), which was promulgated under the right-wing Bharatiya Janata Party-led government in 2002; though it was repealed in 2004 under the centrist government led by Manmohan Singh.

The 'Talibanization' of Terrorism

The most visible form of terrorism and one that receives wide international media interest is its Islamist version in Afghanistan and increasingly in Pakistan. The rise of the Taliban (literally, students) as a political force in the 1980s was an outcome of Cold War geo-politics in South Asia. After the Soviet invasion of Afghanistan in 1979, the US established, with Saudi resources ('the riyalpolitik') and Pakistani intelligence and military support, an army of 'freedom fighters' – mujahideen (fighters of the faith) to take on godless Russian communism (Tripathi, 2011). Nearly five million Afghans were made refugees during the 1980s in Pakistan and Iran. These fighters 'arose from among the youngsters and children who grew up in the refugee camps, with the smell of the gutters in their nostrils and the rage of displacement in their hearts' (Ahmad, 2004: 260).

Indoctrinated in Saudi-sponsored seminaries in Pakistan, these 'fighters of the faith' were able to take power in Kabul in 1996, with American support and general approval from Western media. No international outcry was raised, when in September 1996 Mohammad Najeebullah, the Afghan President, was murdered while he was under the 'protective custody' of the UN and his body hanged for public display. Such barbarity was an early indication of what was to come. The Taliban regime was the most obscurantist in modern history. With their Western and Pakistani backers they plunged Afghanistan, in the words of one commentator 'into chaos, warlordism, rape, plunder, and drug trafficking' (Ahmad, 2004: 261).

It is crucial to understand the role of Pakistani military and especially its Inter-Services Intelligence Directorate (ISI) in supporting and sustaining the Taliban, as an extension of Pakistan's geo-political rivalry with India (Ali, 2008; Rashid, 2008, Rashid 2010). As Haqqani, a distinguished journalist and, in 2011, Pakistan's ambassador to the US, has noted, there is a long and well-established relationship between Islamist groups and Pakistan's military – a mosque-military alliance – as the defender of Pakistan's Islamic identity (Haqqani, 2005). Ever since independence in 1947, Pakistan has experienced long bouts of military dictatorships: the country experienced military coups in 1958, 1969, 1978 and 1999. Aziz has suggested that the army created a 'parallel' state, allied with the US military interests in the region (Aziz, 2009). Such close ties with the US ensured that during Cold War years, Pakistan was a staunch Western ally – being the only Asian member of security pacts, Southeast Asia Treaty Organization (SEATO which it joined in 1954), and the Central Treaty Organization (CENTO, joined in 1958) – both designed to be a regional version of NATO that would block communist advances in Southeast Asia and West Asia respectively.

Other Pakistani commentators have argued that the military is central to the defence and foreign-policy processes in the country, having its own military–industrial complex, giving it economic autonomy (Siddiqa, 2007). Haqqani notes how during the 1980s, Pakistan's military dictator General Zia ul-Haq 'went farther than others in 'Islamizing' Pakistan's legal and educational system' (Haqqani, 2005: 2). Tariq Ali is forthright in his criticism of such policies: Zia 'handed over the ministry of Education and Information to the Jammat-e-Islami, with dire results – Jammati propaganda became embedded in the media' (Ali, 2008: 5).

The subsequent Pakistani governments have differentiated terrorism: while Al-Qaeda affiliated groups are termed as 'terrorists', the militants operating in Kashmir are referred to in policy pronouncements and in the media as 'freedom fighters'. Within the Taliban too, there are 'good' and 'bad' Talibans, the former fighting against regional foes while the latter attack Pakistani civilians.

In the post-9/11 phase, what might be described as the 'Talibanization of terrorism' undermined the control that the ISI had on terrorist outlets as they saw Pakistan operating as a Western ally in the 'war on terror'. One indication of this disruption is the increase in terrorist attacks and fatalities in regions bordering Afghanistan, including Baluchistan, the Federally Administered Tribal Areas (FATA) and the North-West Frontier Province (NWFP). Particularly problematic is the frequency of suicide bombings not only in high-value targets such as military academies, but also public places in major cities including Islamabad, Lahore and Peshawar.

It has been suggested that suicide terrorism has emerged out of the Islamization programme, and the US-led invasion and occupation of Afghanistan and its fall-out on Pakistan. However, the religious motives for such acts are not the primary ones (Hassan, 2010; Pape and Feldman, 2010). The indoctrination of young, very poor boys in ill-equipped Islamic seminaries – which have mush-roomed as state-run secular schools have declined – provides a particularly dis-torted version of jihad against the infidels and their supporters. Noted Pakistani historian Ayesha Jalal writes that the spiritual is 'reduced to a series of formulaic rituals and customs based on a superficial understanding of Islamic ethics' (Jalal, 2008: 287). This, she notes, is a problem not just in Pakistan but in the whole of South Asia. Such a culture generates a fertile ground for anti-US fanaticism. However, as Tariq Ali has suggested, an important reason for the deep hostility to the US 'has little to do with religion', but is based on the knowledge that Washington has backed military dictatorships in Pakistan (Ali, 2008: x).

Drones and democracy: America's Af-Pak War

Even before Pakistan's role in providing shelter and support to Al-Qaeda lead-ers on its soil came under global media scan, the country was viewed with sus-picion. To the question, 'which country poses the greatest terrorist threat to the West today', asked in an international survey of experts conducted by the jour-nal *Foreign Policy*, as many as 79 per cent of those polled said Pakistan; Yemen was second with 12 per cent, while Afghanistan and Iran were at three per cent. The survey, published in the January 2011 issue of the magazine, reported that 'a majority also picked it as the country most likely to have its nukes end up in the hands of terrorists' (*Foreign Policy*, 2011).

That Pakistan is now literally part of America's war on terror in South Asia was indicated when, under President Obama, the theatre of war was renamed as the Af-Pak war. Of 240 reported drone strikes in the past nine years, 53 occurred in 2009 and 116 in 2010. The drones, operated by the CIA and there-fore not subject to military rules of engagement, have claimed nearly 3,000 lives, most of these civilians. Philip Alston, the UN special rapporteur on extra-judicial killings, accused the US of inventing a 'law of 9/11' to issue the CIA with a 'license to kill'. 'Because operators are based thousands of miles from the battlefield ... there is a risk of developing a 'PlayStation' mentality to killing', his report stated (quoted in Walsh, 2010).

Such licence to kill has received scarce media coverage. Instead what we see on news screens around the world with relentless regularity is the footage of gun-totting bearded young Afghans, mired in medieval Islamist tradition and unwilling or unable to manage their own affairs. Their fanaticism and fundamentalism has spawned a whole genre of journalistic writing, documentary and films. The underlying argument of the international community (read the West, led by the US) and one replicated by most of the mainstream Western media, is that the Af-Pak operation is the harbinger of democracy in the region and for protecting human rights of the people. It is often argued that there is no geo-political interest in being involved in a war taking place in a terrain geographically extremely difficult and dangerous and against an elusive enemy representing a 'tribal' culture.

However, beyond this enlightened projection the real picture on the ground is much more complex. Although rarely discussed in mainstream media, which portrays Afghanistan as terrorism-infested lawless land, in geo-political terms the country has, as throughout history, great importance, located as it is, at the intersection of Pakistan, Iran, Turkmenistan, Uzbekistan, Tajikistan and China. In addition to its strategic location, Afghanistan is believed to have substantial deposits of untapped oil and natural gas and is a potential energy corridor for Central Asia producers. The country also has huge mineral potential. Quoting senior US government sources, The *New York Times* reported in June 2010 that the US had discovered nearly $1 trillion in untapped mineral deposits in Afghanistan, including vast quantities of lithium, a key raw material in the manufacture of batteries for computers and mobile devices. The newspaper quoted an internal Pentagon memo, saying that Afghanistan could become the 'Saudi Arabia of lithium' (Risen, 2010). Quoting senior US officials, the newspaper reported that the biggest mineral deposits discovered were of iron and copper. The report added that a Pentagon task force had already set up a system to deal with mineral development, including employing accounting firms to draw up contracts with multinational mining companies and other potential foreign investors (Risen, 2010).

Of course the US is not the only country eyeing these potential trophies from the 'war on terror'. In 2009, Afghanistan's minister of mines was accused by US officials of accepting a $30 million bribe to award China the rights to develop its copper mines (Risen, 2010). Iran and India too have investments in the region – with India committing $1.5 billion in aid spread over several sectors.

It is no coincidence that NATO's first 'out of area' war has taken place in this strategically important area. Its 'Strategic Concept' adopted at the 2010 Lisbon summit of the North Atlantic Treaty Organization envisages its role as a global cop: 'Where conflict prevention proves unsuccessful, NATO will be prepared and capable to manage ongoing hostilities. NATO has unique conflict-management capacities, including the unparalleled capability to deploy and sustain robust military forces in the field' (NATO, 2010). Though it arrived in Afghanistan as part of the UN-mandated ISAF (International Security Assistance Force), with a limited mandate, by 2011, it was in control of all military operations. The declaration the alliance signed with Afghanistan at the Lisbon summit spoke of 'a robust, enduring partnership which complements the ISAF security mission and continues beyond it'. Even after 2014, the supposed date of Western withdrawal from Afghanistan, NATO will maintain its counter-terrorism capability in that country 'until we have the confidence that the Al-Qaeda is no longer operative and is no longer a threat'. The existence of an elusive enemy could ensure a long established presence in an area which is coveted by others and thus to check emerging powers such as China, Russia and India. It may be relevant to mention here that in 2011 NATO also was bombing Libya – the first such incursion in an (oil-rich) Arab country – ostensibly as an act of humanitarianism.

There are other allied benefits too for big powers, arising out of the war on terror in South Asia. Cross-border terrorism features prominently on India's defence thinking and the 'war on terror' gives the hawks among Indian establishment enough ammunition to demand a rise in defence spending: in 2011, India was the world's largest arms importer, according to the Stockholm International Peace Research Institute (SIPRI). India received nine per cent of the volume of international arms transfers during 2006–2010, while Pakistan was the fourth largest importer of conventional weapons during this period, at five per cent of the global total (SIPRI, 2011).

Media Wars in South Asia

Against this geo-political background, a communication war is also being fought by international, regional and local media. Visual media in particular offer a key platform where the war on terror is formulated and fought. At the official level, the US government's Broadcasting Board of Governors – through its Voice of America (VOA) and Radio Free Europe (RFE) and Radio Liberty (RL) – is highly active in its propaganda war in the region. In 2010, VOA and Pakistan's English-language news channel, Express 24/7, launched a joint programme on how to fight terrorism – the first English-language show to be jointly produced by stations in Pakistan and the US. VOA's Radio Deewa, offering Pashto programming, and RFE/RL's Radio Mashaal, are other channels aimed at the Pakistan-Afghanistan border region, while RFE/RL's Radio Free Afghanistan and Radio Farda are in operation to win the 'hearts and minds' of the 'good' Taliban (BBG, 2011). How effective are such messages, arriving as they do along with persistent drone attacks? In the Af-Pak theatre of media war, US messages have to contend not only with a poor communication infrastructure, but also the extremists' own media outlets, especially radio, though the Pakistani government media – both television and FM radio – are also accessible in some border areas. That the terrorists also have their own communication infrastructure, facilitated by new media technologies, was demonstrated during the attacks on Mumbai in 2008.

High-optic Terrorist Attack: Mumbai 26/11

The one global media event to emanate from the region was the terrorist attack on Mumbai on 26 November 2008 when Pakistan-trained terrorists attacked numerous high-profile targets in India's commercial capital. After a 62-hour drama, telecast live on television channels in the region as well as globally, the Indian security forces were able to kill nine out of ten terrorists and arrest the remaining one who is now in judicial custody in India, facing trial for murder (Baweja, 2009). The attacks claimed 165 lives, including 26 foreigners, and aggravated India–Pakistan tensions as well as community relations within India.

The venues for attacks were chosen to provide maximum media impact: the elite Taj Mahal Palace and the Oberoi–Trident hotels, the city's main railway terminal, a Jewish cultural centre and a café frequented by Westerners – the last two aimed at provoking a Western reaction (Tellis, 2008). In addition, the terrorists had access to latest communication technology, including global positioning system handsets, satellite phones, voice over internet protocol phone service and high-resolution satellite pictures of their targets. It has been suggested that the terrorists were able to demonstrate high operational sophistication, indicating organizational support (Acharya and Marwah, 2011).

I have argued elsewhere how the media – especially television – in India was not geared to cover such high-optic unfolding events and tended to sensationalism and shortcuts for Pakistan bashing (Thussu, 2009). Operating in an extremely competitive commercial environment, the news networks were aiming to be first with the 'exclusive', and in the process, the line between objective and subjective coverage and news and entertainment was constantly blurring. The indication of how well orchestrated the terror attack was could be seen in a television documentary screened on Britain's Channel 4 on 30 June 2009. It showed excerpts from the intercepts, of the handler watching TV and deducing how the impact of the attack was shaping up.

The controller, apparently based in Pakistan, tells one of the gunmen in the Taj Hotel: 'My brother, yours is the most important target. The media is covering your target, the Taj hotel, more than any other.' On another occasion, he counsels the young terrorist: 'Give the government an ultimatum. Say, 'This was just the trailer. Just wait till you see the rest of the film. This is just a small example' (quoted in Channel 4, 2009).

Despite its propaganda value for the Indian government, the programme was not broadcast in India until November of the same year, and that too on HBO (Home Box Office – the US entertainment channel) – which reaches very small, largely urban audience. The question that one must raise is how did Channel 4 procure those tapes, which, as the reporter who made the film mentioned, 'was classified material, perhaps some of the most important wiretaps ever recorded by the Indian secret services' (Channel 4, 2009). Was it that the Indian security services wanted to internationalize the terrorism discourse and hoped that by its being screened in London it would receive wider publicity and perhaps greater credibility? Another reason for not showing the film on a mainstream Indian channel could have been not to inflame anti-Muslim sentiment. By screening it, Channel 4 could also place the Mumbai atrocity not as a regional terrorist attack but part of a global 'war on terror'.

Was Mumbai attack part of Pakistan's proxy war against India? Were the factions within ISI supporting Lashkar-e-Taiba (LeT)? Was the attack part of an Al-Qaeda project? The *New York Times* quoted a Pakistani intelligence official as saying 'Lashkar went rogue. Perhaps LeT or dissident factions wanted to emerge as a global player, like Al-Qaeda' (quoted in Polgreen and Mekhennet, 2009).

As Tankel has shown, Lashkar-e-Taiba is one of the most prominent terrorist outfits operating from Pakistan (Tankel, 2011). This puts the Pakistani military establishment in an awkward position. The discovery that Osama bin Laden was ensconced in a house in Abbottabad, down the road from Pakistan's national military academy, raised questions about the complicity or competence, or both, of Pakistan's ISI. As the Guantánamo Bay files, leaked by the whistleblower website WikiLeaks have shown the ISI was listed as a terrorist group by the US (Burke, 2011). WikiLeaks has also released the Afghanistan War Diary – more than 90,000 secret records of actions taken by the US military from 2004 to 2009 – exposing a culture of misinformation and manipulation of information in the war in Afghanistan.

High Optic Imperial Attack – the bin Laden Killing

The global media frenzy unleashed by the CIA assassination of bin Laden on 2 May 2011 was a perfect example of how the old and new imperialism merge. He was killed in a military garrison town, named after a British colonial Major James Abbott. The assassination of an apparently unarmed bin Laden and the hasty sea burial of his body raised both legal and moral questions about the new imperial power. While a majority of the Western media, and particularly the American media, gloated over the success of the mission authorized by a decisive President, the debate about violation of Pakistan's sovereignty received wide media scrutiny in Pakistan, with such news networks as Geo TV providing extensive coverage from their reporters on the ground in Abbottabad. The massive growth in television media in the region – India alone has 80 dedicated news channels – created a competition for macabre footage too. Such was the rush to be first with the news that within hours after bin Laden's death was announced by President Obama in a 'mission accomplished' tone, many news networks were broadcasting pictures of the Al-Qaeda leader's disfigured face – later claimed to be fake. In India, the more popular channels such as STAR News were showing computer-generated graphics of the Navy Seal mission, with suitably Bollywoodized music and heightened commentary. Even on more sober networks such as NDTV 24x7 commentators and anchors were suggesting that the Indian commandos should emulate the CIA and 'take out' the backers of Mumbai attacks based in Pakistan.

Bollywoodization of the 'War on Terror'

I have argued elsewhere that excessive marketization of the media has contributed to an infotainment-driven television news culture globally (Thussu, 2007). In South Asia too, this trend is deeply embedded within the commercialization of the media, especially television, which until the early 1990s was controlled by the state and accurately perceived as the mouthpiece of the government of the day. With globalization, privatization and digitization, the media scene has been transformed, creating an age of media plenty. Terrorism makes good television and in the Indian context – conforming to the global pattern – it is mostly the Islamic version of terrorism that receives widest coverage. In a ratings-driven, fiercely competitive environment news networks borrow popular cultural tropes from Bollywood in terms of dramatization of news narratives, background music and a celebrity-obsessed editorial agenda (Thussu, 2010). Bollywood has itself also tackled the theme of terrorism both in serious and lighter vein. One striking example of the latter was the 2010 satire *Tere Bin Laden* (Without You, Laden), a film about a young Pakistani journalist who is keen to visit the US to further his professional career but cannot obtain a visa. He makes a fake bin Laden video and sells it to news networks. *Tere Bin Laden* is a biting comment on the links between media and terrorism: when the video goes viral, it leads to a global financial crash and conflict. The film, starring Pakistani pop stat Ali Zafar in the lead role, did good business internationally, though it was banned in Pakistan (Waheed, 2010).

Mediation of the war on terror in South Asia, as we have discussed in this chapter, requires a multi-perspectival approach. The phenomenon of terrorism has multiple dimensions: social, geo-political and cultural. Islam is just one of the factors and not necessarily the prime one. It is therefore essential to look at the problem of terrorism in its political context. As we have noted, there are examples from South Asia where external factors have aggravated political struggles emanating from ethnic or economic grievances. Given the rivalries between India and Pakistan and the unresolved status of Kashmir, there is limited scope for regional cooperation in dealing with the problem of terrorism. The media in both countries – with a few exceptions – tend to reflect the dominant discourses of their respective governments (though the degree of dissonance within the elite positions is much more variegated in the case of India, given the size and scale of media in India, its polity, and a deeply entrenched tradition of 'argumentation'). The geo-politics of the region, with the US deepening its 'strategic partnership' with India, and at the same time, needing Pakistan as a frontline state against its 'war on terror', makes external resolution of terrorism extremely difficult. Other terrorist-affected countries in the region, Sri Lanka and Nepal, appear to have tamed the threat, by brute force in the case of the former and by electoral processes in the latter. Despite the prominence of 'cross-border' terrorism in the Indian media, the real threat there remains located in uneven development in some of the poorest districts in India.

As for Afghanistan, the US failure to rebuild a failed state (Jones, 2009; Caldwell, 2011); the corruption and coercion of Afghan politics (Rashid, 2008; Rashid, 2010), as well as the political economy of the narcotics trade (Filkins et al., 2009) will ensure that South Asia, and especially its Af-Pak theatre, is likely to remain at the forefront of the 'war on terror'. The 200,000 American soldiers and other support staff and the massive investments to exploit the mineral and other resources of Afghanistan will create conditions for a long-term presence of the US/NATO in a country of great geo-political and economic interests, especially at a time when US hegemony is being challenged by countries bordering the region. However, the US-dominated global media discourses will continue to present the 'war on terror' as a humanitarian engagement to bring democracy and progress to the region. A partial explanation for such attitudes is the 'deeply moralizing tendency' in American culture and media, as Aijaz Ahmad has noted, 'that goes back to the Puritan forefathers in which collective life becomes the psychodrama of an eternal duel between Good and Evil in which America-the-Good is always exorcising the demons that are out to devour it' (Ahmad, 2004: 267).

References

Acharya, Arabinda and Marwah, Sonal (2011) Nizam, la Tanzim (System, not Organization): Do Organizations Matter in Terrorism Today? A Study of the November 2008 Mumbai Attacks. *Studies in Conflict & Terrorism* 34(1): 1–16.

Ahmad, Aijaz (2004) *Iraq, Afghanistan & the Imperialism of Our Time.* New Delhi: LeftWorld.

Ali, Tariq (2008) *The Duel: Pakistan on the Flight Path of American Power*. London: Simon & Schuster.

Aziz, Mazhar (2009) *Military Control in Pakistan: The Parallel State*. London: Routledge.

Bajpai, Kanti (2002) *Roots of Terrorism*. New Delhi: Penguin.

Baweja, Harinder (ed.) (2009) *26/11 Mumbai Attacked*. New Delhi: Roli Books.

BBG (2011) *Fiscal Year 2010 Performance and Accountability Report*. Washington: Broadcasting Board of Governors.

Burke, Jason (2011) Guantánamo Bay files: Pakistan's ISI spy service listed as terrorist group. *Guardian*, 25 April.

Caldwell, Dan (2011) *Vortex of Conflict: US Policy Toward Afghanistan, Pakistan, and Iraq*. Stanford: Stanford University Press.

Chakravarti, Sudeep (2008) *Red Sun: Travels in Naxalite Country*. New Delhi: Penguin.

Channel 4 (2009) Terror in Mumbai, *Dispatches*, Channel 4 Television, 30 June.

Chellaney, Brahma (2001) Fighting terrorism in Southern Asia: the lessons of history. *International Security* 26(3): 94–116.

DeVotta, Neil (2004) *Blowback: Linguistic Nationalism, Institutional Decay and Ethnic Conflict in Sri Lanka*. Stanford: Stanford University Press.

Filkins, Dexter, Mazzetti, Mark and Risen, James (2009) Brother of Afghan leader said to be paid by C.I.A. *New York Times*, 27 October.

Foreign Policy (2011) The FP Survey: Terrorism, *Foreign Policy*, January/February, Available www.foreignpolicy.com/articles/2011/01/02/the_fp_survey_terrorism, consulted 12 April 2011.

Government of India (2006) *Social, Economic Educational Status of Muslim Community: A Report*. New Delhi: Prime Minister's High Level Committee, Cabinet Secretariat.

Gupta, Dipak (2008) *Understanding Terrorism and Political Violence*. London: Routledge.

Gupta, Ranjit Kumar (2004) *The Crimson Agenda: Maoist Protest and Terror*. Delhi: Wordsmiths.

Haqqani, Husain (2005) *Pakistan between Mosque and Military*. Washington: Carnegie Endowment for International Peace.

Hasan, Mushirul and Roy, Asim (eds.) (2005) *Living Together Separately: Cultural India in History and Politics*. New Delhi: Oxford University Press.

Hassan, Riaz (2010) *Life as a Weapon: The Global Rise of Suicide Bombings*. London: Routledge

Heehs, Peter (1993) *The Bomb in Bengal: The Rise of Revolutionary Terrorism in India, 1900–1910*. New Delhi: Oxford University Press.

Hutt, Michael (ed.) (2004) *Himalayan People's War: Nepal's Maoist Rebellion*. Bloomington: Indiana University Press.

Jaffrelot, Christophe and Gayer, Lauren (eds) (2009) *Armed Militias of South Asia: Fundamentalists, Maoists, and Separatists*. New York: Columbia University Press.

Jalal, Ayesha (2008) *Partisans of Allah: Jihad in South Asia*. Cambridge, MA: Harvard University Press.

Jamal, Arif (2009) *Shadow War: The Untold Story of Jihad in Kashmir*. New York: Melville House.

Jones, Seth (2009) *In the Graveyard of Empires: America's War in Afghanistan*. New York: W. W. Norton.

Lewis, David (2010) The failure of a liberal peace: Sri Lanka's counter-insurgency in global perspective. *Conflict, Security & Development* 10(5): 647–671.

Majumdar, Nivedita (ed.) (2009) *The Other Side of Terror: An Anthology of Writings on Terrorism in South Asia*. New Delhi: Oxford University Press.

NATO (2010) *Active Engagement, Modern Defence*: Strategic Concept for the Defence and Security of the Members of the North Atlantic Treaty Organisation, Adopted by Heads of State and Government in Lisbon, 20 November. Available at www.nato.int/lisbon2010/strategic-concept-2010-eng.pdf (accessed 14 May 2011).

Pape, Robert and Feldman, James (2010) *Cutting the Fuse: The Explosion of Global Suicide Terrorism and How to Stop It*. Chicago: University of Chicago Press.

Polgreen, Lydia and Mekhennet, Souad (2009) ISI knew of 26/11 plan, say LeT men, *New York Times*, 1 October.

Rashid, Ahmed (2008) *Descent into Chaos: The United States and the Failure of Nation Building in Pakistan, Afghanistan, and Central Asia*. London: Viking.

Rashid, Ahmed (2010) *Taliban: Militant Islam, Oil and Fundamentalism in Central Asia*, second edition, London: Yale University Press.

Risen, James (2010) US identifies vast mineral riches in Afghanistan, *New York Times*, 13 June.

Siddiqa, Ayesha (2007) *Military Inc.: Inside Pakistan's Military Economy*. London: Pluto.

SIPRI (2011) *SIPRI Yearbook 2011*. Stockholm: Stockholm International Peace Research Institute.

Sonwalkar, Prasun (2004) Mediating otherness: the English-language national press and Northeast India. *Contemporary South Asia* 3(4): 389–402.

START (2009–10) *Global Terrorism Database*. Available at: www.start.umd.edu/gtd/search/Results.aspx?chart=country&casualties_type=&casualties_max=&country=217 (accessed 26 April 2011).

Swami, Praveen (2007) *India, Pakistan and the Secret Jihad: The Covert War in Kashmir, 1947–2004*. London: Routledge.

Tankel, Stephen (2011) *Storming the World Stage: The Story of Lashkar-e-Taiba* New York: Columbia University Press.

Tellis, Ashley (2008) Terrorists attacking Mumbai have global agenda. *Yale Global*, 8 December.

Thussu, Daya Kishan (2007) *News as Entertainment: The Rise of Global Infotainment*. London: SAGE.

Thussu, Daya Kishan (2009) Turning terrorism into soap opera. *British Journalism Review* 20(1): 13–18.

Thussu, Daya Kishan (2010) The business of 'Bollywoodized' journalism, in *The Changing Business of Journalism and its Implications for Democracy*, edited by David Levy and Rasmus Nielsen, Reuters Institute for the Study of Journalism, University of Oxford.

Tripathi, Deepak (2011) *Breeding Ground: Afghanistan and the Origins of Islamist Terrorism*. New York: Potomac Books.

Waheed, Alia (2010) Bollywood's spoof Osama bin Laden movie proves global hit. *Observer*, 1 August.

Walsh, Declan (2010) Leading UN official criticises CIA's role in drone strikes. *Guardian*, 3 June.

11

COVERING TERRORISM IN RUSSIAN MEDIA

Elena Vartanova and Olga Smirnova

As in South Asia and many Arab nations, state-run TV channels in Russia have been slow and over-cautious in reporting terrorist attacks against civilians compared with private networks and online news sources, which made direct links with the global 'war on terror'. In their chapter, Elena Vartanova and Olga Smirnova, both based at the prestigious Faculty of Journalism of the Moscow State University, track the changes in the presentation of terrorism in the media in Russia over the last two decades. They point out that understanding the phenomenon of 'terrorism' in post-Soviet Russia is a complex issue. Though post-Soviet Russia has been facing armed conflicts in Chechnya since the early 1990s, it was only after 9/11 that the Chechens were represented in the Russian media as terrorists connected to transnational jihadi groups. Vartanova and Smirnova report the findings of the coverage of three high-profile terrorist attacks targeted at civilians: the hostage-taking in Moscow at the Nord-Ost Musical in 2002; the attacks at Beslan secondary school in 2004; and the blasts in the Moscow Underground in 2010. Vartanova and Smirnova note the qualitative changes in the coverage of terrorism in Russian media, in terms of journalists' use of sources, government and civil society response to terrorism, as well as the growing use of hate speech against Chechens in the media.

The media – TV, radio, print and the internet – exercise a significant influence upon public opinion in modern society. In recent decades, the impact of media on their audiences, whether global or national, has become a striking feature of the broader issue of modern terrorism. At the same time terrorism is a key topic for journalists, as terrorists' actions gain more and more media attention, involving innocent people and becoming high on the political agenda, as well as providing sensational media events.

Media researchers are faced, therefore, with a number of important issues in relation to terrorism: professionalism, ethics, citizenship, freedom of speech and responsibility of journalists, editors and media managers that communicate information on terrorist attacks to the audience (Gallimore, 1988; Leeman, 1991; Lockyer, 2003). These issues are especially vital in countries where many civilians have suffered from the violent terrorist attacks and where journalists have found themselves in the midst of events and reported live. The situation in these countries present particular problems for journalists, when terrorists try to use them in order to get through to the wider audience.

The situation in Russia, a country with a long experience in this area, was aggravated by the political complications of the transition period, which began in 1991. After the collapse of the multi-national Soviet Union, the problem of new national divisions in the country became more severe, because many national elites now sought self-determination. In this process, it is still hard to distinguish between their pursuit of power and the struggle for cultural and national identity, between their mechanisms aimed at achieving political authority and efforts to establish their own state (Boudnitzki, 2000; Pronina, 2006). It is these multilevel and internally inconsistent processes that account for both the complexities in understanding the phenomenon of 'terrorism' in post-Soviet Russia, and the tensions in relationships between the authorities, society and the media in relation to covering terrorist acts in the country.

Russian Media in the Post-Socialist Transformation

In analysing Russian media performance and coverage of terrorism it is important to take into account the peculiarities of the national media system that has emerged over the past two decades. Since 1991, Russia has undergone rapid and drastic changes and Russian journalism has had to react to new challenges, above all the problem of terror. Its coverage has been very heterogeneous and all too often unpredictable, which has had negative impacts on society as a whole and on the relationships between mass media and the authorities, i.e. between journalists and the political elite, the legislative powers, and defence and law-enforcement bodies.

After the post-Soviet transformation Russian media represent a unique combination of heterogeneous processes, such as:

- Co-existence of state interests (state-run mass media) and overtly commercial interests (private mass media) with the growing civil sector (significant components in social networks on the internet).
- Innovative technologies (RUnet and mobile telephony) along with survival of print media outlets using outdated technical facilities (those in the Russian provinces).
- Costs of political pluralism, which sometimes results in confrontation (governmental, political and oppositional sites).
- Monopolies (the newspaper markets in Kalmykia, Bashkiria, Belgorod, or Kuban).
- Complementary co-existence of elite editions and channels alongside media that cater for undemanding mass preferences, of private and state-owned media, of state-loyal federal TV channels and openly oppositional newspapers, magazines and internet media.

These features of the Russian media system are important for our understanding of the relationship between media and terror, of which we identify some key ones below.

The growing role of television in providing the audience with news and entertainment

Television today is the most important source of international, national and even regional information for most Russian citizens. More than 90 per cent of Russians obtain their news from TV, about 80 per cent of them trust TV and more than 80 per cent watch it every day. The federal channels cover the key issues of national politics and mass entertainment. Terrestrial television in Russia is available to almost every Russian: 99 per cent of the population have a TV set in their home and receive at least one channel. In 2009, an average of 24 channels were available per household and more than 70 per cent of the population had access to at least seven terrestrial channels. In the late 2000s, there was intense development of non-terrestrial television, already available to 44 per cent of the population. In the new 'division of labour' within the Russian media system, television has gained a centripetal function and taken on the role of shaping national identity, informing Russians about the events in the world, and organizing elections and leisure. Russian TV should be analysed at two levels:

- the federal (national, publicly available) television channels have taken up the tasks of covering the key issues of national politics and of mass entertainment, which is partly accounted for by the presence of global and national advertisers on these channels;

- regional audio-visual media as well as print media have focused on catering for the needs of regional/local audiences, elites and advertisers. (Vartanova and Smirnov, 2010: 80)

Print media, despite the great number of outlets, are mostly focused on serving needs of the regional audiences

The decline of national newspapers in contrast to the growth of regional/local press is evident; in fact, this growth has not contributed to the emergence of daily national quality newspapers. The newspaper sector of the market is clearly divided into three comparatively equal parts: national editions account for 35 per cent of the total circulation figure; regional editions contribute 33 per cent; and local ones 32 per cent ('The Russian Market of Regular Print Media. Condition, tendencies, and prospects for development', 2010). The fact that print media have lost their leading role in the media system has been determined not only by the distribution crisis but also by their loss of superiority in shaping and analyzing the national 'agenda', a role which has been taken over, in recent years, by federal television channels.

The rapid growth of new media has become a vital tendency in the Russian media landscape

In 2010, the monthly audience for RUnet aged over 18 was 40 million (a little less than one third of Russians). Its most active part is made up of young people. In Russian cities with the population over one million, about 70 per cent of young people aged under 22 are internet users. One of the important elements of internet media is social media, which include the blogosphere, social networks, microblogs (Twitter) and the like. As of spring 2010, RUnet hosted 12 million blogs, ten per cent of which were regularly updated.

The internet is increasingly becoming a serious competitor to the traditional media of television, radio and the press. Internet users today are young, active, mostly well educated and also one of the wealthiest sections of the audience. These are professionals, high-school and university students, people who look to the future, that creative class which sets the tone in the context of the globalizing economy.

In fact, the internet as a communication platform has replaced traditional mass media in terms of rapidly delivering information and shaping the political agenda. The Russian internet today is a unique communication and information channel, which provides the user with maximum freedom of choice of content. Political and intellectual preferences are presented on the internet in the form of a whole spectrum of viewpoints. The internet allows for great freedom of choice of diverse content, ranging from information to education and serves as an information menu where people can choose any information they want.

Covering Terrorism: A Complex Story

Terrorism as a global phenomenon has become one of the major topics in media coverage both globally and nationally as evidenced by many studies (Pludowski, 2007; Moeller, 2009; Steger, 2010). However, coverage varies significantly between countries and regions, different media channels and outlets, and the reasons for this are numerous. In different national contexts there is a great discrepancy of views on terrorism because of dissimilar historical and political approaches to this phenomenon. For some scholars, the nature of global terrorism is rooted in fundamentalism, jihadi extremism or religious fanaticism (Sageman, 2004). Others see terrorism as a multifaceted complex phenomenon caused by diverse reasons of a political and economic nature (Sovremennuy terrorism i borba s nim, 2007). In many national contexts, understanding terrorism involves examining not only global and external/international factors, but also internal/domestic factors. Russian approaches to terrorism provide a good example of this, looking at it from a historical point of view.

The first wave of revolutionary terrorism in Imperial Russia dates back to the last quarter of the nineteenth century, when the leftist anarchist movement 'Narodnaya volya' (The People's Will) began its struggle against the Tsarist regime. After the shooting of St Petersburg governor Fedor Trepov (1878) by Vera Zasoulich and the assassination of Tsar Alexander II (1881), the terrorist movement against the Imperial state, its agencies and politicians, not only became one of the most widely covered topics in the Russian-censored press (and abroad), but also started one of the broadest public debates in Russian history about the role of violence and crime in a political struggle. The activities of 'Narodnaya volya' would not have been possible without the new information technologies of the time – newspapers and telegraph – which popularized the ideas and images of the first Russian terrorists. However, Russian anarchists promoted a particular form of ethics, as terrorist attacks were aimed only at state officials, not at the civilian population, in particular women and children.

As some Russian historians argue, this terrorist movement created the foundation for the later successful actions of the Russian Bolsheviks, who widely used violent methods in their struggle for power (Boudnitzky, 2000). The anti-state ideology of the revolutionary social democrats was also paralleled by the separatist struggle of ethnic groups incorporated in the Russian Empire in the nineteenth and early twentieth centuries that reflected both the search for political power by local elites and the struggles of the local population for a better life (Vitoushkin, 2005). As a result, in the twentieth century the very idea of the Socialist (Communist) revolution and liberation movement in Russia had become tightly intertwined with anti-state militant activity targeted at establishing and enlarging the Socialist system worldwide.

Before 1991, the year of the dissolution of the Soviet Union, many events that were considered as (leftist) terrorists' activities in the West were politically, morally and even financially supported by the Socialist states as national-liberation movements of the 'Third World'. After 1991, processes of regional political determination and autonomy, the so-called 'rise of the regions', began in the Russian Federation. Various administrative units such as 'oblast', 'krai' (region) and 'respublika' (republics) called for more autonomy inside established state borders. Real tensions emerged, particularly in the North Caucasus, a predominantly Muslim, multi-ethnic and multi-lingual region. The striving for autonomy was complicated by the contradictory intentions of local elites with regard to economic, political and ethnic, but also religious issues. The struggle between supporters of Wahhabism and Sufism in the region brought about fundamentalist dimensions of global terrorism into military tensions not only in the Caucasus, but also in Russia (Thornburgh, 2010). This contributed to the complex and contradictory circumstances in which the Russian war on terrorism grew and how the Russian media covered this menace.

All over the world media produce a number of stories about terrorism attacks, activities, leaders, since 'terrorism has been the main event of the twenty-first century' (Moeller, 2009: 38). Mediation of terrorism has become one of the most difficult and contradictory professional activities for journalists and media organizations, since it has to include conflicting positions, values, traditions and experiences, to encompass interests of competing powerful forces, to find an uneasy balance between freedom of expression, objectivity and social responsibility, information security, protection of audiences from damaging psychological impact. As Hamelink argues, in news reporting about 9/11 'there are different stories to be told, with sometimes conflicting interpretations. There is hardly ever one single frame that tells it all and many different frames can be all true at the same time' (quoted in Pludowski, 2007: 364).

In media studies, several aspects have gained the particular attention of scholars, laying the foundations for common research approaches. Among them:

- media freedom in conditions of war, state legislation activities concerning the boundaries of freedom of speech (Richter, 2005: 20–36; 2009).
- political economy of 'war on terror' media coverage, including analysis of government influence on media coverage, direct and indirect censorship, media packaging news in relation to government spin (Moeller, 2009: 38), media and government using the global terror events to sustain domestic agenda.

- attention-economy approach, with a focus on how media covering terrorism hold the audience attention, keep them coming back to the content in the same media channel, the same media outlet (Moeller, 2009: 51).
- analysis of agenda setting and journalistic professionalism in respect to covering conflicts by commercially oriented media – journalists' perception of that audiences do not want a multi-layered, complex version of reality (Pludowski, 2007: 363–364).
- textual and cultural examination of journalistic discourse with the focus on creation of enemy images: 'we' versus 'them', in the context of a global 'war on terror' media culture (Wahl-Jorgensen and Hanitzsch, 2009: 111).
- study of professional activity of journalists in particular the reporter–source relationships creating challenges for journalists in case the 'source' is represented by terrorists; the case becoming extremely complicated in the new media where terrorists try either to collaborate with or by-pass journalists (Wieviorka, 1988; Wahl-Jorgensen and Hanitzsch, 2009: 387–388).

This is all relevant to the Russian 'war on terror' and its media coverage. In terms of reporting on the nature and goals of terrorism, the mass media represent and reproduce a whole set of 'frames' in which reality is reflected in the full spectrum of media attitudes – from heavy criticism to acceptance, legitimization of terrorism discourse in Russia. Disagreement between the Russian political leadership, counter-terrorism institutions, civil society organizations and media have resulted not only in a fragmented understanding of the nature of terrorism at the global and especially national level, but also in the impossibility of a consensus in Russian society in relation to domestic terrorist attacks and to defining the limits of information security vs. freedom of speech (Pronina, 2006: 2).

Surviving the 1990s economic and structural crises, the Russian media have poorly performed the role of nation-building and identity formation of Russians as an independent nation since 1991. In addition to the problems of this transitional period, familiar to many states moving towards democracy and a market economy, Russia has experienced a painful shift in cultural paradigms and 'must navigate between a partially rehabilitated Soviet past and an ambivalently viewed, Western-dominated present, and the intensity with which recent terrorist outrages have shaped that navigation' (Hutchings and Rulyova, 2009: 75).

The clash in professional approaches and values in journalists has produced contradictory results. On the one hand, major federal TV channels strongly controlled by politically loyal management were extremely slow and over-cautious in reporting terrorist attacks against civilians in Russia. This reflected the position of the political elite and counter-terrorism forces in the 2002 (Nord-Ost) and 2005 (Beslan) events, when they insisted on limiting or suppressing live media coverage. On the other hand, reporters from commercially oriented or government-critical media often managed to produce fast, live coverage of events, including voices from anti-state military groups or terrorists (the case of Nord-Ost). This division is reflected in the divided views in opinion polls when almost half (47 per cent) of respondents supported censored coverage in 2002 and 2005 while the other half (44 per cent) voted for unrestricted and full coverage of the terrorist attacks (Center for extreme journalism, 2002).

State vs. Self-regulation

The war on terror in Russia is first and foremost related to events in Chechnya and around it. While the first armed conflict in Chechnya (1994–1996) was not defined then as 'anti-terrorist', the conflict that began in the second half of 1999 was referred to as an 'anti-terrorist operation' from the very start, which resulted in numerous legal and political consequences affecting, among other things, the freedom of media.

The Russian state established the political and legal conditions for conducting any anti-terrorist operation in advance. The Federal Law 'On the Fight against Terrorism' was passed in 1998 (further replaced by the Federal Law 'On Counteraction of Terrorism' in 2006.) In spring 2000, this law came to be cited when officially evaluating journalists' material on Chechnya. Article 15 of this law stipulated that the way and degree in which the public should be informed about a terrorist act were to be determined by the leader of the headquarters controlling the anti-terrorist operation. In addition, the article prohibited the dissemination of information 'which served to promote and justify terror and extremism'. The newspapers *Kommersant* and *Novaya Gazeta* were accused of violating this rule, whereby their editorial offices were given an official warning, a measure implying that these media outlets might be banned (Richter, 2005: 20–36).

Attempts to apply the Federal Law 'On the Fight Against Terrorism' to the Chechen conflict had their weaknesses. From the legal viewpoint, the only undeniable reason for sanctions and, under certain conditions, banning a media outlet has always been violation of Article 4 of the Law 'On Mass Media', while the point about 'dissemination of materials containing public calls for terrorist activity or publicly justifying terror' as well as a reference to the privileged role of the leader of the counter-terrorist operation in media activities was unrelated to the disposition of this Article at that time. However, these points were introduced when subsequent events (the tragedy in Beslan, in particular) showed that the degree of legal regulation of media activities sometimes failed to guarantee journalists' appropriate conduct in the zone of a forceful operation, which threatened the safety of hostages and those who took part in it. Dissemination of material containing public calls for terrorist activity or publicly justifying terror was defined as an abuse of the freedom of media. In 2006, Article 205.2 was added to the Criminal Code of the Russian Federation; this established strict restrictions for public calls for terrorist activity or public justification of terror via media (Richter, 2005: 20–36).

There are two documents that can be regarded as tools for media self-regulation in covering the topic of terror: the Ethical Principles of Professional Conduct of Journalists Covering Acts of Terrorism and Counter-Terrorist Operations adopted by the Union of Journalists of Russia in 2003 and the Anti-Terrorism Convention. Rules of Conduct for Mass Media in the Case of a Terrorist Act and an Anti-Terrorist Operation adopted by the Mass Media Industrial Committee in 2003. Related to these two is another document, the Charter of Television Broadcasters 'Against Violence and Cruelty' signed in 2005 by such channels as 'Perviy kanal', 'Rossiya', NTV, TVTS, STS and Ren-TV. This, however, can only be regarded as an indirect tool for the system of media self-regulation in the present context because the word 'terror' and its derivatives do not occur in the text (Vartanova, 2009).

Analyzing the texts of the Ethical Principles of the Union of Journalists of Russia (see www.ruj.ru/about/codex.htm) and the Anti-Terrorism Convention of the Mass Media Industrial Committee (see www.mediasoyuz.ru/docs/antiterr_convent.doc) one will find that these two documents duplicate each other to a great extent. The fact that a number of fundamental provisions coincide is easy to explain as these statements are self-evident to any civilized person, irrespective of their race, nationality, confession, political views and social status.

In order to be fully aware of the existing norms, a journalist needs to review all three documents. Here the first difficulty arises: to do so, one has to know that the Ethical Principles, the Convention and the Charter are not identical but complementary. This seems to be a technical problem whereas the second one has a conceptual quality: comparing the texts of the Ethical Principles and the Convention it becomes obvious that in certain points these two strategic documents contradict each other.

The differences, which, in theory, could be interpreted as nuances, are actually able to mislead a journalist faced with a moral dilemma (for example, in a situation of having to choose between cooperating with security forces or refusing to cooperate). The partial discordance of the Ethical Principles of the Union of Journalists of Russia and the Anti-Terrorism Convention of the Mass Media Industrial Committee, however, is largely removed, 'recompensed' by the fact that they are not extensively used in practice. A major problem here is that the journalistic community in Russia is only slightly aware of the existence of these Acts. These documents are not in regular demand in editorial offices; when a reporter or an editor applies for a job they are not obliged to review the documents. This fact is admitted by both journalists and experts in legal and ethical regulation of media activities. Therefore the available tools for media self-regulation in covering terrorism do not function properly. An attempt to solve the problem has been made by researchers at the Faculty of Journalism of Lomonosov Moscow State University, who worked out and adopted a renewed composite document, the 'Anti-Terrorism Charter of Journalists', wherein they stated the professional ethical norms intended to be a comprehensive guide for action for journalists and other media personnel.

Terrorists Attack Civilians: Coverage of 2002, 2005 and 2010 Events

In the last two decades Russia has survived many terrorist attacks in various regions that had been covered by national and regional media in different ways. Regarding the effects made upon national audiences, several events gained maximum publicity due to their obvious targeting at civilians, live coverage and the potential psychological impact on Russians. The coverage of these events by the Russian media has posed some important questions for media scholars. What are the main characteristics and trends in Russian media coverage of attacks against civilians? How do media behave in cases of terrorist attacks? How do reporters cover the unfolding events and what are the specific features of the activity of Russian media organizations? How does the coverage of events change in the course of time? Are journalists' approaches evolving with every new attack? Are journalists aware of their social responsibility?

The empirical data was collected by a team of researchers at the Faculty of Journalism, Moscow State University, on the coverage of the three most severe terrorist attacks against the civil population: the hostage-taking in Moscow at the Nord-Ost Musical (2002), at Beslan secondary school on the first day of the school year (2004) and the explosions in the Moscow underground (2010). The cases selected have common elements: they have been targeted at civilians; were unexpectedly conducted in public places showing an extreme vulnerability of ordinary people and have not been directly connected with any political acts.

The specific tasks set in the course of the research were to identify the qualitative and quantitative characteristics of the media texts reflecting following:

1 the qualitative changes in terror attacks coverage of the identified topics;
2 the trends in using information sources;
3 the dynamics of assessing the authorities' performance;
4 the dynamics of describing attitudes of civil society institutions and their relation to the media;
5 the dynamics of hate speech presented in researched media texts.

Media texts were selected from eight national Russian newspapers, among them six quality newspapers: the political daily *Izvestiya*, official daily *Rossiyskaya Gazeta*, two business dailies *Kommersant* and *Vedomosti*, investigative and politically oppositional newspaper *Novaya Gazeta*, and two mass-circulation tabloid dailies *Komsomolskaya Pravda* and *Moskovsky Komsomolets*. As noted previously, the role of print media, especially newspapers, as key information providers and as agenda-setting media, is decreasing compared with TV and internet. However, in analysing, commenting and moderating debates among educated professionals and political opinion makers the quality press still plays a role though it is limited to big cities. As for the mass circulation dailies, they remain important sources of national news for different regions in Russia as effective instruments to construct national identity and support continuity of traditional cultural values.

The monitoring periods for each case was the week after each of the incidents took place. They are:

- for Nord-Ost: October 23–30, 2002;
- for Beslan: September 1–8, 2004;
- for Moscow underground: March 29–April 5, 2010.

The monitoring was conducted automatically using the 'Integrum' research and information agency search engine. By identifying several key words, 956 articles on the three terrorist attacks were found. The clear dynamics could be detected in course of the quantitative analysis, with 214 and 437 publications in the year 2002 and the year 2004 respectively. The total number of articles on the latest terror act in 2010, less massive and high-profile than the previous ones, equalled 305. We have also looked at the dynamics of the publications during the first day following the attacks. The number of articles after the hostage taking in Beslan in comparison to that at Nord-Ost went up by more than four times and the media coverage of the Moscow underground attacks was twice as great (10, 44 and 90 articles respectively).

Thus, the quantitative analysis findings show that the newspapers were increasingly efficient and swift when covering each new attack. To a certain extent, this can be explained by the fact that in 2002, the terror attack created profound confusion at all socio-political levels: during the first hours, the authorities, including political elites and counter-intelligence services, the civil society and media professionals felt completely lost. With no previous experience in covering attacks against civilians, the journalists and media were trying to determine what was going on and how this should be covered. With the later incidents, however, journalists had acquired professional skills and developed the technologies for covering counter-terrorist operations.

For the next stage of the research – the qualitative analysis – a step-by-step article selection was carried out, where every third publication from the total pool was analysed. As a result, 238 texts were selected. Content analysis was carried out on the three categories, the use of sources of information on terror attacks, the presence/absence of criticism towards the authorities' actions during the counterterrorist operations and the presence/absence of hate speech.

Use of news sources

The examination of the use of information sources was aimed at revealing the number of information sources employed when covering terror attacks, as well as the dynamics of changes in the information system on the whole. From the prospect of the variety of information sources the following trends were singled out:

- The official sources (by this we mean all government officials' statements, the information provided by the state press offices, such as the Federal Security Service, Internal Affairs Departments, etc.) were leading.
- The next most important sources were the so-called 'live sources', including eye-witnesses, the victims' and hostages' relatives, the hostages set free, the terrorists' families.
- The third most frequently used information source was experts' views.

Not all of the media were striving to use a wide range of information sources and often limited themselves to the official ones. Surprisingly, it was not the government daily *Rossiyskaya Gazeta*, but rather the business periodical like *Vedomosti* that were the leaders in using the official sources. *Novaya Gazeta* demonstrated its lack of trust in the official sources of information and only used information from its own sources and experts.

An important trend which emerged after the 2010 terror attack in the Moscow Underground is the predominance of the unofficial sources (parties involved, eye-witnesses, blogs etc) over the official ones. This results from the increasing use by Russian media of non-professional sources and user-generated content for unique and timely information. This trend appeared already in 2004, when during the Beslan hostage crisis the first unverified news about the attack came through the Echo Moskvy' internet forum. However, after the terrorist attack in the Moscow underground in 2010, the blogging community grew more active than ever. To a certain extent, this can be explained by the fact that the official sources and government information channels kept silent for too long, giving no coverage of the matter for more than an hour. Therefore, most media (notably Moscow FM-radio stations) had to depend on information received from unofficial sources such as blogs, mobile-phone calls, twitter etc. The most

Table 11.1   Timeline of the media coverage of the terrorist attack on 23 October 2002, during the first few hours after the hostage-taking

Time	Media Channel	Type of News
Before 22.00	'Interfax' News Agency	A journalist of the 'Interfax' news agency on his mobile phone from the 'Nord-Ost' theatre hall
22.00	Ren-TV	The first announcement on television about the taking of hostages.
22.00	NTV	Breaking news
22.30	Ren-TV	The first details of the taking of hostages
22.30	Perviy kanal	News bulletin
22.30	TVS	News bulletin
22.48	NTV	Special news bulletin

Source: Center for Journalism in Extreme Situations

often-quoted source at the time was the newly established tabloid-type journalism website LifeNews, which turned out to be the first to deliver the information on the underground attack.

In terms of multi-media strategies, a large proportion of the newspapers in the research study remained quite traditional and they did not use their websites to provide readers with urgent online updates, even in 2010. In fact, only one daily, *Komsomolskaya Pravda*, actively used web sources and user-generated content.

In identifying the sources of the first news reports about the attacks in 2002 and 2010, it was clear that news agencies still have the leading role (see Tables 11.1 and 11.2). TV was undoubtedly both a key medium and source of information, but recently the role of the internet as transmission channel has been substantially increased. However, on the internet it is obvious that major information providers represent both old (news agencies), converged (traditional newspapers' sites) and new (online newspapers, websites and so on) media, thus mixing journalistic and non-journalistic (experts, eye-witnesses) texts.

On the whole, the analysis has demonstrated the following trends: the newspapers' attempts to provide balanced information and employ a wider range of sources; the increasing use of so-called 'live sources' and experts, the increasing use of user-generated content as a source of unique and timely information.

Criticism towards authorities' actions

It is necessary to point out that it was after the Nord-Ost attack that for the first time in the modern Russian War on Terror the authorities have been severely criticized by the non-governmental organizations, civil society and the media for their mistakes in course of the counter-terrorist operation. Allegedly, those

Table 11.2   Timeline of the media coverage of the terrorism attacks on 29 March 2010 during the first few hours after the blasts

Time	Media Channel	Text
8.11 a.m.	RIA novosti	Blast in Moscow underground. Casualties reported
8.12	DNI.ru	A blast erupted in central Moscow underground
8.13	Vzglyad	Blast in central Moscow underground, casualties reported
8.14	Echo of Moscow	Blast in central Moscow underground
8.14	RosBusinessConsulting	Trains on Sokolonicheskaya line moving with big time gaps because of the blast on underground station Lubyanka
8.16	Novye Izvestia – online	Terrorism attacks in Moscow: dozens of victims, injured in grave condition
8.17	ITAR-TASS	A blast occurred in Moscow subway, 15 dead and 15 injured reported
8.21	ITAR-TASS	20 people died in a bomb blast on the underground station Lubyanka
8.22	RIA novosty	According to preliminary information, 15 people have been killed in the bomb blast in Moscow underground
8.27	Lenta.ru	A blast occurred in Moscow underground
8.27	Radio Freedom	Two blasts in Moscow underground, more than 30 people killed
8.28	Rosbalt – Moscow. News	A blast occurred on Lubyanka underground station
8.31	Gazeta.ru	The number of casualties in the bomb blast reached 26 people
8.31	Radio station Mayak	At least 26 killed in the bomb blast on Lubyanka station
8.35	Publishing house Regnum	A blast occurred in Moscow underground
8.36	Interfax	A blast occurred on Lubyanka station, not less then 25 people killed
8.51	ITAR-TASS	Two blasts occurred in Moscow on the underground stations Lubyanka and Park Kultury, numerous casualties reported
9.05	Kommersant news feed	A blast occurred in Moscow underground on Lubyanka underground station
10.30	Vesti 24	Roller captions
11.00	TV-centre	Special report
11.24	REN TV	Special report
11.41	Radio of Russia	Moscow underground: 35 dead, 73 injured
13.00	NTV	News

mistakes led to numerous casualties among hostages. On their part, the authorities fiercely criticized the media. The information on the arrangements to storm the theatre was presented in one of the news-blocks and was thus revealed to the terrorists, which seriously affected the counterterrorist operation.

Generally, the content analysis results show that the intensity of criticism went down after the Nord-Ost attack. In 2002, the share of articles containing criticism of the government actions made up 44 per cent, whereas in 2004 and 2010 it reached 40 per cent. Unexpectedly, it was not the oppositional newspaper *Novaya Gazeta*, but the quality national daily *Izvestiya* that expressed the toughest stance on the authorities (42 per cent and 73 per cent of articles containing criticism, and in the case of *Izvestya*, sharp and direct criticism of the authorities). The government paper *Rossiyskaya Gazeta* met expectations by being the most loyal to the authorities. However, 30 per cent of its articles still contained criticism in all three cases.

The criticism of government actions and its stance is of a subtle and contextual nature. A well-known reporter of *Moskovsky Komsomolets*, Alexander Minkin, began his article on the passiveness of the authorities during the hostage taking at the Beslan school with an improvised interview, implying a typical reaction of government officials to major disasters in Russia:

- What happened to your submarine?
- It drowned.
- What happened to your planes?
- They crashed.
- What happened to your Underground?
- It exploded.
- What's happening to your school?
- It's in the process of normalization (Minkin, 2004).

The government sources which, from the journalists' perspective, were presenting limited amounts of information on terrorist attacks, have became the common object of criticism. 'The TV-set has turned into the magic lantern, and our vast country pays less and less attention to whether the picture coincides with the real life', Minkin wrote in the same article.

We would like to highlight the fact that constructive criticism of the authorities supported by journalistic investigation or experts' insights into the situation is not typical of the Russian press. Instead, there are sweeping criticisms verging on demagogy, with unsubstantiated, emotional claims, such as this one from *Izvestiya*:

> There are numerous questions on our minds. How could a thing like that happen in the city where every dark-haired person is checked, the city packed with special services and military structures? Why haven't the criminal financing channels been blocked? Where are our mighty high precision weapons, which can ostensibly crush even the enemies hiding in the deepest

of holes? Where are our helicopters, said to be the best in the world? Why can't we civilians get armed and protect ourselves since there seems to be no-one else to do that? And all our military officials are just freeloaders! (Izvestia, 2002)

'You are deprived of your right to live. You are just a small change, unnecessary material despised by the mediocre, greedy, cynical and yet dexterous tricksters in their dirty political struggle', the oppositional *Novaya Gazeta* writes, giving the generalized assessment of the military officials, politicians and the government structure on the whole. (Rost, J., *Novaya Gazeta*, 2004)

'The main lesson to be learned by the average Russian citizen after this tragedy is that the authorities and the people now live on their own account. If you are not ready to be killed just like prey, prepare to defend yourself. You can depend on yourself only', the mass newspaper *Moskovsky Komsomolets* calls on its readers (Rechkalov, 2010).

Hate speech analysis

Special attention was paid to the analysis of 'hate speech', as the national and religious aspects of terrorism are probably the most complicated topics to be covered. Each new terror act brings about another round of inter-ethnic confrontation. Sociologists' polls prove that the Caucasians still remain more 'foreign' to most Russians than, for example, the Ukrainians or Belarusians. 'Why is the Northern Caucasus region a matter of constant concern to Russia?' 'Is the formation of the all-Russian identity possible at all?' These questions reflect a common tone in Russian media.

An attempt to narrow terrorism down to the clash of two religions is one of the major mistakes committed by journalists. More often than not, the word 'Muslim' is associated with the word 'terrorist'. In Russia, Muslims are associated with Caucasians, and therefore the array 'terrorist equals Muslim equals Caucasian' comes into life. Even in times of lessening terrorist threat, those of Caucasus origin still remain the main subject of discrimination. Caucasus-phobia is quite typical of Russian newspaper content. Some papers take an anti-Chechen stance, the articles often contain condemnations of Islam or inappropriate comments on ethnic minorities.

Such coverage leaves little doubt about the Caucasian nature of terrorism and are quite surprised when faced with facts contradicting their beliefs: 'It was unexpected for us that the terrorists had no Caucasian accent when giving an interview', a *Komsomolskaya Pravda* reporter states in his comments on the Nord-Ost tragedy (Steshin et al., 2004). In covering the terrorist attack in Moscow Underground, journalists mention they were surprised by the fact that 'The suicide bombers were accompanied by women of 'Slavic type'. Even the reserved business paper *Kommersant* could not help using clichés like 'The explosions are marked by a clear Caucasian pattern' (Sergeev, 2010). Such set expressions as 'the Caucasian trace', a 'Transcaucasian national', the 'Caucasian look', etc.. are also quite frequent. Thanks to government officials, a new idiom, 'the Georgian trace', has come into life after covering the latest terrorist attack in 2010. The newspaper headlines are often quite provocative as well: 'Give Us the Militants' Bodies!' a headline from *Moskovsky Komsomolets* claimed shortly after Nord-Ost. (Maetnaya, 2002)

Some headlines contain chauvinistic or nationalistic stereotypes, such as 'A Terrorist National', which is associated in the mind of any Russian person with the cliché 'a Transcaucasian national'.

Izvestiya, positioning itself as a quality newspaper, turns out to have the largest amount of hate speech in its articles, with about 35 per cent of all publications containing hate speech, this figure being the highest among the editions researched. The newspaper is also marked by the presence of hate speech in its toughest form. Here is an extract from an article titled 'Disinfest Them Like Rats, Crush Them and Destroy Them': 'Terrorists are to be looked for and to be found in their rat holes, disinfested like rats, crushed and destroyed' (Kadyrov, 2010). It also welcomes letters from its readers containing aggressions towards the terrorist suspects ('fanatics', 'bastards', 'swine', 'criminals, running across the Chechen mountains'; 'eradicate the criminal ideology', etc.). A quote from the same newspaper after the 2010 terrorist attack in Moscow: 'The Caucasian women who have lost their husbands, brothers or sons, are characterized by a very peculiar concept of reality. The world no longer exists for them, there is only their craving for revenge …' (Beluza, 2010). The authors of such articles have a habit of generalizing about the whole Caucasus, which accounts for more than 100 nationalities.

Nevertheless, despite the general impression of the presence of hate speech in those newspapers, the data shows that the share of articles containing hate speech between 2002 to 2010 has grown only for two newspapers, *Moskovsky Komsomolets* and *Izvestiya*. As for other newspapers, this figure has gone down, and in some cases gone down dramatically (for example, the business paper *Kommersant*). The overall dynamic is still ambiguous. While the level of hate

Table 11.3   Presence of hate speech

Event covered	Presence of hate speech, no. of articles	Absence of hate speech, no. of articles	% of articles
Nord-Ost hostage	11	44	25
Beslan hostage	14	74	18.9
Blasts in Underground	18	77	23.3
Total	43	195	22

speech from Nord-Ost to Beslan went down (25 to 18.9 per cent), it increased again after the attack in the Underground (22 per cent).

Conclusions

Not surprisingly, the 'war on terror' in the Russian media has become a reflection or even an indication of generic processes that mirror the nature of media–society and media–power relations as well as the character of journalism in post-Soviet Russia. The coverage of the 'war on terror' in general and the three terrorist attacks against the civilian population in 2002, 2004 and 2010 points both to wider general trends in the global media, and inside Russian society, with its own cultural specificities.

The qualitative and quantitative analyses argue that in the past eight years professional approaches, styles of reporting and sources of information for the media coverage of terrorism in Russia have changed considerably. The key trends that have been identified are:

- the more responsible and balanced coverage of different viewpoints by conflicting agents;
- the newspapers are marked by the constructive criticism of the government actions;
- as a negative trend, the stable presence of hate speech in the newspapers;
- the attention to voices from the civil society, and substantial use of bloggers' texts available through new online and mobile technologies (although still insufficient);
- this became especially clear during events in January 2011 (see Table 11.4).

Table 11.4   Timeline of the media coverage of the terrorist attacks in 24 January 2011 during the first few hours after the blast

16.32	Twitter	Breaking news about the blast at Domodedovo airport
16.45	News Agencies	Breaking news about the blast at Domodedovo airport
16.50	Radio	Breaking news about the blast at Domodedovo airport
17.00	TV channel 'Dossh'	Breaking news about the terrorist attack, further live transmission non-stop
17.00	Russia Today	Retranslation of BBC World & CNN
17.22	'Rossiya-24'	Breaking news about the terrorist attack
18.00	Perviy kanal	News. A picture from the archive
18.55	Perviy kanal	News bulletin. A reporter on-the-spot and a witness video from YouTube

Source: Lenta.ru

Concluding the analysis of factors that have shaped the nature of the Russian media's 'war on terror', these might be identified as:

- political: resulting from the struggle of Caucasian ethno-political elites, especially of the Chechens, for autonomy/independence/separatism and its impact on Russian politics;
- economic: resulting from the financial crises of the Russian media and the rise of commercialism, on the one hand, and lack of transparency in financing media production, especially on the internet (sites, publications, videos, etc.);
- cultural: lack of consensus in society on crucial issues, low trust by citizens of the state and the lack of civil society control (silent audiences);
- ethical: blurring of boundaries in the system of social values;
- 'industrial': dictates of owners/editors-in-chief plus lack of professional solidarity and low professional standards as well as psychological vulnerability of media professionals.

References

Alali, A. and Eke, K. (eds) (1991) *Media Coverage of Terrorism: Methods of Diffusion*. London: Sage.

Antiterrorsticheskaya konvenciya Industrialnogo komiteta SMI (2003) (Antiterrorism convention of the Industrial media committee): www.mediasoyuz.ru/docs/antiterr_convent.doc

Beluza, A. (2010) Oni Oderzhimi Zhazdoi Mesti (They are craving for revenge), *Izvestia*, April 2, www.izvestia.ru/news/360250

Boudnitzki, O. (2000) *Terrorism v rossiiskom osvoboditelnom dvizhenii: ideologiya, etika, psihkologiya* (*Terrorism in Russian Liberation Movement: ideology, ethics, psychology*). Moscow: Rosspen.

Clutterbuck, R. (1981) *The Media and Political Violence*. London: Macmillan.

Crelinsten, R. D. (1991) *Terrorism and the Media: Problems, Solutions and Counterproblems*, in David Charters (ed.) *Democratic Responses to International Terrorism*. New York: Transnational Publisher.

Gallimore, T. (1988) *Media Compliance with Voluntary Press Guidelines for Covering Terrorism*, presented at the conference 'Terrorism and the News Media Research Project' in *Communication in Terrorist Events: Functions, Themes and Consequences*. Boston.

Herman, E. and Chomsky, N. (1988) *Manufacturing of Consent: The Political Economy of the Mass Media*. New York: Pantheon.

Hutchings, S. and Rulyova, N. (2009) *Television and Culture in Putin's Russia. Remote Control*. London: Routledge.

Kadyrov, R.(2010), Travit kak kris, davit' I unichtozhat' (Disinfest them like rats, crush them and destroy them), *Izvestia*, March 30, www.izvestia.ru/news/360100

Leeman, R. (1991) *The Rhetoric of Terrorism and Counterterrorism*. New York: Greenwood Press.

Lockyer, A. (2003) *The Relationship between the Media and Terrorism*. Canberra: Australian National University.

Makeenko, M. (2006) Borba s terrorismom i svoboda slova: USA PATRIOT Act – 5 let v efire (Struggle with terrorism and freedom of speech: USA PATRIOT Act – 5 years on air), *Medi@lmanak* 3: 26–30.

Maetnaya E. (2002), Otdayte nam trupy boevikov! (Give us the militants' bodies!), *Moskovskiy Komsomolets*, October 29, www.mk.ru/editions/daily/article/2002/10/29/202434-otdayte-nam-trupyi-boevikov.html

Miller, A. (ed.) (1982) *Terror, the Media and the Law*. New York: Transaction.

Moeller, S. (2009) *Packaging Terrorism. Co-opting the News for Politics and Profit*. Oxford: Wiley-Blackwell.

Minkin, A. (2004) Nas ostalos' malo. I vse mi zalozhniki (There are few of us, and we are all hostages), *Moskovskiy Komsomolets*, September 3.

Nacos, B. (1994) *Terrorism and the Media*. New York: Columbia University Press.

Olshansky, A. (2006) *Terroristicheskie akty v Lonodne 7 iulya 2005 goda'* (Terrorist attacks in London on July 7, 2005), *Medi@lmanak* 3: 30–40.

Paletz, D. and Schmid, A. (eds) (1991) *Terrorism and the Media*. London: Sage.

Pludowsky, T. (ed.) (2007) *How the World News Media Reacted to 9/11*. Washington: Marquette Books.

Pronina, E. (2006) *Grajdanskoe obshetvo i SMI: k edinstvu borby protiv terrorisma* (Civil society and the media: to the unity of the struggle against terrorism), *Medi@lmanak* 3: 20–23.

Rechkalov V., (2010) Vyibirayte puti ob'ezda (Choose bypass routes), *Moskovskiy Komsomolets*, March 29, www.mk.ru/politics/article/2010/03/29/457389-vyibirayte-puti-obezda.html

Richter, A. (2009) *Pravoye osnovy jurnalistiki* (*Legislative Basics of Journalism*). Moscow: Izd-vo Moskovskogo Universiteta.

Richter, A. (2005) Vojna s terrorizmom i svoboda informacii (The war on terrorism and the freedom of information), *Vestnik Moskovskogo Universiteta*, Series Zhounalistika, 3: 20–36.

Rost, J. (2004) Prosnites'! Odni nas ubivayut, drugie unizhayut (Wake up! Ones kill us, others injure our pride), *Novaya Gazeta*, September 6, www.novayagazeta.ru/data/2004/65/09.html

Sageman, M. (2004) *Understanding Terror Networks*. Philadelphia: University of Pennsylvania Press.

Sageman, M. (2005) Jihadi Networks of Terror, in *Countering Modern Terrorism. History, Current Issues and Future Threats. Proceedings of the Third International Security Conference*. Bielefeld: W. Bertelsmann Verlag.

Schlesinger, P. (1991) *Media, State and Nation: Political Violence and Collective Identities*. London: Sage.

Schmid, A. (1989) 'Terrorism and the media: the ethics of publicity'. *Terrorism and Political Violence* (1)4: 539–565.

Schmid, A. and de Graaf, J. (1982) *Violence as Communication: Insurgent Terrorism and the Western News Media*. London: Sage.

Sergeev N. (2010) Poezd Shakhidki (Shahidka's train), *Kommersant*, March 30.

Sovremennuy terrorism i borba s nim: socialno-gumanitarnue izmerenia (Contemporary Terrorism and Fight with It) (2007). Moscow: MCNMO.

Steshin D., Malik E. and Kornienko N. (2004) Nord-Ost prevratilsia v Zuid-Vest? (Nord-Ost has turned into Zuid-West?), *Komsomolskaya Pravda*, September 1, www.kp.ru/daily/23351/31693/

Stenger, M. B. (2005) *Globalism: Market Ideology Meets Terrorism*. Oxford: Rowman & Littlefield Publishers.

Thornburgh, N. (2010) Russia's long war, *Time*, August 16, www.time.com/time/magazine/article/0,9171,2008890,00.html

Tsyganov, V. (2004) *Terrorism i sredstva massovoy informacii (Terrorism and the Mass Media)*. Kiev: Nika-Centre.

Vartanova, E. (2000) *Regulation and Self-Regulation of Internet: A View from Russia*, presented at the conference, International Association for Media and Communication Research (IAMCR). Singapore.

Vartanova, E. (ed.) (2004) Rossia: osnovi setevogo obshestva (Russia: fundamentals of net society), pp. 163–187 in: *Nacionalnie modeli informacionnogo obshestva (National Models of Information Society)*. Moscow: IKAR.

Vartanova, E. (2006) Samoregulirovanie v informacionnom obshestve (Self-regulation in the information society) *Vestnik Moskovskogo Universiteta*, Series Zhounalistika 10: 8–19.

Vartanova, E. (2005) Self-Regulation as a form information security, in *Countering Modern Terrorism: History, Current Issues and Future Threats. Proceedings of the Third International Security Conference*. Bielefeld: W. Bertelsmann Verlag.

Vartanova, E. (2008) Terrorism i SMI: simbioz ili protivisoyaniye? K vorposy o prirode sovremennuh vzaimootno6eniy (Terrorism and media: symbiosis or opposition? To the question of the nature of contemporary relations) in *Materials of the Third International Conference on the Problems of Security and Counteracting Terrorism*. Moscow: MCNMO.

Vartanova, E. (ed.) (2009) *Zhournalistika protiv terrora (Journalism against Terror)*. Moscow: Mediamir.

Vartanova, E. and Smirnov, S. (2010) Modern Tendencies in the development of the Russian media industry and journalism, in *SMI v mejajusheysja Rossii* (*Mass Media in Changing Russia*) E. Vartanova (ed.). Moscow: Aspekt Press.

Vartanova, E. and Tkachyova, N. (2006) SMI pered licom terrorisma (Media facing terrorism), *Medi@lmanak* 3: 14–20.

Vitoushkin, D. (2005) Istoki terrorisma v Rossii: etnonatsionalnay factor (Terrorism roots in Russia: ethnonational factor), pp. 60–63, in *Rossija v mirovom politichesckom processe* (*Russia in the Global Political Process*). St Petersburg.

Wagner-Pacifici, R. (1986) *The Moro Morality Play: Terrorism as Social Drama*. Chicago: University of Chicago Press.

Wahl-Jorgensen, K. and Hanitzsch, T. (2009) *The Handbook of Journalism Studies*. London: Routledge.

Wieviorka, M. (1988) *The Making of Terrorism*. Chicago: University of Chicago Press.

Wilkinson, P. (1997) The media and terrorism: a reassessment, in *Terrorism and Political Violence* (9)2: 51–64. London: Frank Cass.

12

WIKILEAKS AND WAR LAWS

Stig A. Nohrstedt and Rune Ottosen

A Nordic perspective is provided by Stig Nohrstedt and Rune Ottosen – both long-time observers of post-Cold War conflict reporting and peace journalism. Their chapter examines 'new' wars and new media – such as WikiLeaks – and asks how these might impact on war journalism or may even lead to 'peace journalism'. Nohrstedt and Ottosen suggest that war journalism is embedded in national foreign-policy contexts. Focusing on NATO's bombing of Kosovo in 1999, their chapter raises important questions about the legality of that attack – NATO's first war – conducted without authorization from the UN Security Council. The use of humanitarian rhetoric was part of the NATO propaganda to justify the bombing of Kosovo and same logic continues, they argue, in NATO-led attacks in Afghanistan. Nohrstedt and Ottosen recommend that, rather than reproducing propaganda rhetoric from politicians, journalists should carry out their own investigations of the legal basis for warfare in cases like Kosovo and Afghanistan.

In his celebrated memoirs *Travels with Herodotus*, the legendary war journalist Ryszard Kapuściński treated the first history of the Western world, dating back over 2,000 years, as a guide and a source of knowledge and reflection in thinking about the seemingly eternal wars between East and West (Kapuściński, 2007). Like Herodotus, he wondered whether the conflicts in distant places that he reported to the world were completely new, or in fact the most recent instances of humankind's old and tragic fate. He was struck by the 'Old Greek's' thorough descriptions of places and peoples and the fact that he had even formulated historical laws based on the eternal sequences of aggression, revenge and counter-revenge (2007: 82 ff.). And he sympathized with Herodotus' investigative method of listening to every available source, such as the wise old men in Persia and Egypt, as well as his enormous project, the collection of all the knowledge of his time. He even described Herodotus as the first globalist because of this open-minded approach: 'His most important discovery? That there are many worlds. And that each is different' (ibdi: 264); '... in short, he was the first globalist' (ibid.: 77).

A perspective of millennia is perhaps a necessary corrective when reflecting about the terrorist attacks of 9/11 and the consequences for the media, since journalism is, as always, obsessed by the here and now, particularly when dramatic events occur. But with ten years' hindsight we wonder whether the terrorist attacks were actually as much of a historical shift as is sometimes thought. Like Gara LaMarche, we doubt that world-views have been changed through this event – perhaps it is more true to say that 9/11 was seen through different prisms which varied between countries and cultures, although less so in the US (quoted in Lynch and Galtung, 2010: 118).

Should we rather regard 9/11 as but one new conflict point on the historical map, where some trajectory lines cross, and where well-known patterns of a power struggle between a world empire and its opponents repeat themselves? We raise the question, but do not pretend to have the answer. Our task here is less grandiose: the time-frame for our reflections spans from the Gulf War 1990–91 to the Gaza War 2009, and concentrates on the ways that war journalism has developed during this period.

After the fall of the Berlin Wall in 1989 and the dissolution of the Soviet Union in 1991, there was talk of a New World Order holding the promise of international justice and peace. However, the Balkan Wars of the 1990s gave rise to the concept of 'new wars' that, in the wake of the terror attacks of 9/11, have acquired an iconicity rivalling that of fiction films. The 1990–91 Gulf War was the commercial breakthrough for the round-the-clock news channel CNN, as was the war in Afghanistan in 2001 for its competitor Al-Jazeera. The 2003 Iraq War saw the internet's great breakthrough in war journalism with the, at first anonymous, icon Salam Pax of the first generation of war bloggers. And in 2010, WikiLeaks disseminated the video film which showed how two journalists and several other civilians were killed by US soldiers in a helicopter over Baghdad. Later the same year, WikiLeaks published around 90,000 classified documents about the Afghanistan War, which created a wave of reports in the mainstream media about civilian deaths and the US military's cover-ups of illegal operations. A new world order, new wars and new media – what impact is all this having on war journalism? Do we see signs of a new war journalism, or perhaps even the development of 'peace journalism'?

Background

At the level of general social theory, the sobering experiences of the 'new wars', both in the Persian Gulf and in the Balkans in the first years of the 1990s set the scene for wishful thoughts, even though not everyone in academia accepted Huntington's diagnosis of the 'clash of civilizations' as a more adequate credo for the time than 'the end of history'. This was more so after 9/11, when superficial analyses would have it that Huntington's prophecy had come true, with the political implication that one should stand up to defend the Western way of life. More serious analysts objected that globalization, the buzzword of the 1990s, and the ideas of the world becoming 'a single place' (Robertson, 1992) were still relevant. Risk-society – or 'world risk-society' – could also have its 'cosmopolitan moment' (Beck, 2007: 47ff.). In the analyses of the development of international politics and transnational cultural processes it was never either/or but, rather, both/and (Beck, 2006: 4). Researchers have shown that mediated compassion for distant suffering in conflicts was important both for the framing of the news discourse and for the audiences' reception (e.g. Shaw, 1996; Nohrstedt et al., 2002).

However, there are reasons to be sceptical of the impact of mediated representations of suffering in distant places. Emotional news and photos of the victims of wars, famines or diseases may, when these are disseminated en masse, create compassion fatigue. The 'politics of pity' (Boltanski, 1999) is not necessarily successful beyond the realm of local or national identity. Therefore, the media generally are not – owing to their national horizon and audience – fit to support a cosmopolitan disposition. This happens in rare instances of news journalism. But it could be done with media promoting a discourse in which justice is in focus and which is based upon 'effective speech', that is, what can be done to support and empower the victims (Chouliaraki, 2006, 2009). With 'justice' as the key criterion, it seems evident that the attention of the cosmopolitan spectator should be on the norms established in international law and human rights as codified by the UN organizations and other international agencies.

In this New World Order media attention on humanitarian aspects and the sufferings of innocent civilians seems to have an impact – although less impressive when it comes to cosmopolitanism – with regard to the ways Western democracies wage wars (Shaw, 2005). Here we can see the dramatic consequences of the power of media opinion when it colludes with strong political and military interests. On the one hand, the increased scrutiny by media and other institutions (such as humanitarian organizations), on the human costs and agony of the violence, pushes governments and military authorities to plan operations with media coverage in mind: first, with the goal of minimizing losses of their own troops (since growing casualties would weaken public-support on the home-front); second, with considerations for how the use of weapons will influence international opinion. Altogether this has led to what Shaw calls 'risk-transfer war' in which a main strategy is that all risks – physical, political, economic or opinion losses – should be carried by the enemy (Shaw, 2005).

This is a moment of cosmopolitanism in the sense that transnational media reporting creates a global public sphere that makes a difference to military planning and operations. The good thing, of course, is that 'collateral damage' and the killing of innocent civilians must be avoided in order not to risk the operations' political and propaganda objectives. On the other hand, as we will elaborate below, there are other methods than restrictions on the troops that can be applied to 'sanitize' the images of the warfare, e.g. methods that target the journalists rather than the militaries. Hence journalists and media are also involved in modern Western warfare in new ways that pose serious challenges to their professional ambitions.

However, as indicated above, the 'banal nationalism' (Billig, 1995) of the media is far from being replaced by a cosmopolitan outlook. Previous research shows that the national contexts have a substantial framing impact on mediated war discourses. After 9/11 and the Global War on Terror (GWOT), international politics has changed dramatically, with new foreign and security policy alliances emerging. In the Scandinavian region, the previous division between NATO members (Denmark and Norway) and non-aligned countries (Finland and Sweden) is gradually reduced in importance and new patterns of cooperation are taking over. The Nordic countries are presently involved in a formal defence cooperation through NORDCAPS (Nordic Coordinated Arrangement for Peace Support), NORDAC (Nordic Armaments Cooperation) and NORDSUP (Nordic Supportive Defence Structures). These changes will probably in a longer time perspective have an impact on the media framing too.

With these general developments in mind, we will in this chapter present a perspective on how war journalism has changed during the last two decades, in Western countries, and specifically in Scandinavia. We focus on the challenges that war correspondents and media face in the new wars: the increased dangers and threats to which the new way of making war; and the need for a more globalized journalism with competence to report and analyse the legal aspects of the post-9/11 militarized security policy (Magder, 2003).

First, then, the physical risks involved in reporting from the war theatres of today. In spite of the poor and dangerous conditions in which Kapuściński reported from conflicts around the world, it may well be that he would have regarded the new wars as even more threatening for a war correspondent like himself than those he had once covered.

The Real First Casualty and the Globalization of War Journalism

Admittedly, the first-casualty cliché is passé nowadays, mainly because of its foundation in an individualized concept of journalism (Knightley, 1975). Today, at least two other views have more relevance with their focuses, on the one hand, on the organizational-institutional restrictions on war journalism and, on the other, the ways that journalism has become a battleground for warfare – and not only in terms of propaganda war (Thussu and Freedman, 2003). The new Western way of war has led to growing casualties among the journalists – to an alarming degree, with consequences for the reporting of the wars. However, rather than taking truth as the analytical point of departure, it seems to us that one should concentrate on how reporting about civilian casualties and the attempts to manipulate and control the media have developed over time, in order to grasp the ways that the conditions of war journalism affect the content of war reports, including its accuracy and reliability.

In previous publications, we have presented findings about important trends in war journalism since the Cold War (e.g. Nohrstedt and Ottosen, 2010). The results concern mainly Norwegian and Swedish media, but are presumably more widely applicable – at least hypothetically. These trends within war journalism since the Gulf War of 1990–91 are not overwhelmingly dramatic but rather changes in the lower statistical register – that is, from a couple of percentages of the content to around ten per cent.

These trends are:

- Media tend to give increasing attention to war's 'true face', that is, to the sufferings of civilian populations and civilian victims of warfare.
- The conditions of war journalism are increasingly receiving attention and becoming the object of self-critical reflections in the media. The conflicting parties' attempts to manipulate the reporting by more or less sophisticated means and propaganda strategies have become news and this has caused various media to express reservations about the reliability of their reporting and to encourage the audience to be critical.
- Visual materials have been given an increasing amount of space which has, however, not been accompanied by greater visual reflexivity. Unlike the content of written texts, the visual content has not been subjected to the same critical scrutiny or complemented by notes of reservations before the audience (Nohrstedt, 2009).

In discourse-analytic terms, these trends can be described as instances of change within a global discursive order. News reporting from international armed conflicts is characterized, like other foreign news, by a growing international exchange of material. The increasing availability of different transnational news channels enables a diversity that is not always utilized. In this connection, establishment of the satellite TV channel Al Jazeera is one example of the importance of new players in the media market.

Another component of the global discursive order is the development of discourses of compassion that – through live-broadcast charity concerts in which music and film celebrities participate – have directed media attention to human suffering in distant places. Compassion is becoming globalized which, for war journalism, is an incitement to give prominence to 'worthy victims', even those afflicted by the US's and other Western democracies' military operations. In addition, globalization is generally considered to increase reflexivity (Beck, Giddens and Lash, 1994; Hjarvard, 2001), which in this context is closely represented by professional self-criticism and openness about the institutional conditions of war journalism.

These findings, however, should not be interpreted as indicating that the discursive order of war reporting has been revolutionized since the end of the Cold War. The institutional embedding of the media and reporters still means that military, political and economic power structures exert strong influence on news reporting from armed conflicts. Nor do the processes of globalization appear to have caused the cultural mechanisms of discursive inclusion and exclusion to undergo any radical changes compared to the ethnocentrism that Edward Said and others have exposed in Western culture (cf. Nohrstedt, 2005).

This has a lot to do with the fact that media discourses in general, and war journalism in particular, are embedded in a national foreign-policy context and the effect of the warring parties' propaganda on media reporting depends to a large degree on this context. The polarized propaganda discourse that depicts the conflict in black-and-white has, not surprisingly, the greatest impact on the media of the involved parties and, consequently, a lesser impact on the media of uninvolved countries (Nohrstedt and Ottosen, 2001: 255 ff.).

This has consequences for the depiction of the victims. The polarization into worthy and unworthy victims most clearly influences the media of the countries directly involved. Researchers have shown that during the Iraq War of 2003, German media devoted significantly more space to Iraqi victims than did American or British media (Tumber and Palmer, 2004: 97). The degree of a country's involvement in a conflict is an important factor in explaining the influence of war propaganda on its media, and which victims are accorded the status of being 'worthy'. This conclusion, however, does not contradict the argument that in Western countries the reporting from international conflicts are also Westernized – that the reporting is largely framed by cultural stereotypes and prejudiced identity constructions.

On the contrary, the frequent performative expressions that proliferated in European media after 9/11 – and most notably 'Today we are all Americans' – were only the tip of the cultural iceberg that also marks the mediated banal nationalism we see in war journalism. These cultural links and identification with the Western world should not be conceived as separate from the global power relations with the US (the only remaining superpower and therefore with great capacity to influence the rest of the world) and not least when it comes to how the so-called international community interprets and implements international laws and human rights.

New Wars and International Law

In the scholarly debate on the global war on terror many authors refer to the Iraq War and the Bush doctrine[1] as a turning point of American readiness to challenge international law (see for example, Griffin and Scott, 2007; cf. Lynch and Galtung, 2010). We rather see the bombing of former Yugoslavia in 1999 as a test case for US/NATO's policy of ignoring the UN and international law. Even though the bombing happened under the Clinton administration, there is no doubt that respect for international law and human rights decreased dramatically during the presidency of George W. Bush (Nohrstedt and Ottosen, 2010). The lack of respect for the Geneva Conventions and international law was openly admitted by Vice President Dick Cheney at the Meet the Press on the first Sunday after 11 September 2001, when he frankly stated:

> 'We'll have to work sort of the dark side, if you will … We've got to spend time in the shadows in the intelligence world. A lot of what needs to be done here will have to be done quietly, without any discussion, using sources and methods that are available to our intelligence agencies – if we are going to be successful. That's the world these folks operate in. And, uh so it's going to be vital for us to use any means at our disposal basically, to achieve our objectives.' (Cited in Mayer, 2008: 9–10)

The assumption in the US government at the time was that the US had a natural right to decide unilaterally the legal basis for its action rather than follow the rulings of international bodies. McMutry refers to the September 2002 National Security Document: 'We will take the action necessary to ensure that our efforts to meet our global security commitments are not impaired by the International Criminal Court (ICC), whose jurisdiction does not extend to Americans and which we do not accept' (McMutry, 2007: 130). Legally this may be correct since the US did not sign the ICC statute, but from a moral point of view, considering that the US was active and committed in the drafting process, it is a policy open to criticism. The treatment of prisoners at Guantánamo, widely criticized by international lawyers (for example Zerrougui et al., 2006), and Abu Ghraib, as well as kidnapping of suspected terrorist and bringing them to other countries for torture are all examples of practices arising from this policy (Suskind, 2007). In legal terms, the fact that the US has not signed the ICC Statute is not a valid reason for claiming that the country is not liable when it comes to breaches of either – if the Iraq War was in fact a war – the Geneva Convention of treatment of POWs or, if it was not a war, the civil right to be prosecuted by a court. Neither is it a valid argument for not being liable with respect to the customary law prohibition of torture, which is binding for all states regardless of whether they have signed the treaties or not.

The Controversial Legal Basis for the Attack on Yugoslavia

NATO decided to resort to armed force against Yugoslavia on 24 March 1999 unilaterally, without authorization by the UN Security Council. The political rationale given was that there was a humanitarian crisis going on with thousands of Kosovars in danger of being 'ethnically cleansed' if the international community did not intervene militarily against President Slobodan Milosevic and his regime. The seriousness of the situation has been in disputed (Chomsky, 1999). But even if the Kosovo Albanians were driven out in large numbers, this is not a valid argument that the attack was in accordance with international law.

According to a leading Norwegian law professor, Ståle Eskeland, no NATO country could argue that it acted in self-defence (Eskeland, 2004). No resolution that could have authorized the attack was submitted to the UN Security Council. Customary law obliges states to act if human rights are seriously violated and to prevent crimes against humanity, but how this should be implemented is open to debate. As Eskeland has noted, NATO countries argued that the attack was in accordance with international law because the UN Security Council was paralysed. It was expected that Russia would veto a suggestion to authorize the attack, and thus it was never suggested that the matter should be brought before the Security Council. In an article, former state secretary in the Norweigan Foreign Ministry, the lawyer Vidar Helgesen, wrote a solid legal analysis about whether there was a basis in international law for the attack. He concluded: 'I have come to the conclusion such a basis does not exist, neither in the UN Charter or in customary international law. There is no basis for saying that the intervention has created the basis for new international law' (Helgesen, 1999: 43; authors' translation).

What would the legal consequence be if Norway took part in an illegal war? According to Eskeland, members of government can only be prosecuted for impeachment, where Odelstinget, a chamber in Stortinget (the Norwegian Parliament) is the prosecuting authority. It is beyond the political realities of the world to imagine that Odelstinget could have started an investigation to determine whether there is legal basis for an indictment against the then Prime Minister Kjell Magne Bondevik and his former government colleagues. Prime Minister Bondevik insisted that the operation was a 'humanitarian intervention' and not a war. The use of humanitarian rhetoric was part of the NATO propaganda to justify the war (Chomsky, 1999; Hammond and Herman, 2000). Only years after he had left office would Bondevik admit that Norway had taken part in a war (Ottosen, 2009: 28). To have an open and frank debate about whether Norway was about to break international law before the attack took place was beyond the borders of public debate in Norway. Major decisions in military and security policy matters are decided according to Norway's membership in NATO and the alliance with the US (Linneberg, 2001). Thus, loyalty to NATO was more important than international law, which also seemed to be the case with the legal issues in relation to Afghanistan.

9/11 – a Turning Point in Western Policy towards War Journalism?

The US response to 9/11 became, if not a turning point, at least a radicalization of the American practising of double standards – in legal matters in general and in the treatment of media and journalists in particular. Numerous examples of improper interference with freedom of the press in the US after 11 September 2001 have been documented (Ottosen, 2002b). Even more remarkable is that the American authorities have tried to broaden their media control on a global scale. The first step after the attack against Afghanistan on 7 October 2001 was that the Pentagon bought up all the images from commercial satellite companies that could potentially be used to challenge the official US views on the development of the war. Then US authorities tried in vain to push the regime in Qatar to intervene against the broadcasts of Al Jazeera which took the liberty of broadcasting the speeches of bin Laden. When Al Jazeera could not be stopped in this way, US authorities asked their own media to refrain from the use of images from Al Jazeera with footage of, among other things, bin Laden. This was a clear attempt to intervene in the freedom of the press, but even more remarkable, the mainstream American media gave in and stopped 'live' broadcasts from Al Jazeera.

The next intervention came when the government complained that media coverage was placing too much focus on civilian casualties in Afghanistan. CNN staff received instructions from the chairman of the board to 'balance' the coverage of civilian casualties in Afghanistan by reminding viewers that it was because of the Taliban regime's support to Al-Qaeda that the bombing was necessary. This type of detailed directive was also implemented in other media. Finally, the Pentagon took the drastic step of bombing Al Jazeera's Kabul office on 12 November 2001. BBC reporter Nik Gowing has investigated this incident and in an article in the *Guardian* (2 March 2003) he expressed great concern about the attitudes he met when interviewing officials in the Pentagon. To his surprise they did not regard it their responsibility to check whether electronic signals from media offices such as Al Jazeera's in Kabul are normal journalistic activities or part of information warfare. In any case, they were permitted to attack with military forces on the suspicion alone (Gowing, 2003; cf. Suskind, 2006).

One and a half years later, during the Iraq War, the American military attacked journalists on three separate occasions on the same day, 8 April 2003. Al Jazeera had, after the events in Kabul, informed the Pentagon of the coordinates of its office in the Iraqi capital. Nevertheless, one of its photographers was killed and another journalist wounded on the roof of the clearly marked building when it was fired upon from the air. A Reuters photographer and another photographer from the Spanish TV channel Telecino were killed when an American tank opened fire on the Palestine Hotel, well known as the lodgings for Western journalists. US forces also fired on the Baghdad office of Abu Dhabi TV, despite the fact that the name of the station was written in large blue letters on the roof. Knightley is convinced about the purpose: 'The Pentagon is determined that there will be no more reporting from the enemy side, and that a few deaths among correspondents who do so will deter others' (Knightley, 2004: 104; cf. Gowing, 2003: 232–33).

Following these events, the Committee to Protect Journalists started an independent investigation, concluding that, although it could not be proven that Al Jazeera and other media were chosen military targets, they were nevertheless civilian targets and therefore the attacks violated the Geneva Convention. It was further stated that the US invasion force was legally responsible, even if it could not be proved that the television station was struck by intention (Ottosen, 2009). Wadah Khanfar, director general of Al Jazeera, claimed in an open letter in the *Guardian* on 11 December 2010 that there is evidence in the WikiLeaks material proving that president Bush seriously suggested to bomb Al Jazeera headquarters in Qatar, and that this plan had been confirmed to him by a senior US official (Khanfar, 2010).

We have gone into the detail of some examples of how journalists reporting from the new wars are at great risk because they may reveal the propaganda lies and sanitized images of the Western way of war that politicians and military authorities disseminate. But this kind of 'risk-transfer war' policy did not start with the 9/11 terrorist attacks. During the Kosovo conflict NATO had already used weapons against the media, namely when they attacked the Serbian television's building in Belgrade and killed 16 media personnel (Ottosen, 2002a: 149). This was clearly a violation of the Geneva Convention's prohibition on targeting civilians and its rule of proportional warfare.

The eagerness of the parties in conflicts to censor journalists as well as to attack them physically are important obstacles to reporting from conflict areas (Nohrstedt and Ottosen, 2010). Statistics indicate that journalists are often targets in recent wars. According to the IFJ, more than 1,100 journalists and media employees were killed on duty between 1995 and 2007. The number of journalists killed worldwide has risen 244 per cent between 2002 and 2007. Statistically speaking, journalists were ten times more likely than any of the 250,000 American and British soldiers to be killed in Iraq, which has been the most dangerous place to work as a journalist in recent years. A vast majority of the journalists killed in Iraq were not embedded (Gierhart, 2008: 1). The embedded journalists were protected physically by being in military units and, more importantly, their presence was regarded as beneficial by the military. Are other journalists and media facilities perceived to be legitimate targets in modern warfare? This issue should be made a priority for media researchers and journalists in the years to come.

Journalism Based on Rhetoric or Law?

Rather than uncritically reproduce propaganda rhetoric from politicians, we suggest that journalists carry out their own investigations of the legal basis for warfare in cases like Kosovo, Iraq, Afghanistan and other conflicts. The first step could be to listen to what the juridical experts say about the legal issues. Norway's foremost expert on international law, Professor Geir Ulfstein, has argued that the Norwegian approach to the legal issues in NATO-led warfare in Afghanistan can be questioned (Ottosen, 2009). According to Ulfstein, the problem began with the bombing of Yugoslavia in 1999. As mentioned earlier, Norway participated with military support for the bombing despite there being no UN mandate. Ulfstein discusses Prime Minister Bondevik's statement in Parliament on 18 March 1999 in which he approved the use of force. Bondevik referred to a UN Security Council resolution, a report from the UN secretary general and a statement from the Security Council's president. Ulfstein suggested that the reason Bondevik had to rely on these three documents was that none of the three elements separately provided a legal basis for the use of military force. Ulfstein claimed that they do not collectively provide a legitimate basis in international law for war either. Neither did the independent commission on Kosovo find that the war against Yugoslavia was legal even though the commission concluded that it was legitimate because it allegedly stopped the Serbs' ethnic cleansing.

The legal problems, according to Ulfstein, continued after 9/11, when the US chose to attack Afghanistan, putting forward the argument for the right to self-defence. Ulfstein believes that the confusion and weak legal arguments on these issues can create a dangerous precedent. Although he agrees that a right to self-defence against the terrorist attacks on 9/11 can be justified, he doubts that the US has the right to a permanent war against Afghanistan (Ulfstein, 2008). His critique relates to an earlier article in which Ulftstein argued that the attacks on Afghanistan should be seen in light of previous military attacks by the US against countries like Libya in 1986, Iraq in 1993 and Sudan in 1998 (Ulfstein, 2003). He says that such use of force has the character of revenge or punishment, rather than self-defence. International law does not permit the use of force as a reprisal. Ulftstein warns against using Security Council Resolution 1368 to legitimize a large-scale military attack against Afghanistan. However, Norwegian and Swedish politicians have used Resolution 1368 for legitimizing the two countries participation in the ISAF-operations. When Scandinavian politicians speak about the legal aspects, they rarely talk about the attack on Afghanistan, preferring to concentrate on the fact that the ISAF-forces have acquired a UN mandate. Humanitarian rhetoric applied in selective or biased interpretations of international law like in these examples needs to be scrutinized by public media (Ottosen, 2009). Unfortunately we do not see much attempt in that direction by mainstream media in Scandinavian countries.

WikiLeaks – Source of Truth or Target in the Threat-society?

Considering the experiences of a number of attacks on critical media coverage in the new Western way of warfare, with the obvious intent of avoiding or at least restricting reports about 'the true face of war', we welcome the appearance of alternative sources such as WikiLeaks. It is, of course, not a new phenomenon for classified military intelligence to be revealed retrospectively; an earlier example that comes to mind is the Pentagon papers, revealed by Daniel Ellsberg in the *New York Times* in 1971 (Apple, 1996; cf. Cohen, 2010). However, the new Western way of war has changed the conditions and implications of such leaks.

The question here is where it will take us. Probably the revelations will not have a dramatic effect on public opinion. No doubt alternative public information sources like these are important for widening the global public sphere on discourses concerning wars. They offer facts to counter the views that the hegemonic powers promote – both internationally and nationally. However, the facts as such are not entirely new. Therefore the politicians in government are often successful in their efforts to divert attention, and interpretations, from the revelations.

The main question is whether the framing of the GWOT is affected on a larger scale. Factual details, even when they reveal vast numbers of civilian casualties, as in the material WikiLeaks has made public, do not matter that much to general attitudes and opinions or to the media agenda – beyond the moment they are reported. We see this is in the Scandinavian countries where, as we have argued, the humanitarian purposes of the military operations in Afghanistan are emphasized by authorities and in the media. The background information about the true face of the war shakes that propaganda image for a moment, but it does not change the general public opinion. This must be explained partly by the strong self-perception of being a humanitarian and peaceful people, a self-image that rejects contrary information and circumscribes opinion.

Another explanation would be to draw on Entman's cascade model which has a lot to say about how, metaphorically speaking, the force of gravity helps the state-sponsored views to proliferate, but also about the difficulties for opposite frames to find their way up to the ruling elite circles (Entman, 2003). Together with other well-researched theories about the role of the media for shaping public opinion in conflict situations, it does not support any far-reaching hopes that even massive exposure of censored factual information that goes against the views and information from the authorities will change the public opinion or the framing in the media.

The experiences of dead journalists and the case of WikiLeaks should be understood in a context of the emergence of a threat-society as a later phase of the risk-society Beck wrote about more than two decades ago (Beck, 1986). In threat-society there are trends that work as undercurrents, and channel opinions towards accepting violations of human rights and international laws for the sake of security. The culture of fear has a firm grip on popular culture, mediatized discourses and people's minds, and it is exploited for threat policies based upon speculative threat images together with public appeals for patriotism and trust to the leaders in these difficult times. In particular, the militarization of security policy implies that democratic deliberation is moulded into an iron cage of complicity and subordination (Nohrstedt, 2011).

Historically speaking, 9/11 was certainly a world event with wide and tragic consequences, also for the global respect for freedom of expression, civil rights and international law. Dissident voices and alternative information sources are regarded as Fifth Columns instead of as the Fourth Estate, and are targeted as enemies, almost equivalent to illegal combatants. Thus the vagueness of international law when it comes to the responsibility to protect human rights and to prevent crimes against humanity – arguments that the NATO used for its intervention in Yugoslavia – has been exploited and extended to legal areas where there are strict regulations, for example the conduct of war under the Geneva Conventions. This stretching of what is legal (or, at least, not prohibited) is a major problem in the new wars, in particular the GWOT. In addition, it is a huge challenge to journalism since one of its consequences is the dramatically increased risks involved for journalists reporting about these wars. The time is ripe for a 'peace journalism' that questions and challenges 'military humanism' whenever it appears – for the sake of journalists' own safety, for democracy and for an informed global public sphere.

Endnote

1   The Bush Doctrine was declared in the State of the Union address, January 2002, and included three main strands: 1) concept of 'pre-emptive war'; 2) regime change through military action; 3) aggressive promotion of democracy, US-style.

References

Apple Jr., R.W. (1996) Pentagon Papers, *New York Times*, 23 June.

Beck, Ulrich (1986) *Risk Society. Towards a New Modernity*. London: SAGE.

Beck, Ulrich (2006) *The Cosmopolitan Vision*. Cambridge: Polity.

Beck, Ulrich (2007) *World at Risk*. Cambridge: Polity.

Beck, Ulrich, Giddens, Anthony and Lash, Scott (1994) *Reflexive Modernization*. Stanford: Stanford University Press.

Billig, Michael (1995) *Banal Nationalism*. London: SAGE.

Boltanski, L. (1999) *Distant Suffering. Politics, Morality and the Media*. Cambridge: Cambridge University Press.

Chomsky, Noam (1999) The *New Military Humanism. Lessons from Kosovo*. Monroe, ME: Common Courage Press.

Chouliaraki, Lilie (2006) *The Spectatorship of Suffering*. London: SAGE.

Chouliaraki, Lilie (2009) Global Divides in Transnational Media. Managing the Visibility of Suffering. *Nordicom Review* 30: 73–90.

Cohen, Noam (2010) What Would Daniel Ellsberg Do With the Pentagon Papers Today? *New York Times*, 18 April.

Entman, Robert M. (2003) Cascading Activation. Contesting the White House's Frame after 9/11. *Political Communication* 20(4): 415–32.

Eskeland, Ståle (2003) Krig og fredsbevarende operasjoner: Lovlig, ulovlig eller straffbart. *Norsk Militært Tidsskrift* nr. 12.

Gierhart, Cindy (2008) *Targeting Media: The Legal Restrictions on States Attacking Media in Times of War*. Unpublished manuscript, Summer.

Gowing, Nik (2003) Journalists and War: The Troubling New Tensions Post 9/11, in Daya Kishan Thussu and Des Freedman (eds) *War and the Media: Reporting Conflict 24/7*. London: SAGE.

Griffin, David Ray and Scott, Peter Dale (2007) *9/11 and American Empire. Intellectuals Speak Out*. Massachusetts: Olive Branch Press.

Hammond, Philip and Herman, Edward (eds) (2000) *Degraded Capability. The Media and the Kosovo Crisis*. London: Pluto.

Helgesen, Vidar (1999) Kosovo og Folkeretten. *Institutt for forsvarsstudier skriftserie* 4/1999.

Herman, Edward and Chomsky, Noam (1988) *Manufacturing Consent: The Political Economy of the Mass Media*. New York: Pantheon Books.

Hjarvard, Stig (2001) News Media and the Globalization of the Public Sphere, in Stig Hjarvard (ed.) *News in a Globalized Society*. Göteborg: Nordicom.

Hume, Mick (1997) *Whose War is it Anyway? The Dangers of the Journalism of Attachment*. London: BM InformInc.

Kapuściński, Ryszard (2007) *Travels With Herodotus*. London: Penguin.

Khanfar, Wadah (2010) They Bombed My Staff. Now the US is after Our Integrity. *Guardian*, 11 December.

Knightley, Phillip (1975) *The First Casualty*. London: Deutsch.

Knightley, Phillip (2004) History or bunkum?, in David Miller (ed.) *Tell Me Lies. Propaganda and Media Distortion in the Attack on Iraq*. London: Pluto.

Lewis, Charles and Reading-Smith, Mark (2008) *Iraq The War Card*. The Center for Public Integrity.

Linneberg, Arild (2001) *Tretten triste essays om krig og litteratur*. Oslo: Gyldendal.

Lynch, Jake and Galtung, Johan (2010) *Reporting Conflict: New Directions in Peace Journalism*. St.Lucia, Queensland: University of Queensland Press.

Magder, Ted (2003) Watching What We Say: Global Communication in a Time of Fear, in Daya Kishan Thussu and Des Freedman (eds) *War and the Media: Reporting Conflict 24/7*. London: SAGE.

Mayer, Jane (2008) *The Dark Side. The Inside Story of How the War on Terror Turned into a War on American Ideals*. New York: Doubleday.

McMurtry, John (2007) 9/11 and 9/11 Wars: Understanding the Supreme Crimes, in David Ray Griffin and Peter Dale Scott (eds) *9/11 and American Empire. Intellectuals Speak Out*. Massachusetts: Olive Branch Press.

Nohrstedt, Stig (2005) Media Reflexivity in the War on Terror. Three Swedish Dailies and the Iraq War, in Stig Nohrstedt and Rune Ottosen (eds) *Global War – Local Views. Media Images of the Iraq War*. Göteborg: Nordicom.

Nohrstedt, Stig (2009) New War Journalism. Trends and Challenges, *Nordicom Review*, 30(1): 83–100.

Nohrstedt, Stig (2011) Media and Threat-Society, in Nohrstedt, Stig (ed.) *Communicating Risks – Towards the Threat-Society*. Göteborg: Nordicom.

Nohrstedt, Stig and Ottosen, Rune (eds) (2001) *Journalism and the New World Order: Gulf War, National News Discourses and Globalization*. Göteborg: Nordicom.

Nohrstedt, Stig and Ottosen, Rune (eds) (2004) *U.S. and the Others: Global Media Images on the 'War on Terror'*. Göteborg: Nordicom.

Nohrstedt, Stig and Ottosen, Rune (eds) (2005) *Global War – Local Views. Media Images of the Iraq War*. Göteborg: Nordicom.

Nohrstedt, Stig and Ottosen, Rune (2010) Brothers in Arms or Peace? The Media Images of Swedish and Norwegian Defence – and Military Policy. *Conflict and Communication Online*, 9(2), www.cco.regener-online. de/2010_2/pdf/nohrstedt_ottosen.pdf

Nohrstedt, Stig, Höijer, Birgitta and Ottosen, Rune (2002) *Kosovokonflikten, medierna och medlidandet*. Stockholm: Styrelsen för psykologiskt försvar Rapport 190.

Ottosen, Rune (2002a) *Patriotiske virveltrommer eller kritisk krigsjournalistikk. Norske nyhetsmediers dekning av Kosovokrigen i 1999*. PRIO-report No. 8, 2002.

Ottosen, Rune (2002b) Pressefriheten under press etter 11. September. Redaktørinstituttets status 2002. Oslo: Årbok fra Redaktørforeningen 2002.

Ottosen, Rune (2008) Carsten, Hassan and Alaa, *Dagbladet*, 9 February 2008.

Ottosen, Rune (2009) *VG, Saddam og vi. Et kritisk blikk på nyhetsdekning av krig og konflikt*. Kristiansand IJ/Høyskoleforlaget.

Ottosen, Rune (2010) Kampen om bildene, *Dagbladet*, 13 June.

Robertson, Roland (1992) *Globalization. Social Theory and Global Culture*. London: SAGE.

Shaw, Martin (1996) *Civil Society and Media in Global Crisis*. London: Pinter.

Shaw, Martin (2005) *The New Western Way of Warfare*. Cambridge: Polity.

Sjøvaag, Helle (2005) Attached or Detached? Subjective Methods in War Journalism. Masteroppgave Institutt for medievitenskap, Universitetet i Bergen.

Suskind, Ron (2006) *The One Percent Doctrine. Deep Inside America's Pursuit of its Enemies Since 9/11*. New York: Simon & Schuster.

Thussu, Daya Kishan and Freedman, Des (2003) Introduction, in Daya Kishan Thussu and Des Freedman (eds) *War and the Media:* Reporting Conflict 24/7. London: SAGE

Tumber, Howard and Palmer, Jerry (2004) *Media at War.* London: SAGE.

Ulfstein, Geir (2003) Terror og folkerett. *Lov og Rett*, No. 2., 2003

Ulfstein, Geir (2008) Hvor hellig er folkeretten. *Dagbladet*, 22 May.

Zerrougui, Leila et al. (2006) Situation of the Detainees at Guantánamo, U.N. Doc. E/CN.4/2006/120.

13

TELEVISION AND IMMIGRATION IN FRANCE[1]

Tristan Mattelart

If multiculturalism has been undermined by its securitization in Britain, the situation with integration of Muslim minorities into the French mainstream has been fraught with difficulties, as Tristan Mattelart suggests in this chapter, based on an extensive project he is directing about Maghrebi minorities in France. Although the events of 9/11 and the 'war on terror' have contributed to the representations of the Muslim minorities as a 'menace' to the French way of life, Mattelart maps the latent racism which has characterized French attempts at integration and shows interesting historical continuities in the representations of Muslim minorities on French television. He suggests that mainstream French media have represented the 'Arab' living in France as an 'enemy from within', endangering national cultural cohesion – a process aggravated by the availability of the myriad media outlets, not least the bourgeoning Arab satellite channels beaming Arabic programmes into homes in the *banlieues*.

In the aftermath of 11 September 2001 and the subsequent so-called 'war' on Islamist terrorism, populations of Maghrebi origin in France have been depicted in the media as having traits of a growing menace. Among others, Thomas Deltombe and Mathieu Rigouste have analysed how, through 'a series of amalgams and ambivalences around the symbolic categories of the "immigré" and the "foreigner", the "Muslim" and the "Islamist", the "youngster of the banlieues" or the "terrorist", French media have tended since then to represent the 'Arab' living in France as an 'enemy from within', an *'ennemi intérieur'*, a kind of fifth column endangering national cohesion (Deltombe and Rigouste, 2005: 191).

In this chapter, I will first show how French television has historically constructed minorities of Maghrebi origin as a danger for the national community. Indeed, far from constituting a rupture with the preceding periods, post 9/11 media representations of these populations in France have to be seen, in many respects, as a historical continuity.

In a seemingly contradictory way, the aftermath of 9/11 has also coincided with an increased consciousness among French public authorities of the need to foster policies aiming at improving the media representation of ethnic minorities – and more particularly those of Maghrebi origin – on television. As I will try to demonstrate, these policies can be viewed as official attempts to enhance these minorities' 'integration' in French society, at a time when this is seen as endangered by a combination of both local and global threats. Here too, an historical background will be needed in order to understand to what extent the most recent developments in this field are in the continuity of long-established French media policies towards populations of Maghrebi origins.

The Construction of a Threat

In her seminal work on the way in which immigration issues were portrayed in the French newspapers between 1974 and 1984, Simone Bonnafous has showed that, from the 1980s on, coinciding with an economic crisis, Maghreb migrant workers, who until the beginning of the 1970s had mainly been presented as social victims, began to be designated, increasingly, as constituting a social, as well as an economical, a political and a cultural 'problem' (Bonnafous, 1991). This negative portrayal was not so much the result of the discrete words used by journalists to describe the processes at stake than the result of the 'framework of thinking' mobilized to describe them. As the historian Gérard Noiriel explains in his 'Foreword', 'beyond the diversity of views on immigration [...], one discursive matrix unifies all the discourses held on the subject' in the press – a matrix that emphasizes the 'problems' raised by immigration from Maghreb countries and that, in many respects, echoes, even in left-wing French newspapers, the agenda set by the extreme right (Noiriel, 1991: 8).

In tending to reduce the complexity of immigration issues to a set of questionings centered mainly around the 'problems' raised by populations with Maghrebi origins, Bonnafous concludes that French newspapers participated during this period to the building of new 'boundaries' among the populations living in France, making more visible 'the symbols of the separation between "us" and "them"', and underlining the 'extraneity of the "immigrés"' (Bonnafous, 1991: 269).

The media portrayal of Islam has played an important role in the fabric of this image of 'extraneity' associated to the immigrés coming from the Maghreb. As the historian Yvan Gastaut has demonstrated, in France, from the end of the 1970s onwards, 'media representations of immigration have been largely built through the prism of Islam', and, more specifically, through the prism of a frightening Islam (Gastaut, 2000: 517).

In his study *Imaginary Islam* (*L'Islam imaginaire*), Thomas Deltombe stresses the fact that the media representations of this religion in France do not only depend on domestic events, but depend also – increasingly from the end of the 1970s – on international events. The Iranian revolution, in 1979, is a pivotal moment in this respect: it contributed, with its images of angry crowds, threatening bearded men and black chadors – images which were repeated again and again – to the building of the idea that Islam, and, by extension, Muslim immigrés, constitute a menace for France, in cultural as well as in political terms (Deltombe, 2005).

Another important change occurring in the media representations in France in the 1980s has been the progressive substitution of the figure of the migrant worker – dominant throughout the 1960s and 1970s – by that of the 'second-generation' youngster, living in the suburbs of the main French cities. 'Thus immigrants have been supplanted from the field of representation by their children, born in France'. Not without 'confusion', as Édouard Mills-Affif explains: 'those who embody the figure of the immigrant on the small screen are not immigrants'! (Mills-Affif, 2004: 11).

As early as the beginning of the 1980s, with the first large-scale urban violence in the French suburbs, and more particularly the riots in the Minguettes, in the suburbs of Lyon, waged by these 'second generation' youngsters, the socio-economic difficulties experienced by these, as well as the social realities of the banlieues have begun to attract significant media attention (Boyer and Lochard, 1998: 84–90).

The late 1980s brought another break in the television representation of the populations of Maghrebi origin. A conjunction of local, national and international events – *The Satanic Verses* controversy in 1989, the first 'veil affair' in France at the end of the same year, and new riots in the suburbs of Lyon, in Vaulx-en-Velin, at the end of 1990 – filled the screens with images associating immigration, inhabitants of the banlieues and Islam with a danger for national cohesion.

The first veil affair is illustrative of the ways in which media perceptions of French Islam can be framed. Revealingly, the object of the controversy was, during the first weeks of the affair, designated under the name of 'chador'. Borrowing the term from the Iranian imaginary and its Shiite Islam, 'journalists appl[ied] it to an overwhelmingly Maghrebi and Sunnite immigration

[…]: this g[ave] to the veil an "integrist" connotation echoing the vocabulary and the images from Iranian revolution of 1979' (Deltombe, 2005: 101). Under the combined pressure of the Rushdie affair and the veil affair, French television has since 1989, as the preceding example suggests, increasingly focused their attention on the thematic of 'Muslim integrism' or that of the 'Islamist menace', of which the banlieues have been considered as being the main centre of propagation (Boyer and Lochard, 1998: 91–2).

In parallel, under the influence of the outburst of urban revolts in Vaulx-en-Velin in 1990, followed by others in the suburbs of Paris in 1991, the 'crisis of the banlieues' has become the object of increased media coverage. As Henri Boyer and Guy Lochard have shown, the banlieues have been, during this period, set up by French television as 'the symbolic locus of all the evils' of French society (Boyer and Lochard, 1998: 102 and 109). These places have been represented by alarmist television reports as 'lawless areas', where violence and 'insecurity' reign. The inhabitants, with largely migrant origins, especially the youth, have been presented as being 'responsible for all the problems' suffered by French society (Gastaut, 2000: 491).

Moreover, from 1992 with the civil war in Algeria, images associating the banlieues with delinquency and extremist Islamism have become commonplace on French television. Deltombe has analysed how the policy pursued by Charles Pasqua, Minister of the Interior from 1993–1995, targeted Islamist terrorist networks in France, through major, heavily mediatised police operations, resulted in French TV screens – particularly those of the main private TV channel, TF1 – being flooded with sensationalist reports about the rise of extremist Islamism in French suburbs. The main collateral victims were ordinary citizens of these suburbs, stigmatized as being potential terrorists (Deltombe, 2005: 170–218).

This blurring of boundaries on television between immigrants, Islam, or banlieues, on the one hand, and the fear of terrorism, on the other, reached a climax with the series of bombings that hit Paris and the suburbs of Lyon in 1995, attributed at that time to the Algerian Islamist terrorist group GIA, bombing in which were involved French citizens of Maghrebi origins. Over a period of several months, French private and public television broadcast reports linking the banlieues with delinquency and Islamist integrism, going so far, on TF1, as to offer an 'apocalyptic description of [these] suburbs', being controlled by the 'Islamists' (Deltombe, 2005: 244–7).

However, one should not underestimate the contradictions at work in the field of television representation of immigration in France. These representations are indeed by no means uniform. Boyer and Lochard have shown how television journalists, expressing their own 'malaise' in the way they portray the banlieues and their inhabitants through dramatic lenses, have sought to 'balance' their alarmist reports with more positive accounts (Boyer and Lochard, 1998: 127, 135).[2] Facing contradictory constraints – the need to offer credible news while, at the same time, attracting audiences – television journalists increasingly tried, since the beginning of the 1990s, to alternate within the same programmes, reports with an alarmist repertoire with reports dealing with these issues in a more complex way. Through this mechanism, comment Boyer and Lochard, private and public television journalists have endeavoured to 'amend and even totally reverse' the negative stereotypes they have themselves created (Boyer and Lochard, 1998: 111).

Whether they have succeeded or not remains an open question. Considering 'the matrix' through which the 'mediatization of Islam' operated on French television in the 1990s, Deltombe writes that while 'journalists repeatedly describe Muslims in France as practising a peaceful Islam', their reports are 'massively devoted' to the minority 'contaminated' by Islamism (Deltombe, 2005: 218).

The television portrayal of people of Maghrebi origins since 9/11 has thus, in many ways, to be seen as being inscribed in this historical continuity. Under the influence of a global environment marked by the struggle against international Islamist extremism, the boundaries between Islam and terrorism have become, on French television, according to Deltombe, increasingly tenuous. These phenomena, he explains, tend to appear as being 'two contiguous phenomena', the former presented as being at the root of the latter (Deltombe, 2005: 285).

In this context, Islam is, more than ever, treated 'through the prism of Islamism' and of the 'menace' it represents for the 'national body'. As analysed by Vincent Geisser, 'Islam is almost never contemplated as an ordinary social object, but always as a potential danger'. 'The peaceful Muslim in a Bordeaux mosque or the young veiled woman participating in a demonstration in Lille' are then perceived, according to this framework, as being the 'visible elements of a wider group causing problems' (Geisser, 2003: 27–9, 119).

However, other studies emphasize the positive changes that have occurred since the end of the 1990s in the television representation of immigration issues in France. Mills-Affif goes as far as saying that there has been 'a thaw in the debate on immigration' on television, and more particularly on public channels, characterized by 'a real effort to put in perspective immigration history and memory', especially those of Maghreb origins (Mills-Affif, 2007: 56).

These divergent results, gleaned from two different bodies of literature, show how much television representations of immigration and Islam have to be seen as being, on the French small screen, fraught with contradictions. Mills-Affif has sought to explore some of these contradictions which, unfortunately, are still under-researched. He describes televisual space as being a contradictory space whose different segments are not submitted to the same constraints: meanwhile the prime time, with its short formats and its audience-maximisation logics, does not lend itself easily to complex perspectives on immigration, late programmes are better positioned to include them. French television is, then, in a way, 'schizophrenic': it can, during peak hours, give voice to Islamophobia, and, later in the evening, scrutinize the nation's cultural differences (Mills-Affif, 2007: 57); the problem being that French television channels tend 'to relinquish their civic responsibilities during the hours when they reach their widest audiences' (Mills-Affif, 2004: 21).

These works on representation are important: they illustrate how the media, and more especially television, produce particular pictures of the nation of which they define the boundaries, including some and excluding others. However, to explore further the issues raised by these works, it is necessary to question public policies in France to improve the representation of ethnic minorities in the media. Here also, a detour has to be made via the historical background in order to understand recent developments.

From the Defence of Migrants' Cultural Identities to Policies of Integration

In France, the awareness of the need to implement a media policy to deal with migrants living in the country can be dated back to the mid-1970s. The context in which this policy was put in place was one of economic crisis, and of conservative policies carried out by a right-wing government presided over by Valéry Giscard d'Estaing, which decided to fight against immigration by interrupting immigration flows, by inciting migrants to return to their countries of origin, and, even, by trying to expel migrants living in France.

The first television programme that inaugurated this policy was *Immigrés parmi nous* ('Immigrants among us'), launched in 1975, broadcasted by FR3 – the third, recently created, public channel – on alternate Sunday mornings, aimed at both French mainstream and immigrant audiences. Financed by a public agency, the Fonds d'action sociale pour les travailleurs migrants (FAS), the social fund for migrant workers, this programme had the objective of improving, among the French public, the knowledge of immigrants' realities. The idea was that 'a better knowledge of the other and of his culture would expand social peace' (Escafré-Dublet, 2008: 275).

However, it is with the creation of the programme *Mosaïque*, whose title is a reference to the cultural patchwork brought in France by migrant cultures, that this media policy on immigration issues really took shape. Launched in 1976, broadcast by FR3, on Sunday mornings, in French as well as in the migrants' main mother tongues, alternating practical information with relevant news relating to immigration issues and entertainment sequences, the programme quickly became a regular rendez-vous for its migrant viewers and even for a not so negligible proportion of the general public.[3]

Mosaïque's objectives were not without ambiguities. Through this programme, financed by the FAS, the French state offered migrant audiences elements of their cultures of origin – in the form of reports on their homelands, entertainment shows featuring the stars of their mother countries and so on. The programme played, in this respect, an important social function for its migrant public – described as living in the mid-1970s in a 'state of cultural isolation' in France: it was a major means of filling 'an important [cultural] void' (Escafré-Dublet, 2008: 178, 316).

But the programme was also the instrument of an anti-immigration policy. The programme was indeed the televisual arm of a policy that promoted 'the respect for cultural identities' but also encouraged the migrants and their families to 'return' into their countries of origin (Weil, 2004: 119). *Mosaïque* even became, in 1977, a 'key element' of this anti-immigration policy, at a time when this policy resorted to forced returns. Constituting a medium for stimulating nostalgic feelings for the mother country, and thus for improving the efficiency of the return policy, the programme also offered a 'precious means through which building harmonious representations' of this policy, in a context when it was increasingly criticized both at home and in foreign countries (Escafré-Dublet, 2008: 276, 284).

Indeed, this programme was also an instrument of French foreign policy towards emigration countries. From the beginning, contact was made with the authorities of these countries in order to find suitable images for *Mosaïque*'s audiences. Co-production agreements were signed, whereby a certain amount of programmes were to be produced in these countries, at their own cost, for being broadcast on *Mosaïque*. In this context, the programme was also viewed as a means for reassuring the states of emigration countries, and convincing them that, despite the return policy, the French government was 'promoting [in the cultural field] their fellow citizens living in France' (Escafré-Dublet, 2008: 274).

However, as an 'instrument of [French] authorities', *Mosaïque* was also 'a place where divergent voices clashed': the omnipresent voice of the government co-existed with those of the journalists who, through their everyday work, were in tune 'with the living conditions of the immigrants' (Escafré-Dublet, 2008: 316).

Despite the fact that *Mosaïque* was one major instrument of governmental communication towards immigrant populations, the programme encountered many difficulties in trying to ensure its legitimacy within French public television. As an illustration, FR3 has always refused to share the production costs of the programme, forcing the FAS to pay 'much' for having it broadcast (Escafré-Dublet, 2008: 243; Blion et al., 2006: 22–3). Is it not contradictory that a programme aimed at viewers paying their licence fee like the other French viewers had to be produced by the FAS and the television channels of the countries of origin, and not by the French public TV channel broadcasting it? This attitude of FR3 shows how difficult it was for French public channels in the 1970s – in a monopolistic situation – to take into consideration the media needs of the immigrants living in France.

Outside this policy of specific programmes aimed at migrant audiences, no institutional initiative seems to have been taken to address, in generalist programmes, the media needs of these audiences. In some respects, immigrants remaining in France were seen as destined to be integrated into the French cultural mould under the pressure of mainstream media's acculturating force. A report, resulting from the work of a commission established in 1979 to study the relationship between 'Culture and immigration', makes this clear: 'In the host country, the immigrant is "bombarded" with the dominant media [...] culture. In this context, his access to the host country's culture, even though not to the best parts of it, will be a natural phenomenon, taking place little by little' (Culture et immigration, 1979: 44–45).

The election in 1981 of a new, socialist, president, François Mitterrand, opened another phase of these media policies towards immigrants. These were, at least in the first years of the presidency, organized around one principle, which had figured prominently on the program of the socialist party during its campaign: 'the right to be different', '*le droit à la différence*'.

The main objective of the media policies pursued in this context was 'insertion': 'it implied that those concerned could be "inserted" into the social fabric of France while still retaining a distinctive cultural identity'. As Alec Hargreaves has noted, 'although the word "multiculturalism" was almost never used, this was implicitly the direction in which the policies of the left seemed to point during their early years in office' (Hargreaves, 2007: 183).

A report – the first to be entirely devoted to the issue of media policies towards 'immigrant communities in France'– is illustrative of this new approach. Written in 1982, under the direction of Françoise Gaspard, the report first harshly condemned the 'depreciated' image of ethnic minorities and of their countries of origin in the French media, especially on television, and the way in which immigration issues are reduced, in these media, to 'delinquency, social costs, unemployment'. It also criticized the policy of specific programmes, such as *Mosaïque*, inaugurated under Valéry Giscard d'Estaing, considering that this policy, far from reducing the media 'marginalization' suffered by immigrants, increased it (Gaspard, 1982: 29, 35).

Written in the wake of the first large-scale riots in the suburbs of Lyon, the report noted a change in the 'nature' of immigration: this had ceased to be mainly a labour immigration and had become, under the influence of family reunification and the emergence of a 'second generation' born in France, 'a social phenomenon'. In this situation, a new policy of recognition, noted the report, was needed in order to avoid 'the risk of an unprecedented social explosion' (Gaspard, 1982: 59).

Gaspard called for a change in the media representations of immigration-related issues, urging the media 'to fight against the myths that fuel the sus-picions among communities' and that hinder the inclusion of minorities in French society. Likewise, public television channels were asked to increase 'the presence [...] of the cultures of the countries of origin' of the immigrés on their screens. The 'strengthening of a regained identity', far from being, for the immigrants, 'contradictory with a long-term insertion', was presented as being one of its main 'prerequisites' (Gaspard, 1982: 5, 31).

Finally, breaking with the policy of specific programmes pursued by the FAS, the report proposed to force public television channels 'to adapt their programmes to the needs of immigrant populations', by introducing, in their mission statements, provisions compelling them to 'broadcast a minimum quantity of programmes produced by the countries of origin of the immigrants' and, beyond, of programmes that 'reflect France's cultural and ethnic pluralism' (Gaspard, 1982: 58).

However, in practice, the report's conclusions were not realized. Indeed, con-fronted with the first electoral successes of the extreme right National Front, particularly in Dreux, the city of which Gaspard was the mayor, the socialist government was compelled to play down its multiculturalist rhetoric. As the National Front stressed the danger that immigration represented for French national identity, the political vocabulary of the socialist government evolved: from the 'insertion' to the 'integration' of immigrants and their families.

'Integration' is indeed the term around which public policies towards immi-grants, be they implemented by left-wing or by right-wing governments, have been organized since the 1980s. This term has been loosely defined as con-stituting a kind of third way, differing from assimilation, which supposes the erasure of cultural differences, and from insertion, and its associated right to cultural difference. According to the Haut conseil à l'intégration (High Council of Integration, HCI) – the institution that has since 1989 been charged with establishing a doctrine setting the contours of a 'French model of integration' – the policies of integration pursue the following objectives: 'Instead of negating differences, a proper integration policy takes them into account without exalting them, and emphasizes the similarities and convergences in order, with equality of rights and obligations, to establish solidarity among the different ethnic and cultural components of our society' (Haut conseil à l'intégration, 1993: 34–5).

What has become of *Mosaïque* in this new environment? Heavily criticized in Gaspard's report, the programme was compelled to transform itself. New rubrics dealing with immigration in France were added after 1983, more attention was given to 'second-generation' youngsters. But these developments were not sufficient enough to prevent the closure of the programme in 1987 (Blion et al., 2006: 23).

Among the main reasons for this closure was the fact that *Mosaïque* was ill adapted to the new policy towards immigrants. How could a programme survive, in the new era of 'integration', which had promoted the migrants' cultures of origin? A report of the HCI published in 1991 explained that the ending of *Mosaïque* resulted from French public authorities' willingness 'to break everything that could contribute to the creation of cultural "ghettos"' (Haut conseil à l'intégration, 1991: 132).

Different programmes, each with a very short lifespan, succeeded *Mosaïque*: all were more in tune with the new official agenda. A new magazine, *Ensemble aujourd'hui* ('Together today'), was aired at the end of 1987, aiming more 'at integrating [immigrants] to French society than at exploring their identities and their cultures': it was stopped in 1988, just a few months after its creation (Blion et al., 2006: 24). The following programme, *Rencontres* ('Meetings'), which lasted from 1989 to 1991, was conceived as a 'showcase for integration'. However, 'the reports, realized by independent journalists', were quick in offering another, less rosy, picture, at odds with this 'happy conception of integration' (Battegay and Boubeker, 1993: 139).

Paradoxically, at a moment when the FAS, which was funding these programmes, seemed to be unable to find a programme to succeed *Mosaïque*, FR3 agreed, in September 1990, to participate to the financing of *Rencontres* by covering the broadcasting costs (Blion et al., 2006: 25).

In the context of integration policies and of an increasingly deregulated audiovisual market, the FAS changed its modes of intervention in the televisual sector. After 1995, and the failure of *Premier service* ('First service'), it stopped funding regular programmes dealing specifically with the issues of immigration. And, from 1991 on, it began contributing to the financing of programmes aimed at generalist audiences but trying to 'break with the usual stereotypes' on immigration (Blion and al., 2006: 25–6).[4] Apart from these initiatives by the FAS, in the 1990s no policy was implemented to deal with the media representations of minorities. So much so that this decade has been characterized, according to some, by a 'decline of public authorities' engagement' in this field (Blion et al., 2006: 38–39).

The limits of these media policies towards ethnic minorities were made evident when a handful of satellite television channels coming from the Arab world burst onto the French scene in the 1990s. Scholars who have studied this issue make the link between the lack of representation on domestic television and the success with which Arab satellite television channels were received in migrant homes. As Hargreaves notes, minority audiences who 'have been poorly served' by French terrestrial public or private television stations, have been able, thanks to satellite dishes to vote 'increasingly with their feet or, to be more accurate, with their turning buttons, by turning to alternative sources of programming' (Hargreaves, 1997: 93).

An official report, written for the Ministry of Social Affairs in 1995 by Leïla Bouachera, establishes the link between the two phenomena: 'the lack of an overall audiovisual policy towards foreign [sic] populations [...] has had as an effect to direct them towards foreign satellite televisions' (Bouachera, 1995: 2).

The report made it clear that the presence on French soil of an uncontrolled foreign cultural presence was to be considered as a potential problem for the integrative mechanisms of French society. The consumption of satellite channels was 'stirring fears', explained Bouachera, of seeing 'these communities turning in on themselves' (Bouachera, 1995: 68). The programmes in Arabic were described as potentially undermining 'years of literary classes and other efforts at Gallicizing these people'. More, in the context of the civil war in Algeria, 'the religious content of certain programmes will probably increase the Islamization of the banlieues, with the risk of strengthening the propaganda drive of fundamentalist groups' (Bouachera, 1995: 5; quoted by Hargreaves and Mahdjoub, 1997: 461, their translation).

Faced with these risks, French public authorities should, recommended the report, 'improve the television programmes' offered to ethnic minorities, either by increasing their 'visibility' on terrestrial channels, or by creating cable channels specifically aimed at them, or by licensing the 'best [foreign] channels' broadcasting at their émigrés on cable systems. The channels broadcast through cable systems had one major advantage compared to those received through satellite dishes: they could be 'controlled' by the French broadcasting regulatory body, the Conseil supérieur de l'audiovisuel (CSA), the High Council for Audiovisual Media (Bouachera, 1995: 70).

If, in the 1990s, the CSA implemented a policy of selective licensing of foreign channels broadcast through cable systems (Ferjani, 2009: 407–10; see also Hargreaves and Mahdjoub, 1997), it was only at the beginning of the twenty-first century that it began to deal with the issue of the media representation of ethnic minorities on the mainstream terrestrial channels.

Cultural Diversity Policies as Integration Policies

The early 2000s have been characterized by the implementation of public policies aimed at improving media representation of ethnic minorities – policies that have been accompanied by an all-encompassing rhetoric praising the virtues of 'cultural diversity'. The paradox is that these policies are developed at a time, the aftermath of 9/11, when these minorities, more particularly those of Muslim faith, are, as we have seen, increasingly presented as constituting a menace for national cohesion.

Prominent among the factors explaining the implementation of these diversity policies is the role played by different associations lobbying in favour of better representation of ethnic minorities in the French audiovisual landscape. The Collectif Égalité ('the Equality Collective'), created in 1998, headed by the writer Calixthe Beyala, and grouping various artists and intellectuals with African or Caribbean origins, has been instrumental in putting this issue at the forefront of public debates. Having an easy access to the media, multiplying spectacular actions, this association succeeded in giving a wide echo to its claims: it was even received officially by the CSA in 1999. The Club Averroès, founded in 1997 by Amirouche Laïdi, and comprising of a group of media professionals, politicians and businessmen, has also played an important role. They have managed to make senior broadcast and government officials – including Hervé Bourges the then chair of the CSA – aware of the importance of media representation issues (Malonga, 2006: 48–49; Blion et al, 2006: 30).

Reflecting the importance of this new awareness, the CSA commissioned a study on the representation of 'visible minorities' on French television – the first ever commissioned by a regulatory body in France – carried out by Marie-France Malonga, and results of which were released in 2000 (Malonga, 2000). The study, confirming what different academic works had already demonstrated, was met by 'criticisms and a lot of hostility', going far beyond, as Malonga explained, the 'legitimate reproaches' that could be addressed to this kind of work, illustrating the 'French malaise' towards this issue (Malonga, 2007: 60). 'Yet, in the course of the next few years, it became increasingly commonplace', even in government circles, to speak of 'visible minorities' and of their right to a better representation on French television (Hargreaves, 2007: 194).

Prompted by some associations, the claim for a better media representation of ethnic minorities was quickly endorsed by public authorities, and became, in the early 2000s, an object of public concern. One major step of this process was the organization, by the CSA, the HCI and the FASILD (which succeeded FAS in 2001[5]) of a conference, held at the Institut du monde arabe (Institute of the Arab World), in Paris, in 2004, revealingly entitled 'Écrans pâles' ('White screens'). This conference, 'for the first time, with the authority of public institutions, put the issue of the media representation of diversity at the heart of the public arena' (Blion et al., 2006: 36).

At the conference, the organizing principles governing both public and private television were called into question. Participants denounced the existence of 'a non-written law called the law of ratings maximization', considered as being one of the main problems of minority representation. The editorial decisions of channels, particularly those of the private channel TF1, were criticized: 'Not so long ago, when you presented to TF1 fictional programmes projects featuring minorities, you were given the answer that it wasn't good for the ratings' (Écrans pâles, 2004: 45).

Apart from the pressures exerted by associations, another important factor explaining this growing awareness of the need to deal with the issue of ethnic minority media representation was a shift at the end of the 1990s in French public policy towards these minorities. As Hargreaves has shown, from that point, the French authorities devoted a far greater priority to discrimination suffered by minorities. This discrimination was viewed as being at the root of an increasing insecurity in the banlieues and beyond. For the government, 'it became clear that anger and resentment among victims of discrimination was fueling a growing threat to public order'. A threat that took mainly the form of ordinary incivilities, and of 'localized confrontations between disaffected youth and the police'. But there was also, in the eyes of public authorities, the risk of seeing 'the sense of rejection experienced by many young Maghrebis' fuel the rise of Islamist terrorism in the banlieues. It is in this context that, in 1998, Martine Aubry, then the Socialist Ministry for Employment and Solidarity, 'made the fight against racial discrimination a priority area of "integration"' (Hargreaves, 2007: 187–88). It took some more time for public authorities to understand that media discrimination also constituted a threat for national cohesion.

The urban revolts of 2005, with their unprecedented scale, precipitated the awareness of the need of implementing public policies aiming at improving ethnic minorities' media representation. In a televised address to the nation during these revolts on 14 November, President Jacques Chirac emphasizing the need to struggle against 'discrimination' and to acknowledge 'the diversity of French society' for 'our integration policy to be successful', urged the media to 'better reflect today's French realities'.[6]

The law on 'equal opportunities' that was passed a few months later in March 2006 illustrates this increased public willingness to use the media to fight social segregations suffered by ethnic minorities: it includes an important media chapter that, in particular, requires the CSA to act 'in favour of social cohesion' and to struggle 'against discriminations in the field of audiovisual communications'.[7]

After having been neglected for years, the need to improve ethnic minorities' media representation now figures high on the public agenda. Official initiatives have proliferated: studies have been commissioned by the CSA, conferences organized, new provisions introduced in public and private televisions' mission statements, compelling them to improve the cultural diversity of their screens. In addition, a Fund 'Images de la diversité' ('Images of diversity') was inaugurated in 2007; an Observatoire de la diversité dans les médias audiovisuels (a Diversity Observatory) was created in 2008; a 'Diversity Barometer' was launched and measures were taken to require journalism schools and media to increase the diversity in their recruitment policy, and so on.

Wrapped in the rhetoric of cultural diversity, these initiatives could lead one to think that present French public media policies have revived multiculturalist policies of the early 1980s. However, as Hargreaves suggests, if 'a new lexicon' has appeared in the French political discourse, 'in which the buzz words are diversity, anti-discrimination and equal opportunities', many important political orientations 'from the earlier period remain in place' (Hargreaves, 2007: 186–7), starting with the core principle of these: integration.

Indeed, the fact that French television is unable to give 'a representative, that is diversified, image of reality' has, since 2000, been increasingly viewed as being 'detrimental to social cohesion', to quote the introduction of the proceedings of the conference Écrans pâles. French television channels have been encouraged to increase the representation of 'cultural diversity' in order to increase this 'social cohesion'. Far from conflicting with integration policy, the recognition of diversity is part of it. As Blandine Kriegel, then President of the HCI, explained during the same conference, integration must be seen as 'the necessity, for all the elements of a society, [...] to maintain a [national] community within diversity'. And television, according to this philosophy of unity within diversity, has now the duty of increasing the visibility of ethnic minorities, and of providing 'a better place, more diversified' for their representation, in order to 'elaborate ["our"] common culture' (Écrans pâles, 2004: 5, 16).

Another factor can explain the implementation of these diversity policies: the increasing number of Arab satellite channels that can be received in immigrant homes. As Olivier Rousselle, the then general director of the FASILD, has stated, the 'explosion of television choice', thanks to the satellite, 'creates a new situation'. That makes it even more imperative 'to include the immigrant, but also the French with immigrant origins, into television' (Écrans pâles, 2004: 17, 19).

In the 2000s, Arab satellite channels have raised the same kind of fears as in the preceding decade: they have been seen as a force that endangers the 'common culture' that domestic televisions must build. In a research on the rise of anti-Semitism in France, financed, among other institutions, by the Institut national des hautes études de sécurité (National Institute of Advances Security Studies), sociologist Michel Wieviorka draws attention to the increasing role played by these channels in the spread, in the banlieues, of a global 'anti-Semitism', fuelling locally a 'hatred of Jews', particularly among youth of Maghrebi origins who associate the discrimination suffered by Palestinians to those they experience: 'the global and the local blend together, the brutality of the Israeli state, there, echoes the failures of the institutions, here, and the logics of discrimination are viewed as being equivalent in both cases' (Wieviorka, 2005: 113, 159).

In other works, Arab satellite channels are described, in the post 9/11 world, as being the agents of 'an important propaganda campaign of radical Islamism'. The consumption in the banlieues of these channels is presented as constituting 'a major breeding ground for terrorism', and as 'hampering integration processes' (Chiche and Chetrit, 2006: 16–17).

The ban, in 2004, by the CSA, of the satellite broadcasts of Al Manar, the channel of the Lebanese Hezbollah, exemplifies in many respects the fears associated with the reception of Arab satellite television in France. Riadh Ferjani has demonstrated how the banning of this channel was the product of a campaign waged by the Conseil représentatif des institutions juives de France (CRIF, Representative Council of Jewish Institutions in France), during which it provided extracts of Al Manar's programmes with anti-Semitic content to French public authorities, in order to convince them of the harmful nature of these programmes (Ferjani, 2009: 410–11; Koch, 2008; Lamloum, 2009; Sakr, 2008). Ferjani also notes that this ban reflected French authorities' concerns about the risk of seeing the small screen converted into 'a tool for the Islamization of the banlieues' (Ferjani, 2009: 410; Koch, 2008; Lamloum, 2009).

In this context, public policies implemented for improving the media representations of ethnic minorities, particularly those of Maghrebi origin, can be understood as a means of increasing the appeal of domestic French television channels, in order to try to take these minorities away from Arab satellite channels, and to integrate them better into the 'common culture' of French society.

This points to a further dimension of these policies of media inclusion. Mathieu Rigouste has shown how integration policies have been conceived, since the early 1980s, by French authorities, as a 'geopolitical issue', and, as such, as an issue having 'national security imperatives'. In this regard, integration policies are apprehended as a means of containing what is perceived as a 'menace', which would be both global and local in nature, born from the conjunction, from the 1980s onwards, of the rise of Islamist terrorism in the Middle East and the settling in France of immigrant populations of Muslim faith (Rigouste, 2009: 170–2). Cultural diversity policies can thus be seen, according to this perspective – above all in a context, that of the post 9/11, where Muslim populations are described as a danger – as aiming not only at increasing national cohesion, but also, beyond, at national security.

However, despite the fact that they theoretically constitute a priority of the official agenda since the beginning of the twenty-first century, these diversity policies are not without limits, as evidenced by different official documents. Research carried out for the Diversity Observatory of the CSA in 2008 showed for example that ethnic minorities are still largely under-represented on French television: it emphasized the lack of significant progress in this field since 2000 (Macé, 2008). Moreover, a 2010 report evaluating the policies of cultural diversity in the media concludes that there has been 'much talk', but 'less action'. 'The results are mainly negative': there has been 'limited progress, but many problems remain' (Spitz, 2010: 20–1, 36).

The main limit of these policies resides, nevertheless, in their own objectives. To what extent is it possible, to enhance, through 'the "magic" of images', the social integration of ethnic minorities, as these policies intend to do, at a time when the key 'integration instruments, such as the educational system, the employment or the housing policies', fail? (Meyer, 2005: 40).

Endnotes

1 This chapter is part of an international research project funded by the French National Research Agency (ANR) on 'Media and migration in the Euro-Mediterranean space' (Mediamigraterra) which the author is currently coordinating.

2 For another testimony of the 'malaise' expressed by television journalists on that issue, see Peralva and Macé, 2002.

3 According to the available statistics, *Mosaïque* was watched, at the end of 1977, by 54 % of immigrant audiences in France, and by 7 % of mainstream French audiences (Escafré-Dublet, 2008: 290).

4 On the policy of specific programmes pursued by the FAS, see also Humblot, 1989 and Hargreaves, 1993.

5 The FASILD (Fonds d'action et de soutien pour l'intégration et la lutte contre les discriminations) became, in 2006, the ACSÉ (Agence nationale pour la cohésion sociale et l'égalité des chances).

6 See http://www.jacqueschirac-asso.fr/fr/wp-content/uploads/2010/04/Les-évènements-des-banlieues.pdf

7 See http://www.legifrance.gouv.fr/affichTexte.do?cidTexte=JORFTEXT000000268539

References

Battegay, Alain and Boubeker, Ahmed (1993) *Les images publiques de l'immigration*. Paris: L'Harmattan-CIEMI.

Blion, Reynald, Frachon, Claire, Hargreaves, Alec G., Humblot, Catherine and Rigoni, Isabelle (2006) *La représentativité des immigrés au sein des medias. Bilan des connaissances*. Rapport pour le FASILD. Paris.

Bonnafous, Simone (1991) *L'immigration prise aux mots*. Paris: Kimé.

Bouachera, Leïla (1995) *L'offre de programmes télévisuels diffusés par satellite à destination des populations étrangères en France*. Rapport pour le Ministère des Affaires sociales, de la Santé et de la Ville. Paris.

Boyer, Henri and Lochard, Guy (1998) *Scènes de télévision en banlieues, 1950–1994*. Paris: INA-L'Harmattan.

Chiche, Mahor and Chetrit Michaël (2006) Repenser la lutte antiterroriste, *Les cahiers de l'Institut Prospective et Sécurité en Europe*, 87: 16–18.

Culture et immigration: Réflexions et propositions sur les besoins éducatifs, sociaux et culturels des travailleurs immigrés et leurs familles (1979) Rapport de la commission mixte Culture et immigration. Paris: ICEI.

Deltombe, Thomas (2005) *L'Islam imaginaire. La construction médiatique de l'islamophobie en France, 1975–2005*. Paris: La Découverte.

Deltombe, Thomas and Rigouste, Mathieu (2005) L'ennemi intérieur: la construction médiatique de la figure de l 'Arabe' in Pascal Blanchard, Nicolas Bancel and Sandrine Lemaire (eds) *La fracture coloniale. La société française au prisme de l'héritage colonial*. Paris: La Découverte. pp. 191–8.

Écans pâles? Diversité culturelle et culture commune dans l'audiovisuel. Actes du colloque (2004) Paris: La Documentation française.

Escafré-Dublet, Angéline (2008) État, culture, immigration. La dimension culturelle des politiques françaises d'immigration, 1958–1991. PhD Dissertation. Institut d'études politiques. Paris.

Ferjani, Riadh (2009) Arabic-language television in France. Postcolonial transnationality, *Global Media and Communication* 5(3): 405–28.

Gaspard, Françoise (1982) *L'information et l'expression culturelle des communautés immigrées en France*. Rapport au Secrétariat d'État chargé des immigrés. Paris.

Gastaut, Yvan (2000) *L'immigration et l'opinion française sous la Ve République*. Paris: Le Seuil.

Geisser, Vincent (2003) *La nouvelle islamophobie*. Paris: La Découverte.

Hargreaves, Alec G. (1993) Télévision et intégration. La politique audiovisuelle du FAS, *Migrations Société* (5)30: 7–22.

Hargreaves, Alec G. (1997) Gatekeepers and gateways. Post-colonial minorities and French television, in Alec G. Hargreaves and Mark McKinney (eds) *Post-Colonial Cultures in France*. London: Routledge. pp. 84–98.

Hargreaves, Alec G. (2007) *Multi-Ethnic France: Immigration, Politics, Culture and Society*. London: Routledge.

Hargreaves, Alec G. and Mahdjoub Dalila (1997) Satellite television viewing among ethnic minorities in France, *European Journal of Communication* (12)4: 459–77.

Haut conseil à l'intégration (1991) *Les conditions juridiques et culturelles de l'intégration* in Haut conseil à l'intégration (1993) *L'intégration à la française*. Paris: Union générale d'éditions. pp. 59–133.

Haut conseil à l'intégration (1993) *Pour un modèle français d'intégration* in Haut conseil à l'intégration (1993) *L'intégration à la française*. Paris: Union générale d'éditions. pp. 20–58.

Humblot, Catherine (1989) Les émissions spécifiques: de *Mosaïque* à *Rencontres*, *Migrations Société* (1) 4: 7–14.

Koch, Olivier (2008) 'L'affaire Al Manar' en France in Sabrina Mervin (ed.) *Le Hezbollah. État des lieux*. Arles: Actes Sud. pp. 47–64.

Lamloum, Olfa (2009) Hezbollah and the 'Al Manar affair' in Katharina Noetzold and Maha Taki (eds) *Journalism Testing Legal Boundaries: Media Laws and the Reporting of Arab News: Conference Proceedings*. University of Westminster, London: Arab Media Centre.

Macé, Éric (2008) *Représentation de la diversité dans les programmes de télévision*. Rapport pour l'Observatoire de la diversité dans les médias audiovisuels. Paris.

Malonga, Marie-France (2000) *Présence et représentation des minorités visibles à la télévision française*. Rapport interne pour le Conseil supérieur de l'audiovisuel. Paris.

Malonga, Marie-France (2006) Les minorités à la conquête du petit écran, *Médiamorphoses*, 17: 48–51.

Malonga, Marie-France (2007) Les strategies identitaires des minorités noires face à la television française, in Tristan Mattelart (ed.) *Médias, migrations et cultures transnationales*. Paris-Brussels: INA-De Boeck.

Meyer, Vincent (2005) *Les traductions médiatiques de l'immigration: (re)production, représentation et réception des images*. Rapport pour le FASILD. Paris.

Mills-Affif, Édouard (2004) *Filmer les immigrés. Les représentations audiovisuelles de l'immigration à la télévision française*. Paris-Brussels: INA-De Boeck.

Mills-Affif, Édouard (2007) Vu à la télé. La saga des immigrés, in Isabelle Rigoni (ed.) *Qui a peur de la télévision en couleurs? La diversité culturelle dans les médias*. Paris: Aux lieux d'être. pp. 39–57.

Noiriel, Gérard (1991) Préface, in Simone Bonnafous *L'immigration prise aux mots*. Paris: Kimé. pp. 7–10.

Peralva, Angelina and Macé, Éric (2002) *Médias et violences urbaines. Débats politiques et construction journalistique*. Paris: La Documentation française.

Rigouste, Mathieu (2009) *L'ennemi intérieur. La généalogie coloniale et militaire de l'ordre sécuritaire dans la France contemporaine*. Paris: La Découverte.

Sakr, Naomi (2008) Diversity and diaspora. Arab communities and satellite communication in Europe. *Global Media and Communication* 4(3): 277–300.

Spitz, Bernard (2010) Médias et diversités. Rapport de la Commission Médias et Diversités. Paris.

Weil, Patrick (2004) *La France et ses étrangers*. Paris: Gallimard.

Wieviorka, Michel (2005) *La tentation antisémite. Haine des juifs dans la France d'aujourd'hui*. Paris: Robert Laffont.

14

THE 'WAR ON TERROR' IN THE ARAB MEDIA

Helga Tawil-Souri

How do the 300 million people in the Arab world view the 'war on terror'? In her contribution, Helga Tawil-Souri contests the notion of the Arab world as a homogeneous entity or assumptions about the existence of a unified Arab media voice. Instead, she contends, there are a range of Arab media voices, given the diversity of Arab nations, in terms of their histories, levels of socio-economic development, media systems and potential for democratization. Tawil-Souri strongly argues that there are competing Arab and Islamic visions on the war on terror and on the concept of jihad itself. She notes that the war on terror has been used by Arab governments to suppress oppositional voices – whether Islamic, Islamist or jihadist. Dismissing the claim that there is such a thing as a 'global jihad', she argues that the primary targets of Islamists are not the West but Arab governments, which are seen as not practising Islamic conduct. She also debunks the myth about the power and popularity of online 'jihadist media' in the Arab landscape, arguing that broadcasting is the most popular form of media production and consumption, especially pan-Arab satellite channels.

Introduction: What War on Terror?

Standing somewhere in the Arab world one would be hard pressed to have found such a thing as 'the war on terror' in the media landscape over the past decade. There has of course been constant coverage on the war on/in Iraq. And within that, specifics such as the fall of Baghdad, the battles of Fallujah, the trial and execution of Saddam Hussein, images of torture and humiliation at the hands of American soldiers in Abu Ghraib, insurgency campaigns, Sunni–Shia sectarian violence and so on. Likewise there have been ample reports on the US/UK-waged ten-year long war in Afghanistan, from the carpet bombings of Kabul and Tora Bora in 2001 to the precision-guided missiles in 2011 (both of which have killed more innocent by-standers than their purported targets). Osama bin Laden's messages circulate, whether on video, audio or text, as do images and discussions of Guantanamo and extraordinary renditions of 'terrorists'.

There has also been media attention on the increasing anti-Muslim rhetoric and policies across the West, embodied in examples such as the racist vitriol of Dutch parliamentarian Geert Wilders; the French ban on Muslim headscarves; the printing of 'profane' cartoons in the Danish press; Pope Benedict XVI's claim in 2006 that the teachings of the Prophet Muhammad offer 'things only evil and inhuman' (Pope Benedict, 2006); the protests in New York against building a 'mosque' (really a community centre) near Ground Zero. And there is of course the West's complicity in Israel's on-going dispossession of Palestinians.

Taken together, these comprise the 'war on terror' in most Arabs' minds. Implicated as it was with his predecessor's government, in March 2009 US President Obama retired the phrase 'The global war on terror'. We are now supposed to call it 'Overseas Contingency Operation'. This is not to say that the war on terror has ended, did not, or still does not exist. Looking at it from the perspective of Arab media however, the war on terror – understood broadly as the discourse, policies and practices waged in response to the terror attacks on 9/11 – has been a Western construct of the world embedded in Western (read mostly American, and more specifically neo-conservative) political and ideological desires, rather than one adopted by those who, in varying degrees, feel they are its subjects.

Dismantling Arab Media

In the imagined atlas of the war on terror, the core nations of 'the West' are surrounded by a dark periphery of wild places, inhabited by terrorists and homicidal death cults lumped together: the Taliban, Al-Qaeda, Islamic fundamentalists, Hamas, Hizbollah, the Muslim Brotherhood, Muqtada Al-Sadr's Mahdi Army, the Islamic State of Iraq, Somalia's Al-Shabaab, Saudi Salafists, and so on. This wild barbarism emerges from a range of places: from the badlands of Helmand province and the 'failed state' of Somalia to the 'terrorist nests' of Fallujah, Beirut and Gaza. In other words, even if the 'barbaric' world intent on bombing 'civilization' into oblivion is largely an imagined fear and an imagined geography, it overlaps with specific locations.

In the simplistic language of the war on terror, often used synonymously are the terms the 'Arab world,' 'the Middle East' (in which we would have to include non-Arab countries such as Turkey, Israel, Iran) and, much more problematically, 'the Muslim world' (which at its widest would include all the Arab countries and 25 others in which Islam is the official or predominant religion). The 'Arab world' is distinct and specific: it spans 22 countries from the western part of North Africa to the eastern side of the Persian Gulf, with a population of over 300 million people. Even so, it is highly problematic to speak of the 'Arab world' as a homogeneous entity or assume that there is something akin to a unified Arab media voice, unless our objective is to propagate an Orientalist, ahistorical perspective and continue a dangerously Islamophobic discourse (which have much deeper roots than a response to the violent events of 9/11). That is what the rhetoric and practices surrounding the war on terror have done in the West. And that is why I say that it does not exist in and of itself on Arab screens.

Historical, economic, political and cultural differences give each Arab country a unique identity. There are similarities: previously under the control of Western colonial or Mandate rule; largely non-democratic governments since independence mostly backed by the West, and currently experiencing political uprisings; the predominance of the Arabic language; the majority of the population is (Sunni) Muslim as well as young. In the media landscape the 22 Arab countries share some similarities, having had, for the most part, state-owned or state-controlled media as the official (and, for a long time, sole) voice of the country. But it is problematic to suggest that media remain largely under the control of ruling elites; or that television, radio, newspapers, publishing, and internet are all subject to (the same kinds of) regulations that restrict freedom of expression.

Arab countries' histories and state structures are different, as are their adoption of 'open' economic policies, class make-up, racial and ethnic composition, levels of literacy, the influence of civil society, the influence of religion on the political elite, the existence and power of any Islamist opposition. These disparities inform the media landscape (on Arab media and scholarship thereof, see Boyd, 1982; Sakr, 2002, 2007a, 2007b; Tawil-Souri, 2008). Internet infrastructure, policies and uses also vary widely across the Arab world. The Middle East and North African region tends to fall behind in internet penetration rates compared to many other parts of the world (UNDP, 2005; Warf and Vincent, 2007). When focusing on the internet then, we must keep in mind that only a tiny minority of the Arab population uses these technologies. Moreover, one must differentiate between official and institutional voices on the internet – government entities and big media players such as newspapers, radio and television stations – and grass-roots, unofficial, oppositional, alternative and more 'marginal' voices.

Given that it was a jihadist group, al-Qaeda, that waged the violence on 9/11, there has been great concern about the popularity of 'jihadist media' in the Arab landscape – concern emanating from the West, but also from within the Arab world. There is a general fear that a 'radicalization process is occurring more quickly, more widely, and more anonymously in the Internet age'

(US intelligence survey quoted in Hoskins and O'Loughlin, 2010: 145). It is not simply terrorism that is the source of threat, insecurity, and fear, but the internet too. (There is no agreement, neither in the West, nor in the Arab world, nor by its proponents, on what jihad means or what its goals are. Debated in religious and political scholarship for centuries, it continues to be sufficiently ambiguous for different actors to use it, warranting different ideologies, policies and actions; see Mamdani, 2004; Devji, 2005, 2008.) One must contextualize 'jihadist' media and internet use within larger media, political and religious frameworks in the Arab world.

First, if there is overarching media similarity, it is that broadcasting is the most popular form of media production and consumption (radio by far supersedes other media uses, yet continues to be overlooked by most media scholars of the region), and that pan-Arab satellite channels have transformed the landscape. Within that, while news plays an important role, so too do various forms of entertainment such as music videos, talk shows, game shows, Ramadan and regular serials called *musalsallat* (see Hammond, 2007). Even on the internet, the most popular pastimes are chatting, forms of 'cyber-dating', video games, entertainment and news (see Wheeler, 2005; Bunt, 2003, 2009; El-Nawawy and Khamis, 2009). Across all kinds of informative or entertainment media the most popular topics tend to be the ones that are taboo: sex, politics and religion.

Second, when it comes to the intermingling of politics and religion, the most popular online sites are neither overtly political and certainly not 'militant', but those promoting moral guidelines or renewal of Muslim individuals. IslamOnline.net, for example, established in 1997, inspired by the Egyptian preacher Yusuf al-Qaradawi (whose roots lie in the Muslim Brotherhood), has been one of the most popular websites. Al-Qaradawi gained popularity and influence in the 1990s through a program on Al Jazeera. Similarly, Amr Khaled, the 'Muslim-televangelist', a television sensation as much as an internet one, focuses on the role of Islam in everyday life. These two examples, drawing tremendous audiences across the Arab world, highlight the conjuncture of media platforms, as well as the fact that any 'Islamicization' of the media is mostly social and cultural, rather than political or anti-Western (see Moll, 2010 on Islamic televangelists). Moreover, Islamic groups' relative success on the internet began in the early days of the web, in the early 1990s, when Muslim student associations in the US and Europe embraced the new medium to promote a global Islamic consciousness. Thus most of the growth in internet use devoted to Islam and Islamic interpretations has had little to do with the war on terror, and certainly not led by 'Islamists' (see Eickelman and Anderson, 1999; Bunt, 2003, 2009; Hofheinz, 2005; El-Nawawy and Khamis, 2009).

Third, with respect to the war on terror and jihad, there are contending visions within the Arab world. Sunni Arab regimes have used media as a weapon in their battle over who speaks for Islam. In fact, the war on terror has also been used by Arab regimes to suppress oppositional voices – whether Islamic, Islamist, or jihadist, such as in Egypt and Jordan. Finally, even within what might be considered an Islamist or 'radical' discourse, there are contending visions (see Schwedler, 2006, on Islamist movements in Jordan and Yemen). Thus it is important to understand that 'jihad' is by no means the most pervasive or popular subject across Arab media realms.

Decentralized Jihads: From Iraq to Islamophobia

There is no such thing as a 'global jihad'. Rather, there are loosely connected 'networks' of like-minded individuals and groups whose main objective is to restore pure Islam by overthrowing the 'apostate' regimes of the Muslim world, seeking to impose a strict interpretation of Islamic law and defeating the forces of 'unbelief'. There is no widespread agreement on the means by which to do so, although violence is advocated by some. Jihadists also differ greatly in ideology, theology and outlook, including Iraqi insurgent armies (mostly Sunni but including some Shiite militias loosely related to Muqtada al-Sadr's Mahdi Army), Taliban and Al-Qaeda fighters, and leaders in Pakistan and Afghanistan. Historically, the desire to 'Islamize' society has been primarily targeted within Muslim and Arab countries, such as Saudi Arabia and Somalia. Much of the bloodshed in the name of jihad has also largely been targeted within Arab and Muslim countries, and against Western forms of intervention there. Violence towards the 'West', the destruction of the US or Israel, are part of that rhetoric, but largely recent and tangential to the primary objectives (see Mamdani, 2004; Awan, 2007a, 2007b; Devji, 2005, 2008). In fact, despite the 9/11 attacks, neither the US nor the 'West' more generally are the primary targets or problems of jihadists.

The most popular jihadist websites are still those that focus on national issues, where the 'holy war' is targeted towards the Islamicization of local society and/or the state. Al-Mokhtasar lil-Akhbar, founded in November 2002 by radical Wahhabis opposed to the Saudi regime, but not openly agitating against it, is a jihadist news aggregator that is among the most popular Arabic sites. Conservative Islamic sites toeing the line of the Saudi government continue to attract significantly more visitors than their more 'global' jihadist counterparts. Al-Khayma al-Arabiyya, which was established in 1999 as one of the first Arabic web directories, and its affiliates, the portal Raddadi.com and the Wahhabi missionary site Said al-Fawa'id, are also amongst the most accessed. Established in 1998, one of the most popular forums is al-Saha al-Arabiyya. Swalif.net and Arabsgate.com, established in 1999 and 2000 respectively, are two other sites that have been much frequented for years.

While in the West's imagination there exists a unified jihadist push, in practice, it is a chaotic amalgam of transnational cells and localized insurgencies that espouse loosely articulately common goals. As a whole this imagined jihad generally lacks the organizational cohesion of a 'movement'. Moreover, no matter the variants, such groups face official exclusion inside their countries (with the notable exceptions of Somalia and Taliban-era Afghanistan). They face 'security clampdowns' from both their 'host' governments and a larger global security network. The conditions of being loosely organized and being constantly 'on the run' means that jihadists channel their efforts through a variety of decentralized and often transnational structures. That bin Laden was supposedly hiding in a cave somewhere is an apt metaphor for the jihadists movement at large: hiding from both local and international governments. Thus, in the post-9/11 context, the internet was a natural platform through which to remain connected, counter mainstream depictions of jihad and mobilize support.

Websites established by militant Islamists are constantly on a virtual run from clampdowns, as such only able to reach a devoted few who have to follow their tracks on electronic bulletin boards. One of the more persistent examples is Dalil Meshawir that appears in many flavours and at many different addresses. The membership of these groups ranges between a handful and a few hundred at most.

They are not mass platforms but must be understood largely as forums serving internal communication between insiders already converted to a cause. Very few appear online in relatively stable sites: two of those include theislamsun. com, which hosts the Al-Rashedeen Army in Iraq, and press-release.blogspot. com, which until recently offered multiple daily communiqués from the Islamic State of Iraq.

Just as there is no such thing as a unified 'global jihad', in cyberspace too, jihadists spaces are neither homogeneous, uniform, secure, nor static. Jihadist media can be described as 'an 'ordered disorder' of information that is […] diffused' (Hoskins and O'Loughlin, 2010: 10). In general, the more 'radical' the voice, the more on the (virtual) run it is. Only some jihadist groups have official media 'institutions' of their own, most others function as little more than on-line news and information 'aggregators'. Jihadist-oriented websites do not espouse the same views, are not easy to find, nor have huge amounts of followers – largely because of a tension that exists politically as well as technologically, attempting to gain visibility while hiding. They are by and large marginal and marginalized in multiple ways across the Arab world, contrasting the views that Arab media is homogeneously a 'mouthpiece of terrorism' (as one might be led to believe watching Fox News), or that there exists a wide-reaching 'online jihad'.

Osama bin Laden's statements draw wide viewership, but that is true of many globally recognized and important 'leaders'. Similarly, statements by Al-Qaeda number two, Ayman al-Zawahiri, draw significant attention in mainstream media, but also in the West. Al-Qaeda is one of the main groups that has its own media production arm, as well as functions as a large 'cyber-pool' of related jihadist media.

There are three key entities connecting Al-Qaeda and affiliated movements through the internet. Fajr, the Global Islamic Media Front and as-Sahab receive materials from more than one armed group and post those materials on the internet. The agents are dispersed from far across Saudi Arabia, Lebanon, Iraq and Afghanistan, to Chechnya, Somalia, Algeria, and to the US, Asia and Europe. There is no centralized online location for the distribution of Al-Qaeda media. Instead, a shifting array of forums acts as the primary distribution channel.

Over the past ten years, there has been a move to consistently 'brand' media productions. The world's best-known terrorist organizations have spawned a wide variety of regional 'franchises'. The most prominent of these is Al-Qaeda, but so too the Islamic State of Iraq (the successor to Zarqawi's group). Al-Qaeda's media 'network' is both dispersed and mobile, centralized and decentralized, in that the group has increasingly delegated and outsourced the creation of content, and relied on user-generated content to a diffused body of anonymous, but trusted, users, ensuring the breadth and longevity of messages irrespective of attacks on any single node (Awan and Al-Lami, 2009). Put another way, Faisal Devji has argued that 'the Islam of militancy and offence occupies a global arena in which it acts without being an actor' (Devji, 2008: 206). For example, a video of an IED (improvised explosive device) bombing of an American tank in Iraq can be sent to a handful of media producers working with Al-Qaeda (such as As-Sahab), where it is branded (with a logo or song for example), and redistributed through nodes in the jihadist media network. The IED video is likely to appear first on an online forum where members post it, and then circulated back through Al-Qaeda's nodes. Al-Qaeda and all other jihadist media products have constantly modulated between being centralized and de-centralized for obvious reasons. On the one hand, they seek control over the form, content and timing of what is to be communicated, on the other, they are always vulnerable to being shut down. The 'central' sites of jihadists media have disappeared and reappeared in a kind of 'cyber-migration' numerous times over the past ten years.

Moreover, while video is an important component of jihadist media, text products comprise the bulk of the daily media flow in the form of statements, bulletins, periodicals, essays and sometimes books. By far the most important 'analytic' in the online presence of the majority of jihadist media is the web forum which is widely used for online discussions and sharing of files. Web-based discussion sites are filled with pages of threaded postings and comments, some of which are accessible, most of which actually restrict access. In them, news, communiqués, speech transcripts, songs, and still images are posted and exchanged, as well as PDF documents, and video tapes. Ironically, many of these are hosted on commercial fileservers in the West (see Awan, 2007b; Keenan, 2008; Awan and Al-Lami, 2009).

But a review of jihadist media shows that 'Al-Qaeda central' has a relatively minor (quantitative) presence. In fact, the 'original' Al-Qaeda which was led by

Osama bin Laden accounts for a mere fraction of jihadist media production, whether online or offline. Perhaps most surprising is that a large amount of attention draws on some of the same images and examples as those that circulate in the Western media, for a large part of 'jihadist' media is the (re)interpretation of actions taken by Western countries towards Arab countries or Muslims.

The majority of jihadist media focuses on international conflict zones, most notably Iraq, Afghanistan, Palestine and Somalia. It is these four wars that have come to represent, for both jihadists and large parts of the Arab population (many without sympathies to jihadist organizations), the specifics of the war on terror. The conflict in and about Palestine has long pre-dated the 9/11 attacks or the war on terror. Afghanistan, which was the first to bear the brunt of post 9/11 response, is not an Arab nation, even if it was bin Laden's 'headquarters'. Somalia is politically marginalized, both within the Arab world and the international community. As such, it is the war on Iraq, followed by the continued conflict there, that has garnered the most attention in the Arab world vis-à-vis the war on terror (for more on the war in Iraq see Lynch, 2005; Tatham, 2006; Schwartz, 2008).

Iraq has served as the watershed for jihadist media production. The most successful of all jihad-oriented news sites was founded at the beginning of the US-led invasion in March 2003, Mufakkirat al-Islam ('IslamMemo'). With the fight for Fallujah in November 2004, IslamMemo overtook the older Moheet.com, a populist portal appealing to Islamic and Arab national sentiments that had been established in 1998. But the war in Iraq itself has been made up of so many events, each garnering attention from jihadists for different ends. Sometimes, differing political-ideological perspectives were used for groups' own purposes, whether to avoid security forces or to mobilize support. For example, although on differing ends of the ideological and theological spectrum, Al-Zarqawi's media notoriety was partly boosted by Shia counter-insurgency propaganda, which generally preferred to present a 'foreign jihadist' linked to al-Qaeda as a more suitable 'face' for the insurgency.

Some events during the Iraq war were handed on a 'silver platter' to the jihadists by the Coalition forces themselves. For example, the cell-phone footage of Saddam Hussein's execution that was eventually leaked highlighted the disorder of the new Iraqi 'justice' system, and undermined the Coalition and the Iraqi interim government in ways that jihadists could only have prayed for. More catastrophically for the Coalition forces was the footage of a US Marine shooting dead an injured and apparently unarmed man in a mosque in Fallujah, first broadcast on the American network NBC, but then quickly disseminated across the world. The response among Arabs and jihadists was to be expected: an unarmed man killed for no reason only highlighted the barbarity of the Americans. There was widespread belief that the Americans were surely guilty of even worse barbarities, that were either not documented, or purposefully not being aired. Such images only fuelled anger and anti-Americanism, making the 'job' of jihadists all that much easier. And in both the mainstream Arab media and in jihadist online discussions, such examples were often framed within a broader context of American violence towards Iraqi civilians, and often the need to respond to this violence.

It was the Abu Ghraib torture 'scandal' however that served as a pivotal moment, highlighting both the 'real' and symbolic aspects of the war. Abu Ghraib was not an example of one sole Marine acting violently nor the hanging of a much-hated dictator. It was widely interpreted as torture and abuse directed towards the Arab and Muslim man. The war on terror had hit home, with many feeling a profound sense of personal and collective violation. It was also used to mobilize further support by a range of jihadist groups for their own propaganda uses, from mobilizing support to calling attention to human rights abuses against them. Abu Ghraib, and other parts of the war on terror, such as the renditions of 'terrorists' to third countries, denials of fair trials at Guantanamo, CIA 'black sites' and legal formulations paving the way for 'enhanced interrogation techniques' all brought discussions of American barbarity and duplicity further to the fore of Arab consciousness. Before 9/11, many voices including the Islamists had argued that the West only pursued its own interests in the region, but the images of Abu Ghraib sealed that the war in Iraq was nothing short of a war against Arabs and Islam.

Combined with actual military war waged, a secondary important aspect of the Arab world's understanding of the war on terror – and where a lot more media attention is focused both in the 'mainstream' Arab media and among jihadist media – is on the perceived and real rifts between Islam/Arabs and the West. As one scholar has noted:

> many of the most militant of 'jihadi' cultural items available from the Internet are highly ideologically promiscuous, referencing in turns a heady mix of half understood Islamism, Arab nationalism, salafism, the Nation of Islam, conspiracy theories of the left and the right and so on. The logic expressed is not that of a well-worked out theological justification for jihad [...] but rather a loose, but emotive sense that Muslims (as an imagined community more than as adherents to a highly specific creed) are under attack and must be defended. (Ramsey, 2009: 42)

This is contradictory. In the post-9/11 context, it was the 'war on terror' rhetoric that framed the world as experiencing a 'civilization rift'. The response on the part of the West garnered widespread belief among Arabs that this was indeed a 'clash of civilizations' (understood quite differently of course: for Arabs, the Barbarians are the Westerners perpetrating state-sanctioned forms of terrorism). Whether kinetically in Iraq, the complacency with Israeli occupation or the violence wrought on Afghan citizens, these came to be understood as emanating from the same part of the world that was publishing profane cartoons, banning the building of mosques or the wearing of Muslim head-scarves, 'randomly' selecting and searching Muslims boarding flights, and so on.

More than any other example it is France's ban of the headscarf that has been used to mobilize support for jihad, and ironically, not just resulted in the coordination of propaganda, but in furthering the notion of a 'clash of civiliza-tions'. For example, Al Qaeda's Ayman Zawahiri at the global level combines at the local level with a group like the Islamic Army of Iraq, attacking the headscarf ban in France. By using an argument that is emotionally appealing to Muslims around the world who feel oppressed by the West, they deploy anti-Western rhetoric and acts of terror to promote a break between Islam and the West. Zawahiri and the Islamic Army of Iraq leverage this emotional appeal to bring Muslims over to their binary way of thinking – that the world is divided between 'us and them'. The result is a curious and dangerous reductionism that transforms reality into a series of discreet, disconnected facts, and reduces the Other into a series of acts without cause, without history, without reason and without rationality. The way the rhetoric in the West around the war on terror simplified the Arab world, the Middle East and the Muslim world, in effect rendering it a kind of faceless abstract enemy, this was the reverse.

In response to the West's military and cultural 'war' on and against Arabs and Muslims, jihadists positioned themselves as symbols of steadfastness against Western hegemony and aggression, pulling on heartstrings of nationalism, pan-Arabism, the need to defend the Islamic *ummah*, human rights abuses, anti-colonial revolution, conspiracy theories and so on. The same can be said, however, of voices in more 'mainstream' and non-militant Arab media, whether Hizballah's al-Manar television channel or Al Jazeera. What the images of the war on terror achieved in the Arab world is the war's un-framing: inter-pretation now rested outside the West and became increasingly regionalized. Further, all media productions – whether Western or jihadist – demonstrate that those conducting war consider media part of the war itself.

The examples above exemplify the extent to which the role of information in forming opinions, shaping perceptions and manufacturing consciousness have relied on the same events (e.g. the war in Iraq, the French ban on headscarves) and media images from various parts of the world but for different ends. For example, one event in Iraq used by jihadists to target Western public opinion was the ambush and execution by Iraqi resistance fighters in Fallujah in March 2004 of four US mercenaries working for the private security firm Blackwater. The four Americans were dragged from their burning vehicles by a local mob and hacked with shovels before two of their charred bodies were hung from a bridge in front of a chanting crowd of fighters and civilians. The entire sequence was filmed and broadcast across the world, transforming what would have been another routine act of brutality in the ongoing carnage in Iraq into a global media spectacle (see Carr, 2008). To the insurgents who filmed those images, the public lynching of the four contractors was a humiliation of the US, and an attempt to undermine American public support for the occupation. Videos of hostages, beheadings and exploding IEDs are examples of this too – many of which end up circulating again in Western (and often mainstream) media.

The war in Iraq has been a visual 'shock and awe' campaign, as much as a kinetic one; and it is also in response to this media warfare that jihadist media should be understood, on the one hand countering the 'mainstream' Western campaign, on the other, waging its own media propaganda and warfare. Thus one form of violent propaganda is replaced by another, both competing often for the same viewers. As Mirzoeff has suggested, there has been a deliberate effort by the Coalition to reduce the visual impact of the war in Iraq, not simply by embedding journalists or launching pro-Coalition media channels within Iraq, but also 'by saturating our senses with non-stop indistinguishable and undistinguished images' (Mirzoeff, 2005: 14). The same can be said of jihadists.

Thus, thanks to Western (and mostly US) actions since 9/11, there has been a 'consolidation' of a global coalition of anti-Americanism, ironically felt most strongly in the very domain of 'soft power'. What media has established across the Arab world is the atrocities committed in the name of the war on terror that the West has undertaken, in Iraq, in Somalia, in Afghanistan, in Cuba, in France, in Denmark, in the US. The war on terror has largely been re-framed as the terror of the West's wars on Arabs and Islam, both through the military wars in specific places and through cultural means across the globe, thus broadening the geography of where and what the war on terror actually entailed.

Conclusion: From Western Myth to a Global Cultural Space?

Certainly in the aftermath of the 9/11 attacks, the 'jihad' garnered both media attention in the Arab world and resulted in new media outputs. Islamic fundamentalist groups created an information community for both their followers and the world at large, using such outlets as Taliban Online – which outlived the Taliban regime – and Azzam.com to give non-stop alternative coverage of the war in Afghanistan. Movements such as Hawali-'Awda, which previously relied upon faxes and audio-cassettes to circumvent state restrictions, now rely on the internet. Indeed, people seeking schooling in jihad can do so through the Al-Qaeda University of Jihad Studies, a website belonging to the Global Islamic Media Front. But these are marginal and marginalized, even in the Arab world. While for the West it is the 'global jihad' that defines the target of the war on terror, in the Arab world, the 'jihad' is not as prevalent, neither as a political force, as a focus of media attention, nor in terms of 'audience' size. (One only need reflect on the Arab revolutions in spring 2011 to recognize the marginal role played by Islamist or jihadist groups.)

In so far as 9/11 marks a point in time from which to understand shifts in the Arab media landscape, what is significant is the shared sense among Arabs that the West was attacking Islam as a whole, and waging wars on Arab countries and Islam. It is the impact, the aftermath, the practice and the discourses of the specifics of the war on terror that are of importance in the Arab media landscape: the suffering of civilians in Afghanistan, the war in Iraq, the creation of millions of refugees, the brutality of American and Western 'security', the creation of Guantanamo and extra-judicial 'trials', the list goes on. On top of which is a wide-reaching concern about matters outside the Arab/Islamic region which further galvanize the population to believe that the West is attacking Arabs/Muslims wholesale, whether the headscarf ban or the kicking off of 'Arab-looking people' from airplanes. But the amalgam of these examples, along with countless others, have resulted in what has been the war on terror's biggest success and failure: a mythical division between 'us and them' that has become increasingly real.

Most notable has been the war in Iraq and its related 'failures': the rise of sectarian violence, the Abu Ghraib scandal, the continued foreign occupation, the not-so-secret desire by Western governments to exploit Iraqi oil fields, the establishment of corporate security forces, the mockery made of 'democracy', the failure to relieve the impacts of war and occupation on the Iraqi population, the creation of hundreds of thousands of refugees, and so on. Although there is no unified response and 'solution' among Arabs (or the range of jihadist groups) as to what should have happened or what should happen in the future in Iraq (see Lynch, 2005), there is a unanimous belief that it has largely been a botched enterprise. More than anything, it has become the premiere example of the West's attack – kinetically, politically, economically and symbolically – against Arabs and Muslims.

The more dangerous aspect of the war on terror may well be that certain representations have become dominant and hegemonic, and shape the way in which reality is imagined and acted upon: there is a clash of civilizations. Looking through mainstream Western media, mainstream Arab media and jihadist media, it seems that the war on terror has led to the 'clash' achieving a status of certainty in the social imaginary. It has become increasingly impossible to conceptualize reality in other ways.

Thus, the war on terror belongs to our contemporary world and takes part in its transformation. It has become a 'historical agent' with a life of its own, shaping policies, dictating behavior and demanding sacrifices; a regime of discourse and representation, a political project that is reflected in the realm of culture, an elaboration of supposed geographic and 'civilizational' distinctions and a whole series of interests that it creates and maintains. The war on terror may have been driven by the West and the US, based on how they constructed, imagined, described and approached the perceived threat of the other, but it has been the West's and the US's actions in and towards the 'Arab world' that has led the war on terror and its concomitant civilizational division to become an accepted 'cultural space' across the world.

On the whole, however, whether in the realm of jihadist media or elsewhere, the ideological field of the war on terror is structured outside the living conditions of its most exploited layers. The war on terror's discourse and its media manifestations – by mainstream American institutions and by on-the-run jihadists – have more to do with ideological competition among those actors than with any real relevance to the problems facing the victims of war or terrorism.

References

Awan, Akil N. (2007a) Radicalization on the Internet? The Virtual Propagation of Jihadist Media and Their Effects. *RUSI Journal* 152(3): 76–81.

Awan, Akil N. (2007b) Virtual Jihadist Media: Function, Legitimacy, and Radicalizing Efficacy. *European Journal of Cultural Studies* 10(3): 389–408.

Awan, Akil N. and M Al-Lami (2009) Al-Qaida's Virtual Crisis. *RUSI Journal* 154(1): 56–64.

Boyd, Douglas A. (1982) *Broadcasting in the Arab World*. Philadelphia: Temple University Press.

Bunt, Gary R. (2003) *Islam in the Digital Age: E-Jihad, Online Fatwas and Cyber Islamic Environments*. London: Pluto.

Bunt, Gary, R. (2009) *iMuslims: Rewiring the House of Islam*. Chapel Hill, NC: University of North Carolina Press.

Carr, Matt (2008) The Barbarians at Fallujah. *Race & Class* 50(1): 21–36.

Devji, Faisal (2005) *Landscape of Jihad: Militancy, Morality and Modernity*. London: Hurst.

Devji, Faisal (2008) *The Terrorist in Search of Humanity: Militant Islam and Global Politics*. London: Hurst.

Eickelman, Dale F. and Jon W. Anderson (eds) (1999) *New Media in the Muslim World*. Bloomington, IN: Indiana University Press.

El-Nawawy, Mohammed and Sahar Khamis (2009) *Islam Dot Com: Contemporary Islamic Discourses in Cyberspace*. New York: Palgrave Macmillan.

Hammond, Andrew (2007) *Popular Culture in the Arab World*. Cairo: American University in Cairo Press.

Hofheinz, Albrecht (2005) The Internet in the Arab World: Playground for Political Liberalization. *IPG (Internationale Politik und Gesellschaft)* 3: 78–96.

Hoskins, Andrew and Ben O'Loughlin (2010) *War and Media: The Emergence of Diffused War*. Oxford: Polity.

Keenan, Thomas (2008) Jihad Video in *Global Civil Society 2007/8: Communicative Power and Democracy*: 212–17. Retrieved 4 January 2011 from www.comminit.com/en/node/310903/348

Lynch, Mark (2005) *Voices of the New Arab Public: Iraq, al-Jazeera, and Middle East Politics Today*. New York: Columbia University Press.

Mamdani, Mahmoud (2004) *Good Muslim, Bad Muslim: America, the Cold War and the Roots of Terror*. New York: Three Leaves Press.

Mirzoeff, Nicholas (2005) *Watching Babylon: The War in Iraq and Global Visual Culture*. New York: Routledge.

Moll, Yasmin (2010) Islamic Televangelism: Religion, Media and Visuality in Contemporary Egypt. *Arab Media & Society* 10. Retrieved 7 September 2010 from www.arabmediasociety.com/?article=732

Pope Benedict XVI (2006) Speech at University of Regensberg. Retrieved November 23, 2010 from www.catholicculture.org/news/features/index.cfm?recnum=46474

Ramsey, Gilbert (2009) Relocating the Virtual War. *Defense Against Terrorism Review* 2(1): 31–50.

Sakr, Naomi (2002*) Satellite Realms: Transnational Television, Globalization and the Middle Eas*t. London: I. B. Tauris.

Sakr, Naomi (ed.) (2007a) *Arab Media and Political Renewal: Community, Legitimacy, and Public Life*. London: I. B. Tauris.

Sakr, Naomi (2007b) *Arab Television Today*. London: I. B. Tauris.

Schwartz, Michael (2008) *War Without End: The Iraq War in Context*. Chicago: Haymarket Books.

Schwedler, Jillian (2006) *Faith in Moderation: Islamist Parties in Jordan and Yemen*. Cambridge: Cambridge University Press.

Tatham, Steve (2006) *Losing Arab Hearts and Minds: The Coalition, Al Jazeera and Muslim Public Opinion*. London: Hurst.

Tawil-Souri, Helga (2008) Arab Television in Academic Scholarship. *Sociology COMPASS* 2(5): 1400–15.

UNDP (2005) *Arab Human Development Report 2004*. Geneva: United Nations Development Programme.

Warf, Barney and Peter Vincent (2007) Multiple Geographies of the Arab Internet. *Area* 39(1): 83–96.

Wheeler, Deborah (2005) *The Internet in the Middle East: Global Expectations and Local Imaginations in Kuwait*. Albany: SUNY Press.

PART 4
Journalists and the 'War on Terror'

Journalists find themselves in an uncomfortable position when it comes to reporting war. Burdened with the responsibility of holding generals and politicians to account in their pursuit of military objectives, journalists all too often find themselves caught between the duty to report and reflect on what they see on the battlefield and the obligation to appease not just the powerful in government and the military, but indeed their own bosses and editors. They are caught between obeying a professional 'truth-seeking' code and a more immediate duty to provide copy that sells; they are stranded between providing what official figures decide as what the public 'needs to know' and what, according to the journalist's own investigation and presence, it has a right to know.

Moreover, given the increasingly technologized and mediatized nature of war and terrorism, as many chapters in this book have discussed, it is hardly surprising that media personnel are also literally in the line of fire: identified and targeted as combatants whose ability to publicize images of war and terror justifies their re-designation as interested participants rather than disinterested observers. Not surprisingly, then, over 860 journalists have been killed in military operations since 1992 according to figures provided by the Committee to Protect Journalists, 149 of them in Iraq alone.

15

TERRORISM AND NEWS NARRATIVES

Justin Lewis

Justin Lewis argues that terrorism provides a particularly potent story for the media as it has all the perfect ingredients – violence, drama, fear, and so on – to make great news. He contrasts coverage of the 'terror threat' with that of climate change and finds that, while the latter almost certainly poses much greater risks to the future of humanity, the former continues to command our attention. News values, which 'over-represent' terrorism as a threat, coincide with economic and political pressures to fix 'terror' as a decisive narrative in the contemporary media landscape.

Introduction

When asked to define news, journalists tend to shy away from offering anything more than the vaguest criteria, preferring to invoke their own professional instincts for recognizing a 'good story' when they see it (Brighton and Foy, 2007). This is understandable: few in the creative industries want to be seen as mere cogs in a machine, churning out predictable, formulaic copy (Soar, 2006). An explicit codification of news values – why some stories become news and others do not – privileges structure over agency, diminishing a journalist's capacity and freedom to exercise skill and judgement.

But while many stress the importance of retaining this notion of journalistic freedom (e.g. Niblock, 2007), the ability of journalists to pursue their craft is inevitably defined and constrained by the conditions and values of news production, which derive from a series of social practices with rules, traditions and expectations. In the 1960s, the sociologists Galtung and Ruge (1965) attempted to define those features that made some events or issues 'news' while others are ignored. Although their list is suggestive rather than comprehensive, a series of newsroom ethnographies in the 1970s (notably Schlesinger, 1978; Gans, 1979; Tuchman, 1978) confirmed that news-making is more a matter of manufacture than mystery. Galtung and Ruge's typology has since been developed and refined (Harcup and O'Neill, 2001; Harrison, 2006; Brighton and Foy, 2007). At the same time, others have shown how the development of news as a genre tends to privilege certain kinds of ideas and narratives (Williams, 1998; Rantanen, 2009; Lewis, 2010).

In this vein, terrorism contains a number of features making it immediately recognizable as 'news' (Lewis, 2004). This is, of course, part of the point, since one of the main objectives of terrorist activity is to make an impact on political elites, the public, or both. It follows that the terrorist act is a veritable checklist of elements that feature on most definitions of news value: notably violence, conflict, drama, a threat to public safety and an ability to register on the political agenda.

It is hard, in this context, to imagine a more newsworthy event than the terrorist attacks in New York and Washington on 11 September 2001. Hijacked planes crashing in to the World Trade Center and the Pentagon – a devastating attack on the centre of Western military, economic and cultural power – was such an excessive moment in terms of news value that it almost stretched credulity. As Michael Semati writes, this was not only a news story but the stuff of dark, Hollywood dreams, whereby 'geo-political and cultural worlds came together … in a lethal and monstrous moment of blockbuster imagination' (Semati, 2002: 214).

What began on 11 September 2001, I will argue, was determined, in part, by the enormity of the event in news terms, unleashing a series of narrative conventions that had little to do with any credible body of evidence. The idea that 'the world changed' on 11 September was given credence less by indications of a mounting terrorist threat than by the sheer grisly scale of it as a news spectacle. The judgement that this attack signalled the start of a new and distinct threat became an instant cliché and – with the retaliatory 'war on terror' in Afghanistan and Iraq – a self-fulfilling prophecy. This, in turn, created a framework for how stories about terrorism in the twenty-first century would be told.

In this chapter I discuss how news values play a part in the over representation of terrorism as a threat. But there is more than a set of formal properties at play here. The power and shape of the terrorism news story is also formed by its political context, such that some forms of terrorism have become more newsworthy than others. This context has created a coherent – yet misleading – narrative, in which the roots of terrorism are firmly inscribed with the culture and practices of Islam.

Terror Stories

The US State Department keeps a database documenting global terrorist incidents. In early 2004, its analysis of global terrorism over two decades suggested that the volume of terrorist incidents around the world reached a high point in the 1980s, with an uneven but identifiable pattern of decline since that time. Indeed, its figures suggest that the years 2002 and 2003 – when the 'war on terror' was in full swing – contained fewer terrorist incidents than any other years over the previous two decades. Even if we take into account the scale of the death toll on 11 September 2001, State Department figures indicate that more people died in terrorist attacks in 1998 than in 2001. Remarkably, the idea that the 11 September attacks represented a dramatic new threat was undermined by data from the very government who did so much to promote it (Lewis, 2005).

This contradiction was unsustainable, and under pressure from the Bush/Cheney administration the State Department changed its methodology from 2004 onwards (and, retrospectively, its figures for 2002/3) – making longitudinal comparisons difficult. The picture is further complicated by the role of the 'war on terror' itself (notably in Afghanistan and Iraq), which many intelligence analysts saw as a likely catalyst for increasing terrorist activity (Bures, 2010). Before the Iraq War in 2003, for example, British intelligence indicated that a war in Iraq was likely to increase the risk of terrorist attacks in Britain (Norton-Taylor and White, 2003). Such an attack did, of course, materialise in 2005. The extent to which twentieth-century terrorism has actually been fuelled by the military actions of the US and its allies is hard to measure, but it is certainly plausible that the West's military response has, as many predicted, created its own backlash. Either way, any attempt to identify a clear increase in terrorist activity from 2001 – independent of the US-led response in Afghanistan and Iraq – has no basis in any clear, independent body of evidence.

If the data on the scale of the terrorist threat is ambiguous, the news narrative is rather less so, and the notion that the attacks on 11 September 2001 signalled the start of a new era of terrorist attacks became conventional wisdom in the blink of an eye, bypassing any sober analysis. As a consequence, terrorism received significantly more news coverage after 2001, with more terrorism-related stories in 2002 and 2003 than any year before 2001 (Lewis, 2005). Terrorism – and the 'war on terror' – was quickly established as the dominant story of the first decade of the twentieth century.

Ironically, part of terrorism's news value is that fatal terrorist acts – especially those on the scale of 11 September 2001 – are unusual rather than routine. As a consequence, the increases in the volume of coverage was based on a series of sub-plots: documenting threats, arrests, statements by terrorist groups and supporters as well as a stream of alarming tales told by politicians, security and military figures about the scale of the problem. Much of this coverage is speculative, with a range of interested parties – from politicians to the defence and security industries – having a vested interest in amplifying the sense of risk.

This is not to say that the threat of terrorist attacks should not be taken seriously, or to overlook the fact that some of the twentieth century's terrorist attacks in Europe or the US have involved conspicuously high number of casualties. But it is also true that most other forms of risk – many of which may be far more likely to occur – are simply not as newsworthy as terrorism. In 2004, the UK government's (then) chief scientist, Sir David King, made the 'controversial' claim (in the journal *Science*, then later on the BBC) that climate change posed a bigger threat than terrorism (quoted in BBC, 2004). Such a claim is, in many ways, deeply uncontroversial. The evidentiary base about the risk of climate change is voluminous, and the number of potential casualties if climate change continues at the projected rate is genuinely alarming. According to the Intergovernmental Panel on Climate Change, global warming has the capacity to wipe out whole eco-systems, cause widespread extinction and kill millions of people within the next half-century (IPCC, 2007). Indeed, if some of the more pessimistic projections are correct (and the recent history of research in this area thus far has tended to prove the pessimists right), the scale of devastation may alter the sustainability of life on earth as we know it.

Much has been made of the fact that climate science contains elements of uncertainty. Nonetheless, the evidence amassed thus far comes from a wide range of scientific disciplines and is subject to high levels of data analysis and scrutiny (indeed, few scientists have been subject to as much scrutiny and criticism as those researching climate change). Moreover, there is wide agreement on the ways that we might mitigate or reduce the threat of climate change (i.e. reduce our dependence on fossil fuels). The data informing these analyses is less speculative than the evidence used to inform assessments of the terrorist threat. And yet the contrast in the news narrative between the coverage of the two risks is striking: terrorism has received far more coverage and is treated with far more urgency and far less scepticism or scrutiny (Lewis and Boyce, 2009; Lewis and Hunt, 2011).

If, as Sir David King suggested, climate change is a more serious threat than terrorism, why is this not reflected in the news narrative? The answer to this reveals the extent to which the structure of news (and news values) is not politically innocent. If terrorism is an almost perfect expression of how news has come to be defined, climate change is a much more awkward fit. This is manifested in various ways.

First, the time-scale of the terrorist threat is ever-present, in the sense that a terrorist attack could occur at any moment. The time-scale of the climate change story, by contrast, is decades rather than minutes – an extraordinarily brief period in the history of the planet but an achingly long time in the instantaneous culture of 24-hour news (Lewis et al., 2010). Second, while the terrorist threat can be cast as a stereotypical conflict between good (the innocent victims) and evil (the murderous perpetrators), climate change is a consequence of activities generally regarded in the dominant culture as benign – economic growth, consumer culture, travel and the technological development of consumer goods (Lewis, 2011). Thus while the terrorism narrative has an identifiable parade of villains (such as the Islamic preacher Abu Hamza), climate change is a structural condition created with no ill-intent. These conditions may not diminish the level of risk, they simply diminish its value as a news story.

The differences between the two stories is not, however, entirely a product of the typology of news values. While the literature on news values explains some of the features that make terrorism a compelling news story, it is difficult to entirely reduce the creation and repetition of news narratives to a set of transferable properties. The saliency of news – including news about terrorism – is also a matter of history, context and politics.

So, for example, the threat of climate change is further blunted by the pseudo-controversy that surrounds it, and it is here that we can see a set of political contexts which make evidence about the risks of terrorism – as flimsy and ambiguous as it is – much more difficult to challenge than the risks of climate change. There are powerful vested interests who might benefit from the amplification of the terrorist threat. Richard Maxwell (2002) describes how the events of 11 September were used by the Bush administration to promote various military, domestic foreign-policy objectives. Similarly, the defence industry and pro-military establishment, bereft of an enemy in the post-Cold War era, have used the 'war on terror' to maintain levels of military spending which might otherwise have been spent on a 'peace dividend' (Lewis, 2008; Lewis and Hunt, 2011). The terrorists themselves are, of course, more than happy to play their part in this narrative, since it sees their power and potency exaggerated. There are, on the other hand, no powerful lobbies with the same level of interest in deflating the terrorism narrative.

Climate change, by contrast, has significant vested interests stacked up against it. It is not just that nine of the world's 13 biggest corporations (the oil and car industries) are deeply committed to the use of fossils fuels (Lewis and Boyce, 2009), climate change threatens the basic logic of lightly regulated consumer capitalism fuelled by economic growth. As a consequence, there have been well-funded efforts to create the impression that climate science is controversial and unproven, and the risks exaggerated (Holmes, 2009). This, in turn, creates a structural imperative for news coverage to balance claims against counter-claims.

These economic and political pressures combine with news values to push terrorism onto the front pages and make climate change a less urgent, more ambiguous and equivocal story. One of the ironies here is that there is little evidence that the hard response to terrorist attacks – from military action to a number of legislative restrictions on human rights – is effective. On the contrary, it may actually be counter-productive, helping to foster the conditions in which terrorist groups thrive. By contrast, a tough response to the problem of climate change is more likely to deal with the problem, while a soft response may prove dangerously inadequate.

Yet these responses are entirely in keeping with the urgency of the news coverage in one case and the equivocal reporting in the other. This, in turn, helps to shape the character of public response, prompting political action in one instance and inertia in another. During the last decade, public perceptions of the risk posed by terrorist attacks is higher in the UK than in any other EU country except Spain (Bures, 2010).

The threat of climate change generates a more relaxed response. In January 2010, the Pew Research Center for the People & the Press found that dealing with climate change was bottom of a list of 21 priorities for government – with only 28 per cent judging it to be a priority (a fall from 38 per cent in 2007) (Pew Center, 2010). Similarly, an ICM survey for the BBC found that only 26 per cent of British people agreed with a statement that reflected the scientific consensus that climate change is happening and is now established as largely man-made. Almost the same proportion did not believe that climate change was even happening or likely to happen (ICM, 2010).

Behind the Terrorism Narrative

So, while the power of the terrorism narrative is partly a function of its news value, that power is also inflected by a political context that makes some forms of terrorism more newsworthy than others. The resonance of early twenty-first-century terrorism relies, in part, on its connection to a grand narrative (Kitzinger, 2000) played out on the geo-political stage.

This becomes clearer if we recall news coverage of the bombing of the federal building in Oklahoma City in 1995. The first wave of reports of this terrorist attack – which killed 168 people and injured hundreds more – suggested that it had, as one CBS news reporter put it, 'middle eastern terrorism written all over it' (Said, 1998). Two days later, these reports turned out to be mistaken. The perpetrators, it emerged, drew upon a very different, domestic American tradition of terrorist activity motivated by various forms of white, right-wing, Christian extremism. Indeed, the recent history of terrorist activity in the US suggested that this was, and continues to be, one of the most likely sources of terrorist activity in the US.

Reports by the National Consortium for the Study of Terrorism and Responses to Terror (START) at the University of Maryland 'demonstrate a long history of violent crimes and terrorist activity by far-right extremists in the United States' (National Consortium for Study of Terrorism and Responses to Terror, 2010: 3), with 'more than 300 homicide incidents (more than 60 per cent of which were ideologically motivated and/or movement-related) and over 100 additional attempted homicides by far-rightists in the United States since 1990. Excluding the Oklahoma City bombing, these far-rightist homicides have resulted in over 400 fatalities.' In other words, the Oklahoma City bombing – the most serious terrorist attack in the US at that time – had its own, clear narrative, forming part of a well-documented history of far-right terrorist activity in the US.

The fact that, for the first two days of coverage, the Oklahoma bombing was assumed fallaciously by news reporters to have come from the Middle East is itself a testimony to the power of what Edward Said has described as an 'Orientalist' narrative about the terrorist threat (Said, 1979, 1997). Based purely on the evidence, it would have been possible to construct a very different narrative centred on a history of right-wing extremism. This did not happen in mainstream coverage of the aftermath of Oklahoma, and without a clear framework for understanding its significance and meaning the story soon lost its urgency and edge. The story of Timothy McVeigh, one of the terrorists convicted for the Oklahoma City bombing, was treated in isolation, reducible to a particular individual pathology. There was, as a consequence, no war of retribution, no national security legislation and no shifts in the geopolitical map.

This story of far-right terrorism remains absent from the dominant terrorism news narrative, despite evidence of its potency. In April 2009, the US Department of Homeland Security published a report warning against the possibility of terrorist attacks by right-wing extremists. This prediction was manifested most recently in January 2011, by the shooting of liberal Democrat congresswoman Gabrielle Giffords and six others, in Arizona. And while some coverage of the Giffords shooting linked the attack to the rhetoric of right-wingers, little reference was made to a well-established terrorist tradition, and a coherent narrative chronicling far-right terrorist attacks in the US only exists on the margins of news reporting.

As the early coverage of the Oklahoma City bombing suggests, in recent decades the dominant narrative about terrorism has been informed by a framework which pitches the West against the Orient (Said, 1979, 1997). So much so that despite all the evidence, reports rearticulating Oklahoma within an Orientalist narrative are given serious airing in a way that other questionable conspiracy theories are not. During the build-up to the war on Iraq in 2002, for example, the *Evening Standard* reported that 'senior aides to US Attorney-General John Ashcroft have been given compelling evidence that former Iraqi soldiers were directly involved in the 1995 bombing'. The story referred to a 'methodically assembled dossier' which 'could destroy the official version that white supremacists Timothy McVeigh and Terry Nichols were solely responsible for what, at the time, was the worst act of terrorism on American soil'. The article went on to list a group made up of what we might call the usual suspects – in this case 'a group of Arab men with links to Iraqi intelligence,

Palestinian extremists and possibly al-Qaeda' as the sinister forces behind the Oklahoma City bombing (*Evening Standard*, 21 October 2002).

The Orientalist narrative has, traditionally, been vague about questions of motive, conjuring images of dark, sinister forces that, for various unexplained reasons, are antagonistic to what are often referred to as 'Western values' (a phrase which usually refers to the more positive values that might be associated with the West, such as freedom of speech and democracy rather than, say, colonialism, militarism or excessive consumerism). The terrorists responsible for the attacks on 11 September were generally referred to within the vague terms of this antagonism, as evil-doers harbouring a hatred of freedom and democratic traditions (Laquer, 2001; Nacos, 2003).

These characterizations pose as many questions as they answer and are, as a consequence, difficult to sustain without resorting to straightforwardly racist explanations. The idea that such violent antagonism towards the West comes from a people who, for no apparent reason, harbour a hatred of freedom and democracy is, after all, a faintly ludicrous, comic-book account. In the years following 2001, this weakness has been addressed and the question of motive has been gradually developed and refined. In so doing, Samuel Huntingdon's famous 'Clash of Civilizations' (1993) has been narrowed to a specific conflict between Islam and the (Judeo-Christian or multicultural, depending on your perspective) West. This has allowed the perpetrators (actual or potential) of terrorist acts to become more fully fleshed-out characters in the dominant terrorism narrative.

In this more persuasive version, the terrorists' fanaticism is increasingly seen to come from a set of extreme, religious imperatives, derived from and in the pursuit of a radical form of Islam. The couplet 'Islamic terrorism' thereby works in a number of ways: it explains the degree of fervour involved in terrorist activity; it allows us to link a number of Middle Eastern groups (such as the *Evening Standard*'s 'Arab men with links to Iraqi intelligence, Palestinian extremists and possibly al-Qaeda') within a common frame of reference; it forges a symbolic link with the more brutal practices practiced in some Islamic states; and it invokes other appropriate narratives – such as the 'brainwashing' of converts – that help explain the (apparent) spread of terrorist activity.

Coverage of terrorism has often repressed any discussion of political motivations, especially when these involve an examination of the ugly side of Western foreign policy, with its support for and arming of various brutal regimes (Lewis et al., 2009). Any serious analysis of the motivations of 'Islamic terrorism' suggests that it is these political motives – rather than the degree of religiosity involved – that lie behind terrorist activity (O'Duffy, 2008; Stohl, 2008). Indeed, the most likely source of terrorist attacks across the EU does not come from Islamic or international groups, but separatist organizations. So, for example, of the 583 terrorist incidents in EU countries in 2007, 88 per cent were carried out by separatist groups, while Islamic groups were only responsible for a tiny proportion.

The number of people arrested for Islamic terrorist activity is higher, although acquittal rates are conspicuously high (Bures, 2010), suggesting that police operations are heavily weighted in that direction, despite the low number of incidents.

Nonetheless, by providing such a clear and seemingly coherent explanation for 'Islamic terrorism', the role of Islam in the narrative represses the question of political motivation more effectively than the old tautologies (which proclaimed dully that 'terrorists are motivated by their love of terrorism'). The focus on Islam, in other words, has meant that the questionable history of US and British involvement in the Middle East – as well as support for undemocratic regimes in the name of economic, geo-political interests – need not be addressed. Furthermore it sanctions foreign-policy interventions aimed at curtailing Islam or Islamic regimes.

Islam: the Terrorist Religion?

The end of the Cold War left military elites (and their political allies) casting around for a new rationale to justify high levels of public spending (Lewis, 2008; Lewis and Hunt, 2011). A number of scholars saw attempts to amplify the threat of Islamic states – and Islam more generally – as a form of political expedience, whereby the 'Clash of Civilizations' was used as a ready-made replacement for the power struggle between Soviet communism and Western capitalism (Agha, 2000; Mowlana, 2000; Said, 2001; Macdonald, 2003). Before 11 September 2001, however, this discursive shift was nascent rather than overt, with Western pro-military rhetoric coalescing around the threat of dangerous dictators (like Saddam Hussein or Slobodan Milošević) in an uncertain world (Lewis, 2001; Lewis and Hunt, 2011).

The shift towards a more specific focus on Islamic terrorism was, of course, predicated by the attacks on New York and Washington in 2001, but its prominence in media discourse was a more gradual development. One analysis of the coverage of Islam in the UK press between 2000 and 2008 (Lewis et al., 2009) indicated a number of trends which suggested that Islam itself was increasingly identified as a problematic religion, a sinister force driving – and explaining – the terrorist threat.

While the number of stories about Islam or British Muslims increased after 2001, this topic grew more significant in the second half of the decade – the period 2005 to 2008 contained twice as many stories as the years between 2001 and 2004. The main 'news hook' behind these articles alluded to three (related) types of stories: one linking Islam to terrorism (36 per cent of articles about Muslims or Islam); one that focused on controversies around Islamic culture (such as dress codes, Sharia law and fears about the rise of Islamic culture in the UK) that accounted for 22 per cent of articles; and one devoted to tales about

Islamic extremism (11 per cent of articles), with the more vociferous Muslim clerics (like Abu Hamza) playing a leading role.

Taken together, these three stories suggest a clear narrative in which an intolerant Islam is identified in opposition to Western liberal values. More radical or extreme Muslims are thus seen as especially susceptible to committing acts of brutality, of which terrorism is the ultimate expression. Islam and Islamic culture thereby becomes terrorism's back-story, made more vivid by each new account of Muslim intolerance and hostility.

The study found that such stories became an increasingly prominent part of the coverage of Islam in the later part of the decade. Figure 15.1 shows how the proportion of articles about Islam prompted by religious and cultural controversies increased from less than ten per cent of articles in 2002 to more than 30 per cent in 2008. These stories were often highly speculative, casting Islam against a more civilized Christianity.

So, for example, in January 2008, the Bishop of Rochester made comments about Muslim 'no-go areas' – places in Britain where non-Muslims were apparently made to feel unwelcome and unsafe. His fears – as speculative as they were – were widely reported, offering only flimsy or anecdotal evidence. The Muslim population of the UK is not especially high and at 2.7 per cent (in 2008), lower than Germany, France, Belgium, Austria, Sweden and many other EU countries (Bures, 2010). Yet this story – and others like it (such as a dubious story suggesting that mosques would soon outnumber churches in the UK) – created the impression of a non-Muslim population becoming overwhelmed.

The following month Dr Rowan Williams, the Archbishop of Canterbury, caused reactions ranging from concern to outrage following a lecture at the Royal Courts of Justice in London in which, it was reported, he suggested that Muslim Sharia Law would soon become part of British life. The image painted by many newspapers was of a weak Christian leader whose liberal views meant caving in to more ruthless Islamic pressure. Williams became the fall-guy for the weak, Christian response to the Islamic threat, and was variously described as a 'prize chump' (*Daily Star*, 8 February 2008), 'a batty old booby, but dangerous with it' (*Daily Mail*, 8 February 2008) or simply – in a play on words that invoked other controversies about Muslim dress – as 'a burkha' (*Sun*, 8 February 2008).

In fact, the Archbishop's speech was a discussion of the delicate relationship between cultural and religious forms of jurisdiction and the state. Although his address specifically ruled out 'a kind of inhumanity that sometimes appears to be associated with the practice of the law in some Islamic states, the extreme punishments, the attitudes to women as well' (Williams, 2008), a majority of newspaper articles suggested quite the opposite, associating the Archbishop with the most brutal versions of Sharia Law, notably stoning, limb removal and beheading/execution.

The image suggested by these two stories – one Christian leader warning of subjugation to a hostile Islam, the other bowing down before it – is of a hostile,

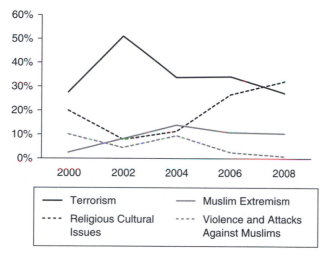

Figure 15.1 Changes in news hooks in coverage of Islam in the UK press, 2000–2008
Source: Lewis et al., 2009

foreign religion uniquely suited to acts of violence. Indeed, by 2008 the power of this narrative was such that many newspapers felt able to describe Rowan Williams's speech explicitly as a triumph for terrorism. As *The Sun* put it, Williams's speech, 'handed al-Qaeda a victory last night' (*Sun*, 8 February 2008). To anyone who had read the careful, nuanced speech, with its assertion of the primacy of a liberal, humane legal system, this interpretation borders on the absurd. Yet the discursive Orientalist climate in the British press made a giant leap between moderate Islamic cultural practices and acts of terror seem but a short step.

Not surprisingly, one of the effects of this coverage was to encourage hostility towards Islam, resulting in forms of discrimination and attacks on Muslims (Armeli et al., 2007). As Figure 15.1 suggests, this story – of a religion subject to distortion, misrepresentation and abuse – became increasingly unlikely to make the news. Such stories simply did not fit within the dominant narrative.

Conclusion

The story of terrorism in the twenty-first century is a compelling one. Cast against a geopolitical landscape which pitches liberal Western values under attack from an aggressive Islam, the terrorist narrative weaves cultural features of everyday life into a hard news story about fear, violence and war. It links stories about Islamic dress codes with the war in Afghanistan, the Qu'ran with repressive 'rogue' states and WMD, and apocryphal scare stories about fearful councils banning Christmas to appease Muslim sensibilities with suicide bombers. And it contains the possibility – in terms of news values – that the blood of innocents may, at any moment, be spilled across the screen in the ultimate 'breaking news' story.

Unfortunately, it is a narrative that conceals more than it reveals. It distorts both the scale and character of the terrorist threat, encouraging ill-informed, aggressive responses in a bid to control the narrative. It represses the political nature of most terrorist acts – inspired by a variety of ideological positions – and substitutes it with one particular form of religious extremism. In so doing, it demonises a whole section of the population who, while they may be seen as moderate in their practice of Islam, are seen to inhabit a position on a continuum with terrorism at one end of it. It is a story that offers glimpses of certain truths (some terrorists are Muslims) in a larger obfuscation. And it shows us that the way the news media choose which stories to tell – and how to tell them – matters.

References

Agha, O. (2000) Islamic Fundamentalism and Its Image in the Western Media: Alternative Views, in K. Hafez (ed.) *Islam and the West in the Mass Media: Fragmented Images in a Globalizing World*. Cresskill, NJ: Hampton Press.

Armeli, S. R., Marandi, S. M., Ahmed, S., Seyfeddin, K. and Merali, A. (2007) *The British Media and Muslim Representation: The Ideology of Demonisation*. London: Islamic Human Rights Commission.

BBC (2004) Scientist Renews Climate Attack, 31 March. Available at: news. bbc.co.uk/1/hi/uk_politics/3584679.stm (accessed 7 March 2011).

Brighton, P. and Foy, D. (2007) *News Values*. London: SAGE.

Bures, O. (2010) Perceptions of the Terrorist Threat Amongst EU Members States. *Central European Journal of International and Security Studies* 4(1): 51–80.

Galtung, J. and Ruge, M. (1965) Structuring and Selecting News, in Cohen, S. and Young, J. (eds) *The Manufacture of News: Deviance, Social Problems and the Mass Media*. London: Constable: 52–64.

Gans, H. (1979) *Deciding What's News*. New York: Random House.

Harcup, T. and O'Neill, D. (2001) What is News? Galtung and Ruge Revisited, *Journalism Studies* 2(2): 261–280.

Harrison, J. (2006) *News*. London: Routledge.

Holmes, T. (2009) Balancing Acts: PR, 'Impartiality,' and Power in Mass Media Coverage of Climate Change, in Boyce, T. and Lewis, J. (eds) *Climate Change and the Media*. New York: Peter Lang.

Huntington, S. (1993) The Clash of Civilizations? *Foreign Affairs* 72(3): 22–49.

ICM Research (2010) Climate Change Survey, 28 Feburary–1 March, prepared for the BBC. Available at: www.bbc.co.uk/insideout/east/docs/OmClimateChange.pdf (accessed 7 March 2011).

Intergovernmental Panel on Climate Change (2007) 4th Assessment Report, www.ipcc.ch.

Kitzinger, J. (2000) Media Templates: Patterns of Association and the (Re) Construction of Meaning Over Time. *Media, Culture and Society* 22(1): 61–84.

Laqueur, W. (2001) *The New Terrorism*. London: Phoenix Press.

Lewis, J. (2001) *Constructing Public Opinion*. New York: Columbia University Press.

Lewis, J (2010) 'Democratic or Disposable? 24 Hour News, Consumer Culture and Built-in Obsolescence' in Cushion, S. and Lewis, J. *The Rise of 24-hour News Television: Global Perspectives*, New York: Peter Lang.

Lewis, J. (2004) September 11th, in Creeber, G. (ed.) *50 Television Texts*, London: Arnold.

Lewis, J. (2005) The Power of Myths: The War on Terror and Military Might, in Nossek, H., Sonwalker, P. and Sreberny, A. (eds) *Media and Political Violence*. Cresskill, NJ: Hampton Press.

Lewis, J. (2008) The Role of the Media in Boosting Military Spending. *Media War and Conflict* 1(1): 108–118.

Lewis, J. (2011) The Dead-End of Consumerism: the Role of the Media and Cultural Industries, in Gates, K. (ed.) *Media Studies Futures*. New York: Blackwell.

Lewis, J. and Boyce, T. (2009) Climate Change and the Media: The Scale of the Challenge, in Boyce, T. and Lewis, J. (eds) *Climate Change and the Media*. New York: Peter Lang.

Lewis, J. and Hunt, J. (2011) Press Coverage of the UK Military Budget: 1988 to 2009, *Media, War and Conflict*. 4: 162–184.

Lewis, J., Brookes, R., Mosdell, N. and Threadgold, T. (2006) *Shoot First and Ask Questions Later: Media Coverage of the War in Iraq*. New York: Peter Lang.

Lewis, J., Mason, P. and Moore, K. (2009) Islamic Terrorism – The Repression of the Political, in Marsden, L. and Savigny, H (eds) *Media, Religion and Conflict*. London: Ashgate.

Lewis, J., Maxwell, R. and Miller, T. (2002) Editorial for special issue of *Television and New Media* on 11 September 2001 3(2): 125–131.

Macdonald, M. (2003) *Exploring Media Discourse*. London: Hodder Arnold.

Maxwell, R. (2002) Honor Among Patriots? *Television & New Media* 3(2): 239–248.

McGaurr, L. and Lester, L. (2009) Complimentary Problems, Competing Risks: Climate Change, Nuclear Energy and the *Australian*, in Boyce, T. and Lewis, J., *Climate Change and the Media*. New York: Peter Lang.

Mowlana, H. (2000) The Renewal of the Global Media Debate: Implications for the Relationship between the West and the Islamic World in Hafez, K. (ed.) *Islam and the West in the Mass Media: Fragmented Images in a Globalizing World*. Cresskill, NJ: Hampton Press.

Nacos, B. (2003) Terrorism as Breaking News: Attack on America. *Political Science Quarterly* 118: 23–53.

National Consortium for Study of Terrorism and Responses to Terror (2010) *Background Report: On the Fifteenth Anniversary of the Oklahoma City Bombing*. College Park. University of Maryland.

Niblock, S. (2007) From 'Knowing How' To 'Being Able' Negotiating the Meanings of Reflective Practice and Reflexive Research in Journalism Studies. *Journalism Practice* 1(1): 20–32.

Norton-Taylor, R. and White, M. (2003) Report Reveals Blair Overruled Terror Warning. *Guardian*, 12 September.

O'Duffy, B. (2008) Radical Atmosphere: Explaining Jihadist Radicalization in the UK. *Political Science and Politics* 41(1): 37–42.

Pew Research Center for the People & the Press (2010) Public's Priorities for 2010: Economy, Jobs, Terrorism, survey report, 25 January. Available at: http://people-press.org/report/584/policy-priorities-2010 (accessed 7 March 2011).

Rantanen, T. (2009) *When News Was New*. London: Wiley-Blackwell.

Said, E. (1979) *Orientalism*. New York: Vintage.

Said, E. (1997) *Covering Islam: How the Media and the Experts Determine How We See the Rest of the World*. London: Vintage.

Said, E (1998) *Edward Said on Orientalism*. Northampton, MA: Media Education Foundation.

Said, E. (2001) The Clash of Ignorance *The Nation*, 22 October.

Schlesinger, P. (1978) *Putting Reality Together*. London: Methuen.

Semati, M. (2002) Imagine the Terror. *Television & New Media* 3(2): 213–218.

Soar, M. (2006) Encoding Advertisements: Ideology and Meaning in Advertising Production, in Bennett, A. (ed.) in *Design Studies: Theory and Research in Graphic Design*. New York: Princeton Press.

Stohl, M (2008) Old Myth, New Fantasies and the Enduring Realities of Terrorism. *Critical Studies on Terrorism* 1(1): 5–16.

Tuchman, G. (1978) *Making News*. New York: Beverley Press.

Williams, K (1998) *'Get Me a Murder a Day!' A History of Mass Communications in Britain*. London: Arnold.

Williams, R. (2008) Interview with BBC *World at One*, 7 February. Available at: www.archbishopofcanterbury.org/1573 (accessed 7 March 2011).

16

ASYLUM-SEEKER ISSUES AS POLITICAL SPECTACLE[1]

Jake Lynch, Annabel McGoldrick and Alex Russell

Lynch et al's chapter uses critical discourse analysis to assess how news stories concerning asylum seekers have been used in the Australian media as sources of hope and fear in the age of the 'war on terror'. Pursuing the notion that popular news narratives function as mediated political spectacles, the authors present the results of a survey where audiences were presented with two types of asylum story: one modelled on 'peace journalism', the other on 'war journalism'. They argue that while 'peace journalism' attempts to include the voices of all participants in order to increase empathy with the 'other', 'war journalism' – with its strident and largely uncritical targeting of the 'other' – actually increases feelings of fear, disgust, anger and distress. Journalists, they suggest, need to learn these lessons: to move away from demonizing and criminalizing representations of asylum seekers and immigrants and to pursue a more socially responsible and humanitarian form of journalism.

Introduction

This chapter traces the evolution of political spectacle in Australia and the UK focused on conflict over immigration and – latterly – asylum-seeker issues. It suggests, following Edelman (1967, 1988), that such issues are transformed into conflicts as a means of political control, where symbolic power inheres in the psychological distance between the symbols involved and the perceptions of the audience, such that would-be incomers to the political community can be constructed as a 'threat' thereby producing an 'aroused' mass response. The residual power of these symbols can then, it is suggested, be made accessible from memory, by the incidence of particular 'cues': framing devices embedded in the representation of immigration and asylum seeker issues that are abundant in political and media discourses, especially at the present time.

Data is presented from an experiment in which two groups of subjects were exposed to different versions of a story about government efforts to administer the asylum system in Australia. Qualitative and quantitative measures were used to gauge audience responses, with noticeable differences between the two. These distinctions are based on the peace journalism model (Galtung, 1998) and are drawn out under a set of headings for deriving evaluative criteria (Shinar, 2007). This chapter traces the process by which framing characteristics were particularized, under these headings, with attention to the representation of asylum-seeker issues, paying attention to the intensification of key threat messages following the 9/11 attacks in the United States and the response by governments, launching the so-called 'war on terror'. This opening section of the chapter takes the form of an exercise in Critical Discourse Analysis (CDA), an approach – or group of approaches – thus characterized by two of its leading theorists: 'CDA sees discourse – language use in speech and writing – as a form of "social practice". Describing discourse as social practice implies a dialectical relationship between a particular discursive event and the situation(s), institution(s) and social structure(s) which frame it: the discursive event is shaped by them, but it also shapes them. That is, discourse is socially constitutive as well as socially conditioned' (Fairclough and Wodak, 1997: 258).

The analysis presented here follows a particular strand of Critical Discourse Analysis (see Fairclough and Wodak, 1997) known as the Discourse Historical Approach (Wodak, 2001), which emphasizes the need for discursive uses of historical analogies and examples to disclose their influence on the potentially accessible inter-textual meanings of particular conflict episodes. In this case, perspectives supplied by the parallel consideration of another context (the UK), in which the symbolic framework of political spectacle around asylum-seeker issues reveals a historical lineage and present-day modalities that overlap to a significant degree with those of their Australian counterpart, enables a hermeneutical commentary.

Anti-Immigrant Discourse in the UK

'If you want a nigger for your neighbour, vote Labour.' The Conservative Party slogan for the 1964 by-election campaign at Smethwick, in the English Midlands, is an infamous example of what Edelman calls 'political spectacle', in which stories are created so as to produce 'a drama that objectifies hopes and fears' (1988: 91). Such stories imbue social situations with definitional power through a spectacle that 'normally rationalizes those conditions' (1988: 103). According to Spencer (2005: 19), it is necessary to 'manage meaning through conflict' because without conflict, 'the issue is not political, by definition' (Edelman, 1988: 104).

Social interactions are transformed into conflicts through spectacles created in media domains as a means of exerting political control. In the UK, later versions of this same spectacle came couched in different language but with similar effects. The 1970s saw the openly racist National Front attain greater prominence, both on the streets and at the ballot box. Strong counter-demonstrations effectively contested their invasion of public space and their electoral advance was stemmed, at the end of the decade, after Margaret Thatcher, in a television interview recorded a few months before she entered Downing Street, expressed sympathy with Britons who feared immigration as a threat of being 'swamped by people with an alien culture'.

These fears dated from the movement of Commonwealth subjects to the old colonial power in the post-war years, but even as memories began to fade, the political utility of such a spectacle remained. The Thatcher government ushered in a 'monetarist' policy – later known as 'neo-liberalism' – which, in Dorling's words, 'turned the tide' (2010: 256) on decades of narrowing economic and social inequalities in Britain, and had the effect of re-opening them. Wilkinson (2005) marshals evidence from social research that life in more unequal societies fosters anti-social attitudes, including racism, as 'relative deprivation' (Gurr, 1970) causes collective frustration, resentment and aggression.

The Conservatives – by then under John Major's leadership – were defeated in 1997, but the incoming New Labour government stuck to the public spending plans set out by its predecessor for the first two years and delayed the introduction of its promised minimum-wage policy for the same period. With important pro-social policies on hold, income inequality had not started to fall significantly by the time of the next General Election in 2001 (Wilkinson and Pickett, 2009). By now, the Conservative opposition was led by William Hague, a declared standard-bearer for the party's right wing. As Labour began to send out a clearer message of 'fairness', Hague and his allies – including some in the media – set out to reframe the agenda for the poll to include curbing immigration.

So, British politics was in need of a scapegoat, and found it, not this time in immigrant communities from India or the Caribbean, but in a new 'wave' of incomers: asylum seekers from the world's conflict zones. A personal recollection: I remember leaving a reporting job at London's High Court (in my former role as a correspondent for Sky News) in mid-2000, and seeing, the capital's then sole daily newspaper, the *Evening Standard*, on sale outside. The front page was dominated by a picture of a Romanian asylum seeker in a headscarf outside an Underground station, with one hand outstretched in mendicancy and a baby in the other, surmounted by an inflammatory headline. The 'starting-gun' on the election campaign had just been fired.

The story of the Romanian beggar proved, indeed, to be the opening scene of a mediated political spectacle that also involved, as a prime mover, the *Daily Mail* – often seen as the 'voice of Middle England' and then owned by the same company as the *Standard* – to demonize asylum seekers by the incessant repetition of conflictual messages: that they were causing various forms of mischief, creaming off state benefits and so forth. The effect on public opinion was an example of what Berger and Luckman call the 'power to produce reality' (1966: 52–3). When Britain's Refugee Council commissioned pollsters to set British people a multiple choice question that asked them how many of the world's asylum seekers were ending up on their shores, the most popular answer was between 25 and 30 per cent. The true figure was actually 1.98 per cent (Lynch and McGoldrick, 2005: 5).

Neither of the two main parties was above collusion with the media in such endeavours. Two political journalists revealed how Labour ministers had collaborated with Rupert Murdoch's *The Sun* newspaper to manage the news on asylum. On hearing that the paper planned to run a week's worth of special reports on 'Britain's immigration crisis', Downing Street devised a cluster of announcements intended to be seen as getting on top of the 'problem'. Then Home Secretary David Blunkett gave the *The Sun* an exclusive interview in which he promised 'tough measures to crack down on asylum cheats' (Walters and Oborne, 2004).

White Australia

In Australia, a similar syndrome was under way, with its roots in the historic switch in the late 1940s away from the 'white Australia' policy enshrined in legislation from the start of 'Federation' nearly half a century earlier. The country's first ever immigration minister, Arthur Calwell, had served as minister for information during World War II when he imposed strict censorship laws. Now, Calwell contrived a political spectacle, with meticulous advance preparation and tight control over its media representation, in what amounted to a highly effective piece of propaganda. Immigration officers were despatched to the refugee camps of war-torn Europe to hand-pick several hundred 'displaced persons' as putative new Australians for the long journey south. Blonde, blue-eyed natives of the Baltic – then the newly established Soviet republics of Estonia, Latvia and Lithuania – were favoured and a shipload of what came to be known as 'beautiful Balts' docked in Sydney in 1947. The story of their voyage was told in newsreel reports, which then played in cinemas across Australia. A 'government film crew' was sent to a refugee camp in Switzerland to take pictures of one of Calwell's officials conducting an apparently 'tough and rigorous' interview with a prospective immigrant (SBS, 2011). The newsreel film culminates in choreographed scenes of their arrival in Australia with smiling young women caught in lingering close-up.

Australia, Calwell declared, had to 'populate or perish': the war had shown the country simply did not have enough people to defend its shores. His policy – of bringing in new citizens whose lives in the northern hemisphere had been wrecked by the upheavals of the 1940s – got off to a bad start, in PR terms, with pictures from the arrival of an earlier boat having shown older, 'foreign' types from the Mediterranean and Middle East disembarking in Melbourne. Hence the political imperative of appearing to discriminate between aspiring new Australians: to control the 'flow' of immigration.

In both Australia and the UK, therefore, there is a stock of symbols and ideas to objectify hopes and fears (in Edelman's terms) that are readily available to be invoked in conflictual dramas as a way to exert political control. There are familiar frames embedded in political and media discourses that can be made accessible to media audiences by the incidence of particular cues for memory-based information processing (Scheufele, 2000). At particular moments of stress, when the premium on political control is increased, such cues are plentiful, in key words and discursive constructions, with abundant evidence of media agenda-setting by political interests.

The symbolic framework for political acts must, Edelman argues, 'evoke a quiescent or an aroused mass response [by] symboliz[ing] a threat or reassurance' (1967: 7). Emotions are intensified through a psychological distance between the symbols and the perceptions of the audience, which is perhaps why, as Lynch and McGoldrick note, a chief characteristic of 'war journalism' – as defined in the peace journalism model conceived by Galtung (1998) – when it comes to stories about asylum seekers, is that they 'do not get a chance to speak for themselves' (2005: 133).

The distance is necessary to construct the threat: the lack of any basis for empathy with the 'other' enables immigrants or asylum seekers to function as empty repositories for hopes and fears, or 'harbingers of all things dreadful' (Crock, 2010: 26). It is in the construction of narratives of identity and alterity that the economic and political interests of the media amplify this effect. As a strategic principle, Tehranian observes, both 'government and commercial media systems tend to dichotomize, dramatize, and demonize 'them' against "us"' (2002: 60). 'We' are the ones who rightfully belong to the political community or aspire to the lifestyle embodied in the advertisements.

The political spectacle of identity and alterity can only evoke an aroused mass response if psychological distance is preserved between their perceptions and the symbols involved. Look beyond those symbols, assign other meanings to refugees or asylum seekers – perceive them as wife, daughters, sons, friends, colleagues – and the threat is dissipated, the conflict defused.

One significant example in Australia of the emergence, and then assimilation into the mainstream of political debate, of racism towards immigrants, similar to that in the UK discussed earlier, is that of Pauline Hanson who was elected to the Federal House of Representatives in 1996, an election that brought 13 years of Labor governments to an end. Her maiden speech carried echoes of Thatcher in 1979: 'I believe we are in danger of being swamped by Asians. They have their own culture and religion, form ghettos and do not assimilate. Of course, I will be called racist but, if I can invite whom I want into my home, then I should have the right to have a say in who comes into my country.'

Hanson's references to the likely response to her remarks indicate an understanding that open expressions of 'old' racism (Hall, 1981) belonged, by then, in what Hallin called the 'zone of deviancy ... [outside] the limits of acceptable conflict' (1989: 117). They played a key role, however, in reactivating a more coded discourse of 'new' racism (van Dijk, 2009) in the zone of 'legitimate controversy' where most journalistic activity takes place.

At her official launch during the campaign by Hanson's One Nation party for the 1998 Federal election, in the economically dispossessed town of Gatton, Hanson concentrated on grievances arising from Australia's own experiment with neo-liberalism, introduced in this case by Labor governments under Bob Hawke and Paul Keating:

> Her audience in Gatton heard that a former Prime Minister, Bob Hawke, in many ways the architect of Australia's modern political settlement, promised the country in the eighties that, by the end of that decade, no child would be living in poverty. He and his successor, Paul Keating, were 'the only prime ministers in Australia's history to become multi-millionaires while in office', Ms Hanson declared; today 700,000 children were living – 'or should I say, surviving' – in households without work (Lynch, 1998).

There were already indications that the ruling Liberal–National Coalition of John Howard was signalling to voters tempted to support openly racist parties that they could find a safe home with him, as the Conservatives under Margaret Thatcher had done 20 years earlier'. There is plenty of evidence that the Coalition has trimmed its sails to the baleful blast of Ms Hanson's rhetoric. Immigration has slowed from 96,000 to 80,000 a year; Liberal campaign literature boasts of introducing tougher criteria to do with an ability to speak English' (Lynch, 1998).

The 'War on Terror' and the Switch from Quiescence to Arousal

These measures were, perhaps, designed to induce a quiescent mass response – in Edelman's terms – rather than an aroused one. But then, in the months leading up to the next election in November 2001, came two events that transformed the political spectacle over immigration and asylum from a threat, to be defused into an opportunity to be exploited: the Tampa affair and the 9/11 attacks in the US.

In August of that year, the Coalition was languishing in the polls as its economic 'reforms' – including, in another echo of the Thatcher government, a newly introduced regressive revenue-raising measure, the General Sales Tax – caused widespread dissatisfaction. Then came deliverance. The government refused permission for the Norwegian freighter *MV Tampa* to enter Australian waters. On board were over 400 Afghan asylum seekers, rescued from a distressed fishing vessel. It triggered a diplomatic dispute with Norway, which accused Canberra of failing to meet obligations to distressed mariners under international law. Within a few days the government introduced the Border Protection Bill into the House of Representatives, promising to confirm Australian sovereignty to 'determine who will enter and reside in Australia'.

An unauthorized biography later claimed that the Prime Minister adopted this stance in order to defuse growing support for One Nation in a marginal electorate – Lindsay, in New South Wales – at the urging of the local MP, Jackie Kelly (Errington and van Onselen, 2007). Kelly was the Sports Minister in Howard's cabinet, but, perhaps more significantly, her political identity was as an icon of the 'Howard battlers': working-class voters who deserted Labor, following 'Reagan Democrats' in the US and 'Essex Man' in the UK. These were the sections of the electorate most prone to feelings of relative deprivation in the face of widening inequalities, while simultaneously being identified as 'aspirational' by media advertisers.

Howard's response to the Tampa succeeded in transforming his party's fortunes, and he went on to win a third term in office with Labor consigned to its lowest share of the primary vote in any election since before the second world war. Howard actually happened to be on a visit to Washington on 11 September of that year, and thus found himself the first world leader to have personal contact with President George W. Bush after the attacks on the World Trade Center and the Pentagon. The coalition exploited the conjunction of events, at home and abroad, notoriously raiding a budget earmarked for measures to curtail domestic violence to send every Australian an 'information pack', including a fridge magnet reminding them to 'be alert, not alarmed'.

The launching of the 'war on terror' allowed the level of 'threat' that could be inscribed in the motif of people attempting to 'enter and reside in Australia' to be ratcheted up. Manning (2004: 12) shows that, of newspaper articles published in Sydney in a two-year period after 9/11, of those referring to refugees or asylum-seekers, 37 per cent also contained references to 'terrorism'. Howard and his ministers made the connection, both in explicit terms and in more subtle forms, on a regular basis. One contemporary newspaper feature article, in the ostensibly (small-'l') liberal *Age* newspaper of Melbourne, drew these threads together in typical fashion:

> In the late 1990s, boatloads of asylum seekers from the Middle East arrived on Australia's shores. At the time, many liberal-minded people hated the government's tough refugee policies. Then September 11 happened. And the Tampa incident. About the same time there was publicity about rapes carried out by Lebanese Muslim gangs in Sydney. Then, last October, the terrible bombings in Bali. Just after the Bali attack, a caller to Australia Talks Back on ABC Radio National, the station of choice for Australia's liberal elite, said: 'We should send all Muslim non-citizens and students home... reintroduce the death penalty for murder ... have no more Muslim or Indonesian immigration or tourism to Australia ... ban Arabs from aeroplanes permanently.' (Bone, 2003)

As with the overtones of the 'White Australia' policy, and the racist posturing of the UK Conservatives, the asylum seeker-as-terrorist frame, once established, tends to become lodged in political and media repertoires: 'a sleeper concern', Maley writes, 'that could be reactivated for political reasons in the future' (2010: 10). Later, as Tamil refugees from the Sri Lanka conflict took to boats to seek asylum in Australia, senior Liberals – by then back in Opposition after their defeat in 2007 – were quick to pronounce their claims unfounded. It was not long before the spectre of 'terrorism' was invoked, in calls for 'tougher' measures to stop them.

Former Attorney-General Philip Ruddock used a newspaper column to explain that these people were now heading for our shores in greater numbers, not because of 'push factors' but because the Australian government had 'gone soft', notably by scrapping the policies of its coalition predecessor such as naval interception of 'people-smugglers', mandatory detention and the issuance of Temporary Protection Visas to successful applicants, rather than a 'migration outcome', thus limiting 'consequential family reunion'. This was, perhaps, a series of cues calculated to make accessible to a latter-day Australian audience the same issue of discernment over the 'right kind' of new Australians that Calwell's film had constructed over 60 years earlier.

The Ruddock line being, evidently, insufficient to arouse a mass response, former minister Wilson Tuckey then weighed in. The refugees now setting sail for Australia were likely to be Tamil Tiger 'terrorists', he declared, who should be denied asylum. This did succeed in creating a political spectacle, especially when a Tamil leader in Australia inadvertently lent credence to it (ABC, 2009). (Indeed, Tuckey had been first into the fray in connecting the two issues in the context of the Tampa incident, as well – see Crock, 2010.)

This latest iteration came as the coalition prepared – under a new, right-wing Liberal leader, Tony Abbott – to reframe the agenda for an upcoming election, as the Conservatives had done under William Hague years earlier. As if to confirm the continuing salience of the 'White Australia' spectacle, an otherwise sympathetic radio interviewer asked Jake Lynch what would happen to 'Australia's cultural stability' if Tamil asylum seekers were to be admitted. In one of the subsequent interventions in the debate, a column for a popular website, Lynch commented on this exchange: 'Decoded? They're darkies, mate! Bloody darkies!' (Lynch, 2010).

The 'Two Versions' Experiment

It was against this backdrop that an experiment was conducted, to illustrate the feasibility of representing the story of asylum seekers coming to Australia in different ways, and to gauge cognitive and emotional responses by audiences. This was part of a wider 15-country study, 'A Global Standard for Reporting Conflict' (Lynch and McGoldrick, 2010) that was based on the peace journalism model first proposed by Johan Galtung (1998).

In it, groups of participants watch two different versions of a set of stories, each highlighting recent conflict issues at home and abroad that are familiar from mainstream news in the country concerned. Each 'pair' of stories are adjusted, in content and presentation, to reflect aspects identified as belonging to categories of 'war journalism' and 'peace journalism' respectively, under five headings developed from an overview of the peace journalism field by Shinar. In this, peace journalism can be recognized as:

- exploring backgrounds and contexts of conflict formation, and presenting causes and options on every side so as to portray conflict in realistic terms, transparent to the audience;
- giving voice to the views of all rival parties;

- offering creative ideas for conflict resolution, development, peacemaking and peacekeeping;
- exposing lies, cover-up attempts and culprits on all sides, and revealing excesses committed by, and suffering inflicted on, peoples of all parties;
- paying attention to peace stories and post-war developments. (Shinar, 2007: 200)

The strategic aim of the study is to enable and foster a Habermasian approach of immanent critique of professional journalism in the target countries, using the system's own legitimating norms to propose institutional reforms: 'the credentials of peace journalism … to be considered as good journalism, make it an important means for media to fulfil their public service role' (Lynch and McGoldrick, 2010: 99).

Before producing each story pair, an exercise in critical discourse analysis was undertaken – as in this chapter – considering historical analogies and examples and their influence on the potentially accessible inter-textual meanings of particular conflict episodes. Additionally, an exercise in content analysis was carried out on two contrasting examples of locally produced television news, monitoring their reporting of all kinds of conflicts over a two-week period, using Shinar's five-point list as the basis for developing a set of evaluative criteria. The 'peace journalism' version of each story could thus be calibrated in such a way as to show what could be realistically aspired to as 'good journalism', in the particular 'mediascape' of its setting.

Lynch and McGoldrick describe the process of content analysis:

> A story that includes material satisfying criteria under each of Shinar's five headings could be allotted one point. One that includes all five would score five points. So each individual story would be 'marked' initially out of five. Following Lee et al. (2006), three indicators of 'passive' PJ [peace journalism] could then be added, for the avoidance of: emotive language; 'labelling' of conflict parties as good and bad, and partisan reporting. To recognize the lesser importance of these indicators, compared with the main framing characteristics, each could be allocated the score of 0.5, to be… subtracted from, the initial score. 'Scores' for each media outlet… could be expressed as mean averages. (2010: 97)

In the case of the asylum story, the critical discourse analysis we have carried out in this chapter pointed to the first, second and fifth of Shinar's headings as the most potentially ideational. In considering the evolution of political spectacle around this conflict in Australia (to take the country chosen for the first phase of the study), Edelman's observations about the need for psychological distance, if representations of conflict are to exert the power to dramatise popular fears to induce an aroused mass response, mean that the most important distinction of any peace journalism treatment is to enable viewers to hear from asylum seekers themselves, thus challenging the hegemonic 'relations of representation' (Hall, 1981) that keep racist attitudes in place.

This was already happening, to some extent, in the actual coverage of the issue offered by the two news programmes chosen for the content analysis exercise – Channel Nine News and SBS World News Australia – during the period of the study. Molotch and Lester (1997) argue that news is generally dominated by those sources who enjoy 'routine access' – usually officials, a category topped by heads of government in the country in which the media are produced – while the resulting patterns are disrupted, from time to time, by 'event promoters' such as 'terrorists'. In this respect, if no other, asylum seekers themselves could indeed be viewed in a similar light: in September 2010, a series of incidents at the Immigration Detention Centre at Villawood, in western Sydney (a few kilometres from the Lindsay electorate) saw inmates stage rooftop protests in a bid to draw attention to their predicament. From there, they spoke to friends outside via mobile phones with some of the conversation relayed to viewers of the two programmes, in a rare opportunity to hear a perspective generally subjugated in political spectacle.

Overall, the two programmes attained very similar 'scores' in content analysis, with a mean average of 1.23 for the stories on Channel Nine News (n = 64) and 1.32 for SBS World News Australia (n = 124). The scores for individual stories ranged from -1 (no qualifying content under any of the five headings, and 0.5 deducted for the presence of two of the three negative indicators) to a full five out of five. Hence, the two versions were framed so as to fall within the upper and lower quintiles of the content analysis scores. Of all the stories examined (n = 188), the boundaries fell at the ratings of 0.5 and 2.5 respectively. All the war journalism stories were coded at 0 and all the peace journalism stories were coded at > 3.

In the case of the asylum story, the peace journalism version scored under the first criterion, by offering to explain why some asylum seekers resort to dangerous journeys by boat, to reach sanctuary. It gave a voice to all parties – not merely the government and main opposition party, the typical 'indexing' pattern according to Bennett (1990) – but also the third political party, the Greens; an opinion pollster who stated that most Australians were happy to welcome asylum seekers as new citizens; and a 'boat person', Ali Jafari, a Hazari man originally from Afghanistan, who featured in extensive personal interview. As Jafari is shown to have successfully settled in Australia, it also scored on the fifth criterion, showing a peace story.

Audience Responses

Thirty-six participants (23 female, 13 male) were recruited via advertisements posted around the University of Sydney and were remunerated for their time. The average age of participants was 25 years, ranging from 18 to 51 years of age. Participants were allocated to watch either the war or peace journalism version of the asylum seekers story, with no participant seeing both versions or at any stage being made aware that a second version existed. Fourteen participants were allocated to the war journalism version and there were no statistically significant differences between the groups in terms of age, gender or any other standard demographic factors.

The Differential Emotion Scale (DES) (Izard, 1977) was employed to test for differences between the groups before and after seeing the asylum-seekers story. The DES is a 30-item questionnaire, consisting of ten fundamental emotions, each assessed by three items. The ten fundamental emotions in this scale are: interest, enjoyment, surprise, distress, anger, disgust, contempt, fear, empathy and guilt. Each of these 30 items is rated on a five-point Likert scale.

Before watching any footage, participants filled in the DES to measure baseline levels on each of the ten subscales. There were no statistically significant pre-existing differences between the two groups in any of the subscales. Participants then watched the asylum seekers story before filling in another copy of the DES. Mixed-model ANOVAs with tests for simple effects and interactions were used to test for differences between the groups in terms of emotional reaction.

The two groups did not differ significantly in any of the baseline measures of the DES subscales. After the story, the war journalism group showed significantly higher levels of distress, anger, disgust, contempt and fear compared with their baseline measures. The level of enjoyment reported by members of the war journalism group dropped significantly more, compared with their baseline, than that of the peace journalism group members. The peace journalism viewers' feelings of guilt also decreased to slightly greater extent than those of the war journalism viewers.

The peace journalism group showed a significant increase in anger and disgust compared to their baseline, albeit to a lesser extent compared with their counterparts in the war journalism group.

Significant interactions were observed for the subscales of distress, anger, disgust and contempt. In every case, the war journalism group showed a significantly stronger reaction in these subscales to the asylum seekers story compared to the peace journalism group. No other significant differences were found.

Thus, both groups had emotional responses to the story, supporting the finding by Unz et al. (2008) that viewers react emotionally to these news stories. The finding that war journalism evoked stronger reactions than peace

Table 16.1 Means and standard deviations for the war and peace journalism groups before and after watching the asylum seekers story on each of the DES subscales

	Pre-test		Post-test	
	War	Peace	War	Peace
Interest	3.31	3.30	3.00	3.02
	0.62	*0.94*	*0.80*	*0.95*
Enjoyment	2.93	3.14	1.50	1.73
	0.92	*1.05*	*0.45*	*0.68*
Surprise	1.38	1.41	2.21	1.64
	0.65	*0.55*	*0.95*	*0.90*
Distress	1.45	1.48	2.40	1.71
	0.84	*0.64*	*0.75*	*0.53*
Anger	1.33	1.25	2.88	1.97
	0.80	*0.41*	*1.08*	*1.07*
Disgust	1.21	1.17	2.90	1.79
	0.55	*0.37*	*1.12*	*1.05*
Contempt	1.31	1.23	2.50	1.52
	0.63	*0.42*	*0.95*	*0.66*
Fear	1.31	1.29	1.64	1.36
	0.65	*0.60*	*0.65*	*0.50*
Guilt	2.02	1.98	1.86	1.71
	0.55	*0.65*	*0.66*	*0.77*
Empathy	2.19	2.54	2.90	2.88
	0.84	*1.04*	*0.88*	*0.57*

Note: Means are shown on the first line, standard deviation on the second for each subscale

journalism indicates that different context or framing can have significantly different effects on emotional reactions to stories, particularly on emotions that could be construed as negative.

It begs the question, of course, of what they were angry, distressed, disgusted, contemptuous and fearful about. In the same experiment, participants also filled in, during the playing of the story, a Thought-Listing Protocol (TLP) (Coleman and Thorson, 2002), inviting them simply to write down any notes of thoughts or feelings prompted by what they were watching. Responses were themed in categories based on Entman's characterization of the cognitive steps involved in framing: 'To frame is to select some aspects of a perceived reality and make them more salient in a communicating text, in such a way as to *promote a particular problem definition, causal interpretation, moral evaluation, and/or treatment recommendation*' (1993: 51–52, emphasis in the original).

The category with the most obvious direct 'read-across' to Edelman's dyad of aroused versus quiescent mass responses is that of moral evaluation, since the problem definition and causal interpretation 'depend' (1993) on that, with the treatment recommendation then logically following. The TLP responses allocated to the moral evaluation theme were grouped into three main sub-themes: of anger towards politicians; empathy towards asylum seekers; and antipathy towards asylum seekers.

The lead 'angle' in the war journalism version of the story is the leak of a letter from the Immigration Department, asking for more staff from across the government bureaucracy, to deal with an increased workload. This formed the basis for criticism of the government, by the Opposition – who obtained the leaked document – for 'going soft' on asylum seekers, along the lines of Ruddock's complaints in his earlier newspaper column.

Responses in the first sub-theme were mostly statements of anger, disgust and contempt towards the Opposition themselves, in particular their leader, Tony Abbott, with some anger also directed towards the Labor government. In the second sub-theme, respondents typically 'felt sorry' for asylum seekers, or professed themselves distressed or disgusted at the conditions they were forced to undergo, being detained in 'processing centres'. In the third, participants either expressed open fear of an increase in the number of asylum seekers entering Australia, or reproduced rationalisations familiar from past iterations of this familiar political spectacle: 'asylum seekers can create a strain on the immigration system', one said, 'and it is unfair for people trying to immigrate by legitimate means'.

It means the DES results are ambivalent in themselves, since the same emotional responses can be triggered by different moral evaluations. The group that watched the war journalism version of the asylum story recorded a total of 61 comments on this theme, with the following totals on each sub-theme:

- Anger towards politicians = 23
- Empathy towards asylum seekers = 8
- Antipathy towards asylum seekers = 17.

In the peace journalism version, the story of the leaked letter is relegated to the second 'angle' after a call by the Greens, via their immigration spokesperson, Senator Sarah Hanson-Young, for more resources to be allocated to the prompt consideration of asylum claims, to avoid people being held for long periods in detention. And it contains the sequence and interview with Jafari, as mentioned on page 281.

In this version, the TLP written responses revealed a different pattern. Anger tended to be directed towards 'mandatory detention' itself and 'the rate of processing' – that is, in furtherance of empathy towards asylum seekers. Empathic statements tended to be linked to the presentation of Jafari as having successfully joined the Australian community – dissolving the psychological distancing on which the power of political spectacle depends. Anger, contempt and disgust towards politicians generally were noticeably less, with the intervention by

Senator Hanson-Young serving to contextualise the debate. In all, 54 comments broke down into sub-themes thus:

- Anger towards politicians = 5
- Empathy towards asylum seekers = 26
- Antipathy towards asylum seekers = 15

(Some comments in the main theme defied categorisation in the sub-themes, which explains the numerical discrepancy in each case.).

Conclusion

Australia has a long tradition of political spectacle around issues of immigration in which politicians have sought, for different reasons at different times, to trigger an aroused or quiescent mass response. Arousal has been used to exert political control, often as a diversion from other issues. The deliberate conflation of asylum issues with concerns arising from the 9/11 attacks and the 'war on terror' was typical – coming, as it did, amid discontent over policies that were exacerbating social and economic inequalities. In this, Australian politics carries abundant echoes of, and correspondences with, its British counterpart. A comparative study in critical discourse analysis can disclose some of the historically transmitted inter-textual influences on meaning-making in response to present-day symbolic experiences.

Past iterations of political spectacle have left a set of potentially accessible legacy frames, to be activated by the provision of highly coded 'cues' to trigger fear and resentment towards asylum seekers. Political leaders have disseminated such cues through their routine access to public debate, ensured by journalistic convention, which elevates 'official sources' to a position of primacy in mass media and commonly frames conflicts as dyadic in shape and character. The power of such political spectacle inheres in its psychological distancing of audience perceptions from the symbols that form the basis for journalistic stories.

Peace journalism is a challenge to such conventions, having been fashioned as a policy response to the structure of foreign news and subsequently extended into a programmatic set of ideational distinctions in the representation of all types of conflict. Content analysis studies, using evaluative criteria derived from the peace journalism model, show there is a certain amount of peace journalism in television news produced and broadcast in Australia, including on stories about asylum issues. The most clearly ideational aspect of peace journalism in reporting asylum stories is to give readers and audiences a chance to hear from, and empathize with, asylum seekers themselves, thus satisfying the peace journalism criterion of hearing 'all sides' – not merely the familiar 'he-said, she-said' of indexed political reporting. This can defuse the power of political spectacle by dissolving the psychological distancing.

Viewers exposed to a war journalism version of a story about the government's handling of the asylum system were more likely to be angry towards politicians, and to reproduce, in a thought-listing protocol, some of the 'classic' framings of this recurrent political spectacle, objectifying fears and anxieties. A separate group, who watched a peace journalism version, exhibited fewer negative emotions, signalling a more quiescent response. They were more likely to be empathetic towards asylum seekers, and less likely to be angry towards politicians.

The way Australian television news reports asylum seeker issues could be reformed within the idiom and range of the medium as locally produced and experienced, with the effect of reducing the opportunity for politicians to activate political spectacles that have had the effect of demonizing and victimizing asylum seekers themselves, notably in the context of the 'war on terror'. This represents a challenge and an opportunity to catalyse immanent critiques of journalistic practice, with the aim of improving the journalism on its own terms. This would, at the same time, create opportunities, for advocates of more humane and socially just responses to asylum-seeker issues, to devise and project their own political spectacles: ones that objectify hopes rather than fears.

Endnote

1   This research was supported under the Australian Research Council's Linkage Projects funding scheme (No. LP0991223) with partnership by the International Federation of Journalists and Act for Peace.

References

ABC (2009) Tigers could be on boats: Tamil leader, *The World Today*. 26 October. Transcript retrieved 31 January from www.abc.net.au/worldtoday/content/2009/s2724040.htm

Bennett, W. L. (1990) Towards a theory of press-state relations, *Journal of Communication* 40 (2): 103–125.

Berger, P. and Luckmann, T. (1966) *The Social Construction of Reality: A Treatise in the Sociology of Knowledge*. Garden City, NY: Anchor Books.

Bone, P. (2003) Bridging the differences: multiculturalism – is it still working?, *The Age*, Melbourne, 4 January.

Coleman, R. and Thorson, E. (2002) The effects of news stories that put crime and violence into context: testing the public health model of reporting, *Journal of Health Communication* 7: 401–425.

Crock, M. (2010) Alien fears: politics and immigration control, *Dialogue* 29 (2): 20–27.

Dorling, D. (2010) *Injustice: Why Social Inequality Persists*. Bristol: Policy Press.

Edelman, M. (1967) *The Symbolic Uses of Politics*. Chicago: University of Illinois Press.

Edelman, M. (1988) *Constructing the Political Spectacle*. Chicago: Chicago University Press.

Entman, R. (1993) Framing: towards clarification of a fractured paradigm, *Journal of Communication* 43: 51–58.

Errington, W. and Van Onselen, P. (2007) *John Winston Howard: The Biography*. Melbourne: Melbourne University Press.

Fairclough, N. and Wodak, R. (1997) Critical discourse analysis, in T. van Dijk (ed.) *Discourse Studies: A Multidisciplinary Introduction*. London: SAGE, 258–284.

Galtung, J. (1998) High road, low road – charting the course for peace journalism, Track Two 7 (4) Cape Town: Centre for Conflict Resolution. E-version, retrieved 23 January 2007 from http://ccrweb.ccr.uct.ac.za/archive/two/7_4/p07_highroad_lowroad.html

Gurr, E. (1970) *Why Men Rebel*. Princeton: Princeton University Press.

Hall, S. (1981) The whites of their eyes: racist ideologies and the media, in G.

Bridges and R. Brunt (eds) *Silver Linings*. London: Lawrence & Wishart, 89–93.

Hallin, D. (1989) *The Uncensored War*. Berkeley: University of California Press.

Herman, E. and Chomsky, N. (2002) *Manufacturing Consent* (2nd edition). New York: Pantheon Books.

Izard, C. (1977) *Human Emotions*. New York: Plenum Press.

Lederach, J. P. (1999) 'Just peace' in *People Building Peace*. Utrecht: European Centre for Conflict Prevention, 27–36.

Lynch, J. (1998) The Saturday Profile: Pauline Hanson, Australian politician – Pauline, queen of the outback, *Independent*, London, 3 October.

Lynch, J. (2010) Memo, 'Cockroach' Kev, show some leadership on asylum, *Crikey*, 19 May, retrieved 1 February 2011 from www.crikey.com.au/2010/05/19/memo-cockroach-kev-show-some-leadership-on-asylum/

Lynch, J. and McGoldrick, A. (2005) *Peace Journalism*. Stroud: Hawthorn Press.

Lynch, J. and McGoldrick, A. (2010) A global standard for reporting conflict and peace, in R. Keeble, J. Tulloch and F. Zollmann (eds) *Peace Journalism, War and Conflict Resolution*. London: Peter Lang.

Maley, W. (2010) Fear, asylum and Hansonism in Australian politics, *Dialogue* 29 (2): 10–17.

Manning, P. (2004) *Dog-whistle Politics and Journalism*. Sydney: Australian Centre for Independent Journalism.

Molotch, H. and Lester, M. (1997) News as purposive behaviour: on the strategic use of routine events, accidents and scandals, in D. Berkowitz (ed.) *Social Meanings of News: A Text-Reader*. London: SAGE.

SBS (2011) *Immigration Nation: The Secret History of Us*, 16 January, SBS One.

Scheufele, Dietram A. (2000) Agenda-setting, priming, and framing revisited: another look at cognitive effects of political communication, *Mass Communication and Society* 3 (2): 297–316.

Shinar, D. (2007) Peace journalism – the state of the art, in D. Shinar and W. Kempf (eds) *Peace Journalism – The State of the Art*. Berlin: Regener, 199–210.

Spencer, G. (2005) *The Media and Peace: From Vietnam to the 'War on Terror'*. London: Palgrave Macmillan.

Tehranian, M. (2002) Peace journalism: negotiating global media ethics, *Harvard International Journal of Press/Politics* 7 (2): 58–83.

Unz, D., Schwab, F. and Winterhoff-Spurk, P. (2008) TV news – the daily horror? Emotional effects of violent television news, *Journal of Media Psychology* 20 (4): 141–155.

Van Dijk, T. (2009) News, discourse and ideology, in K. Wahl-Jorgensen and T. Hanitzsch (eds) *The Handbook of Journalism Studies*. New York: Routledge, 191–204.

Walters, S. and Oborne, P. (2004) *Alastair Campbell*. London: Aurum Press.

Wilkinson, R. (2005) *The Impact of Inequality: How to Make Sick Societies Healthier*. London: Routledge.

Wilkinson, R. and Pickett, K. (2009) *The Spirit Level: Why More Equal Societies Almost Always Do Better*. London: Penguin.

Wodak, R. (2001) The discourse-historical approach, in R. Wodak and M. Meyer (eds) *Methods of Critical Discourse Analysis*. London: SAGE, 63–94.

17

MEDIA MYTH AND GROUND REALITY IN REPORTING FROM IRAQ

Dahr Jamail

The two final chapters are written by journalists themselves. Dahr Jamail is a well-known reporter who was one of the first 'unilaterals' to report from Iraq and beyond. He provides a searing indictment of the complicity between major news coverage of the occupation of Iraq and official military perspectives. Talking about the existence of a 'State/Media combine', he insists that the mainstream media completely missed the dynamics of what was happening on the ground in Iraq and gives many first-hand examples of disinformation, deception and distortion practised by both military sources and news outlets. Jamail asks some very tough questions about the role played by commercial news organizations in securing consent for wars, occupations, bombings, curbs on civil liberties and all the ideological paraphernalia required to sustain an open-ended 'war on terror'.

As we complete the decade following the devastating 9/11 event, of which calamity, incidentally, there has been no official criminal investigation in the last ten years, it is important to evaluate and assess the role of media in what can decidedly be called the age of man-made disasters.

The media has a lot of questions to answer in the period since 9/11: has the media contributed to exacerbating the political, cultural and religious divides within Western societies and the world at large? To what extent has the media, in all its forms, questioned, celebrated or simply accepted the unleashing of the so-called 'war on terror'? Today these questions are as inevitable as they are imperative. This chapter argues that mainstream media blatantly abdicated its role of objective informer to the public and responsible critic of the presiding powers. Nowhere has this abdication been as thorough as in the US. I have attempted to deal with the implications of this phenomenon particularly with reference to the so-called war in Iraq and the ongoing occupation of the country. The same conditions apply to Afghanistan but constraints of space compel me to deal only with the former here.

I have tried to underscore the enormity of the fraud, for no other word can represent the large-scale deception that all sections of the media have perpetrated on its readers and viewers, at the behest of the American administrative system. It is my contention however, that a larger segment of the American public is fully complicit in this fraud. There is no other way to explain how a population with an allegedly 99 per cent literacy rate can exercise such a willing suspension of disbelief in the face of all manner of evidence that what they have been and are still being told, shown and offered as news is a travesty of reality. For those seeking the truth the media is actually redundant as there is no dearth of authentic official material outlining the plans, proposed strategies, rationales and defence of the indefensible mandate that America has of leading the world by ruling it and securing control over its resources.

When in 2003, I decided that I had to personally cover the invasion of Iraq, little did I know that I was embarking on a long war of my own against the mighty allied forces that constitute a ruthless state machinery supported by several military establishments. I saved some money, bought a laptop, a camera and a plane ticket, and armed with elementary information gleaned through the internet, headed for the Middle East. I had few contacts, no work space appointed with private guards, no protection, as I was going as an independent journalist, but above all I had no media outlet to write for. Perhaps that was just as well since the rampant media repression in 'liberated' land would not have allowed me to accomplish my two-point agenda of witnessing for myself and presenting to American citizens accounts of the occupation as it impacted on the lives of Iraqis.

Order 65 of the '100 Orders' penned by former US administrator in Iraq, Paul Bremer, established an Iraqi Communications and Media Commission, which was authorized to control and regulate the entire telecommunication system in the country. When in June 2004, the United States handed over power to a 'sovereign' Iraqi interim government, Bremer passed on the authority to the US-installed interim Prime Minister Ayad Allawi who had longstanding ties with the British intelligence service MI6 and the CIA.

Media outlets and media representatives in Iraq that chose to operate autonomously and not follow the diktat of the US have been punished. In 2004,

I reported from Baghdad how journalists were being detained and threatened by the US-installed interim government. There were draconian constraints on covering the occupation in Iraq. A glaring instance is the curbs placed on Al-Jazeera. Within days of the 'handover' of power, the Baghdad office of the channel was raided and closed by security forces on charges of inaccurate reporting. A ban was imposed initially for one month and later extended 'indefinitely'.

As early as 2004, the Media Commission sent out an order on the letterhead of Allawi to news organizations, asking them to 'stick to the government line on the US-led offensive in Fallujah or face legal action'. Additionally it instructed the recipients to set aside space in their 'news coverage to make the position of the Iraqi government, which expresses the aspirations of most Iraqis, clear'.

To highlight the broad pattern of mainstream media coverage of America's 'War on Terror' in the last decade, I have picked a few specific episodes from the Iraqi occupation and juxtaposed media myth against ground reality as witnessed by me and a handful of my colleagues, who, like me, do not have the option of disowning reality.

My main difficulty in undertaking such an exercise is that the lines blur and I find myself critiquing and condemning the policies and strategies of the US 'War on Terror' rather than the media's projection of the war. That nothing separates the two should perhaps be one of our biggest concerns. What needs serious and sustained attention is the fact that the Pentagon has dominated not only the battlefield but the media landscape in which that battlefield is reported. My observations do not seek to engage the media, which I believe has been proved guilty of deception, beyond reasonable doubt, but I hope to underscore the role and liability of civil society in remedying the situation. Ultimately it is this amorphous body of ordinary citizens alone that can reinforce the element of accountability in all institutions that dominate the public sphere, media being the foremost.

Fallujah

My first case offers a look at major US coverage of the siege of Fallujah in November 2004, one of the most guarded military campaigns in Iraq. The biggest issue for the US Department of Defense here was to explain the waging of war upon a population, on behalf of that population. It is an issue that has been deftly tackled on prior occasions. In the Vietnam era it was the 'counterinsurgency doctrine'. When this began to be associated with unprecedented civilian deaths, less than desirable interventions of the US foreign policy gained the nomenclature of 'foreign internal defense'. More recently we have been looking into 'internal security and stability'. In Iraq, the language of counter-insurgency has been redeployed and never more effectively than during the bombardment and invasion of Fallujah. Major US media outlets succeeded in framing their reportage accordingly.

The US misadventure in Iraq abounds in ironies: the American government defines insurgency as 'a small, ideological armed group which gradually encroaches on a state to win over its people and take its territory' (Slim, 2004). To anyone possessed of reason, it would be obvious that the definition marks, as insurgents, the forces that bombed and invaded the city, rather than the Iraqis residing within. Reinforcing the irony we had Rumsfeld's statement even as US soldiers went on the rampage in Fallujah that 'no government can allow terrorists and foreign fighters to use its soil to attack its people and to attack its government, and to intimidate the Iraqi people' (US Department of Defense, 2004).

If the media noted the irony, they were careful not to acknowledge it. Instead there was almost unanimous projection of the invasion of Fallujah as a desperate bid to tackle insurgency. The *New York Times* reportage represents the trend of the entire mainstream media so I have used it as my basic parameter of reference, confident that differences in accounts of different agencies, if they did exist, were superficial only. Of the Fallujah siege the *New York Times* said: 'With only three months to go until the country's first democratic elections, American and Iraqi officials are grasping for any tool at their command to bring the insurgency under control' (Oppel and Worth, 2004). Although a mass boycott of elections was already being widely reported, this stated objective of the invasion remained totally unquestioned. With the exception of a single news article, moreover, an offer for peace contingent on the 'ambitious demand' that US soldiers remain on base during an Iraqi election day went entirely unreported (Vick, 2004).

Similar silence has prevailed over previous US interventions in Fallujah. For instance nowhere in the media was any mention made of the fact that armed resistance in Fallujah developed only after the US military opened fire on a crowd of civilians, killing 17 and injuring some 70 more in what was described as 'appropriate action' (*San Francisco Gate*, 2003) – perhaps because the 'collateral damage estimate was within permissible limits', a justification given for a later bombardment of the city that killed 20 (Cody, 2004). A Human Rights Watch report conducted thereafter could find 'no compelling evidence' that any guns had been fired upon US soldiers (2003).

More disturbing was the absence in the November military campaign of any discussion about the precedent set by the US attacks on Fallujah in April. A *New York Times* article devoted to the US takeover of the Fallujah General Hospital (Oppel, 2004) which, like all major US coverage, was uninterested in the levelling of another Fallujah hospital around the same time, said only that the hospital had been 'considered a refuge for insurgents and a center of propaganda against allied forces' (BBC News, 2004).

The alleged propaganda remained unstated for understandable reasons since it dealt with the doctors' reports of US military use of cluster bombs, shooting of ambulances and civilians, and related war crimes (Jamail, 2004a). That a US military takeover of an Iraqi hospital may exacerbate the precarious condition of serious occupation victims merited even less attention (Jamail, 2004b). During the April 2004 attack on Fallujah I had reported on *Democracy Now!* that a doctor had been instructed by US and Iraqi forces entering to raid the Fallujah General Hospital that, if information about the raids were disclosed, the hospital staff would be fired or arrested by orders of the Iraqi health minister. Violating the order, the doctor had described to me how soldiers and the Iraqi forces had pulled wounded people out of their beds, interrupted operations that were in progress, tied doctors' hands behind their backs and essentially appropriated control of the hospital from its legitimate monitors before going on to detain several patients, overthrowing their need for emergency medical care (Jamail, 2004c).

Media attention during the November siege was directed to promising aspects of the invasion. A *New York Times* photo of a soldier poised to open fire had the caption: 'Protecting the Islamic cultural center in Falluja was one of the marines' objectives today' (Filkins and Glanza, 2004). The article emphasized Iraqi participation in the assault: '"For cultural reasons, we think it is much better for the Iraqis to search the mosques", General Metz said in Iraq, adding that Iraqi forces had found a large number of weapons inside a mosque in the city.'

Just as Iraqi soldiers have been deployed by the US military, Iraqi voices have been deployed by the US media to highlight implicit support of the invasion. In fact the account in the *New York Times* could easily mislead a reader to believe the Fallujah attack to be an Iraqi-led action: 'In Baghdad on Monday, Allawi announced that he had given the go-ahead for the operation. "I have given my authority to the multinational forces", he said at a news conference inside the fortified compound housing the headquarters of the interim Iraqi government. 'We are determined to clean Falluja of terrorists' (Filkins and Glanza, 2004).

Another *New York Times* article discusses the ambivalence of the Iraqi response to the siege of Fallujah within a frame that opens with apparent dissent ('the country's most prominent Sunni political party said today that it was withdrawing from the interim Iraqi government') and closes with an Iraqi answer ('"Nobody is in favor of using force, but the problem is you need sovereignty over all the parts of Iraq", [Hassani] said. "I haven't heard any party come up with a single suggestion that we can solve the problems in these places without using force"') (Wong, 2004).

In reporting the siege, I focused entirely on the recalcitrance of Iraqi citizens in the face of the American military campaign. I was interested in what they had to say and in seeing why they seemed not to understand that freedom comes with sacrifice – such as that of Artica Salim, seven months pregnant, killed at 3.30 a.m. on 1 November while she slept when two rockets from US warplanes struck her home (Jamail, 2004d).

Nisan al-Samarra'i, a 55-year-old merchant in the Karrada district of Baghdad, said, 'The people of Falluja have the right to fight for their city, because if the Americans are invading their city, they have to defend it.' Former commander of the Iraqi police in Baghdad, 80-year-old Mahmoud Shakir, said 'Fallujans should fight for their city. They are not terrorists, and there has been no proof of foreign fighters in Fallujah. And if there are Arabs there, they are more accepted than the Americans and coalition forces. In the name of liberty, they must fight.' Hamad Abdulla Raziz, an unemployed electrician doing odd jobs at a hotel in central Baghdad, said the US-led coalition failed to see that 'we are having now to fight for our liberation against them' (Jamail, 2004e).

I found and reported that in order to bring freedom to Fallujah, the 'US troops have sprayed chemical and nerve gases on resistance fighters' and that 'residents have been further burnt beyond treatment by poisonous gases'. I had evidence too since the US had admitted having used napalm, an internationally banned weapon, in Iraq during the initial invasion of the country (Jamail, 2004f).

I had eyewitness accounts to back my claims. Ahmed Abdulla, a 21-year-old student whose father like all male civilians of 'fighting age' was denied exit from Fallujah by the US army, described how 'shops had even been bombed; bodies with arms and legs lying near them were tossed about on the sidewalks in places just after the bombs fell. I still can't get the smell of dead bodies to leave me' (Jamail, 2004g). The top marine commander in Iraq informed the *New York Times*, 'We're sweeping through the city now. We're clearing out pockets of resistance. It ought to go down in the history books' (Filkins and Worth, 2004).

Frequently during the course of my reporting from Iraq I found myself asking, what gives violence legitimacy? I am convinced that the humanitarian crisis in Iraq would not have been possible without a widespread dehumanization of Iraqis among American soldiers and a deep-set, if largely unexpressed and little considered, conviction on the American 'home front' that Iraqi lives were worth little. If, four decades ago, the Vietnamese were 'gooks', 'dinks' and 'slopes', the Iraqis of the American occupation are 'hajis', 'sand-niggers' and 'towel heads'. Latent racism abets the dehumanization process, ably assisted by a mainstream media that tends, with honourable exceptions, to accept Pentagon announcements as at least an initial approximation of reality in Iraq.

Abu Hanifa

My second case is a comparison of two accounts of this attack on a Baghdad mosque. On Friday 19 November 2004, after noon prayers at Abu Hanifa mosque in Baghdad were interrupted by a US-led military assault. My story, 'As US Forces Raided a Mosque', opens with the statement that 'US soldiers raided the Abu Hanifa mosque in Baghdad during Friday prayers, killing at least four and wounding up to 20 worshippers.' As a sequence of events, the episode is explained with an onset ('about 50 US soldiers with 20 Iraqi National Guardsmen entered the mosque') at a specified time ('12:30 pm') (Jamail, 2004h).

This report was a phone relay of the proceedings by an eyewitness who also happened to be my interpreter. He conveyed a minute by minute account, 'Everyone started yelling "Allah u Akbar" (God is great) because they were frightened. Then the soldiers started shooting the people praying! They are holding our heads to the ground.' Testimony from two further witnesses corroborates this account, as does the extended audio version of this report that includes a recording of gunfire inside the mosque.

Both versions of the incident noted that the US military prevented medical personnel from entering the mosque to treat the wounded. About 30 men were led out with hoods over their heads and their hands tied behind them. Soldiers loaded them into a military vehicle and took them away around 3.15 p.m. It was almost three hours before the Red Crescent officials were able to attend to those inside the mosque, confirming nine wounded and four dead.

The *New York Times* story, though similarly titled, 'GI's and Iraqis Raid Mosque, Killing 3' provides a different account. The article begins by amplifying its explicit subject ('American and Iraqi troops raided a prominent Sunni mosque in Baghdad on Friday') for which a possible cause is given (it 'may have been aimed at a cleric said to have incited insurgent violence'). This cause is then substantiated: 'In Mosul, in the north, Iraqi commanders staged numerous raids in search of rebel hideouts as up to a dozen decapitated bodies were found strewn about the city' (Glanz and Oppel, 2004).

Returning 200 miles to the south, the article describes a 'chaotic raid' following a 'melee'; 'blood splattered on the floor' – whose is unsaid. It is to be understood therefore that it follows from the actions of 'enraged worshipers' rather than that of those who opened fire on them. In contrast to the previous article, Iraqi rather than American soldiers are said to have opened fire, and it is they who supply the rationale for the attack, both at the highest and at ordinary levels: 'Ayad Allawi said imams who incited violence would be arrested' and 'Louay Ibrahim, an Iraqi police officer who was praying', recounts that 'the imam at the mosque was giving a sermon that urged his audience to make Mosul and other Iraqi cities into embattled places' (Glanz and Oppel, 2004).

The assault on Abu Hanifa is represented first as a response to murderousness elsewhere in Iraq and upon a more studied look, as a necessary preventative to such murderousness. The killings in Abu Hanifa – the subject of the report – appear a slight cost, relatively benign albeit unfortunate, as against the evils unearthed in Mosul. The article contains a larger, grander narrative of the American mission in Iraq. There is little or no place for mundane details – the denial of medical care to those wounded inside the mosque, and that men were afterward bound, hooded and detained. Any mention that those subject to the shootings were civilians likewise did not suit the heroism of mission, heroism that is depicted in the print edition of the article by an adjacent photo of two US soldiers, steadily converging on a Mosul mosque, their long shadows following them. The shooting inside the mosque is depicted as part of an immediate response to 'resistance' on the part of frenzied worshipers. In this account, Iraqi soldiers do all of the shooting – there is but passing mention that American soldiers even entered the mosque.

Most fundamentally, the second article is a departure from the first and a literal departure from Abu Hanifa in the view it offers of the episode: the attack on a house of worship is no more than a frame for expounding on 'the militants' organization' and operations in Mosul and elsewhere, operations that emanate from prayer services of the sort that the US military interrupted. This account, falling under the heading 'Insurgents' in its print version legitimizes the unprovoked assault. This second account is the authoritative or official account of the episode at Abu Hanifa. Like so many other authoritative or official accounts of violence in Iraq, this contained within it the word 'terrorist'. But the subjects of violence in Abu Hanifa were civilians; why is it that the attack on them is not described as terrorist?

In his lecture 'Terrorism: Theirs and Ours', Eqbal Ahmad (2002) has said that 'inconsistency necessarily evades definition. If you are not going to be consistent, you're not going to define'.

This is as true of the discussion of violence in Iraq as it is of public discussion generally. The US Joint Chiefs of Staff define terrorism as 'the calculated use of violence or threat of unlawful violence to inculcate fear; intended to coerce or intimidate governments or societies in the pursuit of goals that are generally political, religious, or ideological' (Institute for Homeland Security, 2001; the 'institute preferred definition'). The US State Department has used another definition of terrorism:

> The term 'terrorism' means premeditated, politically motivated violence perpetrated against noncombatant targets by sub national groups or clandestine agents, usually intended to influence an audience. The term 'international terrorism' means terrorism involving citizens or the territory of more than one country. The term 'terrorist group' means any group practicing, or that has significant subgroups that practice, international terrorism. (US State Department, 2010)

Operations of the sort in Fallujah and on a smaller scale, in the Abu Hanifa mosque (and most of the military action that has occurred in Iraq under the aegis of the US Military), would be terrorist actions according to the criteria of the State Department as they target those unengaged in armed conflict. These operations, moreover, ably fit the psychological objective common to both definitions – that terrorism is used to 'intimidate' and is 'intended to influence an audience'.

However, there is a stipulation in the State Department definition of terrorism that exempts the actions of the US military in Fallujah and Abu Hanifa. Such actions are terrorist (actions) only when they are undertaken by 'sub national groups or clandestine agents'. This condition disqualifies actions of US armed forces as terrorist, even though such actions would qualify as 'attack directed against a civilian population' and the 'deportation or forcible transfer of population' – crimes against humanity as considered by the International Criminal Court.

The assumption that terrorism cannot come from a state, explicit in at least one definition, tacitly circumscribes public discussion of terrorism, and accordingly of what constitutes legitimate and illegitimate uses of violence. It seems that such legitimacy depends less on the violence deployed than on the individual or agency that deploys it.

The Ongoing War on Truth in Iraq

In 1920, T. E. Lawrence (a.k.a. Lawrence of Arabia), wrote in the *Sunday Times*:

> The people of England have been led in Mesopotamia into a trap from which it will be hard to escape with dignity and honour. They have been tricked into it by a steady withholding of information. The Baghdad communiqués are belated, insincere, incomplete. Things have been far worse than we have been told, our administration more bloody and inefficient than the public knows … We are today not far from a disaster.

If the date is withheld it could well be a note on the current occupation in Iraq. From the beginning of the American occupation in Iraq, air strikes and attacks by the US military have only killed 'militants', 'criminals', 'suspected insurgents', 'IED [Improvised Explosive Device] emplacers', 'anti-American fighters', 'terrorists', 'military age males', 'armed men', 'extremists' or 'Al-Qaeda'.

The pattern for reporting on such attacks has remained the same. Invariably the official version of an incident differs vastly from the version offered by locals. In October 2007, in a helicopter strike in a heavily populated urban neighbourhood, American soldiers claimed to have killed 49 'armed men' in a 'gun battle' in Sadr City, a sprawling Shi'ite neighbourhood in eastern Baghdad. The military initially insisted 'no civilians were killed or injured'. A Shi'ite citizens' council and other Shi'ite groups responded that many innocent bystanders had died. Among the 13 dead mentioned in initial reports by local Iraqi police were three children and a woman. Other Iraqi authorities announced that 69 people had been injured.

The official American account went like this:

> The operation's objective was an individual reported to be a long time Special Groups member specializing in kidnapping operations. Intelligence indicates he is a well-known cell leader and has previously sought funding from Iran to carry out high profile kidnappings. Upon arrival, the ground force began to clear a series of buildings in the target area and received sustained heavy fire from adjacent structures, from automatic weapons and rocket propelled grenades, or RPGs. Responding in self-defense, Coalition forces engaged, killing an estimated 33 criminals. Supporting aircraft was also called in to engage enemy personnel maneuvering with RPGs toward the ground force, killing an estimated six criminals. Upon departing the target area, Coalition forces continued to receive heavy fire from automatic weapons and RPGs and were also attacked by an improvised explosive device. Responding in self-defense, the ground force engaged the hostile threat, killing an additional estimated 10 combatants. In total, Coalition forces estimate that 49 criminals were killed in three separate engagements during this operation. Ground forces reported they were unaware of any innocent civilians being killed as a result of this operation. (US Defense Department Briefing, 18 November 2004)

After the 'operation', television news outlets broadcast images of grieving families in the streets of Sadr City. One man reported that his neighbour's six-year-old child had been killed and a two-year-old wounded. Arab television outlets caught scenes of ambulances with wailing sirens carrying the injured to the Imam Ali hospital, the largest in Sadr City, where doctors were shown treating the casualties, including children. Typically with such incidents, those 49 dead 'criminals' turned back into civilians when local police began checking, including two (not three) children in their final count. The US military, as far as we know, still stands by its assertion that no civilians were killed or wounded.

In 2006 Colonel Jeffrey Snow was reported by AFP as saying, 'My personal opinion is that the only way we will lose this war is if we pull out prematurely.' On the same day Reuters reported Snow admitting that resistance attacks in

Baghdad have risen despite the then recent security crackdown that brought tens of thousands of American and Iraqi soldiers, new checkpoints and curfews in the capital city.

Snow, unable (or more likely, unwilling) to provide statistics on the increased number of attacks, used the excuse that the steps the US military took to tell the Iraqi people about the new security measures kept resistance fighters informed of the military's plans. He seemed to be less concerned with the reality on the ground than he was with public perception of the hell that Iraq had become. His professional critique of media coverage on the failed state of Iraq was:

> Our soldiers may be in the crosshairs every day, but it is the American voter who is a real target, and it is the media that carries the message back each day across the airwaves. So when the news is not balanced and it's always bad, that clearly leads to negative perceptions back home. (DOD news briefing 30 June 2006)

'In wartime, truth is so precious that she should always be attended by a bodyguard of lies', said Winston Churchill, British Prime Minister during World War II, to Stalin at the 1943 Tehran conference. This bodyguard of lies is what constitutes propaganda through which the Western corporate media tries to influence public opinion in favour of the Iraq War by consistently tampering with truth and distorting reality. It is to be recognized for what it is. On occasions when the media does its job responsibly and reports events like the Haditha Massacre on 19 November 2005, it must also be willing and able to anticipate and counter propaganda campaigns that will inevitably follow. It is to be expected that the responsible members of the media fraternity will stick to their guns and not join the propagandists

Al-Jazeera, which had already been banned in Iraq after being hounded relentlessly, had their anchorperson interview journalist Walid Khalid in Bahgdad about the Haditha massacre. Khalid's report, translated by MidEastWire.com (from an Al Jazeera phone interview), was as follows:

> Yesterday evening, an explosive charge went off under a US Marines vehicle in the al-Subhani area, destroying it completely. Half an hour later, the US reaction was violent. US aircraft bombarded four houses near the scene of the incident, causing the immediate death of five Iraqis. Afterward, the US troops stormed three adjacent houses where three families were living near the scene of the explosion. Medical sources and eyewitnesses close to these families affirmed that the US troops, along with the Iraqi Army, executed 21 persons; that is, three families, including nine children and boys, seven women, and three elderly people.

The reportage of the slaughter by the *New York Times*, on the other hand, unquestioningly parroted the military press release:

> The Marine Corps said Sunday that 15 Iraqi civilians and a Marine were killed Saturday when a roadside bomb exploded in Haditha, 140 miles northwest of Baghdad. The bombing on Saturday in Haditha, on the Euphrates in the Sunni-dominated province of Anbar, was aimed at a convoy of American Marines and Iraqi Army soldiers, said Capt. Jeffrey S. Pool, a Marine spokesman. After the explosion, gunmen opened fire on the convoy. At least eight insurgents were killed in the firefight, the captain said. (November 2005 Marine Press Release frm Camp Blue Diamond, Ramadi)

It was not until four months after the event that the Western corporate media attempted to straighten out the story. On 19 March 2006, it was *Time* magazine that 'broke' the Haditha story in a piece titled 'Collateral Damage or Civilian Massacre in Haditha' (reported by Tim McGirk from Baghdad). The primary sources for this piece were a video shot by an Iraqi journalism student produced the day after the massacre and interviews conducted with witnesses. This proves once again that a few simple interviews with Iraqis and some readily available photographs and video can drastically correct the glaring errors in the Western media's representations of the occupation.

The Haditha massacre is not the only story that the Western corporate media has delayed covering. The five most commonly deployed crisis-management propaganda tactics which the state and media combine have deployed in the US, and I daresay elsewhere, are: delay, distract, discredit, spotlight and scapegoat. Although connected with the common thread of a singular objective, to mislead and misinform, they are applied variously in different situations in the context of conflict.

In all instances of excessive consequences of conflict the state–media combine has delayed its reportage of the situation, while independent journalists and unaffiliated eyewitnesses have been prompt in recording and disseminating information. Perhaps the delay comes from the need to give an acceptably favourable spin to the story, and the further removed from reality the better. There is a simultaneous attempt to distract the reader/viewer from the incident at hand by drawing attention to other occurrences that will possibly downscale the magnitude of the horror. When the alternative media report stories of atrocities substantiated by irrefutable proof, the mainstream media set up a strident campaign to discredit those reports, as being generated by left-wing, unpatriotic individuals and groups.

In cases where reporting an incident becomes inevitable, the media try hard to place the spotlight on a minor issue thereby attempting to obfuscate the larger violation. This was clearly visible in the case of the Abu Ghraib reports. Repeated mention of a few kinds of torture left no room for mention or discussion of torture as a war crime. Finally the scapegoat of 'bad apples' absolves the state as well as its stenographer, the mainstream media, of the need to own responsibility.

According to media critic Norman Solomon, the Associated Press and other mainstream news networks are able to get away with agreeable paraphrases of 'official' statements on the occupation because it is similar to the kind they have provided in the past. Their coverage does not seem conspicuously shoddy to most readers because it fits in with previous shoddy reportage.

There are the usual token scraps of truth in the stories lending them a hue of credibility. Regarding the loose usage of pejorative terms, Solomon said,

> ... it's an unwritten rule of US media coverage that the 'terrorism' label can only be used, or quoted with credence being given to the sources, if 'terrorism' applies to murderous violence opposed by the US government – in contrast to murderous violence inflicted or otherwise supported by the US government, in which case that violence is routinely presumed to be positive.

The precious few media persons who have dared to tell the truth have met with dire consequences. In February 2007, I reported for the Inter Press Service along with Ali al-Fadhily how US soldiers raided and ransacked the offices of the Iraq Syndicate of Journalists (ISJ) in central Baghdad. Ten armed guards were arrested, and ten computers and 15 small electricity generators kept for donation to families of killed journalists were seized. Many Iraqis believe the US soldiers did all they could to deliver the message from their leaders to Iraqi journalists to keep their mouth shut about anything going wrong with the US-led occupation.

'The Americans have delivered so many messages to us, but we simply refused all of them,' Youssif al-Tamimi of the ISJ in Baghdad told IPS. 'They killed our colleagues, closed so many newspapers, arrested hundreds of us and now they are shooting at our hearts by raiding our headquarters. This is the freedom of speech we received' (al Fadhily and Jamail, 2007).

The incident occurred just two days after the Iraqi Union covering journalists received formal recognition from the government, which status allowed the Syndicate access to its previously blocked bank account, and it had just purchased new computers and satellite equipment. International Federation of Journalists General Secretary Aidan White referred to the raid as a 'shocking violation of journalists' rights' and an 'unprovoked act of intimidation'. He said in a statement:

> Just at the point when the Syndicate achieves formal recognition
> for its work as an independent body of professionals, the
> American military carries out a brutal and unprovoked assault.
> Anyone working for media that does not endorse US policy and
> actions could now be at risk.(Jamail, 2008)

Lawyer Hashim Jawad of the Iraqi Lawyers Union in Baghdad told IPS: 'The
Americans and their Iraqi government followers are destroying social activities
and civil unions so that no group can oppose their crimes and plans. The press
is our remaining lung to breathe democracy in this country and now it is being
targeted' (Jamail, 2008). The Press Emblem Campaign (PEC), an independent humanitarian association based in Geneva, which seeks to strengthen legal
protection and safety of journalists around the world, also strongly condemned
the US military raid.

The media watchdog group Reporters Without Borders lists at least 148
journalists and media workers killed in Iraq since the beginning of the US-led
invasion in March 2003. In July 2008 I wrote a report for the Inter Press Service
about US journalist Zoriah who was fired for having photographed US Marines
who died in a suicide bombing in Fallujah, along with two interpreters and
20 Iraqis, including the mayor of the nearby town of Karmah, two prominent
sheikhs and their sons, and another sheikh and his brother, assembled for a
meeting of the local 'awakening council', one of the US-backed militias that have
taken up arms against Al-Qaeda in Iraq, according to US and Iraqi authorities.

Zoriah was embedded with Marines on a patrol one block from the attack
when it occurred. I quote from his description of the scene given to me by
phone as part of an interview:

> As I ran I saw human pieces … a skull cap with hair, bone shards.
> When we arrived at the building it was chaotic. There were
> Iraqis, police and civilians running around screaming. Bodies
> were being pulled out of the building … I went in and there were
> over 20 people's remains all over the place … Of the Marines I
> jogged in with, someone started to vomit. Others were standing
> around, not knowing what to do. It was completely surreal.

> At that moment I realized this was far beyond anything I'd
> experienced, and I realized I wanted to focus and make sure I
> could capture what it felt like, and the visual horror. I thought,
> 'Nobody in the US has any idea what it means when they hear
> that 20 people died in a suicide bombing.' I want people to be
> able to associate those numbers with the scene and the actual
> loss of human life. I want to show why soldiers are suffering from
> PTSD.(Jamail, 2008)

When the Naval Criminal Investigative Service was brought in to investigate the bombing, Zoriah's photos were the only ones of the scene, so he made copies but was told to delete the memory card. He refused. He said he was following the rules for embedded journalists. He posted the photos on his blog about 96 hours after the bombing and after having shared and discussed with the Marines that it would not be offensive to the affected families. He was immediately asked by the Public Affairs Officer at Camp Fallujah to take his blog down because he had supposedly broken his contract by showing photos of dead Americans with US uniforms and boots.' (Jamail, 2008)

His embed was terminated on grounds of his having photographed the remains of US soldiers and having posted these images along with detailed commentary and thereby violating 14 H and O of the news media agreement he had signed. In addition, the termination letter stated, 'By providing detailed information of the effectiveness of the attack and the response of US forces to it, you have put all US forces in Iraq at greater risk for harm.' Zoriah feels the reason for his dismissal is otherwise.

'The media is guilty': was the verdict passed by the World Tribunal on Iraq (WTI), an international people's initiative seeking the truth about the war and occupation in Iraq. More than five years after attending the final session of the WTI in Rome, I find that the media remains as culpable and as complicit in its distortion of truth as it was at that time. I conclude the chapter with the findings of the tribunal in the hope that redrawing attention to the charges might help us in 'liberating' the media from its shackles and facilitate its restoration as an unbiased source of information in times of war and peace alike.

The judges at the tribunal charged the United States and the British governments with impeding journalists in performing their task, and intentionally producing lies and misinformation. They also held much of Western media guilty of inciting violence and deceiving people in its reporting of Iraq. The panel further accused Western corporate media of filtering and suppressing information, and of marginalizing and endangering independent journalists. More journalists were killed in a 14-month period (till the time of the tribunal, the numbers now are far greater) in Iraq than in the entire Vietnam War.

The tribunal said mainstream media reportage on Iraq violated Article 6 of the Nuremberg Tribunal which states:

> Leaders, organizers, instigators and accomplices participating in the formulation or execution of a common plan or conspiracy to commit any of the foregoing crimes (crimes against peace, war crimes and crimes against humanity) are responsible for all acts performed by any persons in execution of such a plan.

Tony Alessandrini, a human rights activist and scholar of the US colonization of Iraq and co-organizer of the WTI. said, 'What we are being asked to consider is not simply media bias, but rather the active complicity of media in crimes that have been committed and are being committed on a daily basis against the people in Iraq.'(IPS, 2005)

The most telling testimony at the tribunal came from Fernando Suarez, who lost his son Jesus during the invasion of Iraq, when he is said to have stepped on an illegal US cluster bomb:

> I never had the truth from them, and the truth was very simple. On March 26 the Army dropped 20,000 cluster bombs in Iraq, but only about 20 per cent exploded. The other 80 per cent are in the cities and the schools and acting like mines ... Bush sent my son because he said Iraq had illegal weapons, and my son died from an illegal American weapon, and nobody has spoken about this. The media will not talk about the illegal American weapons. (IPS, 2005)

It is my hope-filled plea to media academics and professionals to develop and implement a framework of transparency and accountability for the media that will make them immune and impervious to the pressure of state power.

References

Ahmad, E. (2002) *Terrorism: Theirs and Ours*. New York: Seven Stories Press.

al Fadhily, A. and Jamail, D. (2007) Another US Military Assault in Media, Inter Press Service, 23rd February.

BBC News (2004) US Strikes Raze Falluja Hospital, 6 November.

Cody, E. (2004) US Strike in Fallujah Kills 20, *Washington Post*, 20 June.

Filkins, D. and J. Glanza (2004) American Forces Reach Center of Falluja Amid Fierce Fighting, *New York Times*, 9 November.

Filkins, D. and R. Worth (2004) Insurgents Routed in Falluja; Smaller Bands Still Resist, *New York Times*, 14 November.

Glanz, J. and R. Oppel (2004) GI's and Iraqis Raid Mosque, Killing 3, *New York Times*, 20 November.

Human Rights Watch (2003) Report on Falluja. New York, Available at: www.hrw.org/reports/2003/iraqfalluja/Iraqfalluja-04.htm#TopOfPage

Institute for Homeland Security (2001) *A Primer on Homeland Security*. Washington: Institute for Homeland Security.

International Criminal Court (1998) Rome Statute of the International Criminal Court: International weapons conventions in Iran, Iraq articles 7(1) and 7(2).

Inter Press Service (2005) Media Held Guilty of Deception, February 14th.

Jamail, D. (2004a) Atrocities Continue to Emerge from the Rubble of Fallujah, 11 May.

Jamail, D. (2004b) Detained, Bludgeoned and Electrocuted into a Coma, 7 January.

Jamail, D. (2004c) Fallujah Devastated: Witnesses Describe Humanitarian Crisis and Civilian Death Toll, *Democracy Now!* 15 November.

Jamail, D. (2004d) As Slaughter Continues in Fallujah, Anger Swells in Baghdad, *Open Democracy*, 11 November.

Jamail, D. (2004e) Condemnation of Falluja Siege in Baghdad as Violence Escalates across Iraq, *Inter Press Service*, 7 November.

Jamail, D. (2004f) As Slaughter Continues in Fallujah, Anger Swells in Baghdad, *Open Democracy*, 11 November.

Jamail, D. (2004g) The Ghosts of Fallujah Emerge, *Sunday Herald*, 12 November.

Jamail, D. (2004h) Propaganda and Haditha. Available at www.dahrjamail. net/?s=000125

Jamail, D. (2008) Journalist Charges Censorship by US Military in Fallujah, *Inter Press Service*, 3 July.

Oppel, R. and R. Worth (2004) US Forces Begin Moving Into Falluja, *New York Times*, 7 November.

Oppel, R. (2004) Early Target of Offensive Is a Hospital, *New York Times*, 8 November.

San Francisco Gate (2003) 24 November.

Slim, H. (2004) Humanitarian Agencies and Coalition Counter-Insurgency, Center for Humanitarian Dialogue, July, Geneva.

US Department of Defense (2004) Press Briefing, 8 November.

US State Department (2010) *Patterns of Global Terrorism*. Washington: United States Department of State.

Vick, K. (2004) Battle Near, Iraqi Sunnis Make Offer, *Washington Post*, 6 November.

Wong, E. (2004) Falluja Assault Roils Iraqi Politics, *New York Times*, 9 November.

18

CHALLENGING THE MEDIA WAR

Danny Schechter

Danny Schechter is a US-based filmmaker, former TV network producer and journalist who provides a powerful critique of the failures of domestic media to hold US officials to account and who, instead, acted mostly as cheerleaders for the 'war on terror'. He argues that 'weapons of mass deception' have been unleashed on a US public in order to sell the wars in Iraq and Afghanistan and that commercial television, in particular, has acted effectively as a state broadcasting machine. This is not the responsibility of individual journalists or broadcasters but is the result of a more systemic failure inside the US media, a failure that in the context of the 'war on terror' constitutes a 'crime against democracy'. Schechter presents a picture of a media system that has mostly collapsed its responsibility to think independently and act unilaterally in the face of systematic pressure from political and military administrations determined to secure favourable narratives for its recent adventures. A combination of dodgy dossiers, sophisticated media management machines, the lure of exclusives, the temptation of embedding – all of these are now familiar techniques used to incorporate often submissive mainstream media into reproducing and promoting the agenda of the 'war on terror'.

In writing about class identities in America, Henry Giroux (2006) makes a point that speaks powerfully about the media coverage and representations of the GWOT, America's Global War on Terror: it seems to have morphed since its inception from a war against the world's 'bad guys' into a 'blowback' attack on American traditions and journalistic truth. He writes: 'its traces and effects can also be found in acts of real violence that now run like a highly charged electric current through the mainstream media, which both reproduces representations of … violence while failing to comment on it critically'.

As a result of its deference to this vague and all encompassing war and even enthusiastic complicity with those who wage it, major American television media outlets became a casualty of the war too, to the degree that their credibility has been questioned and, increasingly, seen as an extension of an increasingly protracted and unpopular war without end.

After an initial surge in viewing, thanks to wall-to-wall coverage/promotion in an environment of fear and uncertainty during events like 9/11 and the invasion of Iraq, viewers began to turn away, some seeking other news sources, often in other countries. Millions of Americans, for example, turned to BBC and British newspaper websites because they appeared more objective.

Some were, some weren't. The BBC, for example, was far more balanced in its international broadcasts than in its pro-war, domestic news bulletins. The same was true in the US between CNN domestic and CNN International feeds that mounted separate coverage teams. UK newspapers like the *Independent*, the *Guardian* and the *Daily Mirror* offered a counter-narrative; no mainstream US media outlet did the same.

Soon, as the war dragged on, it was being covered less and less, except for anniversaries and special events like staged elections. At home (in what became described by politicians as 'the homeland'), the national initial consensus/ appearance of a united American nation, as with the media, soon fragmented along domestic political lines. Fox News, more an ideological channel than an information outlet, emerged to bait the 'liberal' media and polarize the audience.

This led to a new war, fought out in the media, a still ongoing, partisan, political war couched in the language of combat, denunciation, demonization and pervasive propaganda, where hard-line opinion displaced any pretence of reporting. Fox may have been the most consistent from the right. But soon MSNBC took them on with a similar approach from the liberal centre. The only serious criticism emerged on the Comedy Channel and humour outlets, with the exception of alternative media programmes including *Democracy Now!*

One consequence: network news soon had less and less appeal to younger viewers, as new entertainment channels surfaced offering faux 'reality' television formats, while marginalizing reality-based news. An internal war for ratings and revenues within and between the networks soon raged as the viewing experience changed with the emergence of social media and a plethora of cable outlets. More money was spent on branding promos than programming.

We have all seen and heard about the portrayal of war as a form of militainment and its reduction to the familiar American narrative of good versus evil, playing on a cultivated and sanitized national memory of civilization versus evil-doers, of cowboys versus Indians. Later, when Navy Seals killed Osama bin Laden, it was revealed that they called him by the name of American Indian leader Geronimo.

The Iraq War was neatly packaged within this narrative, reduced initially to a fight between the evil-doer Saddam Hussein and the forces of civilization. More recently, Libya's Muammar Gaddafi has replaced Saddam as the Arab leader in the cross hairs, a man we loved to hate.

We know about how the cultural patrimony and pre-war reality of Iraq was turned into a picture of a one-dimensional hell-hole presided over by two-bit dictator frequently compared to Adolf Hitler. This process of institutionalized demonization associated him with the holocaust and worse. It was repetitive by design, driven by clearly designed message points intended to fuel attitudes of outrage. Hussein was pictured as an enemy on a par with the Führer; *Time* magazine even literally used the same cover castigating Hitler on Hussein, who had, in a similar fashion, oppressed his people who, ironically, were then made to pay for his sins with more than a million dead.

As in Hitler's war for his thousand-year Reich, no stereotype would be avoided, no exaggeration downplayed, no nuance allowed to complicate a benevolent view of the US and UK mission (and symbolic coalition of the good serving humanity in its hour of need). The war became a focus on the troops with 'thank you for your service', a mantra 'deployed' for depoliticizing its purpose and methods.

There were two wars going on in Iraq – one was fought with armies of soldiers, bombs and a fearsome military force. The other was fought alongside it with cameras, satellites, armies of journalists and propaganda techniques. One war was rationalized as an effort to find and disarm WMDs – weapons of mass destruction; the other was carried out by even more powerful WMDs, weapons of mass deception.

The TV networks in America considered their non-stop coverage their finest hour, pointing to the use of embedded journalists and new technologies sports-like and graphics that permitted viewers to see a war up close for the first time.

Different countries saw different wars. Why? For those of us in America watching the coverage, the war became more of a spectacle, as part of an around-the-clock global media marathon, pitting media outlets against each other in ways that distorted truth and raised as many questions about the methods used by TV news as the armed intervention it was covering – and in many cases – promoting.

It was more than traditional censorship. Censorship, self-censorship and 'spinning' are common in every war, as governments try to limit negative coverage and maximize reporting that will galvanize support on the home front. Every war inspires elite-led jingoism in sections of the media and deception.

Sun Tsu, the great Chinese analyst of war, said that deception is by definition a tool in every war. He understood wars happen because of deception. They are fought with deception. But what was often discussed in the past as a tactic or a tool has become a well-deployed strategy with sophisticated, high-tech information warfare doctrines guiding attempts to achieve strategic influence based on policies built on calculated deception.

This concept was deeply grounded in neo-conservative ideologies based on the work of the late University of Chicago philosopher Leo Strauss, who counselled deception as policy. It has become deeply institutionalized, in part because the media is the place and platform for where our politics plays itself out. Every war needs its media handmaidens. For many 'journalists', covering wars has become a speciality often carried out in cooperation, if not collusion with war-making bodies. This practice became a programme called 'embedding'. It is not accidental. It is deliberate.

Modern corporate media and even their competitors in the public interest sphere, like BBC or PBS, only rarely probed, investigated and exposed. Instead reports reflected a repetition of the official narrative, promoting news personalities – frequently commended on air for their bravery. Its intent was only incidentally informing the public. Its real goal was building their brand while raising revenues and ratings by turning war into an audience-attracting form of programming, sacrificing truth in the service of a false sense of duty and patriotic correctness.

The journalists in the field, and more importantly back in their network newsrooms and appropriately named control rooms, became bound by a consensus view that not only missed the story but also distorted it. For one example, they underestimated the extent of Iraqi resistance that was barely acknowledged, much less covered. For another, they avoided reporting on civilian casualties.

Critics were silent, while official claims went largely unscrutinized as an armada of ex-generals recommended, placed or vetted by the Pentagon were recruited to offer background and colour commentary on network news shows. There was soon no distance between the mentality that waged the war and the one commenting on it. This itself became an exercise in information warfare. Television outlets integrated their war 'coverage' into their pre-existing and expanded formats, driven by anchormen, field reporters, electronic graphics, pundits, and military experts the Pentagon trusted and cleared. These were formats the audience had long been conditioned to accept and feel comfortable with, turning news business into show business and commercial television into state television. Some critics asked how the coverage would have been different if we had a state-run television system in place. There were no answers.

Focusing on the 'action' in Iraq, they avoided putting the war into the larger global context that US strategists did, that is, the context of the GWOT that saw the expansion of American military power and bases into over a hundred countries, all in the name of fighting a ubiquitous and vague enemy that seemed to be everywhere at once, i.e. faceless and menacing 'terrorists'.

Just as deception characterizes war operations, deception moved from the battleground to the media ground and drove its information component. With few journalists critiquing the blizzard of 'news' coming from official sources in an environment of intense competitive pressure, it is not surprising that the government view largely became the dominant view.

When the war in Iraq supposedly ended in 2010 with the withdrawal of what were called combat troops, a TV comic satirized it as 'been there, won that'.

The views of such conservative-libertarians on the right as Republican Ron Paul were barely heard in the media chatter, even as some troops were withdrawn. Paul said:

> Considering the continued public frustration with the war effort, and with the growing laundry list of broken promises, this was merely another one of the administration's operations in political maneuvering and semantics in order to convince an increasingly war-weary public that the Iraq War is at last ending. However, military officials confirm that we are committed to intervention in that country for years to come, and our operations have in fact, changed minimally, if really at all.

The coverage of the war in Iraq could be faulted on two levels: commission and omission. What was not covered was often more telling than what was. News managers tightly controlled the output. Critics were screened out. At MSNBC popular talk-show host Phil Donahue was ordered to have two pro-war guests for every critic. CNN introduced pre-screening to ensure that all correspondent scripts were 'responsible'. NBC fired veteran war correspondent and Pulitzer Prize winner Peter Arnett who had anchored CNN's coverage of 'Operation Desert Storm'.

Former White House press secretary Scott McClellan later called the media 'complicit enablers'. At Fox News, pro-war support was mandated by the management, which issued daily memos and edicts to its producers and staffers on how the news was to be spun, even specifying what buzz words were to be used. Their message points were spelled out and used in all programs like a drumbeat, in the belief that propaganda needs repetition to be successful.

Veteran former CBS News anchor Dan Rather, later forced out of his anchor's chair for a critical report on President Bush, became an outspoken critic, but also offered some context:

> In the wake of 9/11 and in the run-up to Iraq, these news organizations made a decision – consciously or unconsciously,

but unquestionably in a climate of fear – to accept the overall narrative frame given them by the White House, a narrative that went like this: Saddam Hussein, brutal dictator, harbored weapons of mass destruction and, because of his supposed links to al Qaeda, this could not be tolerated in a post-9/11 world....

Now, cut back to your evening news, or your daily newspaper ... where that White House Correspondent dutifully repeats the question he asked of the president or his press secretary, and dutifully relates the answer he was given – the same non-answer we've already heard dozens of times, which amounts to a pitch for the administration's point of view, whether or not the answer had anything to do with the actual question that was asked. And then: 'Thank you Jack'. In other news today... (Rather, 2008)

Media writer Michael Wolff zeroed in on two rather basic factual questions that were rarely asked and are largely still not answered:

Beyond getting rid of Saddam Hussein himself, what then? What was the larger goal – and, by the way, how would we accomplish it? Once in, if it all went wrong, how would we get out?

The perfect obviousness of these questions, the clear necessity of having to ask these questions, and the failure of the media to make them a central part of the story demonstrates, rather painfully, that the American media was either hopelessly asleep at the switch, or so conflicted in its desires (to curry favor with the Bush Administration, to please the managers of the media corporations that owned the news outlets, not to disturb the shareholders of these corporations, not to look foolish when, if as the administration was promising, the war got over fast) that it was unable to do its job. (Wolff, 2006)

Let us not re-fight, or as policy makers like to say, 're-litigate' this battle on the field of facts. What is there still to say about the discredited WMD threat and other invented rationalizations justifying the war? All of that will be further blown away once the next Wikileaks on the Iraq War drops from the virtual world into the real world, as internal reports from within the military operation begin to surface.

There is, however, another question, often missed by analysts and journalists stuck in outdated understandings of what we were seeing or that we now live in a post-journalism era. In this era, TV programmes once defined as a noun has become programming, a verb, programming not the networks but public understandings.

Could it be that our new, fine-tuned hi-tech and heavily controlled media system was in fact doing its job, the job it had been assigned, a job that was at first modelled and then largely overseen and heavily influenced and managed by the Pentagon/government and its own octopus-like network of news mechanics, media monitors, consultants and specialists; who reorganized reporters as embeds, neutralized and, then, even killed off unembedded independents who wouldn't go along with their mission of running an pre-planned exercise in sanitized information deprivation?

A job of selling, not telling, became the job of pushing for 'the home team' in a media that makes so much more money and builds far bigger audiences by televising sporting events. Reporters often sounded like sportscasters as they measured the speed and pace of the invasion with colour commentary, profiles of the key players and human-interest stories. It became clear that the reporting was structured on an 'AAU' basis – 'all about US' – with the focus on American television on Americans: our good intentions as liberators, our humanitarian methods, and so on.

The country of Iraq soon became a set for TV coverage; Iraqis the 'enemy' or the extras in a foreign production in their own country. Think about it: how many Iraqi civilians did we ever hear from, how much did we learn about this country's long history and deep culture? When President Obama withdrew some 'combat troops', there was barely any mention on the air of the estimates of more than a million Iraqi dead.

I came at all this not as an academic or dispassionate researcher but as a journalist in the trenches who saw how journalists were pushed to the side during the first Gulf War, a.k.a. 'Desert Storm'. I then decided to closely follow the details of its successor 'Operation Iraqi Freedom'. I did so by using that tool of media observation – the remote control in my living room – obsessively flipping through the dials and reporting every day on what I saw. Those reports became the basis of my book, *Embedded: Weapons of Mass Deception*, a book that tried to document the unfolding coverage on TV in all its absurdity and with all its distortions. To my knowledge, it was the first book out on the Iraq war in July 2003. It was also largely ignored.

While I was focusing on TV, perhaps because of my experience as a network producer and because 80 per cent of the population get all or most of their information from TV, many on the left were bashing the more elite *New York Times*, especially its former reporter Judith Miller, who they turned into the poster-symbol of a degraded press, the press they relied on. There were later mea culpas and mild apologies of sorts in many press outlets who admitted they were used, but all rather late to make a difference in perceptions by the public. I then decided that writing about all this didn't do it justice. If my focus was television, I felt I had to show what was happening, and then did that with a 2004 film, *WMD – Weapons of Mass Deception*. It included my own interviews with some of the key players and top journalists.

During this period, I also wrote feverishly about the media and the war, not only in the US but also across the world with interviews in Europe, Africa, Brazil and the Middle East. By 2006 when my third media 'product' on the subject appeared, the book *When News Lies*, the invasion phase of the war was all but over for most media outlets and even a shrinking but ineffectual anti-war movement. I had moved from angry analysis to political condemnation, indicting media complicity as a key component of the war and calling for a media crimes tribunal to hold media institutions accountable for their blatant propaganda roles. That call went nowhere.

In point of fact, in earlier wars, media outlets and personalities have been indicted for their role in instigating conflict and contributing to it. The special International Tribunal on Rwanda has pointed to the role of hate-radio stations in inflaming genocide. In the former Yugoslavia, TV stations in Serbia and Croatia became propaganda organs that incited ethnic cleansing and mass murder.

The post-World War II Nuremberg Trial established a precedent in this regard. I cite one article on what happened there: the prosecution case, argued by Drexel Sprecher, an American, placed considerable stress on the role of media propaganda in enabling the Hitler regime to prepare and carry out aggression that violated the laws of war. The use made by the Nazi conspirators of psychological warfare is well known. Before each major aggression, with some few exceptions based on expediency, they initiated a press campaign calculated to weaken their victims and to prepare the German people psychologically for the attack. They used the press, after their earlier conquests, as a means for further influencing foreign politics and in manoeuvring for each following invasion. Thus, the presentation of an illegal invasion of a foreign country as a 'preventative' or pre-emptive war did not originate with Bush, Blair, Cheney or Rumsfeld.

The Nuremberg prosecution raised an issue that is of the greatest relevance today: the role of Nazi media propaganda in inuring the German population to the sufferings of other peoples and, indeed, urging Germans to commit war crimes. Historical parallels are never exact and I am not here to argue that because the Nazis distorted their media, the US or British media are Nazis. That is specious reasoning. But a broader point, also argued at Nuremberg, does have resonance today. Many in the Pentagon believe to this day that it was the media coverage that was responsible for the loss of the Vietnam War. That led to large amounts of money and manpower invested in controlling the media in preparation for future wars.

At the same time, with mounting media consolidation, with the corporatization of TV news, there was a sea change inside the media business making external manipulation easier. This is the context that is often missed with all the Bush (or Blair) bashing. One man did not organize this war: it took powerful institutions – a military–industrial–media complex – to achieve the desired outcome.

We have to put it in the context not just of US foreign policy but of the way our modern media system works. Viewers in Italy have watched how their TV system – from RAI to private channels – has been Berlusconized with porn-like programming dominating the airwaves and more serious fare discarded. In the US, corporate media has become a handmaiden of special interests. News managers who were not journalists took over and bottom-line pressures begat infotainment and more and more celebrity coverage. Pundits soon outnumbered journalists. Journalism schools started producing more PR experts than reporters. The government took PR to a new level: it is now called PM for 'perception management' and it treats war as a product to be 'rolled out' and promoted. It is serious and systematic. It branded the war and used advertising-like slogans to sell it. This approach went beyond traditional PR.

Twenty-four-hour cable news channels offered more news, not better news. They soon degenerated into a headline hit parade. Investigative reporting had long since given way to 'breaking news' free of context and background. In-depth documentaries disappeared from the prime-time environment. Reality-based programming replaced reports anchored in reality. Anchormen complained that the media had gone from being a watchdog to a lap dog, but did nothing about it.

It was this transformation of the media system – implemented over 20 years with an assist by the deregulation of public interest laws – that made the media a willing accomplice and promoter, especially in the post-9/11 environment of fear and patriotic correctness. When news anchors started emulating politicians, politicians were given 'media training' to more effectively use the airwaves to promote their policies and personas. Is it any wonder that honesty, candour and truth are in such short supply?

One result: out of 800 experts on all the US channels from the run-up to the war until 9 April 2003, when the statues were brought down by the US military and a carefully assembled crowd of US supporters, only six opposed the war. The media environment was soon charged with a mix of seductive co-optation that gave selected journalists access to the frontlines and military protection and intimation, attacks on critical reporting, denunciations of journalists who stepped out of line and even, some charge, the deliberate targeting and killing of journalists in incidents such as the one at the Palestine Hotel. My film, *WMD: Weapons of Mass Deception*, reports on these incidents and quotes the distinguished historian of the media and war Phillip Knightley as saying that he now believes that the firing on media sites was deliberate. CNN's Eason

Jordan told a panel at the World Economic Forum in January 2005 that journalists were targeted. When challenged, he seems to have backed away.

It is important to understand that this does not add up to a critique of a few lapses or media mistakes. The Iraq War was more than a catalogue of errors or flaws. The war was shaped for coverage, planned and formatted, pre-produced and aired with high production values, designed to persuade, not just inform. What we saw and are seeing is a crime against democracy and the public's right to know.

In a book I wrote after my film was released, *When News Lies: Media, complicity and the Iraq War*, I called for Nuremberg like Media Crimes Tribunals similar to the panels that indicted the role played by Serbian and Croatian TV in sparking the Balkan Wars and Hate Radio Stations that sparked the genocide in Rwanda. The Media, in my view, must be held accountable for its role in promoting aggressive war, a certified war crime.

It is a crime against the people of Iraq and Afghanistan, who have suffered and died in large numbers in war, even though the extent of it is not reported. We have had coverage of torture incidents but no real investigation of the responsibility of decision-makers. Only a handful of journalists follow that story closely, including Seymour Hersh who exposed the My Lai massacre in Vietnam. He publishes in a smaller magazine, not a big newspaper.

This is a crime against our soldiers too whose gruelling experience goes largely unreported, as do their casualties and psychological traumas. It is a crime against the profession of journalism that has been shamelessly distorted even as many conscientious reporters soldier on, often in an alternative media that reaches a smaller audience.

Wars come home and this one has spawned a dangerous and calculated outbreak of domestic Islamophobia. This kind of media complicity has to be challenged, refuted, condemned and opposed. We acknowledge the existence of war crimes. We now have to recognize and oppose **media crimes** like those that are still being committed in Iraq, Afghanistan and many other so-called 'theaters of war'. I am confident that when critics and scholars examine the Western intervention in and over Libya of 2011, they will find the same pattern of deception. Just one example offered up by MSNBC in its critique of President Obama's speech justifying American bombing of Libya, which implied that Washington's role was shrinking because NATO's was expanding. This is what went unsaid: 'In transferring command and control to NATO, the US is turning the reins over to an organization dominated by the US, both militarily and politically. In essence, the US runs the show that is taking over running the show.'

Studying this phenomenon is not enough. We need a full investigation with testimony by reporters of conscience and a full compilation of all the critical studies that have been done over the years. We need to make the coverage as much of an issue as the war. We have to actively expose it and oppose it. We also have to honour those journalists who performed honourably and the many others who died trying to get the truth out. To quote the late Malcolm X, 'by every means necessary', and, I would add, possible.

References

Giroux, H. (2006) *America on the Edge: Henry Giroux on politics, culture and education*. New York: Palgrave MacMillan.

Rather, D. (2008) Speech to the National Conference for Media Reform, Minneapolis. June 7.

Schechter, D. (2006) *When News Lies: Media complicity and the Iraq War*. New York: Select Books.

Wolff, M. (2006) Foreword, in D. Schechter, *When News Lies: Media complicity and the Iraq War*. New York: Select Books.

INDEX

Abbott, Tony, 279, 284
Abdel Jawwad, Saleh, 28
Abdulla, Ahmed, 294
Abdulmutallab, Umar
  Farouk, 74
Abu Graibh prison, 85–6, 122,
  213, 241–2, 249, 252, 301
Abu Hamza, 261, 266
Abu Hanifa mosque, 294–7
Abukhalil, As'ad, 86–7
academic links with the US
  military, 97, 107–11
Afghanistan, 1, 4, 12, 14, 28, 55,
  59, 71, 74, 100, 124, 167,
  172–6, 180, 206–7, 215–18,
  242, 290, 315
Afghanistan War Diary, 178
Ahmad, Aijaz, 180
Ahmad, Eqbal, 296
Ahmad, Mahmoud, 124
aid policies, 5
airborne warning and control
  system (AWACS)
  planes, 57
Al Aqsa Television, 70
Alessandrini, Tony, 303
Alexander II, Tsar, 188
Ali, Tariq, 173–4
Al-Jazeera, 15, 40, 55, 207, 211,
  214–16, 250, 291, 299
Allard, Kenneth, 83
Allawi, Ayad, 290–5
Al-Qaeda, 2, 5, 13–14, 30–2, 49,
  63, 66–7, 71–5, 110, 167–8,
  173, 176, 215, 243–8,
  263–4, 267
Alston, Philip, 174
American Academy of
  Pediatrics, 110
American exceptionalism, 100
Amis, Martin, 136–7, 140, 143
Amnesty International, 152
Angola, 4
Animal Liberation Front, 6
anti-Americanism, 251
anti-communism, 12

anti-Semitism, 236–7
Anti-terrorism and Security Act
  (UK, 2001), 144
'Arab spring' (2011), 15, 24, 33,
  41, 252
'Arab world', the, distinctiveness
  of, 242–3
Arafat, Cairo, 69–70
Arbenz, Jacobo, 122–3
Archer, Lawrence, 82
Arnett, Peter, 310
assimilation, 145
Association for the
  Advancement of Artificial
  Intelligence, 107
Atari (company), 106
Atta, Mohamed, 124
Aubry, Martine, 235
Australia, 271, 274–86
al-Awlaki, Anwar, 74–5
Aziz, Mazhar, 173
al-Azmeh, Aziz, 138

Baader-Meinhof group, 3
Banakar, R., 146
Barthes, Roland, 36
Baum, M., 12
Bawdon, Fiona, 82
Beck, Ulrich, 218
Ben Ali, Zine el Abidine,
  31, 33
Benedict XVI, Pope, 25, 242
Bennett, Ronan, 143
Bennett, W.L., 281
Bergen, P., 4
Berger, P., 274
Beslan school terrorist attack
  (2004), 194, 198
Beyala, Calixthe, 234
bin Laden, Osama, 2, 11, 14, 66,
  72, 124, 126, 167–8, 178,
  214–15, 242, 246–8, 308
Blackwater (company), 39,
  250–1
Blair, Tony, 33, 141, 156–7
blogs and blogging, 86–7, 187

Blum, W., 122
Blunkett, David, 274
Body of Lies (film), 126
'Bollywoodization', 179–80
Bondevik, Kjell Magne, 214, 217
Bonnafous, Simone, 224
Bouachera, Leila, 233
Bourges, Hervé, 234
Boyer, Henri, 226–7
Bremer, Paul, 290
British Broadcasting
  Corporation (BBC), 154–8,
  163, 307
Broadcasting Board of
  Governors (BBG),
  13–14, 176
Brown, Gordon, 141
Burleigh, Michael, 137
Bush, George W., 2, 80, 104,
  122, 153, 212, 216, 259,
  261, 277–8

Callinicos, Alex, 140
Calwell, Arthur, 274–5, 279
Cameron, David, 137,
  141–2, 145
Campbell, Alastair, 80–1
capitalism, 47–52, 55, 58–9
Carlile, Lord, 7
Carlson, T., 56
Carnegie-Mellon University,
  107, 110
Castells, Manuel, 3
Castro, Fidel, 122
'Caucasian' terrorism, 199–200
censorship, 11–12, 191, 308
Central Intelligence Agency
  (CIA), 2–4, 30, 80,
  174, 178
  cinematic depictions of,
  116–32
Chakravarti, Sudeep, 170
Channel 4 Television, 177–8
Charlie Wilson's War (film),
  125–6
Chechnya, 5, 184, 191

Cheney, Dick, 30, 212, 259
Chetrit, Michaël, 237
Chiche, Mahor, 237
China, 5, 15, 49, 58, 118
Chirac, Jacques, 235
Chomsky, Noam, 8, 29, 32–3, 78, 105
Churchill, Winston, 299
Civil Contingencies Act (UK, 2004), 144
Civil Contingencies Secretariat, 82
climate change, 260–2
Clinton, Bill, 212
Club Averroès, 234
CNN, 55–6, 207, 215, 307, 310
'CNN effect', 15
Cold War, 3, 68, 98, 100, 105, 123, 172–3, 265
collateral damage, 209, 292, 300
Collectif Égalité, 234
Committee to Protect Journalists, 215, 255
The Company (film), 118–20
Conseil supérieur de l'audiovisuel (CSA), 233–5, 237
content analysis, 280, 285
control orders, 144
Corner, John, 78–9
cosmopolitanism, 208–9
Counterinsurgency Field Manual of the US military, 13
counter-terrorism, 8, 12, 63, 73
covert operations, 117
Criminal Justice Act (UK, 2003), 144
critical discourse analysis (CDA), 272, 280, 285
Crock, M., 275
cultural diversity, 142–3
policies for, 233–8
culturalization of terror, 134–41
culture, terrorization of, 141–7
Curtis, Adam, 14

Daily Mail, 274
deception as policy, 308–10
Defense Advanced Research Projects Agency (DARPA), 107, 110–11
De Graaf, J., 10
DeLappe, Joseph, 110

Deleuze, Gilles, 56
Deltombe, Thomas, 223, 225–7
Der Derian, James, 11
Devji, Faisal, 247
diplomacy, 63, 99; *see also* public diplomacy
discourse historical approach, 272
discrimination, ethnic, 235
Dr Strangelove (film), 103
'Dodgy Dossier' (2003), 81
Domodedovo Airport attack (2011), 201
Donahue, Phil, 310
Dorling, D., 273
Dulles, Allen, 122–3

Eagleton, Terry, 143
The Economist, 69, 139
'Écrans pâles' conference (Paris, 2004), 234–6
Edelman, N., 271–2, 275, 277, 281
Eisenhower, Dwight D., 122–3
electronic gaming, 98, 103–11; *see also* video games
Ellsberg, Daniel, 218
'embedding' of journalists, 55–6, 81, 105, 216, 302–3, 308–9
emergency measures against terrorism, 143–5
England, Lyndie, 85
English Defence League, 143
entertainment industries' links to the military, 13
Entman, Robert M., 10–11, 218, 283
Escafré-Dublet, Angéline, 228–9
Eskeland, Ståle, 213
Eteraz, Ali, 87
Europol, 6, 30, 87

Facebook, 68–9
al-Fadhily, Ali, 301
Fair Game (film), 129–30, 132
Fairclough, N., 272
Fallujah, 250, 291–4, 297
Fatah, 154
Fazlullah, Mullah, 71
Federal Bureau of Investigation (FBI), 6
Fekete, Liz, 143, 145
Feldman, J., 3

Ferjani, Riadh, 237
films depicting the CIA, 116–32
financialization, 47–54
First World War, 48, 59
Fitzgerald, Pat, 128–9
Fordism, 53, 55
Forest Gate raid (2006), 89
Fortier, Anne-Marie, 138
Foucault, Michel, 39
Fox News, 56, 106, 246, 307, 310
France, 223–38, 250
freedom of speech, 26
Friedman, Thomas, 72
Fryer, P., 138
Fukuyama, Francis, 140–1
'full spectrum dominance', 82–3
fundamentalism, 27, 136, 189, 251

Gaddafi, Muammar, 5, 31, 308
Galtung, Johan, 258, 275, 279
game theory, 106
Gandhi, Indira, 170
Gandhi, Rajiv, 170–1
Gardels, N., 13–14
Garfinkel, Harold, 105
Gaspard, Françoise, 230–1
Gastaut, Yvan, 225
Gates, Robert, 67–8
Gavan, Terrence, 146
Gaza, 33–6, 39, 70, 151–9
Geisser, Vincent, 227
Gelb, Leslie H., 30
The Ghost Writer (film), 130
Giffin, John, 83
Giffords, Gabrielle, 263
Gilleard, Martyn, 146
Gindin, Sam, 49
Giroux, Henry, 306
Giscard d'Estaing, Valéry, 228, 230
Gizbert, Richard, 103
global economic crisis (2008), 48–9
Global Islamic Media Front, 110
Global Positioning System (GPS), 57–8
Global Terrorism Database, 1, 6, 169
globalization, 50, 53, 208, 211
The Good Shepherd (film), 121–2
Gowing, Nik, 215
Graham, P., 40–1

Graham, S., 29
Green, Michael, 158
Green Zone (film), 130–1
Greene, Graham, 120
Greenwald, G., 40
Gregory, Derek, 28–9
Groeling, T., 12
Guantánamo, 213
Guatemala, 122
Gulf War (1991), 56, 207

Habermas, Jürgen, 50, 280
Haditha massacre (2005),
    299–300
Hague, William, 273, 279
al-Haj, Sami, 40
Halevy, Ephraim, 153–4
Halliday, F., 2
Hallin, D., 12, 276
Hamas, 66, 152–62
Hanson, Pauline, 276–7
Hanson-Young, Sarah, 274–5
Haqqani, Husain, 173
Hardt, M., 50–2
Hargreaves, Alec, 230, 233,
    235–6
Harriman, Averell, 119
Hartmann, Thom, 193
Harvey, D., 50–3
Hasan, Nidal Malik, 6, 72
Hassan, R., 3
'hate speech', 26, 199–201
Hawali-'Awda movement, 251
Hawke, Bob, 276
Headrick, D., 4
Hebert, James, 98
Helgesen, Vidar, 213–14
Herman, E., 32
Hermann, E., 29
Herodotus, 206–7
Hersh, Seymour, 85, 315
Hitchens, Christopher, 142
Hoffman, Michael, 7–8
Hoskins, Andrew, 11, 246
Howard, John, 276–8
Howell, J., 5
human rights, 213, 219
Human Rights Watch, 292
humanitarian interventions, 214
Huntington, Samuel, 24, 138–9,
    208, 264
Hussein, Saddam, 80, 109, 131,
    241–2, 248, 265, 308, 311
Hutchings, S., 190

Ibrahim, Louay, 295
Ikenberry, J., 15
'immaterial labor' (Hardt and
    Negri), 51
Immerman, Richard, 4
immigration
    into France, 224–32
    into Australia, 274–7, 285
imperialism, 47–8, 59, 138, 140
    American, 4, 98, 101
    see also new imperialism
Independent Police Complaints
    Commission (IPCC), 89
India, 5, 15, 167–72, 176–80
information and communication
    technology (ICT), 49–55,
    58–9
integration policies, 231–8
International Criminal Court
    (ICC), 212–13, 297
international law, 31, 208,
    212–13, 217–19, 277
international relations theory,
    99–100
internet resources, 54–5, 187–8,
    196, 243–6, 251
internment, 144
Iran, 123, 174, 225–6
Iraq, 1, 3, 12, 27–30, 39, 55, 57,
    59, 83, 100, 103, 207, 211,
    248–52, 255, 259, 289–304,
    312, 315
Irish Republican Army
    (IRA), 3
Islam, perceptions of, 13, 135–9,
    147, 225, 227, 265–7
Islamic Army of Iraq, 250
'Islamic' or 'Islamist' terrorism,
    2–3, 6, 30, 87–90, 168–71,
    179, 199, 227, 237, 258,
    264–7
Islamism, 136, 141, 143, 226–7,
    237, 241, 245, 249, 252
IslamOnline, 244
Islamophobia, 27, 37, 135–7,
    228, 243, 315
Israel, state of, 35, 151–61,
    236, 242
Ivanov, Igor, 5
Izvestiya, 198–200

Jafari, Ali, 281, 284
Jalal, Ayesha, 174
Jawad, Hashim, 302

Jenkins, Roy, 142–3
jihadism, 241–52
Joint Direct Attack Munitions
    (JDAMs), 57
Jones, Seth, 73
Jongman, A., 7, 11
Jordan, Eason, 314–15
journalistic freedom, 257
journalists
    risks faced by, 215–16, 219,
        255, 301–3, 314
    see also 'embedding' of
        journalists; 'peace
        journalism'; 'war
        journalism'

Kalam, Abdul Kahar, 89
Kapuściński, Ryszard, 206,
    209–10
Kashmir, 171, 173
Katovsky, B., 56
Kavanagh, Trevor, 135
Keating, Paul, 276
Kellner, B., 10
Kellner, D., 32
Kelly, Jackie, 277
Kennedy, John F., 122
Khalid, Walid, 299
Khalid Sheikh Mohammed,
    124–5
Khalistan, 170
Khanfar, Wadah, 215–16
Kilcullen, David, 79, 84
Kimmage, Daniel, 66
'kinetic' power, 84
King, Sir David, 260
King, Peter, 27
Kissinger, Henry, 119
Knightley, Phillip, 215, 314
Kosovo, 70, 206, 213
Kovach, B., 15
Kriegel, Blandine, 236
Ku Klux Klan, 6
Kuma War, 106–7
Kundnani, Arun, 136,
    142, 146
Kuttab, Daoud, 69–70

Laïdi, Amirouche, 234
LaMarche, Gara, 207
Laqueur, Walter, 7–8, 11
The Last Starfighter, 107
Lawrence, T.E., 297
legitimacy, 31–3

'legitimate' targets, 8
Lenin, V.I., 47–8, 59
Lester, M., 281
Libbey, Lewis, 129
Libicki, Martin, 73
Libya, 1, 5, 12, 33, 176, 315
Liddle, Rod, 137
Liddy, G. Gordon, 100
LifeNews website, 196
Liman, Doug, 129–30
Lind, J., 5
Livni, Eti, 36
Lochard, Guy, 226–7
Lockheed Martin
    (company), 108
London bombings (2005), 74,
    87, 259
Loughner, Jared Lee, 6
Louw, P.E., 10
Lucas, George, 107
Luckman, T., 274
Lumumba, Patrice, 123
Lurie, Rod, 128–9
Lynch, J., 275, 279–80

McChesney, Bob, 103
McClellan, Scott, 310
McGirk, Tim, 300
McGoldrick, A., 275, 280
McGovern, Mark, 143
McGreal, Chris, 153–4
Macintosh, Jamie, 82
McMurtry, John, 212
McVeigh, Timothy, 263
Major, John, 273
Majumdar, Nivedita, 169
Malcolm X, 316
Maley, W., 278
Malonga, Marie-France, 234
Manning, P., 278
Marx, Karl, 53
Maxwell, Richard, 261
Mazumdar, Charu, 169
Mearsheimer, J.J., 156
Medavoy, M., 13–14
mercenaries, 27
Merkel, Angela, 145
Meyer, Vincent, 238
Mideast Youth Foundation, 68
A Mighty Heart (film), 123–4
military equipment, trade in,
    5, 176
military expenditure, 3, 5,
    100–1, 261

military service, 102
Miller, Judith, 128–31, 312
Mills-Affif, Édouard,
    225, 227–8
Milošević, Slobodan, 213, 265
Minkin, Alexander, 198
Mirzoeff, Nicholas, 251
Mitterrand, François, 230
Mobutu, Joseph, 123
Moeller, S., 189
Molotch, H., 281
Mosaique (television
    programme), 228–32
Moscow underground attack
    (2010), 194, 197–201
Mossadegh, Mohammad, 123
MSNBC, 307, 310, 315
Mubarak, Hosni, 31, 33
Muhammad the Prophet,
    25, 242
    cartoons of, 26, 64, 242
multiculturalism, 142–5, 230, 236
Mumbai, 171–2, 177–8
Munich (film), 123
Murdoch, Rupert, 56
Musharraf, Pervaiz, 124
Muslim populations, 139–40,
    237, 266, 268

Nacos, B., 12
Najeebullah, Mohammad, 172–3
Narodnaya volya movement, 188
National Academy of
    Sciences, 107
National Consortium for the
    Study of Terrorism and
    Responses to Terrorism
    (START), 1, 262–3
National Counterterrorism
    Centre (NCTC), 7
National Front, 273
National Research Council, 107
National Security Agency, 103
Naxalite Movement, 169
Negri, A., 50–2
neo-conservative ideology, 102,
    141–2, 242, 309
neo-liberal ideology, 48–55,
    147, 273
Nepal, 167, 170, 180
new imperialism, 48, 55, 58
    information and communication
    technology in the theory
    of, 49–52

'new wars', 212–13
'new world order', 207–8
New York Times, 292–5,
    300, 312
news reporting and news values,
    151, 154, 162–3, 211,
    255–62, 300–1, 312–16
newspapers
    in France, 224
    in Russia, 187, 194–200
Nicaragua, 3–4
Nichols, Terry, 263
Nikonorow, Basia, 70
Noiriel, Gérard, 224
Non-classified Internet
    Protocol Router Network
    (NIPRNET), 58
Nord-Ost terrorist attack
    (2002), 194–200
Nordic countries, 209
Norris, P., 10
North Atlantic Treaty
    Organization (NATO), 1,
    5, 33, 175–6, 180, 206, 209,
    212–16, 219, 315
Northern Ireland, 70, 87–8
Norway, 213–14, 216–17
Nothing But the Truth (film),
    128–9, 132
Nuremberg Trial, 313
Nye, Joseph, 72

Obama, Barack, 2, 11, 14, 30,
    68, 98, 102, 174, 179, 242,
    312, 315
Oborne, Peter, 137
Office for Security and
    Counter-Terrorism
    (OSCT), 81–2, 146
Oklahoma City bombing
    (1995), 6, 262–4
O'Loughlin, Ben, 11, 246
O'Loughlin, Toni, 152
Oppenheimer, J. Robert, 110
Orientalism, 24, 126, 243,
    263–4, 267

Pakistan, 28, 124, 126, 167–8,
    171–80
Palestine conflict, 152–62, 236,
    242, 248
Panitch, Leo, 49
Pape, R., 3
Pasqua, Charles, 226

Paul, Ron, 310
'peace journalism', 271–2, 275, 279–86
Pentagon, the *see* United States Department of Defense
'Pentagon papers' (1971), 218
Pew Research Center, 139, 262
Philby, Kim, 119
Pilger, John, 157–8
Plame, Valerie, 129
political correctness, 142
Pool, Jeffrey S., 300
Poole, Elizabeth, 135
post-Fordism, 54
Powell, Colin, 125, 131
Press Complaints Commission, 135
Press Emblem Campaign, 302
Prevention of Terrorism Acts (UK), 144
private security companies, 5
privatization, 51, 53, 108, 147
Project on Defense Alternatives, 31
Project for a New American Century, 38
propaganda, 67–70, 77–90, 151, 211, 218, 251, 292–3, 313
impacts of, 87–90
as political action, 90
in practice, 85–7
propaganda doctrine, 82–4
propaganda institutions, 80–2
public diplomacy, 64–72, 75, 77, 99
as a counter-terrorism tool, 65–72
definition of, 64

al-Qaddafi, Muammar *see* Gaddafi
al-Qaradawi, Yusuf, 244
Qatar, 214, 216
Quantum 3-D (company), 106
The Quiet American (film), 120
Qur'an, the, burning of, 27

racism, 23, 26, 36, 136–7, 140, 145, 147, 223, 264, 273, 276, 278, 281, 294
radio broadcasts, 71, 244
Ramsey, Gilbert, 249

RAND Corporation, 73
al-Rashed, Abdul Rahman, 75
Rather, Dan, 310–11
Raziz, Hamad Abdulla, 294
'regime change' policy, 1
Regulation of Investigatory Powers Act (UK, 2000), 144
Reid, Richard, 124–5
rendition, 122, 130
Rendition (film), 127–8
Reporters Without Borders, 302
Research, Information and Communication Unit (RICU), 67, 81–2, 86
Rice, Condoleeza, 29
Rigouste, Mathieu, 223, 237
'risk-transfer war', 209, 216
Robinson, W., 50
Roosevelt, Franklin D., 98
Rosenstiel, T., 15
Rousselle, Olivier, 236
Ruddock, Philip, 278, 284
Ruge, M., 258
Rules of Engagement (film), 37
Rulyova, N., 190
Rumsfeld, Donald, 80, 292
RUnet, 187
Rushdie, Salman, 225–6
Russia, 5, 184–202
Rwanda, 71, 313

al-Sadr, Muqtada, 245
Said, Edward, 9, 24, 211, 263
Salim, Artica, 293
al-Samarra'i, Nisan, 294
Sanders, Bernie, 103
Sanyal, Kanu, 169
Sayafi, Omid Reza Mir, 68
Schmid, A., 7, 10–11
Schumpeter, Joseph, 105
Second World War, 101
Secret Internet Protocol Router Network (SIPRNET), 58
self-censorship by the media, 56
self-regulation by the media, 192
September 11th 2001 attacks, 10, 12, 30, 59, 124, 189, 207, 214–16, 219, 223–4, 252, 259, 261, 264–5, 289–90
Serious Organised Crime and Police Act (UK, 2005), 144

Sesame Street and Sesame Workshop, 69–71
Shaheen, J., 13
Shakir, Mahmoud, 294
Shaw, Martin, 209
Shinar, D., 279–80
Shlaim, Avi, 162
Simpson, Christopher, 85
Singh, Manmohan, 172
Sklair, L., 49–50
Slim, H., 292
Snow, Jeffrey, 298–9
social fabric, 28
social networking, 65, 67, 108, 187
'sociocide' (Abdel Jawwad), 28
Soffer, Arnon, 34
'soft power', 68, 72, 99–100, 251
Solomon, Norman, 301
Somalia, 74, 248
South Asia
media wars in, 176–7
terrorism in, 167–72, 176, 179–80
Soviet Union, 101
speculative capital flows, 54
Spencer, G., 273
Spider-Man 2 (film), 109
Sprecher, Drexel, 313
Spy Game (film), 117–18
Sri Lanka, 167, 170–1, 180, 278
Stahl, R., 13
stealth bombers, 57
Stepanova, E., 5
Stevens, David, 86
Stockholm International Peace Research Institute (SIPRI), 176
stop-and-search powers, 144–5
'strategic communication', 83–4
Strategic Horizons Unit (SHU), 82
Strauss, Leo, 309
Suarez, Fernando, 304
suicide bombings, 3, 170–1, 174, 267–8
most common locations for, 168
The Sun, 274
Sun Tsu, 309
Swami, Praveen, 171
Switzerland, 25, 69–71
Syriana (film), 120–1

Taliban regime, 71, 124
'Talibanization' of terrorism,
    167, 172–4
al-Tamimi, Youssif, 301
Tampa incident (2001), 277, 279
Tankel, Stephen, 178
Tatham, Steve, 82, 84
Taylor, Philip, 79
Teather, Sarah, 152, 162
Tebbit, Lord, 137
technological determinism, 52
Tehranian, M., 275
television, 11, 70
    in France, 224–33, 236–7
    in Russia, 186–7, 190, 198
Tenet, George, 131
Tere Bin Laden (film), 179
terrorism
    as communication, 9–12
    definitions of, 5–10, 32–3,
        78, 296–7
    ending of, 72–5
    mediatization of, 11–12
    motivations for, 264
    as 'news', 258
    'optical' character of, 11
    as resistance, 32–3
    scale of threat from, 259–63,
        268, 278
    as a symbolic act, 10
Terrorism Acts (UK), 144–5
'terrorism pyramid', 66, 69, 73
terrorism studies, 78
terrorist attacks
    countries most affected by, 1–2
    number of, 1, 6, 30, 88,
        168–9, 259
terrorist plots, number of, 88
Thatcher, Margaret, 273, 276
Thornton, Thomas, 10
'threat-society' concept,
    218–19
Time magazine, 6
Tobin, Angela, 143
Tokyo subway attack (1995), 6
torture, use of, 85–6, 118, 122,
    213, 249, 301, 315
Toynbee, Polly, 135–6
transnational corporations, 48
Travis, Alan, 86

Trepov, Fedor, 188
Tuckey, Wilson, 279
Tunisia, 33
Turk, A., 7

Ulfstein, Geir, 216–17
UNITA, 4
United Fruit Company (UFC),
    122–3
United Nations
    Charter, 31–2, 214
    Children's Fund (UNICEF), 69
    Security Council Resolution
        13, 68, 217
United States
    Department of Defense, 27,
        53, 94, 96, 109, 112,
        115–17, 119–24, 144,
        189, 228, 291, 309, 313
    Navy, 101–2
    State Department, 8, 10, 259,
        291, 296–7
University of Central Florida, 108
University of Southern California
    (USC), 97–8, 108, 110
unmanned combat air vehicles
    (UCAVs), 57
Unz, D., 282
user-generated media content,
    195–6, 247

veiling of Muslim women, 24–5,
    225–6, 250
video games, 13, 105; *see also*
    electronic gaming
Vietnam War, 313

Wall Street Journal, 6, 131
Walt, S.M., 156
war crimes, 90, 152, 301
'war journalism', 206–12, 255–6,
    271, 275, 282–6
'war on terror', 1–7, 23–6, 29–40,
    73, 81, 97, 106–9, 116, 122,
    126–7, 134, 147, 167–8,
    171–5, 212, 218–19, 223,
    241–5, 249–53, 258–61,
    272, 278, 285–6, 289,
    306–7
    Arab understanding of, 249

'war on terror' *cont.*
    'Bollywoodization' of, 179–80
    framing of, 12–14
    looking beyond, 14–16
    in Russia, 189–91, 196,
        201–2
warfare, 27–9, 54–60
    mediatization of, 47
    role in the economy and
        society, 102–3
Warsi, Sayeeda, 137
water-boarding, 125
'weapons of mass deception',
    306, 308
weapons of mass destruction
    (WMD), 81, 103–4, 131,
        308, 311
White, Aidan, 301–2
'White Australia' policy,
    274
Wieviorka, Michel, 236
WikiLeaks, 15, 99, 178, 207,
    216–19
Wilders, Geert, 242
Wilkinson, R., 273
Williams, Rowan, 266–7
Wilson, Amrit, 138
Wilson, Joseph, 129
Winters, Jim, 83
Wittgenstein, Ludwig,
    26, 37–8
Wodak, R., 272
Wolff, Michael, 311
Wood, E.M., 50
World Tribunal on Iraq, 303
Wright, Micah Ian, 103

Yale University, 122
Yemen, 74, 174
YouTube, 15, 74–5
Yugoslavia, 213–14, 217,
    219, 313

al-Zarqawi, Abu Musab,
    72–3, 107
Zasoulich, Vera, 188
al-Zawahiri, Ayman, 66–7,
    246, 250
Zia-ul-Haq, Mummad, 125,
    171, 173